SHELDON JACOBS'

GUIDE TO
Successful No-Load Fund Investing

Also by the same author

**The Handbook for No-Load
Fund Investors**

The No-Load Fund Investor

SHELDON JACOBS'

GUIDE TO
Successful
No-Load Fund
Investing

The No-Load Fund Investor, Inc.
Post Office Box 318, Irvington-on-Hudson, NY 10533
Telephone: 914-693-7420, 800-252-2042

The No-Load Fund Investor, Inc. publishes *Sheldon Jacobs' Guide to Successful No-Load Mutual Fund Investing*, the annual *Handbook for No-Load Fund Investors*, and the monthly *No-Load Fund Investor* newsletter. The *Handbook* is regularly $45; twelve monthly *No-Load Fund Investor* newsletter issues are $119. Both publications are available to new subscribers only at a special introductory rate of $99. Additional copies of the *Guide* are $25. A sample issue of the *Investor* newsletter can be obtained free from *The No-Load Fund Investor.*

Unless otherwise indicated, the mutual fund data in this book originate in *The No-Load Fund Investor* newsletter or *The Handbook for No-Load Fund Investors*. Where necessary, we will refer to these two publications as the *Investor* and the *Handbook*.

If you have any suggestions for future editions of this *Guide*, or have spotted any mistakes, I would be glad to hear from you. Please write me at *The No-Load Fund Investor*. SJ.

Library of Congress Catalog Card No. 95—79688

ISBN: 0-7863-0436-7

To my loving wife, Liz,
whose help and support I depend on.

To my loving wife, Liz,
whose help and support I depend on.

CONTENTS

TABLES AND CHARTS

What you are about to read is the third incarnation of the first book ever written on how to invest in no-load funds. The first was called *Put Money in Your Pocket*, subtitled *The Art of Selecting No-Load Mutual Funds for Maximum Gain*. It was published by Simon & Schuster in 1974. *Put Money in Your Pocket* was an instant success. *Money* and *Financial World* magazines published chapters. The reviews were good. Even today—more than two decades later—people tell me how much the book influenced them.

I received the following letter in 1990, and it meant a lot to me.

> I feel compelled to write a note to you and send it with my application for a one year subscription to your *No-Load Fund Investor.*
>
> One day during 1975, I was drifting through the aisles of my local library. A book entitled *Put Money in Your Pocket* caught my eye. I checked it out, read it, and became fascinated by what you had written. That book planted the seed that was to change my outlook on investing. Through me, it also changed the outlook of quite a few of my friends and relatives.
>
> Five years later, I retired (4 years earlier than required) and with a philosophy of investing that began with the seed planted by your book, we have enjoyed seeing our investments grow at a compound rate in excess of 16%. So you see, subscribing to your service is really a small "Thank You" for what you started with *Put Money in Your Pocket*, more than 15 years ago. Thank you.

I wrote *Put Money In Your Pocket* when I was simply a private investor who believed that no-load funds were the best way for the individual to build a nestegg.

The popularity of *Put Money In Your Pocket* enabled me to become a professional investment advisor. I wrote for others for several years, and then in 1979 I started my own newsletter, *The No-Load Fund Investor*. Two years later I complemented the newsletter with a companion publication, *The Handbook For No-Load Fund Investors*.

The *Handbook* had three sections: 1) an editorial how-to section, 2) a statistical section with detailed 10-year performance data, and 3) a comprehensive Directory providing purchase and selection information for virtually all no-load mutual funds available to individual investors.

To write the editorial section, I went back to Simon & Schuster and obtained the rights to *Put Money in Your Pocket*. Thoroughly updated, that book became the first section of *The Handbook For No-Load Fund Investors*, an annual book that is published by my company, The No-Load Fund Investor, Inc.

The *Handbook*'s first edition, published in 1981, was a 160-page book covering 291 funds. By 1994 it had grown to a huge 565-page book that covered 1,742 funds.

We're still publishing the *Handbook*, but with the 1995 Edition covering 2,045 funds, we made the decision to produce it in two volumes. The *Handbook* now includes the statistical and directory data only. The editorial how-to section is contained in this volume. Thus, *Sheldon Jacobs' Guide to Successful No-Load Fund Investing* is the third generation of my original book, *Put Money In Your Pocket*. This "new book" actually is the culmination of over 20 years of study, advising, writing and rewriting.

The *Guide* can provide useful guidance to both beginning and expert investors. In addition, it is designed to enable subscribers of the *No-Load Fund Investor* newsletter to maximize their investing results from the newsletter's recommendations. Other newsletters provide little or no guidance to their subscribers, merely asking them to accept their newsletter's recommendations. You can accept our newsletter's recommendations too. But we believe you will be a better and more confident investor, and will make better use of the *Investor's* recommendations, if you really understand the art of no-load fund investing. Other newsletters offer at most a short pamphlet on the basics. We think the subject is so important that it deserves a whole book. I hope that you will find it worthwhile.

Sheldon Jacobs
Irvington-on-Hudson, NY

PART I

The Case For Mutual Funds

C H A P T E R   1

Mutual funds — investments for the 1990s, and beyond

It is a myth that the way to make money in the stock market is to find the "big" stock—the romantic stock that will double, triple, even quintuple. Driven by those few stocks that do achieve enormous gains, that myth looks even more credible in an era of highly publicized leveraged buyouts. Some fortunate investors who own these stocks are not shy about boasting of their good fortune. They may believe that the rewards are due to their skill as investors. All too often, it's not skill at all but luck. Of course some sophisticated investors spend hundreds of hours looking for that terrific value (or for inside information). And sometimes they buy at bargain prices, and sell near the peak. If you are an unusually perceptive securities analyst, willing to spend much of your leisure time ferreting out facts unknown to the financial community, then go for big winners. However, very few of us fit this description—including most Wall Street professionals.

Let's look at some facts. In 1991, a strong bull market year in which the New York Stock Exchange Index rose 27.1%, only 21% of the stocks listed on the Big Board increased in value by more than 50%. And only 8% rose 100% or more (a double). Real bragging gains? Forget it. Only 39 stocks (out of more than 2,200) did 200%

or better. On the other hand 20% of the NYSE stocks declined in this tremendous bull market year. An investor who picked the wrong stocks could have seen as much as 94% of his investment melt away.

Conversely, 1994 was a year in which the Dow Jones Industrial Average gained. But it's comprised of just 30 large, blue chip companies. Overall, most stocks lost ground, as reflected by the declines in the broader market averages.

More to the point for most investors are the results found by academic researchers who developed the efficient market theory—the so-called "random walk." In essence, the theory says that by and large, stocks are priced about where they should be in light of all the information available at a given time. Thus subsequent changes in prices depend on new information, which develops randomly. Contrary to what Wall Street analysts would have us believe, stocks are not ordinarily undervalued or overvalued. The reason, academics explain, is that thousands of knowledgeable stock market professionals and informed laymen closely follow a relatively few stocks. They quickly buy and sell when they spot a stock whose price they feel is out of line.

Although the efficient market hypothesis is now decades old, it is still controversial. Some observers believe that a number of "anomalies" disprove the theory. Yet, for the vast majority of investors, spending precious time selecting a portfolio of stocks on their own does not make sense. Luck aside, it is most unlikely that the average layperson will beat the pros over an extended period. The reason is simple. In the stock market, average ability gets you almost nowhere. To beat the professionals you have to have the facts about stocks before they do, or be able to analyze the available data better than they do. This takes time, effort and money.

Here's how *Stock Market Logic*, published by the Institute for Econometric Research, explains the task of finding profitable investments:

> The ability to foresee and profit from future price changes in the stock market rests upon: (1) an ability to assimilate, correctly interpret, and act on available information before it is fully appreciated by most market participants and fully reflected in prices; and (2) an ability to measure the mood of market participants.
>
> As to the first, most information, although disseminated almost instantly, is assimilated slowly and ultimately fully understood by a

small portion of the investing public. Such information may lead to price adjustments that are drawn out over long periods of time and may not even be recognized by most investors. For example, while the first drop in interest rates is never sufficient to wipe away the gloom of a bear market, as one piece of encouraging news after another emerges, we find fear replaced with hope and a bull market beginning. To cite another example, a glamour stock selling at an astronomical price/earnings ratio does not lose 90% of its value the day the first quarterly earnings figures reflecting a decelerating rate of growth is announced; as quarter after quarter of increasingly disappointing results are reported, the stock enters a lengthy downtrend, returning to the realm of more prosaic issues.

Information which is obscure or difficult to comprehend is the most useful, as that is the type of information which is also most slowly assimilated by market participants.

The second essential element of successful stock market prediction is an ability to measure the mood of market participants. It is axiomatic that when everyone is bullish and has adjusted their portfolios to their bullish expectations, few potential buyers remain. The converse is true in extreme bear markets. That explains the success of contrary opinion.

Most investors buy stock because they *expect* prices to advance, and most sellers are in the market because they *expect* prices to decline. Changes in these expectations are the underlying forces of all stock price movements.

In short, if you're going to succeed in the market, you've got to correctly forecast the expectations of other market participants whose motivations are similar to yours. Lord Keynes, who propounded his economic theories more than a half century ago, spelled out the difficulty of the task:

Professional investment may be likened to those newspaper competitions in which the competitors have to pick out the six prettiest faces from a hundred photographs, the prize being awarded to the competitor whose choice most nearly corresponds to the average preferences of the competitors as a whole; so each competitor has to pick, not those faces which he himself finds prettiest, but those which he thinks likeliest to catch the fancy of the other competitors, all of whom are looking at the problem from the same point of view. It is not a case of choosing those which, to the best of one's judgment, are really the prettiest, nor even those which average opinion genuinely thinks the prettiest. We have reached the third degree where we devote our intelligences to anticipating what average opinion expects the average opinion to be. And there are some, I believe, who practice the fourth, fifth and higher degrees.

Keynes, in addition to being a renowned economist, amassed a fortune speculating in the stock market.

Obtaining information is not nearly as difficult as interpreting it correctly. Are you as quick to understand the significance of corporate earnings reports as the knowledgeable professionals who spend their working hours following companies? How good are you at analyzing the footnotes to the earnings statements?

It's not getting any easier. A study by the accounting firm of Ernst & Young found that between 1972 and 1992, the number of pages in the annual reports of 25 large, well-known companies including AT&T, GE, GM and IBM increased by 83% (from 35 to 64 pages). The average number of pages of footnotes increased 325%—from four to 17—during those same 20 years. In addition, the average number of pages of managements' discussion and analysis went from three to 12 pages, a 300% increase.

Why stocks move

Stock prices fluctuate for many reasons. Some of the more important have to do with events relating to the company, the industry, and overall stock market cycles. (This last factor is influenced by a host of variables—inflation, interest rates, changes in the money supply, earnings and dividends, to name the most important)

Astonishingly, research shows that *events pertaining to an individual company account for less than half the price movement of most stocks.* Benjamin King, using factor and cluster analysis, studied the price variation of 63 stocks in six industries for the years 1952-1960. (Source: Richard A. Brealey, *An Introduction to Risk and Return from Common Stocks,* MIT Press, 1969.) King found that on average, only 20 percent of the variation in stock prices could be attributed to the individual company. The study was repeated for the 1927-1952 period with similar results. Another study by James L. Farrell in the Journal of Business (Apr. 19, 1974) determined that the company accounted for 45% of a stock's variation. You must inevitably conclude that devoting hours to studying stocks is a waste of time. You will do as well or better by buying a diversified mutual fund portfolio and relying on the expertise of sophisticated fund managers who, with their skills, training, and research staffs, are much better equipped to deal successfully with the markets.

Table 1

Variation in common stock prices			
Factor	**1927-1952**	**1952-1960**	**1961-1969**
General Market	52%	31%	30%
Industry	13%	12%	10%
Other	23%	37%	15%
Company	12%	20%	45%

"Just an hour a day"

This is a cost-conscious age. But if you think you can save money by providing your own investment expertise, rather than delegating the job to professional money managers, you might do a little informal cost analysis.

Does an hour a day seem like a reasonable amount of time for you to spend supervising your own investment program? If so, consider this: taking even this modest amount of time from your normal business or professional schedule to mind your investments costs you dearly. The "time expense" is equivalent to one-eighth of your earned income assuming you generally put in an eight-hour day. If you earn $48,000 a year, essentially you are expending $6,000 worth of your time to manage your portfolio. For a lot less you can get professional management. A typical mutual fund investment management fee is 0.5% to 1% of the fund's average assets—or $50 to $100 a year for each $10,000 the fund manages.

Does it surprise you to learn that at that rate you'd need to have more than $1 million in your investment account before it would be worth your while—on a dollar-for-dollar basis—to use just an hour a day of your business time to "save money" on investment management by doing it yourself? And that assumes that your investment results would be equivalent to the manager's.

Your broker may not know more than you do

Just how good is the guidance provided by the typical broker? In a book written by a broker, *Heads You Win, Tails You Win,* Ray Dirks talked about his fellow brokers. In an early chapter titled "The Case Against Your Broker," Dirks writes:

> The average stock broker is not the man you should listen to when

you invest your money. Your interests and his interests are inherently contradictory. Most of the time it's in your interest to hold securities for a long time. He earns a commission only when you buy and sell securities.

Second, there is the matter of a broker's qualifications. There are striking exceptions, of course, but the average broker is not a trained investment counselor. He is a salesman... What the average broker does is pass along to you information developed by his firm. He represents his firm as having strong research capabilities, analytical prowess, and the kinds of contacts that can develop inside information. He conveys to you the sense that he is an equal partner in this information-gathering process.

In fact, the average retail broker is the least well-informed person in his firm. In the pecking order of the securities business, he is the last to know. The dangers of this for you are enormous. It is highly likely that everyone else in the firm has already acted on the information before it gets to your broker.

Dirks goes on to illustrate the negative consequences for the investor. A stock can rise from 5% to 30% before you even hear about it. In fact, Dirks charges, "It is not at all inconceivable that, while your broker is urging you to buy, others higher up in the brokerage firm are advising their clients to sell."

This practice has been confirmed to us by mutual fund money managers. One told us that a personal friend once passed along a retail research report from a large, well-known stock brokerage firm. The report was so bullish on a certain housing stock, that our money manager was intrigued. However, noting that the stock had risen quite a bit since the report was issued, he called the research analyst who had authored the report to confirm that it was still a buy. As a professional, he was able to speak with the analyst. When he realized he was speaking to a professional, the brokerage house analyst reacted in horror. "This stock isn't for you!" he said. "This report is just the last big retail push so that our institutional clients can realize their profits."

And then there are the inevitable broker abuses. Brokers and their employers are compensated by the commissions they receive for buying and selling securities. As a result, their advice comes with an inherent conflict of interest. They are under great pressure to "produce," that is, generate the maximum commission income. An all-too-frequent result is that a broker will sell products which produce high commissions, but which are not necessarily suitable for their clients—you. Our advice: The average layman should not buy individual stocks. The only exception to this rule would be to consider buying stocks where you are more knowledgeable about a company than Wall Street. Once in a blue moon, you may learn of developments at your own or a friend's company, or you may spot a new product in the marketplace before Wall Street becomes aware of it. That may be a reason to buy. But if you hear about a stock from a broker, or even if you read about it in the popular press, forget it. You won't have any edge over Wall Street. There's no chance of buying at an undervalued price.

This writer talks to many mutual fund portfolio managers, and occasionally receives stock tips. Even though they are probably pretty good tips, I never buy. One major reason: I know the portfolio manager will never remember to call me when he sells. If I really like his tip, I buy his fund.

So don't spend hours poring over charts, earnings' statements, and annual reports, searching for rare undervalued stocks. Instead, let a professional mutual fund manager make the selections for you.

Hear what Nobel Prize-winning economist Paul Samuelson, a random-walk proponent, said back in 1971: "A small man—anyone with a portfolio of, say, under $100,000—is unlikely to do as well investing his own money as he can do in a no-load fund." Inflation-adjusted, that $100,000 would be about $377,000 in 1994's dollars.

Mutual funds are pools of investors' dollars. The money is used to purchase a diversified portfolio of stocks, bonds or money market instruments under the continuous supervision of professional managers. Mutual funds seek to do for the individual what he might do for himself if he had the time, inclination, background, experience and resources to spread his investments among many securities.

A fund's investors share in its income and expenses, and profits and losses, in proportion to the number of shares they own. When a mutual fund provides joint ownership of securities—stocks and bonds—that can fluctuate in value, the fund cannot guarantee a specific return to its investors. It is thus fundamentally different from a bank savings account or certificate of deposit. Bank accounts do guarantee a fixed rate of return to depositors, who are lenders, rather than owners.

So just what are mutual funds?

Mutual funds are owned by their shareholders. However, they are seldom managed along conventional corporate lines by their own officers and directors. A typical fund is "externally managed," meaning that most or all of its work is done for it by a separate company usually called the *investment adviser*, who presides over a fund's birth and generally remains in control throughout its life. Almost invariably, a fund's shareholders vote to renew the adviser's management contract.

Some funds are organized as Massachusetts Business Trusts. By doing so they are able to issue an unlimited number of shares without specific shareholder approval and avoid the requirement that they hold annual shareholder meetings. The latter is no big loss, few shareholders ever attended. All other shareholder rights are intact.

Funds have been around since the 20s

Mutual funds evolved from investment trusts and investment companies that were founded toward the close of the nineteenth century in Boston, New York, Philadelphia, and other cities. These trusts were established by bankers, brokers, investment counselors and others who saw the need for making professional financial management available to investors of moderate means.

The first mutual fund, or open-end investment company, was formed in 1924 when the Massachusetts Investors Trust (M.I.T.) granted its shareholders the right to redeem their shares at net asset value—total assets held by the fund divided by the number of shares outstanding—minus a discount of $2 per share. However, mutual funds did not achieve significant growth until after the passage of the Investment Company Act of 1940, which eliminated abuses of the 1920s and provided statutory safeguards for investors. This act provided the essential framework for the substantial growth of the mutual fund industry in the past six decades.

The term "mutual fund" seems to have arisen in the late '30s. Some think it was coined to take the onus off the word "Trust." Investors' faith in "trusts" was severely shaken by the 1929 crash.

While mutual funds initially were started for investors of moderate means, many wealthy individuals and institutions have found them to be a good way to achieve their investment objectives. In 1993, 37 per cent ($559 billion) of reported long-term mutual fund assets and 49% of money fund assets ($277 billion) were held in 14 million different institutional accounts—bank trust departments, fiduciaries, pension funds, foundations, unions, and businesses.

Large institutional investors buy mutual funds for good reasons, and those reasons apply even more to small investors. These attributes, which we will investigate more thoroughly in later chapters are especially compelling for the "sophisticated" individual investor:

■ Funds offer professional management.

■ Past performance records are readily available for systematic evaluation.

■ In their prospectuses, funds must disclose unfavorable facts, such as being sued.

■ Funds are diversified.

■ They have low transaction costs.

■ They can provide access to inaccessible markets.

■ They can automatically reinvest your dividends.

■ Funds' risk-reward ratios can be determined fairly accurately, and the ratios are generally acceptable.

■ The entire field can be adequately researched and mastered by a layman.

■ Purchasing and redeeming shares is easy.

Mutual fund shareholders receive *professional management* at rock-bottom fees. Years ago Bernard Baruch made the cogent comparison:

> It would never occur to anyone to open a department store in competition with Macy's or Gimbel's or to make motor cars against Ford and General Motors without prior training or preparation. Yet many people will cheerfully toss their savings into a market dominated by professionals who are as expert in their line as the department stores and auto makers are in theirs.

The second reason is by far the more important and bears emphasis. *Past performance records are easily available.* From the layperson's point of view, this is unique and terribly important. There is no way to compare the performance of stockbrokers or, in most cases, even investment counselors. Only mutual funds publish industry-wide performance records that are readily accessible. With this indispensable data bank, the lay investor can make intelligent investment decisions.

When you buy a mutual fund you will always receive a *prospectus*. It will tell you in detail what the fund is all about. You can learn its objective—whether the fund seeks growth, income or a combination; what kinds of securities the fund will invest in; and the amount of risk the fund plans to take. In addition, the prospectus may give you unfavorable facts about the fund, as well as the favorable information that fund management would like to convey. The SEC requires information on pending lawsuits, management changes, etc. This makes the prospectus a valuable data source, one not available when you select an investment counselor or buy stock, unless it's a new issue. Chapter 23 shows you how to get the most out of a prospectus.

Diversification, owning a large portfolio of stocks, is a key reason for buying funds. The point is simple. There are two basic risks in owning stocks. The risk that the market will go down, and the risk that an individual company will do poorly. Diversification can eliminate the latter risk. And since the wise investor is risk averse, it makes sense to avoid taking any risk that's unnecessary. In fact, academic studies have found that investors who don't diversify are *not* rewarded for taking on this additional risk. Every time a stock plummets, be happy that your investments are diversified in mutual funds.

The art of diversification is more complicated than it might appear. It is not enough to own a dozen or more stocks. Proper diversification demands investments in stocks of different industries that are unlikely to behave the same way at the same time. Some examples: cyclical industries versus moderate or high-growth industries that are relatively insensitive to business cycles. This distinction is lost on the average stock broker; most do not seem to understand the importance of diversifying into a range of industries. Their conventional "widows and orphans" portfolio—supposedly ultraconservatively designed to provide safety and high income—tends to be heavily invested in bonds and utility stocks, all of which decline simultaneously when interest rates rise. In 1994, these portfolios did far worse than other portfolios invested more aggressively.

Diversity is a major advantage that mutual funds have over stock advisory letters or stockbrokers' recommended lists. There is always great variation in the performances of individual stocks. But with funds, it is the portfolio's overall performance that counts.

In many cases it is important to diversify among markets—U.S. stocks, U.S. bonds, international stocks, international bonds, and cash. You can buy funds that provide this kind of diversification, often within a single large mutual fund company.

Mutual funds can provide *access* to foreign markets that you might find difficult to trade in yourself.

One of the truisms in investing is that greater *risks* and greater *rewards* go hand in hand. Investors are usually advised to seek situations where the probability of profit is greater than the possibility of loss. But with stocks, it is hard to apply this generalization. We're certain that many investors have had the experience of buying a conservative stock, often with a low price-earnings ratio, and still suffering a substantial loss.

Mutual funds have similar risk-reward ratios. Speculative funds offer the greatest profit potential, of course. But they also can be counted on to decline the most sharply during bear market downturns. However with funds, the risk-reward ratios are generally acceptable and probably significantly more favorable than with stocks. Even more important, the risk-reward ratios are far more easily ascertainable than with stocks. Since funds range from very speculative to very conservative, you can easily find those funds best suited to your needs.

An average person can do the sort of analysis with funds that only professionals do well with stocks. The *entire field can be well researched and mastered,* even if the time you have for investing is very limited. Uniform data for most no-load funds are readily available from mutual fund advisory services, such as our companion publications, *The Handbook for No-Load Fund Investors* and *Investor* newsletter. Both contain performance computations, as well as rankings and comparisons of similar funds. So you can easily spot the best, virtually forcing you into an organized approach to investing. You look automatically for the best performers and eliminate the rest. You thus have an excellent chance to maximize your profits, and need to expend relatively little energy. The sizeable increase in the number of funds over the past few years has not altered this fact. In contrast, most investors don't compare the relative merits of stocks because data are seldom complete or uniform.

Funds have low transaction costs

On May 1, 1975, the Securities and Exchange Commission finally abolished the last vestiges of the fixed-commission-rate system that had for so long enriched brokers. Immediately commission rates declined. Large institutions were the primary beneficiaries. Today mutual funds pay far lower commissions to trade stocks than you do—in some cases as low as two cents per share traded. In contrast, a 1987 study showed individuals paid an average 42 cents per share. The cost may be higher today, since brokerage firms have tacked on new account charges. The lower institutional commissions help offset the funds' management fee expense. These commissions are also less than individuals can typically obtain from a discount broker. And using a discount broker, you receive no investment advice.

How profitable are mutual funds?

Until the late 40s, most mutual funds followed similarly conservative investment policies. The funds that survived the Depression had names like Massachusetts Investors Trust, Investment Company of America, American Business Shares, Dividend Shares, Founders Mutual, Income Foundation, and Lexington Income Trust. As a result, they were considered stodgy, beneficial only to small investors who were incapable of understanding the basic principles of investing. In those days, "smart" investors bought stocks. In fact in 1952, the entire mutual fund industry had assets of only $3.9 billion. Today, scores of individual funds are larger.

Then, performance became an important element in mutual fund competition. It soon became clear that funds such as Dreyfus and Fidelity Capital were regularly outpacing the market averages. Fund salesmen, who had once talked retirement goals, began to stress appreciation. New funds were formed which frankly stated that their objective was to achieve maximum capital gains. Gas Industries Fund changed its name to Colonial Growth & Energy Shares. Massachusetts Investors Second Fund was transformed into Massachusetts Investors Growth Stock Fund. Foreign Bond Associates became the Winfield Growth Fund. "Smart" money moved into well-managed aggressive funds. The mutual fund industry was, in fact, revolutionized. In 1949 only two funds used the word "growth" in their name; today, it's commonplace.

Top mutual funds delivered impressive performance in the 1950s and 1960s as the stock market boomed. Then in the late 1960s and early 1970s, profits virtually disappeared when three brutal bear markets wiped out many of the gains of the previous two decades. The tide has turned. Since 1975 the long-term trend of the market has once again been up. As a result, the mutual fund industry has soared in popularity. It is now the preeminent place for the individual investor to take care of his retirement and financial needs.

The most striking fact about individual stock funds is that their performance varies tremendously. And it's easy to understand why: Their objectives differ. Individual funds range in size from less than one hundred thousand dollars to over $36 billion, and the number of stocks in their portfolios ranges from a handful to hundreds.

You can't buy and forget

In most years, the performance of individual funds varies from gains of 50% or more—occasionally 100% or more—on the high side to significant losses at the other extreme. Note that "performance" as used in the mutual fund industry and in this book means the fund's performance, not an investor's experience. Your results will vary depending on when you bought a fund, whether it has a load and your personal tax situation.

For various reasons, which we will discuss in detail in the chapters on mutual fund selection, it is highly unlikely that any fund will maintain an outstanding growth record over a long period of time. There are good reasons why funds don't turn in outstanding performances year in, year out. Some are victims of their own success. They become gigantic and complacent. As they get unwieldy, they lose the sharp edge of aggressiveness that originally distinguished their approach. Others become casualties of the market's cyclical ups and downs. It is axiomatic that the aggressive, performance-oriented funds that surpass all others in bull markets are, by nature, the funds that decline most when the inevitable bear market arrives.

What to do

The implications are clear. It is no trick at all to buy a fund that has been an above-average performer in the past. Moreover, with the help of *The No-Load Fund Investor* and with your own study, you can select funds that will perform substantially better than average for a time—perhaps one to four years. But if you want above-average performance year after year, *you are going to have to switch funds from time to time*.

The mutual fund industry has always correctly pointed out that the greatest rewards come to the long-term investor. But that doesn't mean you should marry a particular fund. Holding one fund for your investing lifetime is definitely not the way to maximize your profits.

When you realize that you have to move from one fund to another periodically, you then must consider the cost of buying and selling—the sales charge—and its effect on your investment program. We think you will agree that a sales charge, while legitimately compensating salespeople, is an entrance fee that prevents you from making the wisest investment decisions.

The only way to avoid this entrance fee is by buying no-load mutual funds, an investment type that is unique in that you can obtain it without paying any sales commission. For the sophisticated investor, the absence of an entrance charge allows for greater liquidity and flexibility, and removes the psychological restraints that lock investors into holding when they should be selling. With no-loads, it's easy to switch from poorly performing funds to better performers. It's easy to sell a fund if you feel that it will be adversely affected by a looming bear market. And it's just as easy to move back in when better times arrive.

No-load funds:
The modern way to
make money grow

Can you imagine an investment that is free of commissions, completely liquid and as safe—or as risky—as you want it to be? That sounds almost too good to be true. What's the catch?

There isn't any, really. No-load mutual funds are as close to the perfect investment vehicle as you can find. You buy them directly from the investment company, so there is never a sales charge. You can cash in—or move your money quickly. And you can invest in almost any type of stocks, bonds or money market instruments. If there weren't such a thing as a no-load fund, someone surely would have to invent it.

Actually no-loads have been around for decades. The first funds to be offered without commissions came out in 1928, only four years after the first mutual fund. Only since the financial explosion of the 70s and 80s, however, have they reached their ultimate flowering.

Now no-load funds come in wild profusion. Anyone who wants to can invest exclusively in everything from municipal bonds to hi-tech stocks—or in a broader range of securities. You have a wide choice, from funds that buy the stocks of very volatile companies to those investing in the money market. Most firms let you switch your money among different types of funds by telephone. You pay nothing.

Once you have decided how you want to invest your money, no-load funds give you the advantage of professional management. You don't have to worry about picking the best stocks or bonds yourself. A professional makes those decisions for you. For most investors, this is the soundest way to make money.

No-load funds are exactly like their more expensive counterparts, the load funds, in every respect except one. *No-loads are sold without a sales commission* (which in the jargon of the industry is called a "load"). Selling funds without a sales charge is possible if no salespeople are involved in the purchase. No-load fund companies work directly with you, the investor, and you must take the initiative.

The beginnings

The first no-loads were started by investment counseling firms. They needed a depository for accounts too small to warrant individual handling. T. Rowe Price got its start that way, as did Scudder, Stevens & Clark. These counseling firms now view their mutual funds as a "showcase" for their investment acumen and expertise.

Later, some brokerage firms set up their own no-load funds, seeing in them vehicles that would provide a steady flow of new commissions from their portfolio transactions. The Lehman Bros. brokerage house at one time had two such funds. One still survives as the Salomon Opportunity Fund. The Wayne Hummer Fund is managed by a brokerage house.

There was a pronounced trend to no-loads during the 70s and 80s, with more than 75 old-line load funds "firing" their salespeople and marketing shares directly to investors. Fund groups that were originally 100% load but are now partially or wholly no-load include the Invesco, Vanguard, Twentieth Century, Dreyfus, and Fidelity funds. Later, funds sponsored by insurance companies followed suit. The SAFECO and Selected Funds are now no-load. In the 90s such groups as Skyline, PBHG and Heartland have gone no-load.

The newer money market funds are 100% no-load; early attempts to sell money funds with loads failed completely. No wonder. One dictionary definition of a load is "a heavy burden or weight." No investor needs such a burden, but especially not one who is investing in a cash fund.

Including money market funds, no-loads now account for over half of the industry's total assets.

To understand what distinguishes loads from no-loads, you must understand how funds are sold, managed and valued.

First, you need to understand the NAV, or net asset value per share. The NAV constitutes the real worth of a fund. It is derived by computing each day the total market value of a fund's portfolio, including cash on hand, then dividing this sum by the total number of investors' shares outstanding. You could think of the net asset value as the liquidation value of a fund if it were to sell everything at the end of the day and divide the proceeds among its shareholders. It is what you get when you sell your shares back to the fund. On any given day, you can determine the value of your holdings by multiplying the NAV by the number of shares you own.

The offer price is what you pay to buy shares in a fund. With a load fund, the difference between the offer price and the NAV is the sales charge. Since no-loads carry no sales charge, the NAV and the offer price are the same.

Both load and no-load mutual funds are managed by professional investment advisers who are paid fees for selecting the best stocks, providing judgment in timing the purchase and sale of securities and safeguarding the investor's money. The fee for this service does not come out of the sales commission paid to load funds. It is a common misconception that some—or all—of a sales charge compensates management. Not true. The sales commission is essentially a distribution expense. That commission is shared by the salesperson and the selling organization, a firm which generally is owned by the same corporation that owns the mutual fund company itself.

But don't grieve for the investment managers. In both load and no-load families, they are paid separately—typically 0.5% to 1.0% of a fund's net asset value annually. The management of a mutual fund with $100 million of assets will normally be compensated between $500,000 and $1 million per year for providing investment counsel and services to the fund. In the case of load funds, this is in addition to the sales charge.

The difference between loads and no-loads

It is important for you to know that as far as the funds are concerned, it is strictly a marketing decision whether to distribute shares through sales people or directly to investors. If a fund group chooses the commission route, it must decide on the size of the load and which funds to apply it to. Some companies offer nothing but no-load funds, oth-

Load or no-load is a fund marketing decision

ers charge commissions on all their funds, and some firms have both load and no-load funds. Fidelity markets its funds four different ways: no-load, low-loads marketed directly to investors, front-end load funds sold by brokers, and contractual plans (a kind of super load). Even Vanguard, a virtually pure no-load fund group, has utilized salesmen to launch closed-end funds.

There is nothing evil about selling products through salesmen—virtually every industry does it. Since funds are compensated on the basis of the amount of assets under management, the greater the assets, the more profitable they are. If a fund company can attract more assets by selling directly to investors, no-load, it will do so. If employing salesmen is more profitable, the company will do that.

The funds' perspective is in sharp contrast to our own point of view. We look at these alternatives solely from the investor's perspective. Since our research proves that no-loads are better for the investor, we are zealous in advocating that you confine your mutual fund investing to no-loads.

The marketing of mutual funds is in constant flux. In general, there's been a gradual narrowing of fee schedules throughout the mutual fund industry. Years ago, the vast majority of load funds charged the maximum 8.5% because of fierce competition back then to get the salesmen to sell their funds instead of somebody else's. Nowadays the majority of load funds come to market with lower fees because investors are a lot smarter. Fees in the 4%-6% range are common; bond funds may be slightly lower. On the other hand, some funds that have mid-range loads impose an extra annual fee of around one-quarter of 1% a year (called a "trail") to compensate salesmen for servicing their clients' accounts. And here's something else to watch out for. It's legal to exact a sales commission for reinvesting dividends! A few funds do so.

Beware! Some funds that look like no-loads aren't

If you buy a fund through a broker, you will most likely pay some sort of commission. Even some funds that are sold directly to investors charge commissions. Not all of these fees are obvious. Here are some of the types of distribution fees that you might encounter along the mutual fund landscape.

12b-1 plans.   The name refers to the 1980 Securities and Exchange Commission rule that permits them. Originally, the SEC used Section 12b-1 to enable funds to pass along to investors their marketing and distribution expenses—for example, advertising and the costs of printing and mailing prospectuses and sales literature to prospective investors. These expenses had traditionally been covered by the management fee. Very quickly, though, load fund groups realized that they could use the 12b-1 fee to compensate sales personnel and broker-dealers for their services. Collecting a 12b-1 fee in lieu of a front-end load gave commissionable funds a terrific marketing advantage because the 12b-1 fee is paid to fund management at regular intervals out of the fund's net assets, in just the way that the management fee is collected. Unless a prospective fund purchaser reads the prospectus carefully, the fee is hidden, for all practical purposes. It will come as no surprise to learn that salesmen seldom explain this fee. And until 1988 these funds were listed as N.L. in newspaper price quotations. Consequently, salesmen frequently told their clients they were buying no-loads. What they meant, of course, was that the client didn't pay an up-front sales charge. That's not the same as *no* load. With only occasional exceptions, if a salesman is selling it, assume he is being compensated for his efforts. Ask him what's in it for him and where the money is coming from. You will usually find out you're the one paying the tariff, no matter what it's called.

Contingent deferred sales charges.   A few funds have always had redemption fees. Traditionally these fees, typically 1% and never more that 2%, were used to deter trading and were rescinded after an investor had held a fund's shares from two months to a year. Now, a marketing wrinkle has been introduced to complement the 12b-1 fee: the contingent deferred sales charge (CDSC). At first glance it seems to be a cousin of the redemption fee. But it is really quite different. The deferred sales charge, like the upfront sales charge, is paid to salesmen and their selling organizations. Deferred sales charges can be as much as 5% to 6% for shareholders redeeming in their first year, declining by 1% per year for the next five to six years.

The CDSC makes 12b-1 plans practical. Here's how the system works. The broker or fund salesman is paid 4%-5% to sell the fund shares—compensation the salesman receives at the time of the sale. If the fund were using a front-end sales charge, there would be no problem, but under a 12b-1 plan, the shareholder is charged no more than 1% a year. At that rate it can easily take four to five years for the fund's sponsor to recoup the money that it paid the salesman. And what if the shareholder redeems in the meantime? Without the CDSC, the sponsors would be out the money. With the CDSC, fund companies are assured of being able to recoup the money that was advanced to the salesman. The shareholder pays one way or the other—via the 12b-1 fee or the CDSC.

An increasing number of load fund groups now market some of their funds three ways: Series A funds with a front-end load, Series B funds with a 12b-1 plan coupled to a 5%-1% CDSC in lieu of a front-end load, and Series C, the level load—usually 1% per year. The shareholder has a choice. He pays about the same either way, although you wouldn't necessarily know it from the performance. For example, in 1994 the Merrill Basic Value Fund A gained 2.0% while the Merrill Basic Value Fund B gained 0.9%. The fund was the same, the only difference being that in the A version the sales commission was paid up front and didn't affect the reported performance. In the B version, the commission came out of net assets and did affect reported performance. To be sure, reported performance and your performance are not the same. With these funds you fall behind either way.

In recent years, 12b-1 plans have spread like wildfire. More than half of all funds have them. Several years ago, an ICI study found that dealer compensation is the most frequent use of the 12b-1 plan. Over 85% of funds basing 12b-1 dollars on a percentage of assets are sold through a sales force.

Sometimes called *broker* no-loads, these 12b-1 funds have become a salesman's paradise. The lack of a front-end sales charge, a deferred sales charge that the salesman argues can be avoided if the fund is held long enough, and a 12b-1 charge that is essentially hidden, all combine to make these funds easier to sell than conventional load funds. It's against regulations to call these funds no-load, but unfortunately, what a salesman says in a private conversation can't be policed. Brokers frequently call these 12b-1, CDSC funds "no-loads." You should avoid broker no-loads just as you would traditional front-end loads. They levy the same high sales fees.

There is another category of 12b-1 plan you should be aware of. These are the "defensive" 12b-1 plans. About 13% of funds have installed them for contingency or legal reasons. In many cases the managers of these funds have no present plans to activate the 12b-1 provisions, i.e., levy fees against the fund and its shareholders. Some of these plans have been put in place because of a long-standing SEC rule that provides that if a fund acts as a distributor of its shares, a written plan must be adopted. Before the existence of 12b-1 plans, fund managers often didn't bother to set up a written plan. Some funds fear that because of the profusion of 12b-1 plans, the SEC may reinterpret its rules to mean that sales expenses, even if paid by the manager, must be detailed in a plan. Other funds believe that by setting up plans now, they may be grandfathered, and thus be unaffected by future changes in securities laws.

The giant Fidelity group has "defensive" 12b-1 plans for most of its no-loads. The plan, labeled Distribution and Service Plan in the prospectus, permits Fidelity to pay distribution costs out of its own pocket. It would take a shareholder vote to enable Fidelity to charge them 12b-1 fees. Generally speaking, you should not be concerned about defensive plans, but you should carefully examine future proxy statements to make sure that the policy hasn't changed.

The *Guide's* companion publications, *The No-Load Fund Investor* and *The Handbook for No-Load Fund Investors*, list a number of 12b-1 funds, but for the most part they are funds with nominal fees of .25% of assets per year or less that are direct-marketed, not sold by brokers. Realize, also, that many 12b-1 funds deduct only the actual marketing expenses incurred, often less than the maximum allowed in the prospectus. Under government regulations which took effect in 1993, funds without a front-end or back-end sales charge and 12b-1 fees no more than .25% can still call themselves no-loads. We suggest you examine a fund's expense ratio in evaluating this charge. While modest 12b-1 fees are not usually a problem, other things equal, *we strongly believe that your first preference should always be for pure no-loads*.

When petitioning the SEC to permit 12b-1 plans, funds argued that they would benefit the investor by enabling the fund to grow larger. This would spread expenses over a larger asset base. As it worked out, these new charges have basically benefited the fund managers, not the investor. Incidentally, the picture is not entirely bleak. At least one group that collects both a 12b-1 fee and a deferred sales charge mitigates the fees under one circumstance. If you are lucky enough to die during the contingent deferred sales charge period, the fund waives that charge!

Because the financial press has done such a good job alerting investors to the liabilities of 12b-1s, some funds— including Neuberger-Berman's and the Harbor Growth Fund—which had been collecting minimal fees, have discontinued their 12b-1 plans to avoid the negative image that the fees engender.

Historically, there was no time limit on 12b-1 fees. Over the years, they could easily add up to more than the front-end load. Since this was clearly unwarranted, regulators have now put a cap on 12b-1 fees. The NASD (the National Association of Securities Dealers) has capped these asset-based charges at 7.25% of new gross sales if there is no continuing .25% service fee, and at 6.25% of new gross sales if there is a service fee. Annual fees are capped at .75% (plus a .25% service fee). While this new ruling is welcome, for administrative reasons it is applied to the fund, not to the individual accounts. So its benefits to individual investors will vary and, in fact, may be non-existent if the fund's assets grow rapidly.

Low-loads. A few funds have always carried "low-loads," up-front sales charges typically in the 2-3% range. Historically, the low-load concept was not particularly successful because the low-load did not provide sufficient incentive to salesmen who, for obvious reasons, preferred to put their efforts into selling funds with the standard 8.5% commission. Low-loads were even less attractive to no-load fund investors.

Fidelity has found a way to make low-load funds sold directly to investors work for them in a substantial way. Since 1983, Fidelity has selectively added commission charges to a number of the family's best performing equity funds, and it has found many investors willing to pay the charges in order to obtain superior performance. These low loads don't compensate salesmen, but rather are a marketing charge that Fidelity keeps for itself. Fidelity claims to send out more prospectuses and spend more time on the phone before people buy equity funds than the firm did previously when the easier-to-explain money market funds were the fund group's most sought after product. However, it seems clear that these low-load fees are being used more to establish advertising dominance than to provide customer service.

What's worked for Fidelity, hasn't really worked for smaller groups. Few other funds have followed Fidelity's lead. The Strong

Funds added a 1%-2% sales charge in 1985, but then dropped the loads in 1992 to regain their pure no-load status.

Besides 12b-1 and redemption fees, a savvy investor needs to be alert to other anomalies, even in the no-load arena. The Permanent Portfolio Fund, while it is a no-load, has a $35 start-up fee and an account maintenance fee of $1.50 per month. Some of the Vanguard Index Funds have account maintenance fees, which while they serve to apportion fixed expenses fairly, also serve to lower reported expense ratios. For small accounts, these fees can represent a sizable percentage of assets.

When a sales charge isn't

Most sales charges are payable to the adviser or to a sales organization, but a few funds, generally index funds which stay fully invested at all times, collect sales fees that are *payable to the fund*. That means the fee is payable to *you*, since you are one of the owners of the fund. The sums spent come back to you in the fund's return. These fees, generally in the 1/2 to 1 percent range, are levied to ensure that entering and departing shareholders pay their own transaction costs. This is fair since every time a new shareholder signs on, the fund has to buy more stock, and every time a shareholder leaves they must sell stock. If the fund didn't collect this fee, those transaction costs would be mostly borne by existing shareholders. Since many existing investors bought their shares with the intention of holding for the long term, it would be unfair for them to have to shoulder the cost of newcomers. With this charge, the new shareholder pays his own way. In effect this system raises costs for the short-term trader and lowers costs for the long-term investor.

Secondly, this system deters market timers who like index funds because they guarantee participation in a market move. (Market timers become quite annoyed if they buy into a fund just before a big upmove only to find that the fund is not participating in the market advance because the fund's manager has become defensive and sold much of the fund's stocks or, just as bad, has picked the wrong stocks to invest in.)

Some of Vanguard's and DFA's index funds have sales charges payable to the fund. We consider these funds to be *pure* no-loads. Net, net, sales charges paid to the fund are beneficial. In these particular cases, don't avoid funds that have them.

How to identify no-loads in the newspaper

If you turn to the financial pages of a daily newspaper, there is usually a listing of mutual fund quotations. While there is considerable variation from paper to paper, Chart 2 lists the salient points. Usually the first two columns which appear after each fund's name are titled "NAV," and "Offer Price." No-loads can be identified by the "NL" in the second column. Where there is a number in the "offer price" column that is higher than the NAV, it is a front-end load fund; the difference between the NAV and the offer price is the front-end commission that goes to the mutual fund salesperson and his or her selling organization. Low-loads can be identified in the papers by the

---

Chart 2

Mutual fund listings

	NAV	Offer Price	Chg
Bernstein Fds:			
ShCAMu	12.50	12.50	
ShDvMu	12.50	12.50	
ShNYMu	12.45	12.45	−.01
GvSh	12.34	12.34	+.02
ShtDur	12.32	12.32	+.02
IntDur	12.71	12.71	+.04
Ca Mu	13.16	13.16	+.01
DivMu	13.10	13.10	+.01
NYMu	13.07	13.07	+.01
IntlVal	14.74	14.74	−.04
BerwynFd	17.71	17.71	−.08
BerwynInc	11.18	11.18	−.01
BhirudMc	8.44	8.95	+.06
Biltmore Funds:			
Balncd	10.18	10.66	+.01
Equity	10.58	11.08	−.01
EqIndx	10.89	11.40	+.01
Fixedin	9.26	9.70	+.03
QuantEq	10.14	10.62	+.01
STFIxIn	9.70	9.95	+.01
Blanchard Funds:			
AmerEq	9.47	9.47	
EmGrln	5.73	5.73	−.06
FlxTFB	4.97	NL	
FlexInc	4.65	NL	+.01
GlGrp	9.13	9.13	
PrcMp	6.54	6.54	+.09
ST Gl	1.65	NL	
ST Bd	2.92	NL	
BramwlGp			
	10.72	NL	
Brndyw	24.66	NL	+.03
Brinson Funds:			
US Bal	10.43	NL	+.01
Bruce	96.78	96.78	+.50
BrundgSl	10.18	10.18	+.02
BuffBal	10.01	NL	+.02
Bull & Bear Gp:			
Glbincp	7.62	7.62	+.01
Goldp	12.35	12.35	+.25
GovtScp	14.58	14.58	+.06
Mulncp	15.95	15.95	+.04
QualGtp	13.28	13.28	−.02
SpEqp	20.54	20.54	+.17
USOvsp	7.13	7.13	+.04
Burnhmp	19.72	20.33	+.03
C&SRlty	31.81	NL	+.02
CGM Funds:			
AmerTF	9.15	NL	+.01
CapDv	20.64	NL	−.02
Fxdinc	9.90	NL	+.02
Mutl	25.09	NL	−.01
Realty	9.56	NL	−.02
Calmos p	12.13	12.70	+.02
C&OAggG	11.60	NL	
California Trust:			
CA Ins	10.09	10.09	+.02
CalUS	10.15	NL	+.04
S&P500	11.53	NL	+.01
S&PMld	11.69	NL	+.02
Calvert Group:			
GlobEq	15.59	16.37	+.02

	NAV	Offer Price	Chg
FirstMut	8.46	NL	+.03
First Omaha:			
Equity	11.27	NL	+.01
FxdInc	9.57	NL	+.05
SIFxIn	9.64	NL	+.02
First Priority:			
Balancd	10.31	10.52	+.02
Equity	10.22	NL	+.01
Fxdinc	9.70	NL	+.03
LtdMGv	9.73	9.93	+.02
First Union:			
BalAp	11.63	12.21	+.02
BalBT	11.63	11.63	+.02
BalY	11.64	NL	+.02
FxInAp	9.73	10.22	+.03
FxInY	9.73	NL	+.02
HiGdAp	10.35	10.87	+.01
HiGdY	10.35	10.35	+.01
MnBdY	9.60	NL	+.03
USGAp	9.31	9.77	+.03
USGBr	9.31	9.31	+.03
UtilityBT	9.09	9.09	+.04
ValueB1	17.66	18.54	−.02
ValueBt	17.64	17.64	−.02
ValueY	17.66	17.66	−.02
Flag Investors:			
EmGtp	13.95	14.61	−.02
Intincp	9.86	10.01	+.02
IntlTrp	11.58	12.13	−.06
MMunp	10.17	10.65	+.03
QuiGp	12.16	12.73	−.02
Telinp	12.48	13.07	+.06
TRTsp	9.38	9.82	+.02
Valuep	11.64	12.19	+.01
Flagship Group:			
AATEAp			
	10.46	10.92	+.02
AATECp			
	10.45	10.45	+.02
AZTEAp			
	10.48	10.94	+.03
GldRbp	17.06	17.06	+.05
IntTEp	9.97	10.28	+.01
LtTEp	10.43	10.70	+.01
UtilAp	9.72	10.15	+.01
Flex Funds:			
Bondp	19.57	NL	+.08
Glblnp	9.32	NL	
Grthp	13.57	NL	
Mulrp	10.45	NL	+.01
Fontaine	11.18	NL	+.08
Fortis Funds:			
AstAIAp	14.62	15.31	+.03
CapitIAp	17.52	18.39	
CaApAp	24.16	25.30	+.01
FldcrAp	29.25	30.71	−.03
GlbGrAp			
	14.17	14.88	+.01
GvTRAp	7.81	8.18	+.03
GrwthAp			
	26.16	27.46	−.01
HIYIdAp	7.78	8.15	
TFNatE	10.50	10.99	+.02

■ The second column is the Net Asset Value (NAV) per share as of the close of the preceding business day. In some newspapers, the NAV is identified as the sell or the bid price—the amount, per share, you would receive if you sold your shares, less any deferred sales charges.

■ The third column is the offering price or, in some papers, the buy or asked price—the price you would pay if you purchased shares. The buy price is the NAV plus any sales charges. NL for no-load, appears in this column, and the buy price is the same as the NAV. If the NAV and the offer price are the same, it means the fund has no initial load, but it does have a CDSC.

■ The fourth column shows the change, if any, in net asset value from the preceding quotation—in other words, the change over the most recent one-day trading period.

■ "p" means the fund has a 12b-1 plan.

■ A "t" indicates the fund has both a "p" and an "r." (the "t" stands for terrible!)

■ An "r" after the name indicates the fund has either a redemption fee or a CDSC (a contingent deferred sales charge).

■ An "f" after the fund's name indicates the price is for the previous day.

■ "x" indicates the fund went ex-dividend the previous day.

■ "e" is "ex" a capital gains distribution

■ "s" the fund split its shares or declared a stock dividend.

small spread between the bid and asked prices. For example, Fidelity Select Energy Services Fund was listed one day with an NAV of $10.00, and an offer price of $10.20. This 2% difference is the load. In other cases, where the numbers in the first and second columns are the same, the fund is charging a sales commission, either buried in the price (the infamous 12b-1 or hidden-load fee) or paid at the back-end, the CDSC. Letter symbols after the names of many of the loaded funds explain just what fees are being charged.

Performance should always be paramount in your selection of a fund. If no-loads don't perform as well as the loads, you would be foolish to buy an inferior fund simply to save the sales charge. Poor performance costs many times more than any commission you might save.

No-loads and loads perform equally well

However, no-load funds are every bit as good as load funds. Independent research has consistently shown no difference in performance, on average, between the two types when the load is disregarded.

As far back as 1962, a special study prepared by the Wharton School of Finance for the Securities and Exchange Commission found "no evidence that higher sales charges go hand-in-hand with better investment performance." Indeed, the study showed that fund shareholders paying higher sales charges had a less favorable investment experience than those paying less.

One of the best studies was an exhaustive comparison of no-loads versus loads covering income, growth, and stability. It was conducted in 1971 by FundScope, formerly a financial publisher, and concluded: "In the end, because so many no-load and so many load funds perform above average and so many below average, you must reach the conclusion that there just is no relationship, no correlation, between load and results."

In 1979, Computer Directions Advisors, Inc. (now CDA/Wiesenberger), compared 82 no-load mutual funds with assets of $7.3 billion with 138 load mutual funds with assets of $22.0 billion. They found there was no significant difference in risk, diversification, rate of return or risk-adjusted performance over the one-, three-, and five-year periods ending June 30, 1979.

Consumer Reports looked at the performance of more than 1,000 stock funds over a five-year period 1988 to 1992, and found that no-load funds had an average annual return of 13.5%, compared to 13.3% for load funds.

In 1994, the average diversified no-load equity fund lost 1.5% compared to a loss of 1.7% for all diversified equity funds tracked in the comprehensive Lipper Mutual Fund Performance Analysis, which rates all funds regardless of loads.

Look at it this way. The load is a *marketing* expense, and has no bearing on investment management expertise. If a load fund group drops the load, there is no reason for its performance to change. Its management has not changed. In the same vein several groups, for example Dreyfus and Fidelity, manage both load and no-load funds—and in some cases, individual portfolio managers manage both no-load and load funds. What difference would the load make to the performance of their investment managers?

In sum, a sales charge—or lack of it—is not a factor in achieving performance. The conclusion is inescapable: load or no-load, the basic product is the same. So it's only logical to go no-load and save the commission expense.

The high cost of the load

By law, the maximum sales charge load funds are allowed to collect is 8.5%. And for many years the majority of load funds were sold at that level. In recent years, though, competition from no-load funds and increased consumer awareness has forced most load funds to lower their fees somewhat. But even at the lower levels, the costs are far more damaging to your wealth than you may suspect.

First of all, the sales charge that you actually pay is understated because it is expressed as a percentage of the total purchase price (net asset value plus sales charge) rather than as a percentage of the amount you invest in a fund. The 8.5% maximum load is really 9.3%—it's 8.5% of the money you pay out, but 9.3% of what you invest. That's because if you put $10,000 into a load fund, $850 goes to the sales organization; the balance—$9,150—would actually be invested in stocks and bonds. Divide the $850 by $9,150 and you get 9.3%. If you want $10,000 working for you in a load fund, you must pay $10,930 total. Similarly, a 5.75% load, when calculated correctly, is really 6.1%.

It is amazing that so many investors accept these costs with equanimity. If these same investors bought a stock or a fund that suffered an instantaneous loss of 6% or more, they would be beside themselves with anguish. But that's exactly the same as the loss you incur paying the load.

Over the years, mutual fund salesmen have offered many arguments to justify their commissions. One common rationale is to claim that the load amortizes over the years. They argue that over a period of nine years, for instance, an 8 1/2% charge is amortized to only 1% per year. They then conclude that 1% a year doesn't have any real impact, and then imply that after nine years you are home free and clear. This is not only not true, it is in fact the opposite of the truth. The longer you hold a fund, the greater the cost of the load. That's because commission money paid to the broker compounds each year. This constant compounding increases the spread between a no-load's and a load fund's returns.

For example: Take two funds, one a pure no-load, the other one carrying a 6% front-end load. You invest $10,000 in each. The load fund starts out 6% — or $600 — behind. If both funds grow at the same rate, the load fund will always be 6% behind—30 years, 40 years, even 50 years later. Now the salesman will argue "it's 40 years later, your fund is up 2,000%; the no-load is up 2,006%. Big deal."

Well it is a big deal. The $10,000 investment in the load fund may now be worth $1 million. But the no-load will be worth 6% more. That 6% now represents a *$60,000 advantage*, six times your original investment! Moral: you spend dollars, not percentages.

The above example is fairly realistic for many investors. We checked this with another comparison based on an 8.5% load. Assume a person starts investing in no-loads at age 20. For the next five years he invests $100 a month. At age 25 he increases it to $250 a month, at 30 to $500 a month, and finally from age 40 to 65 he invests $1,000 a month. At the same 10% annual growth rate he will have amassed $1,421,574 by age 65, that is *$121,684 more* than a comparable load fund investor. *This is the real difference the load makes.*

These comparisons also presume growth during a bull market. But there are also bear markets; then the no-load investor doesn't suffer the instantaneous commission loss on top of his declining net asset values.

Furthermore, there are no savings paying with asset-based sales charges (series B or C). A 12b-1 fee of one percent, which results in a high expense ratio, cuts performance just as the front-end load cuts performance. There's a high cost to a load, whether it's paid up-front, back-end or level.

No-load mutual funds are investing's greatest bargain. Suppose you wanted to invest $100,000 through a broker. Table 3 shows how much commission you would pay for various investments.

With no-loads there's no commission. And not only that, you don't have to deal with a broker!

Table 3

Commissions on a $100,000 investment	
Type of investment	**Commission range**
No-load mutual fund	zero
Treasury securities	$50
Municipal bond	$500- $2,000
Common stock	$500- $3,000
Unit investment trust	$3,000- $4,900
Load mutual fund	$1,000- $9,300
New stock offering	$3,000-$10,000
Limited partnership	$6,000-$10,000

CHAPTER 3

You can select a top-performing no-load yourself

Choosing the best funds is crucial. You have hundreds of different no-load stock and bond funds to choose from, with a wide range of objectives. They vary enormously in performance, and picking the wrong fund can be costly.

The typical investor—and certainly you—can select top-performing funds without any salesperson's help. A comparison of past selections made by no-load and load investors proves this point. As we noted earlier, both load and no-load fund categories feature superior and inferior funds—and money is invested in all of them. In the case of load funds, the investor is assisted in his choice by an adviser or salesperson. With no-loads, the investor is the sole decision maker.

We can prove that no-load fund investors are more sophisticated and do a better job of picking funds than investors working with salesmen. We do that by looking at where the money is going. In other words, are the best funds getting the most money?

Even though the proportion of good and bad funds is roughly the same in the load and no-load categories, we found that no-load fund investors, acting on their own, are more likely to put their money into the best performing funds than are load fund investors, assisted by salesmen or brokers. And here's the proof: fully 49% of no-load assets, we discovered, are in funds whose returns ranked in the top

20% of all equity funds over a five-year period; only 33% of load fund assets are in these top-performing funds.

Since many investments remain in the same fund for years, it is possible that some of these funds were better at the time they were purchased than they are now. If this is the case, the load has obviously inhibited these investors from selling when the performance of their funds faltered. How else could so much money remain invested in mediocre load funds?

This study was first done in 1972 and has been repeated periodically ever since. The results have been consistent over the years. We think the reason the no-load fund investors continually win is that they have only one interest: the superior performance of *their own money.* Salesmen, alas, have other interests in addition to performance: some funds pay higher commissions than others, or they may

Chart 4
___

Where investors put their money

Percent distribution of

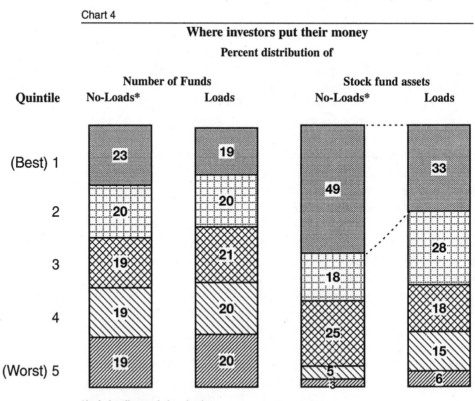

Quintile	Number of Funds		Stock fund assets	
	No-Loads*	Loads	No-Loads*	Loads
(Best) 1	23	19	49	33
2	20	20		28
3	19	21	18	18
4	19	20	25	15
(Worst) 5	19	20	5 / 3	6

*includes direct sale low-loads
Source: Quintile returns, five years ending 1994. Assets Dec. 1994.

not be able to sell the best funds. (In some cases, the universe of load funds they can sell is quite small.) Some brokerage houses reward brokers by giving them a greater percent of the gross commission earned for selling internal funds than for outside funds. These differentials make dollars and sense to the brokerage firms because when an in-house fund is sold, the company receives a management fee for as long as the customer's money remains in that fund. The differential doesn't necessarily serve the investor well, though. There have also been studies that conclude that brokerage-house funds are largely inferior in terms of performance.

Here's another caveat: brokerage firms frequently put on educational seminars for potential customers. It's fine to go to learn, but realize that they will inevitably wind up trying to sell you commissionable products.

Shouldn't I buy the best fund regardless of the load?

We're frequently asked that question. The answer is yes, but... Certainly you would be better off if you invested in a load fund that outperforms all no-loads—*but* only if you could count on that fund to continue its superior performance. You can't be certain of such results. Past performance is no guarantee of future results, as the saying goes, particularly when you are "marrying" the fund, as you are likely to do with the loads.

Out of the thousands of funds in existence over the years, only two could possibly claim they had a chance of beating *all* no-loads: Templeton Growth, and Fidelity Magellan. Templeton Growth was the number one fund, load and no-load, for the 20 years ending December 1981. Fidelity Magellan is the number one fund for the 15 years ending 1994. Magellan isn't exactly a load or a no-load, but rather a low-load, that is marketed directly to investors. Templeton Growth, though it still has a respectable record, has no chance of coming anywhere close to beating all no-loads anymore. Similarly, Magellan, at $37 billion, has its best days behind it. And we've identified these funds on the basis of very long-term track records, the kind salesmen love to cite. At this writing there is no new Templeton Growth or Magellan in sight. The top diversified load fund for the 10 years ending 1994 is the $3.7 billion AIM Constellation. Its long-time manager retired in December 1993, and its chances of beating all no-loads is slight.

No-load investors vs. salesmen

The differing sales patterns between no-load fund investors and those who purchase funds through an adviser or salesperson confirm the results of our broad-based studies. It is a fact that over the long-term equity funds outperform bond funds. Yet salesmen continually emphasize bond funds. The data in Table 5 from the Investment Company Institute compare equity and fixed-income fund sales for funds distributed by sales forces versus those marketed directly. The column labeled Sales Force essentially shows load fund purchases. The next column, labeled Direct Marketed, shows no-load and direct marketed low-load fund sales.

In 1992, 60% of no-load sales were equity mutual funds, and 40% were fixed-income funds. In the case of load funds sold by salesmen, the figures were almost exactly the opposite. In 1993, a better year for equities, a higher proportion of no-load purchases went into equity funds. But on the load fund side, brokers still sold more bond funds than equity funds. In 1994, when the performance of fixed-income securities was awful, direct marketed sales of bond funds dropped to just 20% of total sales. Yet, the sales of loaded fixed-income funds were more than twice as high, accounting for almost 38% of investments into load funds.

Considering the brokers' actions, you might say there are four kinds of yields: current yield, yield to call, yield to maturity—and yield to broker!

Mutual fund salesmen have other tactics to win clients away from the no-loads. One is to scare prospective customers by telling them that no-loads have higher expense ratios than load funds and that in

Table 5

Mutual fund sales by objective

Total (in $M)	1992		1993		1994	
	Direct marketed	Sales force	Direct marketed	Sales force	Direct marketed	Sales force
Equity	$76,993	$89,031	$126,375	$134,383	$152,316	$151,473
Bond & Inc	$51,295	$125,491	$56,569	$156,080	$39,453	$91,858
Percentage						
Equity	60.0%	41.5%	69.1%	46.3%	79.4%	62.3%
Bond & Inc	40.0%	58.5%	31.0%	53.7%	20.6%	37.8%

Source: ICI

the long run will prove to be more expensive even taking the load into account. That argument, to put it mildly, is disingenuous. The average no-load doesn't have a higher expense ratio than the average load fund (this is documented in Chapter 14), and in individual cases only a handful of no-loads have higher overall costs. So while it is theoretically possible for commission funds to end up charging lower fees, even including the load, in practice it's quite rare.

Moreover, one of the beauties of no-loads is that you can select the best; there is no salesmen to fast-talk you into buying an inferior fund. It's easy to avoid a no-load with a high expense ratio. If you'd like to be certain of finding a no-load with an expense ratio lower than whatever fund a salesman is pushing, deal with Vanguard. That no-load company has led the way in reducing overhead costs. The average Vanguard equity fund has an expense ratio of .36; the average Vanguard bond, municipal bond, and money market funds have expense ratios of .27%, .20% and .28%, respectively.

Another tactic that brokers sometimes use is to complain that "no-loads are not no-load." By this they mean that no-loads also have marketing costs, which ultimately have to be paid by the customer. One load fund advisor asked, "Who pays for all those no-load advertisements in the popular financial press? (The very same press that promotes no-load fund investing.)"

Our response here is that of course no-loads advertise—and of course that costs money. But the expense is picayune compared to the cost of a personal one-on-one sales call. Fidelity is the heaviest advertiser, but the group's ad money comes primarily from the 3% low-load commission sales. The second heaviest advertiser is Dreyfus. This group's no-load funds have a very modest average expense ratio of .72%. The company's heaviest advertising is frequently for new funds that are waiving expenses. Vanguard, which is a sizeable advertiser, breaks out its marketing expenses in its fund prospectuses. It amounts to about .03% of assets—that's three one-hundreds of one percent. Their Tax-Advantaged Funds have a .02% marketing cost. Advertising is cheap. Even commercials on the Super Bowl, probably the most expensive ads on TV, cost advertisers only about two cents per each viewing home they reach. A broker can't make a sales call for two cents. Nobody ever claimed no-loads were a free lunch. They have to make themselves known, and advertising is a cheap way to do so. Don't forget, the cost of distributing no-load funds is included in the funds' expense ratios.

You can't take it with you

By now most of the liabilities of load fund investing have been well publicized. So it's of some interest that we report on a liability few readers are likely to be aware of: most in-house, proprietary brokerage funds lack portability.

Let's say your long-time, highly-competent PaineWebber broker tells you that he is leaving PaineWebber to go across the street to Merrill Lynch. Naturally, he wants you to move with him. You will find that your stocks can be transferred; but if you own a PaineWebber fund, it can't be transferred with the rest of your securities. And if you decide to sell in order to follow him, you could very well face a capital gains tax.

Here's another situation. You want your securities to be managed on a discretionary basis by a money manager who executes transactions through a discount broker like Charles Schwab. You can move the stocks, bonds and other mutual fund shares from your Dean Witter account over to Schwab. But you can't move your shares in Dean Witter's in-house funds.

While we've used PaineWebber and Dean Witter as examples, similar restrictions apply to in-house mutual funds at other major retail brokerage firms. And even though some brokerage firms, Prudential and Smith Barney, for instance, will let you transfer out their proprietary funds, you are apt to have difficulty at the other end. The new brokerage firm may very well refuse to accept them.

You do have some alternatives, but they are inferior. 1) You can sell the shares ... but then there are tax consequences, and a possible back-end sales charge. 2) You can leave the fund shares in the old firm's account ... but then you may have to contend with a strange broker, or there may be an inactive-account charge, or an annual IRA fee. 3) In some cases you can send the shares to the transfer agent for holding. But that's probably no improvement. Future transactions will have to be handled by a letter that contains a signature guarantee. 4) In a few cases you can send the certificates to the new broker, but only for safekeeping. That means dividends can't be reinvested, no additional purchases can be made, and if you want to sell, the shares must be sent back to the original brokerage firm or its transfer agent, causing a delay, which could be costly. These alternatives don't accomplish your goal: to move to a new brokerage account.

This overview is somewhat oversimplified, of course, and there can be exceptions. In individual cases, it may be possible to set up ways to ease the difficulty. But in an age when fund and brokerage accounts are increasingly integrated, lack of portability is a serious drawback.

Let's stress that this inflexibility we're describing applies only to these firms' in-house funds. If you hold funds in the American, Franklin, Putnam or other load fund families in your brokerage account, they will usually be transferrable.

Active no-load fund investors often keep their funds in accounts at discount brokerage houses to consolidate their holdings. Unfortunately, this great convenience, with some minor exceptions, doesn't apply to in-house brokerage funds.

If you are willing to spend some time learning about mutual funds and to do some work evaluating them, you can easily pick top mutual funds on your own. Other no-load investors are doing it right now. So can you. No-load mutual funds can make your money grow and perhaps will do so more conveniently and more consistently than other investment approaches.

It's worth buying no-loads

PART II

Finding the Right Funds For You

CHAPTER 4

Your first steps to profitable investing in no-loads

Buying no-load funds is a challenging do-it-yourself program in which you have to take the initiative. It requires time and know-how. But once you've learned the fundamentals, your periodic review shouldn't take more than one hour a month. It's well worth the effort. When you follow a logical plan, the psychic and monetary rewards of investing in no-loads are great.

Here are the steps you'll need to take to initiate a no-load investment program. We'll discuss each of them in more detail in subsequent chapters.

1. Analyze your specific investment objectives. How much risk are you willing to take? Could you accept great risks for maximum gains? Or would you prefer a more conservative course of investing, with less risk and less potential?

2. Learn to recognize which mutual funds are designed to meet your specific investment objectives. This vital step is the one most often neglected by investors. Far too many unknowingly buy funds that are either too speculative or too conservative for them, and their investment programs suffer as a result.

3. Select no-load funds whose objectives coincide with your own. No matter what your investing style, allocate a percentage of your assets to a *core holding* of mutual funds that you can hold long-term

throughout both bull and bear markets. These are generally conservative funds or, occasionally, more aggressive funds that have a history of selling stocks and sitting with cash when market conditions are uncertain or adverse.

4. Analyze past performance to determine the best two or three funds among those that meet your objective.

5. Learn the criteria for selecting those funds that are most likely to perform well in the future.

6. Write or phone for prospectuses of two or three top-performing funds.

7. Read the prospectus, in particular the sections detailing the fund's investment philosophy and allowable investments. Look carefully at the fee table and the expense ratio.

8. Then make a decision and invest in one or more funds.

9. Continue to follow the performance of these and other top-ranked funds.

With this plan of action you can design your own financially rewarding investment program. For the details, read on.

Making your peace with risk

Understanding and managing risk is by far the most important skill that you must master in order to be a skilled investor—in mutual funds or any other kind of investment. Here's why. First, *there's no way you can avoid risk*. While everyone understands the risk of losing principal—i.e., seeing the value of a security decline in nominal terms—fewer realize that there are numerous other risks that can be just as deadly. For example, the loss of income that occurs when CD rates decline, or the loss of an investment's value in real terms due to inflation.

You need to take equity risks

Generally speaking, stocks are riskier than fixed-income investments and, for that reason, provide greater rewards. Research by Ibbotson Associates indicates that over the long term—69 years—we can expect a total return on common stocks of 10.2% annually. During this period, the Consumer Price Index rose 3.1% a year, on average, which means that the real returns from stocks were about 7% annually. On the other hand, fixed-income investments, as typified by long-term corporate bonds, averaged 5.4% a year—leaving you only a 2% edge over inflation.

While the Ibbotson numbers commonly are quoted back to 1926, we have broken out the data for the last 50 years. By doing so, we eliminated the effect of the Great Depression, which we don't see ever recurring. When the Depression is removed from the numbers, we find that stocks have averaged almost 12% a year and inflation has risen to 4.4% a year. But bonds remained about the same, meaning that a conservative fixed-income investor whose investments were entirely in bonds or bills would have seen the purchasing power of his money actually contract after the impact of income taxes was taken into account.

Of course, returns varied greatly during this half-century. Standard deviation is a statistical measure showing variation over a period of time. It is typically used as a proxy for risk. A high standard deviation indicates high volatility: large swings between gains and loses. A lower standard deviation indicates a more conservative security. The standard deviation for stocks over the 50 year period was 16.5, far greater than the deviations for either bonds or Treasury bills, which were respectively 9.9 and 3.2. Look at it this way, if stocks weren't riskier investments than, say, CD's, they wouldn't have better returns than CDs.

Table 6

Long-term historical returns:
Compounded annual returns with income reinvested

	69 years 1/1/26- 12/31/94	50 years 1/1/45 12/31/94	50 years Standard deviations
Common stocks (the S&P 500)	10.19%	11.92%	16.5
20-year Corporate bonds	5.38	5.31	9.6
20-year Government bonds	4.84	5.01	9.9
Treasury bills	3.68	4.69	3.2
Inflation (Consumer Price Index)	3.13	4.36	3.8

While we like to think that low single digit inflation is acceptable, it really isn't. Even a 4% inflation rate can seriously erode your assets in 15 to 20 years. Today's senior citizens usually live at least that long after retirement. Therefore, investing too conservatively can jeopardize the purchasing power of your assets over a long period of time.

In short, stocks are riskier than fixed-return investments, since they fluctuate more in value. Yet, over long periods of time they are

Table 7

Value of $1,000 at various inflation rates
Average annual rate of inflation

Years	4%	5%	6%
5	$815	$774	$734
10	665	599	539
15	542	463	395
20	442	358	290
25	360	277	213

the only investment to decisively outpace inflation. Consequently, it is imperative that every investor keep at least a portion of his assets in equities. As we describe the many varieties of mutual funds in the following chapters, keep this overriding principal in mind.

Risk ordains reward

Usually, over a long period of time the relationship between risk and reward is reasonably fixed. The greater the risk, the greater the reward—and vice versa. Novice investors often make certain demands of financial advisers and money managers: "I'd like an investment that gains 20% annually," is a frequent request. Another common assumption: "If you've earned 15% annually in the past, can I assume you'll make 15% a year for me once I've signed up with your organization?"

Sorry, it doesn't work that way. Reward is ephemeral. It depends on the market conditions, the economy and other factors that are difficult to predict. Risk, on the other hand, is easier to evaluate and predict. Thus in the long run the amount of risk you undertake will determine your investment reward.

Match funds to your investment objectives

As in any carefully planned investment program, the first step in selecting mutual funds is to establish your investment objectives. Next, identify those funds—out of hundreds catering to a wide range of objectives—that meet your goals.

Typically, young investors look for growth. They need to build up their savings for a variety of reasons—emergencies, a new house, their children's college education, eventual retirement. Older investors, who already have an estate, need income to live on in retirement and safety

of principal. Since many funds serve each need, you first have to know
how to classify mutual funds by their investment objective.

At one end of the spectrum are funds committed to a policy of
conservative investing, specifically, to conserve capital and produce
income. At the other extreme are funds that invest speculatively for
maximum capital gains. In between, funds are spread across every
segment of the investment horizon, and it is often difficult to determine minor differences in their investment philosophies.

In Chart 8, we've graphically depicted the wide spectrum of
objectives as a dial. Conservative funds, appropriate for the investor
who wants minimum risk, are at the far left; aggressive funds, that
offer the possibility of high returns and the accompanying risks, are
on the right. The analogy holds because it is a continuous spectrum.
The differences between an income fund and one called growth-

Chart 8

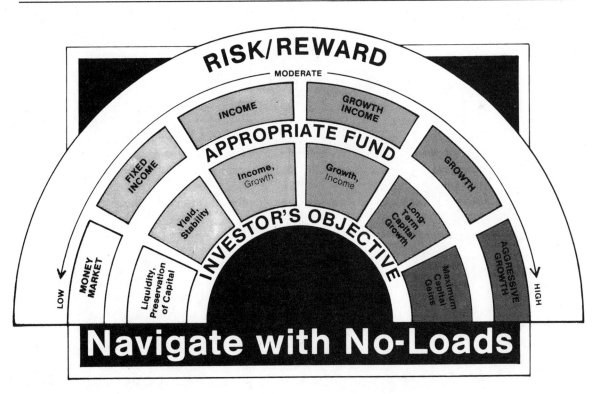

income may be slight, just as the difference between traveling 50 versus 55 miles per hour is not great. But at the opposite ends of the dial, the differences are huge.

In Chapters 5 though 13, we explain the differences between the various types of funds so as to provide you with the proper grounding to make your selections. We start with the most speculative funds, and then chapter by chapter proceed down the risk spectrum.

In Chapters 14-21, we describe the strategies, techniques and even "tricks" that you can use to obtain the best performance from your no-load funds.

Finally, in Chapters 22 and 23 we guide you through the administrative maze of do-it-yourself no-load investing.

CHAPTER 5

Aggressive growth funds

Funds that invest for the greatest possible gain are called aggressive growth funds. They also go by several other names: "maximum capital gains," "capital appreciation" and "performance" funds. In the 1960s such funds were called "go-go," a term that fell into disrepute after the 1973-74 stock market debacle, when the go-go's went-went.

The principal characteristics of the aggressive growth funds are:

■ They are oriented toward achieving capital gains.

■ To achieve their gains, they must take risks, investing in speculative stocks.

■ They are volatile, doing very well in bull markets and very badly in bear markets.

■ They may occasionally use adventurous investing techniques — margined portfolios, options and short selling.

The objective of an aggressive growth fund is to grow faster than all the other funds by buying stocks that can outperform the market to the fullest possible extent. Top growth means top returns for management because money pours into the current best performers. Since management fees are determined basically by the size of the fund, superior growth is a good way for fund management to increase its income. This is especially true for no-load funds. Because they have no sales agents and their advertising budgets are generally limited, an impressive growth record is imperative. With an outstanding record, the fund's advertising stands out and fund management finds it easy to get noticed by the media. That's how no-loads grow.

Greater rewards entail bigger risks

Those who manage aggressive growth funds are not afraid to take risks in order to grow rapidly. Some attempt to call turns in the market. They buy stocks they think have the greatest potential, often highly volatile stocks in vogue industries. They are quick to sell those that don't measure up.

The profit potential for investors willing to accept the risks these funds take is tremendous. In a bull market, the best aggressive growth funds can give you heady performance. For example, in 1993 more aggressive growth funds appeared in the top 50 best performing diversified funds than any other category. In 1994, some of these funds did well, primarily those with heavy technology stock weightings. But aggressive funds that did not contain technology stocks did poorly. Over a half-dozen no-loads suffered double digit losses.

Mutual fund performance should be calculated in terms of percent changes. However, the psychological impact is greater when you see a spectacular fund's performance expressed in dollars and cents. Top-ranked Fidelity Magellan, for example, went from $3.86 in 1975 to a high of $75.16 a share in 1994, and also distributed $64.15 a share in capital gains.

Now, some investors held individual stocks that performed well in this period but how many had whole portfolios that duplicated the performance of these top-ranked funds? Their growth was achieved over an entire portfolio, including cash reserves held along the way. In contrast to the popular stock averages, this represents net growth after management fees, expenses and transaction costs have been deducted.

On the other hand, we should emphasize that the variations in the performance of aggressive growth funds are particularly wide because the managers are taking great risks. The American Heritage Fund ranked number one among all funds for the three years ending 1993, gaining 230%. In 1994, the fund went to fifth worst, declining 35.4%.

In the October 1987 meltdown, the average aggressive growth fund lost 26%. The most volatile funds in the group lost more than 30%. And that included well-managed funds like Twentieth Century Vista, which lost 33%. In the milder downturn that began in the third quarter of 1990, the average aggressive growth fund declined 21.9%, while the worst, the Prudent Speculator Leveraged Fund, declined 46.4%. It made the disastrous mistake of being 40% leveraged at the outset.

Because performances vary so dramatically, you have to take great care in selecting aggressive growth funds. And then, keep a sharp eye on them!

A 1991 study by the Systems & Forecasts newsletter quantified the aggressive growth funds' lack of consistency over a five-year period. The study examined the standard deviations (see definition in Appendix B) of 963 funds that invest in U.S. equities and found that the range for results for high volatility funds was far greater than for low volatility funds.

The study broke the universe into four groups with standard deviations ranging from below 1.5 to above 3.0. Funds in the under 1.5 standard deviation group had an average five-year gain of 8.86% with almost all funds gaining between 5% and 10%. On the other hand, the funds with standard deviations over 3.0 averaged a 13% gain, but the dispersion around the average was far greater, ranging from a 2.5% annual gain to a 20% return. In fact the range in performance did not even peak around the average but at a higher level—17.5%. Selectivity among this group is thus far more important than among the lower volatility funds. Chart 9 provides the details.

Small company growth funds

These are funds that specialize in the stocks of small, or sometimes, medium-sized firms. One definition used by some funds: companies that rank in the smallest 20% of NYSE stocks in terms of market capitalization. (Which means a stock's market price times the number of its shares outstanding. In other words, market capitalization is the total value of all its shares.) Most small company growth funds are in the aggressive growth category. They exhibit the volatility and accompanying risk of aggressive growth funds.

There are three varieties of small company growth funds: those that invest in high growth stocks; funds that invest in undervalued stocks or asset situations; and index funds, which tend to invest across the size spectrum. Most small company growth funds are in the first category. An example of a small company asset fund is Pennsylvania Mutual. Two index funds are the Vanguard Small Cap Stock Fund and the Vanguard Extended Market Fund; the latter has stocks with larger capitalizations than the former. In addition, there are also small company global and international funds.

You can usually identify these funds by the language in the objectives section of their prospectuses and by inspecting their portfolios.

Chart 9

Fund performance ranges by volatility

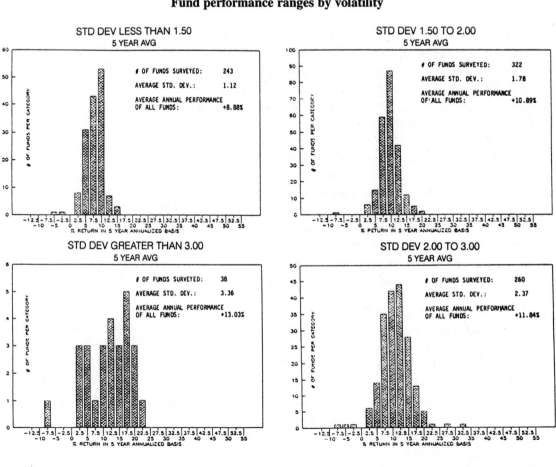

Source: Systems & Forecasts

Shares of smaller companies, such as those traded on the American Stock Exchange and NASDAQ, as well as secondary issues on the New York Stock Exchange, have generally outperformed the blue chips over the years. A study by Roger Ibbotson and Rex Sinquefield found that a dollar invested in the average small cap stock in 1926 would have been worth $2,440 at the end of 1994! By comparison, a dollar invested in the S&P 500 stocks would have grown to only $811 in this 69-year period. And a dollar invested to exactly match inflation would now be worth $8.36. That equates to average annual rates of 12.0%., 10.2%. and 3.1%., respectively.

Other studies have found that the returns from small company stocks are sufficient to offset their greater volatility and lack of liquidity. On a risk-adjusted basis, the smallest companies' returns are still significantly higher than the returns from larger company stocks.

A distinction can be drawn between small cap stocks and emerging growth stocks. The latter are untried and have high failure rates. Most small company funds do not invest in start-up companies. For example, Twentieth Century Ultra stipulates that the companies it invests in must have at least three years of continuous operation.

Similarly, small cap may not correspond to small company as measured by sales or assets. While the words small cap and small company tend to be used interchangably, they are not the same. A good-sized company unloved by Wall Street may sell at a low price, and thus have a small market capitalization. Conversely, some very small companies whose stocks are wildly overpriced will have large market caps. The studies that have proven small company stocks are superior are mostly based on market cap, typically listed stocks (which excludes most emerging companies).

Small companies don't always outperform large companies, but there are good reasons why they may in the long run:

■ The mathematics of growth are more favorable in small companies. A new product or service will usually have a greater impact on revenues and profits in a small company than in a large company.

■ Small companies are more entrepreneurial. Their management owns more stock and works harder. With their simpler structure and leaner bureaucracy, they are more flexible and make decisions more rapidly. Each decision maker has a greater impact on the business.

■ Small companies are more innovative. Over half of all the important innovations in the U.S. during the last 40 years have come from small businesses and individuals on their own.

■ Small firms are closer to their customers and to the marketplace.

One rough gauge of this category's attractiveness is small companies' price/earnings ratios compared to those of large companies. Chart 10, which shows this relationship, is frequently included with quarterly reports distributed by the T. Rowe Price New Horizons Fund. When small company p/e's are only slightly higher than those of large companies (as exemplified by those corporations that comprise Standard & Poor Corp.'s 500-stock index), small company funds generally are a good buy. When their p/e's are twice as high as the S&P 500's they are a sell.

Chart 10

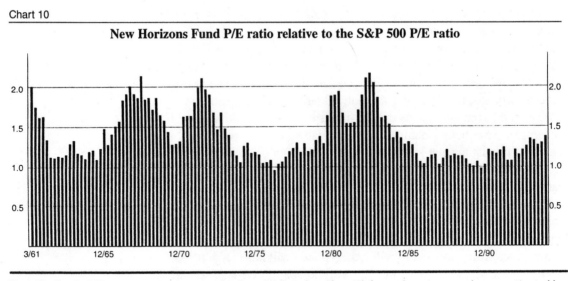

New Horizons Fund P/E ratio relative to the S&P 500 P/E ratio

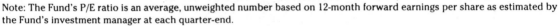

Note: The Fund's P/E ratio is an average, unweighted number based on 12-month forward earnings per share as estimated by the Fund's investment manager at each quarter-end.

We should reiterate one point. If you choose a small fund in order to maximize performance, realize that it is likely to excel primarily because of its maneuverability and its greater propensity to take risks, not because of inherently superior management. The large growth funds own the stocks of multibillion-dollar companies which are unlikely to go bankrupt in any recession. The same cannot be said of small companies; and even in booming times there have been bankruptcies in highly competitive fields, especially in the high-tech area.

How small is small?

Small means different things to different funds. At one extreme is the DFA U.S. Small Company Fund, which buys the ninth and tenth decile stocks (the bottom 20%) on the New York Stock Exchange. At the other extreme are "small company funds" that buy stocks that may rank near the median capitalization of all listed companies. The record for stretching the definition may be held by an institutional fund, the Regis FMA Small Company Portfolio, which is permitted to own stocks with capitalizations as large as $2 billion!

Another tactic: some small company funds have been known to vary the size of stocks they hold in their portfolios depending on market conditions. When small stocks are booming, they buy the smallest; when large cap stocks are popular, as they were throughout much of the 80s, these funds edge up to medium cap stocks. To give you some insight into market capitalizations, Table 11 shows the largest companies in each decile group among those stocks listed on the New York Stock Exchange, and how those companies relate to AMEX and NASDAQ stocks.

The great advantage that aggressive growth funds have is that they are the best way for an investor to buy a portfolio of stocks that's likely to grow dramatically. Because funds are diversified, it's less risky for them to buy secondary stocks than for you to. Even if one company goes bankrupt, it isn't catastrophic if that stock accounts for only 2% or 3% of a diversified portfolio, and possibly a good deal less than that.

Pros and cons of aggressive growth funds

Table 11

Decile sizes

Market capitalization deciles	Size ($MM)	NYSE Largest company	No. of companies*		
			NYSE	AMEX	NAT'L NASDAQ
1	84,752	AT&T	166	1	10
2	5,143	Union Carbide	166	1	17
3	2,661	Sherwin Williams	166	7	42
4	1,528	Boston Scientific	166	9	58
5	962	Morrison Restaurants	166	9	82
6	642	Flowers Inds	166	14	134
7	417	Standard Products	166	23	203
8	262	Aztar Corp.	166	35	329
9	157	Imco Recycling	166	93	763
10	71	Kollmorgen	166	429	1622

Market capitalization = price x shares outstanding as of 12/31/94
excludes ADRs, REITs, foreign companies and closed-end funds

The principal disadvantages of aggressive growth funds are their extreme price fluctuations, lack of defensive strengths in a bear market, and inconsistent performance. However, you can minimize these disadvantages by diversifying your investments. Buy shares in more than one fund, then follow the performances closely.

While the aggressive growth funds' volatility can be a disadvantage in the short run, it has been an advantage in the long run. Since World War II, bull markets have lasted longer and gone further than bear markets.

But ... watch out!

To make money in aggressive growth funds you have to be invested during those times when the market is making strong upward moves. Often, bull markets begin with a pop. So, you need to be invested at the end of a bear market. That's when the risks are lowest and the potential rewards the greatest.

On the other hand, investing after strong upward moves in the market diminishes your prospects. Buying stocks in periods of consolidation or, worse yet, near the end of a market advance, changes the risk/reward relationship dramatically.

It's more fun to see your money grow, naturally. The problem is that aggressive growth funds will fluctuate wildly in both directions. Chart 12 shows how the American Heritage Fund performed in 1994. Its 33.0% decline far exceeded the drop in the market. This a good example of the sort of volatility you should expect from an aggressive growth fund that is usually completely invested in stocks.

Chart 12

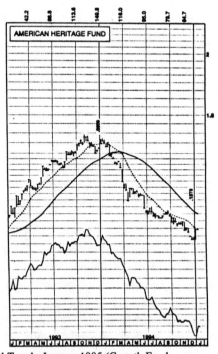

AMERICAN HERITAGE FUND

Source: Mutual Fund Trends, January 1995 (Growth Fund Research Bldg., Box 6600, Rapid City, SD 57709).

A few aggressive growth funds use leverage to increase their volatility. At times when the market is moving dramatically, these funds are frequently among the best—or the worst—performers.

At least half of all aggressive growth funds stay relatively fully invested at all times, even during bear markets. The reason is the difficulty in anticipating market tops and bottoms, and the cost of selling out and buying back a sizeable portfolio of stocks. It has been estimated that the stock market has to decline about 25% in order to justify a move to cash. Thus, funds are strongly inclined to ride out what may be a minor dip.

Furthermore, fund managers are greatly affected by what their competition does. Savvy investors recognize that aggressive growth funds will perform poorly in a bear market and they will get out themselves when the market declines. These investors are primarily interested in up-market performance. Thus, by staying fully invested during bear markets, a fund is assured of a fast start when the new bull market begins. Too many aggressive fund managers don't care if their fund declines during a bear market; they just don't want it to decline more than their competitors' funds.

So, holding aggressive growth funds in a bear market can be hazardous. If you have a low tolerance for large declines, or a short time horizon, you are best advised to stand clear of aggressive funds. Put another way, you should limit your investment in these funds to an amount you can do without, and invest only those dollars that you can afford to keep invested over a long period, at least three to five years.

And, if you're a sport and can take losses in stride, in Chapter 19 we'll give you some strategies for maximizing profits in aggressive growth stock funds throughout the market cycle.

The bear could get you if you don't get out

We use four criteria to determine whether a fund should be classified as aggressive growth. Our tests are (1) volatility, (2) analysis of a fund's objectives as stated in its prospectus, (3) dividend yield and (4) the fund's portfolio.

Volatility can be determined by noting a fund's fluctuations over various periods. You can get an up-to-the-minute guide by checking mutual fund prices in the daily newspaper on any day when there has been a large movement in the market. Pick a day when the Dow moves one per-

Identifying aggressive growth funds

cent or more. Let's assume the Dow Jones Industrial Average rose 40 points in one day. If the index was around 4000, this would mean an increase of 1%. Next, scan the mutual funds section in the financial pages to see which funds outpaced the Dow and by how big a margin. You have to do this quick analysis using percentages; looking at a fund's net asset value in terms of dollars-and-cents changes won't give you a meaningful comparison. *The Wall Street Journal* and a few other papers now provide percentage changes. If your newspaper doesn't, you can easily calculate the change.

For example: If the Dow was up 1% on a given day and a fund with a net asset value of $10 advanced 10 cents, then that fund's rise matched the Dow's; if it was up 20 cents — 2% — it went up twice as much as the Dow. Obviously, the calculation is the same when the market is declining. The point is how much a fund moves above or below the market.

On active days, some funds will move from one-and-one-half to three times as much as the market indexes. These are the aggressive growth funds. Naturally, price movements on any one day can be atypical; but, if you follow the prices over a number of such active days, you can get a pretty good idea which funds are the most volatile.

An easy way to make this comparison without having to flip all over the paper is to compare a fund's daily market action to the Vanguard Index funds. The Small Capitalization Stock Fund is an excellent proxy for small cap funds; the 500 Portfolio, which owns all the stocks that comprise the S&P 500 average, is a representative stand-in for the funds owning large capitalization stocks. (Look for Idx 500 under the Vanguard listings in the mutual fund tables.)

One caution: This is not a method for selecting funds to buy, nor is it a method of predicting future growth. The most volatile funds aren't always the biggest gainers in the long run.

Follow the bouncing betas

A more sophisticated way to measure the volatility of individual stocks, as well as entire portfolios, is called the beta coefficient. The theory behind it is based on two simple ideas: (1) that there is a fairly close correlation between the movement of most stocks and portfolios and the movement of the market as a whole, and (2) that to get higher rewards, you must take greater risks. The beta coefficient measures a fund's sensitivity to, or volatility relative to, the stock market in general. Using the beta is different from the method described in the paragraphs above because it ignores all other factors influencing the price of a stock or a portfolio.

A beta computed for a portfolio of stocks measures the riskiness of that portfolio in relation to the risk of the market. Funds with the same volatility as the market, as measured by a broad based index, have a beta of 1.00. Funds with higher betas are more volatile; those with lower betas are less volatile. The share price of a fund with a beta of 1.20 will typically rise or fall 12% when the broad index rises or falls 10%. On the other hand, the price of a fund with a beta of .80 will rise or fall 8% when the index moves 10%. This makes high beta funds the most desirable in up markets, while low beta funds are preferred in adverse markets.

The average no-load aggressive growth fund had a beta of 1.16 in 1994; the average small company fund, a beta of 1.04. Among the aggressive growth funds, SAFECO Growth had the highest beta (1.72). Both categories are considerably higher than the average equity fund (.91).

Table 13

No-load funds	
3 yrs ending 1994	
Objective	**Avg. Beta**
Aggressive growth	1.16
Sector	1.07
Small company growth	1.04
Growth	.93
Growth-income	.86
Global	.76
International	.74
Income	.62
Tax-free	.39
Precious metals	.37
Fixed-income	.21
Avg stock	.91
Avg diversified stock	.94

We use the beta as a measure of risk because it allows us to distinguish between two components of total risk—that which is caused by the market's variability and that due uniquely to the securities within an individual fund's portfolio. Betas work best for diversified domestic equity funds. They are far less meaningful for specialized funds such as gold funds, which march to their own drummer, and for bond funds.

Beta has two companions: the alpha and the coefficient of determination. The alpha, which measures non-market-related variability, is considered by some to be an indicator of management ability. The other measure, notated as "r²," measures the percentage of variability due to the market. Betas are included in the *Handbook* and in *The No-Load Fund Investor* newsletter. Because beta measurements can be relatively volatile over short periods of time, they are generally calculated over a three year period to produce a more stable, useful comparative tool.

Two other measures of risk you should be aware of are the standard deviation and the Sharpe ratio. Standard deviation measures a security's periodic variations from its own average performance. This differs from beta which measures the variation from a separate index. The Sharpe ratio, developed by Nobel prize winning economist William F. Sharpe, measures reward per unit of risk. The latter measure attempts to reduce all portfolio results to the same risk level in order to assess management's ability, i.e. a management which produces a mediocre return while taking a large risk with your capital is inferior to one which can produce that same return with much lower risk.

Analyze a fund's objectives

The second test of an aggressive growth fund is to see what the fund considers its "objectives" to be. Following SEC regulations, every sale of a mutual fund must be made by prospectus, and in every prospectus there is a section labeled "objectives." Aggressive growth funds typically describe their objectives in the following manner:

> Principal growth through investment primarily in equity securities of small companies which are deemed to have better than average prospects for appreciation. Fund is not intended to constitute a complete investment program; nor is it designed for investors seeking dividend income. It is designed primarily for the investment of that portion of an investor's funds which can appropriately be invested in special risks of various kinds. There is no assurance that its objective can be obtained — *Kaufmann*.

> Seeks significant capital appreciation by investing in securities, primarily common stocks, that management believes are more aggressive and carry a greater degree of risk than the market as a whole (as measured by the S&P 500 Stock Index) — *Columbia Special Fund*.

> Sole investment objective is to realize capital growth. The fund

may employ "leverage" by borrowing money and using it for the purchase of additional securities. Borrowing for investment increases both investment opportunity and investment risk—*Value Line Leveraged Growth Investors.*

Seeks long-term growth of capital through investment in common stocks of small, rapidly growing companies—*Price New Horizons.*

Capital growth by investing in a broadly diversified list of special situations. Investing in special situations may increase the risk of possible loss but it may also offer greater appreciation potential — *Value Line Special Situations.*

The statement of objective is not always as explicit as we would like. On the front page of its prospectus, Fidelity Magellan merely says it seeks to increase the value of its shares over the long term by investing in companies with growth potential, but on later pages it goes on to note that it seeks capital appreciation and that no emphasis is placed on dividend income. Thus, Magellan is more aggressive than the impression it conveys in its front-page description. (Magellan's beta is an above-average 1.05.)

Some other aggressive growth funds are even less explicit. For example the prospectus of the Vanguard Explorer Fund merely says of its objective: ". . . long-term growth in capital." That's why the volatility tests are so important.

The third criteria is dividend income. Funds with the lowest yields are the most aggressive, since a high percentage of their portfolios is invested in stocks that reinvest their profits for future growth rather than paying their shareholders hefty dividends. The average aggressive growth fund yielded only 0.5% in 1994; many paid no income dividends at all.

Dividends make a difference

Finally, the fourth way to determine the fund's attitude toward growth and risk-taking is to examine the composition of its portfolio. Aggressive growth funds will frequently have heavy weightings in high-tech stocks. So if you see a lot of "ix" and "onic" at the ends of the names of unfamiliar companies in the portfolio, chances are the fund takes an aggressive stance.

Portfolio composition

Are aggressive growth funds for you?

Yes . . . if you are interested in making your money grow as fast as possible and are able to sustain losses without worrying.

Yes . . . if your income is substantial enough to sustain a "businessman's risk."

Yes . . . if you currently buy volatile stocks, new issues, options and futures, maintain a margin account, sell short, or are a serious student of the market.

Yes . . . if you are willing to take the time necessary to follow the fund and the market.

Yes . . . if you can discipline yourself to sell at the outset of a bear market or when the fund's performance falters.

Performance funds aren't for everyone. But if you found yourself nodding in agreement with—rather than shuddering in terror at—these criteria, consider putting some of your capital into aggressive no-load growth funds.

Note that older or retired investors should not automatically shrink reflexively from volatile funds. If in retirement your wealth is substantial, and you can sustain losses without jeopardizing your standard of living, then it makes sense to consider the merits of taking above-average risks for above-average gains, at least with a modest portion of your assets. An excessive preoccupation with security can be a mistake. Life is an exercise in uncertainty; often, safety is an illusion that carries its own high price.

CHAPTER 6

Growth funds

Growth funds, often called "long-term growth" funds, focus their attention on capital appreciation over a period of years. They do not attempt to win the yearly performance derby. On the contrary, their aim is to *prudently* grow the money entrusted to them by investors. Some were "go-go" funds in their early years, but have since matured, becoming too big to maintain the percentage increases needed to keep up the performance pace.

Less hyperactive than their aggressive cousins, growth funds do not employ speculative investing techniques such as leveraging or selling short. And, they are more likely to hold the stocks of large established companies—GM, GE, 3M, IBM, Bristol-Myers, Time-Warner, Wal-Mart and so on.

They are more stable than aggressive growth funds, and as a result, are more consistent performers. In bear markets their losses can be substantial, but they are generally less than the aggressive growth funds'. In bull markets, they grow fast enough to do a superior job of combating inflation, but certainly are not in the vvrroom-vvrroom league of the high-performance aggressive growth funds.

In terms of their level of risk, the growth group's betas are on average about 7% *less* volatile than the index, while the average aggressive growth fund is 16% *more* volatile than the stock market as a whole. On the other hand, most other stock mutual fund groups are more stable still. (The only group, besides aggressive growth funds, to have higher betas than growth funds are the highly risky, non-diversified sector funds.)

Chart 14 shows the performance of Founders Growth Fund. It was far less volatile than the American Heritage Fund in 1994, as shown on Chart 12.

Chart 14

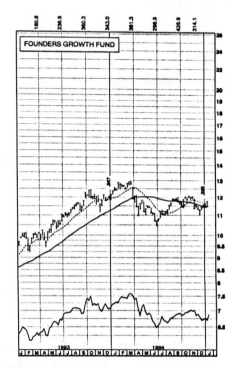

Source: Mutual Fund Trends, January 1995.

Throughout much of the 80s, the most popular growth funds were those that bought blue-chip stocks (large, well-established companies). Now, many types of funds have such stocks in their portfolios. The following funds have a preponderance of their assets in blue-chips:

Aggressive growth: Dreyfus Appreciation, Janus Twenty, SteinRoe Growth Stock, Twentieth Century Growth.

Growth: Babson Growth, Benham Equity Growth, Columbia Common Stocks, Dreyfus Growth Opportunity, Fidelity Blue Chip Growth, Invesco Growth, Janus Fund, Neuberger-Berman Guardian, Neuberger-Berman Focus, T. Rowe Price Growth Stock, Scudder Quality Growth, Twentieth Century Select, Vanguard US Growth.

Growth-income: Benham Income & Growth, Dodge & Cox Stock, Dreyfus Fund, Fidelity Fund, Founders Blue Chip, Invesco Industrial Income, Janus Growth & Income, T. Rowe Price Dividend Growth, T. Rowe Price Growth & Income, Schwab 1000, Vanguard Index 500, Quantitative and Windsor II.

Income: Dodge & Cox Balanced, Dreyfus Balanced, Invesco Total Return, T. Rowe Price Equity Income, SAFECO Income, SteinRoe Total Return, USAA Income Stock, Vanguard Equity Income.

A typical growth fund's prospectus will describe its objectives in terms like these:

> Objective will be achieved by investing substantially all of its assets in common stock and other equity-type securities which, in the opinion of the investment adviser, have long-term appreciation possibilities—*Stein Roe & Farnham Stock Fund.*
>
> Primary objective is capital appreciation, and its secondary objective is current income. Invests in readily marketable common stocks of established companies. In many cases dividends are paid on these investments, but the amount of dividends is not a major factor in selecting stocks—*Founders Growth.*
>
> Growth of capital through investment in securities of well-known and established companies as well as smaller, less well-known companies—*Fidelity Trend.*

Sometimes what a growth fund won't do is the key to distinguishing it from an aggressive growth fund. In the "Restrictions" section of the prospectus or the "Statement of Additional Information," many growth funds note that they will not utilize margin, short sales or options, nor will they invest in restricted securities, commodities, nor use other types of investment techniques involving a significant degree of risk.

How growth funds talk about themselves

Growth can be achieved by buying either "growth" stocks or "value" stocks, or both. This distinction has become increasingly important and more widely understood by investors. Because this issue is so vital to understanding a mutual fund, many publications—newsletters, magazines and analytical periodicals—now specify the sort of companies that funds invest in.

Growth versus value

Growth funds buy the stocks of companies whose earnings are increasing, stocks that have relatively high price to book ratios, high price-earnings ratios and low dividend payouts.

Value funds look for undervalued securities. The stocks they buy generally have the following characteristics: their price/earnings ratios and price/book value ratios are low compared to other stocks, and their dividend yields are higher than average. Value fund managers pay lots of attention to the precepts of Graham and Dodd (two professors who wrote the definitive book on stock valuation more than half a century ago). Such funds can often be identified by the words *value* or *asset* in their name, or by a close reading of the objective section of the prospectus.

Vanguard, which now manages both S&P Growth and Value Index funds, provides this breakout concerning their relative characteristics.

Table 15

	Dividend yield	Price/earnings ratio	Price/book ratio
S&P Growth Index	2.1%	18.1x	4.3x
S&P Value Index	3.8%	12.8x	1.8x

(as of 12/31/94)

In terms of performance, growth funds and value funds alternate in cycles. Here's how they've performed since 1975.

Chart 16

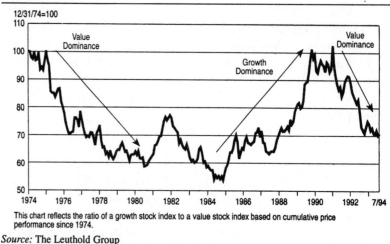

This chart reflects the ratio of a growth stock index to a value stock index based on cumulative price performance since 1974.

Source: The Leuthold Group

Notwithstanding the cycles, other studies show that over the long-term, value has outperformed growth. Perhaps that's because growth stocks, with their higher price/earnings multiples, are simply poorer bargains. An interesting study developing this point of view was published in 1987 using both "excellent" and "unexcellent" companies described in the Tom Peters book, *In Search of Excellence*. The excellent companies were far superior based on all the standards that accountants use to measure success. Yet, as shown in Table 18, the unexcellent companies' stocks posted far greater returns.

Finally, just to confuse the issue, some portfolio managers—Tony Orphanos of Warburg Pincus Growth & Income, for one—feel that growth and value are two sides of the same coin. These managers search for undervalued companies that have good growth potential.

Table 17

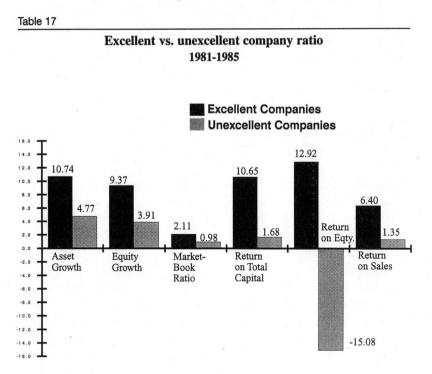

Excellent vs. unexcellent company ratio
1981-1985

Source: Clayman, M., "In Search of Excellence: The Investor's Viewpoint"
Financial Analysts Journal, May-June 1987

Table 18

**Excellent vs. unexcellent company portfolio returns
1981-1985**

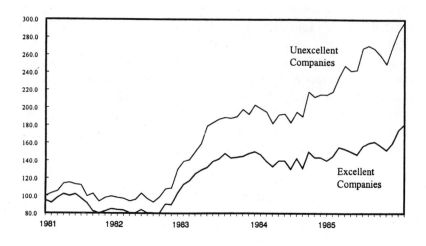

Source: Clayman, M., "In Search of Excellence: The Investor's Viewpoint"
Financial Analysts Journal, May-June 1987

Style boxes

Style boxes are a useful innovation in maximizing diversification. As popularized by the *Morningstar* rating service, they are a nine box grid, with two variables. In the case of equity funds they are growth versus value and cap size. Thus, funds can be categorized as large cap value, or small cap growth, etc.

Morningstar determines categories by an inspection of the fund's portfolio. The growth/value placement is determined by relating the funds' average price/earnings ratio to that of the S&P 500. Consequently, the categories can and do change from time to time. Also keep in mind that the style boxes represent the average stock in a portfolio and, thus, may be a simplification of the fund's actual policies. A fund designated medium cap might actually hold mostly large and small cap stocks. Usually this isn't a problem, but if you are combining a number of funds, you probably won't get exactly the diversification you are aiming for.

Chart 19
_____

Equity style box

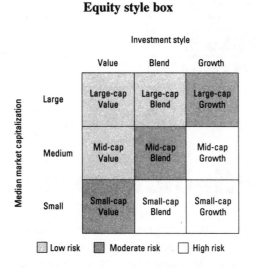

Within the equity style-box grid, nine possible combinations
exist, ranging from large-cap value for the safest funds to
small-cap growth for the riskiest.

_____

Source: Morningstar
_____

Yes . . . if you don't want the risks of an aggressive growth fund.

Yes . . . if you do want your money to grow, keeping you ahead of
inflation.

Yes . . . if current income is not a pressing need.

Growth funds are suitable for almost all investors. Nearly everyone
should consider putting some investment dollars into them.

Are growth funds for you?

CHAPTER 7

Growth-income funds

Growth-income funds aim to give their investors a combination of price appreciation and current income—called *total return* in the industry, resulting in a reasonable, though usually not stupendous, return. Here's an easy way to distinguish between the three different categories of common stock funds. In 1994, the average no-load growth-income fund had a dividend yield of 2.1%; the growth funds' dividend yield averaged 1.1% and aggressive growth funds' just 0.5%.

Because dividends helps cushion market volatility, growth-income funds provide relative stability for an equity investment. They are ideally suited for conservative investors and, in uncertain times, aggressive investors who want to reduce their risk.

An above-average growth-income fund over the past few years is Scudder Growth & Income. As Chart 20 shows, it had a very stable performance in 1994. Compare its performance with those of more speculative funds shown in Charts 12 and 14.

The case for conservative equity funds

Growth-income and income funds have done very well in recent years. Here are some of the reasons:

Characteristically, they hold stocks with higher yields than do growth funds. Generally, high-income stocks are more conservative because the yields provide downside protection. But somewhat surprisingly, it doesn't necessarily mean that they lack upside potential. It's possible for them to be conservative on the downside, yet not necessarily conservative on the upside.

Chart 20

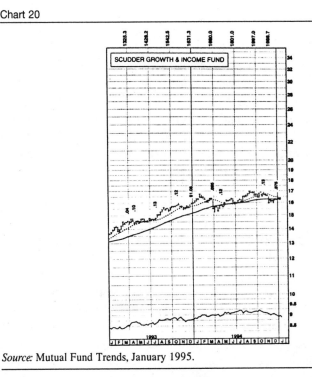

Source: Mutual Fund Trends, January 1995.

Growth-income funds can perform well compared to growth funds because their dividend yield gives them a headstart. A growth fund has to beat its growth-income cousins by the amount of the yield differential during any particular year just to tie. That's not as easy as it may seem.

Advocates of growth-income stocks point out the two ways you can make money on this type of stock. One is that the company's prospects may improve relative to analysts' expectations, and the stock may thus appreciate in value. The other is that, even if it doesn't, the stock market may have already oversold it and discounted its problems (or apparent problems). Thus these funds are, in any event, left holding cheap stocks.

Furthermore, the income portion of the return always gets underestimated. People do not adequately take into account the compounding effect of income, which is an enormous part of the total return. Here's an example: The Standard & Poor's 500 Stock Index, from year-end 1979 to year-end 1994, a 15-year period, went from

107.94 to 459.27—351 points, not counting dividends. But when you include reinvested dividends, the index shoots up not just from 107 to 459, but in effect to 823! The Index has a 663 percent increase in value by reinvesting the dividends, but only a 325 percent increase if you don't include the reinvested dividends. You get a doubling in performance simply from the compounding effect of income. Because income is such an important component of total return, an investor ignores it at his or her peril.

Finally, in years when the market favors large established companies, that's an additional plus for growth-income funds, since these stocks are among their favorite holdings.

In 1984, the American Telephone and Telegraph Company (now AT&T) broke into eight separate companies. Thousands of shareholders found themselves with a greatly increased administrative burden, and the problem of deciding what to do about it. Some chose to sidestep the issue by swapping their shares for an interest in special funds and trusts set up for the purpose. Those doing so usually paid some sort of sales fee. Before the breakup, AT&T was a stock commonly held in conservative mutual fund portfolios. Investors who owned AT&T as part of their mutual fund holdings were spared the necessity of making these decisions. The fund managers automatically restructured their AT&T holdings to conform with the fund's objective.

Growth-income objectives

In their prospectuses, growth-income funds state their objectives as follows:

Long-term growth of capital and reasonable current income— *Lepercq-Istel.*

Long-term capital growth. However, in order to provide a reasonable current return to shareholders, the fund to some extent limits the emphasis on the growth objective by investing a portion of its portfolio in securities selected for their current income characteristics— *Fidelity Fund.*

Seeks long-term growth of capital, a reasonable level of current income and an increase in future income through investment in income-producing equity securities which have prospects for both growth of capital and dividend income—*T. Rowe Price Growth & Income.*

Sometimes, it is difficult to place funds in their proper categories. If you are still wondering after you have applied the four tests of stated objective, portfolio, dividend yield, and volatility, rely most heavily on volatility. Reason: some funds change their tactics with market conditions and at times can be out of phase with or have outgrown their stated objective, while others deliberately push the outer limits of their category in order to be the best performers within the particular category.

On occasion, a fund's category needs to be revaluated. For example, our newsletter used to place the Neuberger-Berman Guardian Fund in the growth-income category, but because of its then 1.00 beta we moved it to the growth category. (Some other rating services still call it growth-income; we disagree.) If an aggressive-growth fund has grown larger and is buying the stocks of bigger companies, we may recategorize the fund to growth or growth-income. For example: the Dreyfus Fund, once the epitome of aggressive growth, is now a growth-income fund. Conversely, some funds with "income" in their name may be managed quite aggressively. We may move these funds from our income category to growth-income, or perhaps even growth.

Occasionally, the impetus comes from a renaming. Back in the 70s, Twentieth Century had a fund named Twentieth Century Income Investors. We categorized it as a growth-income fund because of its name, even though the fund's fine growth record, dividend payout, and prospectus language were more characteristic of a growth fund. Twentieth eventually recognized the incongruity and changed the name to Twentieth Century Select Investors. With the name change, the *Investor* moved the fund to the growth category, where it remains. So you need to look behind a name before you invest.

Yes . . . if financially or psychologically you cannot accept the greater risks of the growth or aggressive growth funds.

Yes . . . if the market is favoring the blue-chip, dividend-paying stocks held by growth-income funds.

Yes . . . if you have been investing yourself—and not too successfully—in blue-chip stocks.

A word of warning

Are growth-income funds for you?

CHAPTER 8

THE
NO-LOAD
FUND INVESTOR

Income funds

Income funds are the most conservative category of funds that hold common stocks. Also known as equity-income funds, they usually invest half of their assets or more in income-producing stocks, though at times they take defensive measures. The balance of their portfolios contain convertibles and bonds. At year-end 1994, the portfolio of the average no-load income fund, excluding the cash portion, was 60% invested in equities, 40% in bonds. By comparison, no-load growth-income funds had 87% in equities, 13% in bonds; growth funds were 97% in equities, and aggressive-growth funds were 99% in equities. Simply put, if a fund is almost entirely stocks, it's probably not an income fund. If it is an income fund, its risk, growth potential and dividend yield put will place it somewhere between growth-income and bond funds.

Accenting income even more than the growth-income funds do, the income funds' average yield was 3.6% in 1994. While exceeding the yield of other diversified equity funds, it was still substantially less than the 6.3% that the typical long-term corporate bond fund achieved. For much of the 80s and early 90s, income funds did almost as well as the other, more speculative, categories—and with far less risk. This unusual performance resulted from an unprecedented situation. The dozen years or so from the early 1980s to the mid-1990s were probably the best time for both stocks and bonds in history, due to the nearly uninterrupted, and very steep, decline in interest rates.

While typically their objectives focus on income, it is not uncommon for these funds to have growth as a secondary objective. Note these prospectus extracts:

As much income as possible, consistent with the preservation and conservation of capital—*Fidelity Puritan*.

As much current income as in management's judgment is consistent with reasonable risk—*Wellesley Income*.

Income, as high and dependable as is consistent with reasonable risk. The secondary objective is capital growth—*Value Line Income*.

Regular income, conservation of principal and an opportunity for long-term growth of principal and income—*Dodge & Cox Balanced*.

Categorizing mutual funds is a judgemental process. Authorities may and do differ in their classifications. We use the income category as a catch-all for a number of different types of mutual funds that have the common attributes of relatively low volatility and reasonable dividend income. These include the balanced funds, asset allocation funds and convertible securities funds.

Among the earliest mutual funds organized in the United States, balanced funds offer a "complete investment program," as a matter of policy, keeping percentages of their assets in a combination of common stocks, preferred stocks and bonds. Their prospectuses usually require that 20%-50% of their assets be in interest-bearing securities. This differentiates them from common stock funds, which are not required to hold any bonds.

In the inflationary and high interest rate environment of the 70s, balanced funds tended to underperform both growth-income and equity income funds. That was primarily attributable to the losses suffered by the bonds in their portfolios. Thus, for many years the industry shied away from balanced funds. The oldest no-load fund, the Scudder Stevens & Clark Balanced Fund, changed its name to Scudder Income and dropped its policy of balance in 1977. At the time, Scudder said the change was a "progressive step that would enhance current income." In 1984 the Stein Roe Farnham Balanced Fund became the SteinRoe Total Return Fund.

Still, there is life in the genre. With inflation low, interest rates dropping and bond prices rising for many years, the balanced funds have staged a strong recovery. In fact, from 1984 to 1994, the balanced funds out-performed the equity income category.

Roughly speaking, balanced funds can fall into one of three types: 1) Regular, which typically have a ratio of about 60% stocks to 40%

Balanced funds

bonds. Vanguard Wellington is an example. 2) Income oriented, where the ratio is weighted in favor of bonds. Vanguard Wellesley is an example, with only typically about a third of its portfolio in stocks, and 3) Domestic asset allocation funds, where the ratio between stocks, bonds and cash is more variable. Many, but not all, balanced funds have "Balanced" in their names. The asset allocation funds typically have Asset Allocation or Asset Manager (or some variant) in their names.

Since balance is a policy, not an objective per se, balanced funds can have income, growth-income and, occasionally, even growth as their objective, depending on their volatility.

The advantage of a balanced fund is that it provides diversification, a low minimum investment and a professional manager to do the required reweighting or make the asset allocation decisions. Thus, you need not take such an active role in the apportionment of your portfolio. If you have only a small sum to invest, it's by far the best approach.

On the other hand, almost all medium and large fund families now offer both stock and bond funds. Thus you can "balance" your own holdings fairly easily, simply by apportioning your investments among two or more stock and bond funds to suit your objectives. If you are in a high tax bracket, we strongly recommend that you do your own balancing, since you'll want tax-free funds in your portfolio, and the vast majority of balanced funds hold taxable fixed-income securities. One exception: USAA Balanced Fund, which owns both long- and short-term muni bonds. Additionally, the Fidelity Bond Strategist Fund can invest in either taxable or tax-free bonds depending on their relative desirability.

Similarly, most balanced funds hold long-term bonds. In periods of rising interest rates, you are better off doing your own balancing, in order to keep the maturities of the fixed-income portion short.

Global asset allocation funds

Also known as flexible portfolio funds or global flexible portfolio funds, they provide broad diversification across a number of markets. Their goal is to obtain returns greater than those of a risk-free investment, yet with low volatility. Traditional equity funds invest in one market—usually the U.S. stock market. This strategy provides protection against specific-company risk, but does nothing to insulate investors from a general market decline. In fact, the typical diversified fund may provide an investor with less protection when the market is tanking than owning individual stocks would. A particular stock can resist a decline if the company is doing well. A few exceptionally performing stocks, that may account for less than 5% of the assets of a diversified fund, aren't sufficient to buck a general downtrend.

Global asset allocation funds typically invest in five or six different markets (or asset classes), which do not necessarily move in tandem with the U.S. stock market. As a result, losses in one or two markets may be offset by gains in others.

These funds started in the mid 80s and performed very well for a time, particularly in 1987, when their gold and international sectors buoyed performance and offset sharp declines in the U.S. stock market that year. From 1988 to 1992, they were underachievers because their gold and international sectors underperformed, and because they have fairly high expense ratios due to their wide diversification. With performance lagging, in late 1991 two of the best known no-load funds in the category both made changes to give themselves more flexibility.

The Blanchard Global Growth Fund established new, wider maximum and minimum allocations. (1) With two exceptions, its sector allocations are now varied from 0%-65%. Previously the range was 5%-50% or 5%-35%. Precious metals can now be eliminated entirely. (2) The fund added two new sectors: international bonds (which had previously been grouped with domestic bonds) and emerging markets such as Mexico, Chile and Malaysia. The allocation range in this new sector is 0%-15%.

The USAA Cornerstone Fund, which for years had a policy of investing a fixed 20% of its portfolio in each of five different asset classes, altered its portfolio mix by reducing its gold allocation to only 8%-12% and introducing some flexibility into its other four categories. Foreign stocks, real estate stocks, U.S. government securities and basic value stocks can now vary from 20% to 25%. In making the change, USAA noted that "the fund was conceived in 1984, in the aftermath of a period of high inflation...During the periods of moderate and low inflation which followed, the fund's investments in gold stocks increased volatility without a commensurate increase in total return." While these two funds' move to greater flexibility didn't help them in 1992, it did wonders for their performances in 1993; both were up about 24%.

The following table summarizes the range of each fund's asset allocations.

Table 21

| Portfolio | Global asset allocation funds | |
	Blanchard Global Growth	USAA Cornerstone
U.S. stocks	0%-65%	—
Basic value stocks	—	20%-25%
Real estate stocks	—	20%-25%
Int'l stocks	0%-65%	20%-25%
Emerging markets	0%-15%	—
Precious metals	0%-65%	—
Gold	—	8%-12%
U.S. bonds	0%-65%	—
Int'l bonds	0%-65%	—
U.S. gov sec.	—	20%-25%
Cash, U.S.	0%-100%	—
Cash, int'l	0%-100%	—
Betas	0.71	0.65

Convertible securities funds

Until 1985, no no-loads invested exclusively in convertibles. Since then, funds with this specialty have been launched by Vanguard, Fidelity, Value Line and others. In addition, several closed-end funds invest in convertibles.

Convertible securities are bonds or preferred stock that can be converted to a fixed number of shares of another security—usually common stock—issued by the underlying company whenever the investor wants. Convertible funds really are equity substitutes. Companies usually sell convertible securities when conditions (for instance, low stock prices) make it difficult to issue common stock and/or the credit markets demand such unacceptably high interest rates that issuing straight debt (bonds) is unappealing.

The conversion feature of a convertible is a "sweetener" to persuade investors to accept a lower interest rate in the hope that eventually the company's stock, into which the issue can be converted, will appreciate in value, thus increasing the worth of the convertible. When the company's common stock is valued below the conversion price, the value of its convertible bonds are based on their yield, without regard to the conversion feature. But when the common rises above the conversion price, the convertible's value moves up with the stock price.

Proponents of convertibles believe that they offer the best of both worlds. They believe that convertibles will rise more when stock prices are advancing than they will fall when prices are declining. That's because when stocks rise, convertibles will rise too (but not usually as fast as the common stock). When stocks fall, convertibles will often fall less than the common stock because at some point the convertible becomes attractive for its yield.

Detractors argue the opposite. They think convertibles get the worst of both worlds. Investors, they feel, don't get the maximum gain during rising stock markets. Just as bad, the yield an investor receives is less than the straight bonds issued by the company would produce. In 1987, the detractors had the best case. In the October-December quarter, the Dreyfus Convertible Fund (merged out of existence in late 1993) declined 20.5%; Fidelity Convertible, 16.8%; Value Line Convertible, 18.1%; and Vanguard Convertible, 17%. That's only slightly less volatility than the 19.9% decline for the average diversified equity fund.

Top-rated Fidelity Convertible Fund has performed well in recent years. It posted a 24.0% average annual gain between 1991 and 1993, while declining only 1.7% in 1994's rising interest rate environment. That's because, notwithstanding their higher yields, convertible funds are not nearly as interest-rate sensitive as bond funds. The action of the equity markets is a stronger influence on their performance.

Yes . . . if you are a conservative investor who needs income and is willing to accept a moderate amount of risk to achieve some growth.

Yes . . . if you have fixed-income investments that are not providing the total return you desire.

Yes . . . if you have been investing yourself—and not too successfully—in income-producing stocks.

Are income funds for you?

Bond funds

An item of interest that you've probably never considered. If you're typical, you'll receive over your lifetime four times as much interest income as you'll spend in interest payments. You'll lend money to banks, corporations and governments. And in this enterprise, no-load bond funds can be an important ally, providing you with maximum returns at reasonable risk.

From 1981, when inflation began to ebb and interest rates started their long plunge from historic highs, through 1993, bond funds delivered an enviable combination of interest and capital gains with very low price volatility.

This great performance is something of a historic anomaly, though. For many years before, and in 1994, when the Federal Reserve Bank raised interest rates repeatedly, bond funds were very poor investments; their returns were eroded by inflation, their prices fluctuated wildly with swings in interest rates, the purchasing power of their interest payments steadily declined. If inflation stays low, bond funds will continue to be outstanding investments in the 90s. On the other hand a resurgence of inflation will give bond funds the negative total returns that they often had in the 70s.

Bond funds have two advantages over individual bonds: liquidity and diversification. Regarding the former attribute, a no-load bond fund can always be sold at net asset value with no commission cost, whereas there can be a sizeable commission cost in disposing of individual bonds. As to diversification, bond issuers occasionally default on their obligations, and a fund spreads your risk over a large portfo-

lio. That allows you to hold a portfolio of bonds of a lower grade than
would make sense if you were buying a few indi-
vidual bonds yourself.

It is important to understand that owning a
bond fund is not the same as owning individual
bonds. The latter have a specific maturity, when
you can get your principal back in full, at least in
nominal terms. This is not true of bond funds,
which is a disadvantage in times of rising interest
rates. For all practical purposes, a bond fund has
no maturity. For example, a fund portfolio that
currently has an average life of five years, will
usually have an average life of five years at any
time in the future. The reason: when one bond
matures it is replaced by another with a similar
maturity. This means you always sell a bond fund at its current market value, not its face value.

Price impacts yield

The price volatility of fixed-income investments can significantly increase or reduce their yield. For example, if a bond fund yielding 6% and selling for $10.00 per share has a change in price of a single penny, that's the equivalent of gaining or losing six days' interest.

While the real risk of holding bonds or bond funds is the risk that
inflation will erode their value, there is also the default risk. Bond
funds offer various degrees of protection from that risk. Some invest
in government bonds that are totally safe from default, others in
bonds that are insured. Some funds buy high quality, investment-
grade bonds issued by corporations. Others invest in low-grade speculative issues, termed "junk" bonds, which may have a significant
likelihood of default.

Risk is usually evaluated by the two national rating agencies,
Standard & Poor's and Moody's. The prospectuses of many bond
funds list their quality standards using these ratings. Annual reports
sometimes summarize the portfolio bonds using these ratings. The
lower the rating of a portfolio, the more speculative it is, and the higher its return should be. Bonds rated in the first four grades (AAA to
BBB in S&P) are called investment grade; those with ratings below
the first four grades (BB and below) are called high-yield or "junk"
bonds.

The second major determinant of risk is the average maturity of the
portfolio bonds. With long-maturity bonds, the risk of losing principal is high, while the risk of losing income, at least over a period of

Choose your risk

years, is low. With short-term bonds, the reverse is true: the risk of losing principal is low while the risk of losing income is high. Witness the decline in money market rates. In 1994, a time of rising interest rates, the average long-term government bond fund lost 6.0% while the average short-term government fund lost only 1.2%

How changes in interest rates affect principal

When the economy slows, interest rates are likely to drop. As a result, bond fund NAVs rise. Conversely, when the economy heats up again, interest rates are likely to rise. That's when bond fund prices fall. How far depends mainly on the maturity of the holdings in the fund's portfolio. The following table illustrates the approximate changes in value that can be expected from a $10,000 investment in various government securities when interest rates change 1%. The longer the maturity, the greater the change you should expect.

Table 22

$10,000 investment

U.S. gov. security	Change in value if interest rates move:	
	Up 1%	Down 1%
3-mo. Treasury bill	$ -24	$ 24
1-year Treasury bill	-93	94
5-year Treasury note	-383	401
10-year Treasury note	-617	672
30-year Treasury bond	-940	1,123
30-year zero coupon bond	-1,989	2,665

Source: Benham Management Corp.

What to do

We recommend that the long term fixed-income investor is generally better off buying bond funds with intermediate term maturities, typically in the five-to-ten year range. Intermediate bonds capture most of the yield of the long-term bond funds, but with substantially less volatility.

Short-term bond funds are a great substitute for money funds when interest rates are falling. But when interest rates are rising, you are better off scuttling back to the money funds, even if their yield is substantially less. You will come out ahead on total return. Another way to beat money fund rates when prices are falling is to buy one- or two-year Treasuries. They're less liquid, but you can hold them to maturity and be assured that your principal is safe.

Significant differences exist in the yields of bond funds. One major reason is the varying average maturities of the bonds in their portfolios. Funds with bonds maturing in the near future typically yield less than funds holding long-term bonds. This offsets the fact that their prices will almost always fluctuate less than the funds that buy longer term bonds.

Illustrating this principle, Table 23 shows the maturities and yields of the bond funds offered by three major fund groups: Vanguard, Fidelity and T. Rowe Price. Vanguard offers a number of separate U.S. Treasury portfolios ranging from a short-maturity money market fund to a long-term bond fund. The Money Fund's investments had an average maturity of only 39 days at year-end 1994. It yielded 3.8%. Its price, like those of virtually all money funds, is fixed at $1.00. Next, the Vanguard Short-

From here to maturities

Table 23

Bond funds
How average maturity affects yield and volatility

	Average maturity 12/31/94	1994 Yield	1994 Net asset value High	Low	Volatility
Vanguard					
Treas. Money Mkt	39 days	3.8%	$1.00	$1.00	0.0%
Treasury Short	2.5 yrs	5.3	10.45	9.78	6.9
Treasury Intermediate	8.6 yrs	6.2	11.17	9.57	16.7
Treasury Long	22.0 yrs	7.3	10.84	8.87	22.2
Fidelity Spartan					
US Gov. MM	42 days	3.9	1.00	1.00	0.0
Limited Mat. Gov.	4.7 yrs	5.9	10.07	9.35	7.7
Government Income	10.4 yrs	7.4	10.80	9.59	12.6
Long-Term Gov.	23.2 yrs	5.1	12.77	9.94	28.5
Rowe Price					
Tx Expt Money Mkt	38 days	2.5	1.00	1.00	0.0
TF Short-Inter	3.2 yrs	4.2	5.39	5.16	4.5
Tax-Free Inc	17.3 yrs	6.0	9.97	8.47	17.7
TF High-Yield	19.2 yrs	6.5	12.55	10.90	15.1

Term Treasury Portfolio had an average maturity of 2.5 years and yielded 5.3%. Its price varied by 6.9% from high to low in 1994. Vanguard's Intermediate and Long-Term Treasury Portfolios, had longer maturities and consequently higher yields and greater volatility.

We've shown similar data for Fidelity government and the Rowe Price tax-free funds. Their volatilities and yields also varied with maturities. All the variations were extreme in 1994. In previous years, the variations were less than half those of 1994.

Duration

While average maturity is useful, there is a better measure—called duration. It differs from average maturity in that it takes into account a bond's cash flows from current interest payments. Average maturity doesn't take cash flows into account. Here's an example that shows the difference. The AARP High Quality Bond Fund and the Benham Target 2005 Fund both had similar average maturities, about 11 years, at year-end 1994. But the AARP Fund had a far shorter duration, 5.2 years vs. 10.8 years for the Benham Target Fund.

Table 24

Duration vs. average maturity			
Fund	Avg. maturity	Duration	1994 total return
AARP High Quality	11.0	5.2	-4.5
Benham Target 2005	10.8	10.8	-8.9
AARP diff.		-51.9%	-49.4%

The reason for the difference is that the AARP Fund makes regular interest payments, which shorten the time needed to receive the sum total of interest and principal due you over the life of the bond. The Benham Fund is a zero coupon bond fund that doesn't make any distributions until its zero coupon bonds mature. With lower duration, the AARP Fund lost less in 1994s rising interest rate environment. Its total return declined 4.5%, while the Benham 2005 Fund declined 8.9%, twice as much.

Duration is a far more accurate measure of volatility due to interest rate changes. You can multiply a fund's duration by a change in interest rates and get its price movement. A fund with a duration of five will lose 5% of its value with a 1% increase in interest rates. A fund with a duration of 10 would lose 10% of its value. Conversely, a 1% decline in interest rates would result in 5% and 10% gains in total value, respectively. If interest rates change by 2%, then double the figures. You can't use average maturity to make these determinations.

However, while average maturity data are universally available, that's not the case with the duration figures. Funds and reporting services have only recently begun to provide such information to the public. If you can get duration information, by all means use it. Because otherwise you must rely on average maturities when you analyze bond funds.

Here are some of the subtleties of duration to be aware of:

■ Generally speaking longer-term bonds have higher yields and thus have higher durations. However, if two bonds both mature at the same time—say 20 years, the bond with the higher yield will have a shorter duration, and thus be less volatile. That's because more interest is paid along the way. By the same token, changes in interest rates and yields will shorten or lengthen durations.

■ Like maturity, duration can be calculated more than one way. In addition to figuring duration to the maturities of the bonds in the portfolio, it can also be calculated to the dates that the bonds may be called—that is, redeemed early by the issuer.

■ Several factors can reduce the accuracy of duration figures. If a fund holds convertible bonds, they may be excluded from the calculations. Similarly, foreign bonds, which may not track domestic interest rates, can throw the figures off. Derivatives are another problem. They may have different volatilities and a lack of liquidity can affect their prices, regardless of their theoretical value. Sometimes nobody will buy them at a fair price, or even at any price).

■ Duration is less meaningful for junk bonds. Interest rate changes are only a small part of the risk of holding them.

Careful about the name

A fund's name should tell you a lot about its average maturity. Short, Intermediate and Long in a name has a fairly consistent meaning, but the name Limited can mean either Short or Intermediate. Some examples:

Fund	Avg. maturity (Dec. 1994)
Neuberger-Berman Limited Maturity	2.2
Vanguard Muni Limited Term	2.6
Fidelity Spartan Ltd Maturity Gov.	4.7
Fidelity Limited Term Muni	8.9

Emphasize a fund's total return

Don't make the mistake of thinking that bond funds with high yields are always better buys than funds with lower yields. Compare total return—the sum of yield and changes in NAV. In 1993, Dreyfus A Bonds Plus had a yield of 6.3%, and a total return of 14.9%. In contrast, the Dreyfus GNMA Fund had a higher yield, 6.8%, but a far lower total return, 7.1%. In 1990, junk bonds boasted high double-digit yields, yet had negative total returns.

When the yield is higher than the total return, you are losing principal. The truest measure of your return is total return. Some retired investors who live on their investments may say that they don't care what happens to the price of their bonds as long as they continue to receive their interest income. We think this point of view is incorrect, particularly if virulent inflation were to return. Back in the 1950s, 30 year corporate bonds provided 2-3% yields. If you bought one of those bonds for $1,000 and held it until the 1980s, you lost your shirt, even though you received your $1,000 back at maturity.

Similarly, during periods of high inflation it's a mistake to spend all your interest distributions. The reason: high interest rates primarily reflect high inflation and thus provide a return of capital.

Economists believe that during times of no inflation, bonds should return about 3% per year. During inflationary periods, interest rates above 3% compensate a lender for the loss of purchasing power on his principal when it is paid back. Let's say that inflation is running at a 4% rate and bonds are yielding 7%. Three percentage points is pure interest; the balance, four percentage points, is demanded by lenders to preserve what they believe to be the real value of the principal.

How does this affect you? If you are holding $10,000 worth of bonds for the long-term, and they pay $700 per year, don't spend the entire $700 unless you want to eat into your principal. Spend only $300 and reinvest the balance. If you don't, you will suffer when non-inflationary times return. That's because when your bonds mature, they will have to be rolled over into new bonds yielding far less. We've used the example of individual bonds to make the point clearly, but the same holds true for bond funds. The fund's portfolio holdings mature or are called, and the managers must replace them with lower yielding bonds. Similarly, if the fund sells more shares it must dilute its high-coupon bonds with newer ones that have lower coupons.

While total return is the best measure to use when looking at past performance, it's a poor gauge of future performance. Under SEC regulations, when the funds quote yields, they must also show total return performance figures for the latest one-, five-, and ten-year periods (or the life of the fund, if less). In some respects this policy is ill-advised.

If you examine only total returns when you purchase a long-term bond fund, there are occasions when you may be riding for a fall. Here's why. Total return figures look best after a long decline in interest rates. Yet, if the trend reverses and interest rates start rising, that will be the worst time to buy. The best time to buy long-term bond funds is when interest rates are high—and starting to decline. Unfortunately, that is the time when total returns look the worst. In sum, total return tells you how you have done, but is of little help in predicting how you will do in the future. It is best ignored when timing purchases. Yield is a better forecaster of the future.

Two other variables in determining performance are a fund's willingness to protect against price declines either by going to cash equivalents or by shortening the maturities of its portfolio during periods of falling bond prices. The funds most likely to vary their maturities this way are those with the word "flexible" in their names.

There is a tendency to ignore expense ratios, in part because the total return and yield figures used to analyze performance are net of all expenses. Too often we excuse high expenses if a fund is doing well or if it fills a niche in the investment spectrum. It's very important to keep investment expenses as low as possible, particularly in the case of bond funds.

To illustrate, we've compiled a comprehensive list of all domestic,

Watch expense ratios

Table 25

Bond funds with expense ratios of 1.5% or more

**Percent distributions
by five-year quintile performances**

Quintiles	# funds	% Distribution
1 (best)	4	10%
2	3	7%
3	3	7%
4	5	12%
5 (worst)	26	63%
Total	41	100%

Source: Returns, Lipper, 5 yrs ending 1994, exp. ratios latest through Nov. 1994

investment-grade bond funds, load and no-load, that meet two criteria: a five year performance history and a 1994 expense ratio of 1.5% or more. (The median no-load bond fund has an expense ratio of .70%.) Out of a universe of 760 bond funds, 41 funds met the criteria, about 5% of all funds. We next compared the performances of these 41 high-expense bond funds to all bond funds and found that over the five-year period, high-expense bond funds were far more likely to be underperformers. Using our standard quintile analysis, only 17% of them were above average (1st and 2nd quintiles) while a full 75% ranked in the bottom two quintiles.

You can find a fund's expense ratio in the prospectus in the chart usually titled "Per Share Income and Capital Changes." Table 37 in Chapter 14 provides averages you can use as benchmarks. Make a point of checking this important figure before buying any fund.

Other selection criteria

Don't waste your time looking for "star" fixed-income managers. There is expertise out there, but fixed-income managers (with the possible exception of PIMCO's widely respected guru William Gross) just don't get the publicity treatment accorded hot equity fund managers. It's best to make your investment decisions based on a group's fixed-income expertise and a particular fund's long-term performance record—a minimum of a year, preferably three to five years.

It's not necessary to select insured bond funds. In most cases the loss from defaults is less than the cost of the insurance. (Single state munis, described in the next Chapter, may be an exception.)

Most bond funds pay interest monthly; however, a few pay quarterly and even annually. If you need the income to live on, you may prefer to receive your dividends monthly.

We'll now provide an overview of some of the major bond categories of interest to investors.

Corporate bond funds

These are short, intermediate, or long-term bond funds in which corporate bonds predominate in the portfolio. Many of the funds also own government bonds. (The SEC only requires that 65% of a fund's portfolio be in assets that are implied by its name.) The prospectuses of most corporate bond funds simply call for the purchase of investment grade bonds, which are the four highest grades: AAA, AA, A, and BBB. However, some funds in this category restrict themselves to a higher standard, usually A-rated or better. Funds in the latter category include Dreyfus A Bonds Plus, D. L. Babson Bond Trust L, which mandates that 80% of the portfolio be in the top three grades and/or government bonds, and the AARP High Quality Bond Fund, which keeps 80% of its portfolio in the top two highest quality grades, or in government-issued securities.

Government bond funds

Government bonds are the ultimate in credit safety. They are backed by the "full faith and credit" pledge of the U.S. government, and include instruments such as Treasury bills, notes, and bonds as well as government agency securities that are fully backed by the government such as GNMAs and FNMAs. Nevertheless, government bonds, like all bonds, fluctuate with interest rates. Since 1980, annual total returns on long-treasury bonds has been as high as 40.4% (in 1982) and as low as -7.8% (in 1994).

For years, government bond funds have been popular among investors. Interestingly, most of the action centers on load funds, which are heavily pushed by salesmen. They have accounted for over three-fourths of the sales in past years. While their total returns have been relatively high through much of the past decade, equities usually offer more potential over the long-term. This may be another case of salesmen making the easy sale instead of doing what is best for the investor.

In many large states, avoiding state and local taxes can be almost as important as avoiding federal taxation. Thus, you may reap substantial benefits from some bond funds that invest only in Treasury bonds. They may be tax-free at the state level. The funds can usually tell you the tax status in your own state.

While we almost always prefer using professionally managed mutual funds to holding individual securities, whether they be stocks or bonds, Treasury bond funds may be an exception for the long-term holder. Since there is no credit or call risk, you are better off holding individual Treasury bonds, particularly if you want the money back at some pre-determined time in the future. This way you save the management fees which add up over the years.

GNMA funds

These government funds invest in mortgage-backed GNMA (or "Ginnie Mae") certificates endorsed by the Government National

All fixed-income funds are not created equal

Fixed-income investing may seem simple, but don't be fooled. More than 30 categories of funds could nestle in your fixed-income portfolio. And they have wide variations in performance.

Fixed-income funds
Ranked by 5-year returns

# funds		1990-1994
111	High current yield (junk bonds)	65.7
31	Convertible securities	57.1
3	Short World Single-Mkt Income	53.6
44	Short World Multi-Mkt Income	47.8
59	General bond	46.5
84	Corporate bond - BBB rated	46.5
12	Target maturity	45.9
150	World income, general	43.8
24	Flexible income	43.8
110	Corporate bond - A rated	41.7
149	Intermediate inv grade debt	41.4
16	Intermediate US Treasury	40.3
16	General US Treasury	39.8
69	GNMA	38.8
174	General US Government	37.4
96	Intermediate US gov	36.9
62	US Mortgage	36.8
141	Short inv grade debt	36.3
20	Short US Treasury	36.0
216	General muni debt	36.0
41	High yield muni	35.2
51	Insured muni debt	35.0
108	Intermediate muni debt	34.9
133	Short US government	34.3
22	Ultra Short Obligations	30.1
55	Short muni debt	29.3
87	Adjustable rate mortgage	26.5
262	General money market	25.2
92	US Treasury MM	24.8
109	U.S. Government money market	24.5
125	Tax exempt MM	17.6

Source: Lipper Fixed-Income Performance Analysis

Mortgage Association. The principal and interest are guaranteed by the United States government. GNMA certificates are created by an "issuer," which is an FHA-approved mortgage banker who assembles a pool of FHA, FmHA, or VA-insured mortgages that have similar interest rates, maturities and dwelling types. The certificates are most commonly marketed to investors as "passthroughs," in denominations of $25,000. There are also $5,000 participation certificates, but they pay interest semi-annually, not monthly, as the passthroughs do.

These Ginnie Mae certificates have a stated life of 25 to 30 years, but because some mortgages are prepaid or are foreclosed, the typical certificate has about a 12-year life. In periods of declining interest rates this is a disadvantage since this limits their potential price gain and reduces the ability to lock in good yields for long periods of time, because maturities will shorten as home owners pay off their old mortgages. That was a dramatic drawback in 1993 as rates plunged and refinancings soared. The average GNMA gained only 6.8% that year, well below the returns for other intermediate and long-term funds. However, by actively managing the underlying GNMA certificates, funds can control maturities better than individuals generally are able to.

Holders of GNMA certificates receive both interest and return of principal. If you own the certificates themselves you have to be careful not to spend your monthly returns, because doing so wouldn't just be spending your interest, you'd actually be eating into your capital as well. When you buy a GNMA fund, your capital distributions are automatically reinvested, thus maintaining your equity.

Many large fund groups now have GNMA

funds. In addition, other fixed income funds like Fidelity Mortgage Securities Fund, invest in GNMAs, as well as in other mortgage-backed securities, such as Fannie Maes and Freddie Macs.

GNMA bond funds are not all the same. They can hold GNMA certificates at par, or at a discount or premium. Discount GNMA certificates represent mortgages with interest rates significantly below current market rates. As refinancing in these circumstances gives homeowners few advantages, such GNMAs have a low repayment risk and their maturities are longer than average. They have a high sensitivity to interest rate changes.

Premium GNMAs, which have coupon rates above current market rates, have greater repayment risk and shorter-than-average maturities. They are less interest rate sensitive and their prices are more stable. Current-coupon GNMAs, at around the current market rate, are the most sensitive of all to interest rate changes.

When interest rates are rising, premium GNMAs can offer the most stable returns. When rates are falling, discount GNMAs generally have the greatest potential for price appreciation. (GNMA fund managers can move from one to another, or may even have some of both. You're relying on the manager's expertise to pick the best ones.)

Junk bond funds

When you see the words "high yield" in a fund's name, that's usually a dead giveaway. Such funds invest in bonds rated below the top four grades—in other words, BB or lower. There are two types of junk bonds, "fallen angels" and "original issue." Fallen angels are bonds that once were investment grade; original issue bonds, pioneered by Michael Milken, enable young companies with poor credit ratings to tap public markets. Junk bond funds hold both types of securities. They also differ from each other in the grades they hold. Some junk bond funds stick to the BB issues—almost investment grade. Others dip down to the far more speculative CC and C grades.

A prudent investor should think of high-yield bonds not as safe debt, but as an equity substitute—a way to achieve appreciation along with generous income. Well-known mutual fund manager Mario Gabelli calls them "SID's," stocks in drag. They are not as interest rate sensitive as higher quality bonds, which perhaps gave them an aura of safety until a few years ago. But the risk of default is many times higher. According to Standard & Poors, roughly one-third of all speculative-grade rated securities have defaulted since 1981. This is about seven times the default rate of investment grade securities. Investors who thought they were "CDS's" (CD substitutes), couldn't have been more wrong.

The following table compares the total return of junk bond funds with diversified equity funds and intermediate term investment grade bond funds. We used the intermediate term category since most junk bond funds are not of long maturity. As you can see, in most years the junk bond funds track equities somewhat better than they do other bond funds.

Table 26

Junk bond funds vs equities and investment grade bond funds

Total return percent

| | | | Fixed-income investment grade | |
	Hi-yield	**Diversified equity**	**Corporate intermediate**	**Gov. intermediate**
1983	14.3	21.4	8.3	8.4
1984	10.6	-0.5	12.5	14.3
1985	23.4	27.0	18.8	19.0
1986	15.0	14.1	12.6	11.1
1987	1.0	0.6	1.6	2.1
1988	12.9	15.8	7.7	6.4
1989	1.1	22.9	12.0	12.9
1990	-6.3	-5.8	7.3	9.0
1991	29.6	33.5	15.1	15.0
1992	15.8	9.0	7.1	6.6
1993	18.9	13.2	9.7	8.2
1994	-2.2	-1.5	-2.8	-3.4

Junk bonds turned in terrible performances in 1989 and 1990 primarily as a result of the S&L crisis. This resulted in their being oversold. Junk bonds then bounced back with a vengeance in 1991, up 30.4% on average, and continued to make strong gains in 1992 and 1993. In 1994s bear market for bonds they did comparatively well precisely because they are not as interest-rate sensitive as other types of bonds are. As a general rule junk bonds will do well when the economy is strong, because that reduces the chances of default by the bond issuers. Conversely, when the economy is weak, the number of defaults will increase, often sharply, and junk bond funds will be poor investments.

High yield bond funds are not for investors who need dependable income. Look what happened to these bonds since 1989. All of them had to reduce their dividend payouts to reflect the problems in the market, general declines in interest rates, and refundings of their highest-yielding portfolio bonds. It was only in the last two years that the declines moderated. Table 27 shows the percent change in the cents per share dividend payouts for the high-yield bond funds we have followed since 1989.

Table 27

Nine junk bond funds

Average income	per share distributions
1989	1.11
1990	0.99
1991	0.86
1992	0.79
1993	0.77
1994	0.75
94 vs. '89	-32%

Junk bond funds are most appropriate for equity investors. When buying, look for the best managed funds. You need a manager who knows credit analysis because avoiding defaults is the name of the game. Diversification is a must; do not buy individual junk bonds. Choose funds with a large number of different issues and no disproportionately large individual holding. A very high-yield probably indicates that the fund is buying the riskiest junk; lower yields, a somewhat better grade. Ironically, when these funds are doing well, the riskier variety does best. But don't look just at yield; the real bottom line is total return.

We previously noted that you should not spend that part of the interest distribution that reflects an inflation premium. Similarly, in the case of junk bond fund investments, don't spend that part of your distribution that compensates you for loss through defaults. If you spend all the interest you receive you are, in a very real sense, eating into your capital. In 1994, the average no-load junk bond fund we follow yielded 9.6%, while the average long-term corporate bond fund holding investment grade bonds had a yield of just 6.3%. That extra yield is not a free lunch.

Flexible bond funds

As the name indicates, these funds can move between various types of fixed-income bonds and vary their maturities. They can invest in corporate, government, mortgage-backed, international and junk bonds, convertibles and income producing common stocks. Maturities can vary from very short to very long. These funds have the advantage of being able to move into the fixed-income sectors that are currently the best performers, saving you the chore of switching. Their disadvantages are: 1) their selections and timing can be off, and 2) you never know exactly how the fund is invested.

Our newsletter follows six flexible funds: Blanchard Flexible Income, Flex-Fund Bond, Janus Flexible Income, Merriman Flexible Bond, Price Spectrum Income, and USAA Income. In 1994, as grizzly a year for bonds as we are ever likely to see, these funds did quite well. By keeping their maturities short to intermediate, they had an average loss of only 3.0%.

International bond funds

A new genre was started in 1986 when the T. Rowe Price International Bond Fund was launched. For the first time, it provided no-load fund investors with the possibility of higher returns by investing in foreign bonds. Other groups such as Scudder, Fidelity and Warburg, Pincus followed with international and global fixed-income funds.

International bond funds are attractive because they benefit from weaknesses in the dollar, and because of the high yields being paid in many foreign countries. Of course, a rising dollar can shrink and even offset foreign bond returns, so the returns on these funds are erratic. They did well in 1991 with a weak dollar, but were laggards in 1992 when the dollar strengthened. In 1987, the Price International Bond Fund gained 28.1%, to rank 14th among all no-load funds. The next year it lost 1.3% and was one of the worst performing of all funds.

International bond funds tend to invest in high-quality, intermediate-term securities, frequently issued by foreign governments. They may enter into currency hedges in countries where a fund's manager feels that the currency is weak against the dollar.

In 1990 and 1991 a number of fund organizations—including Scudder, Fidelity, and Blanchard—launched short-term global bond funds that sought to obtain high yields by investing in high-quality, short-term debt instruments, many of them government backed, both here and abroad.

These funds minimize interest rate risk by investing in securities with maturities of three years or less. Credit risk is reduced by investing mostly in government obligations, and currency risk is reduced — *but not eliminated* — by hedging techniques. Some of these funds, principally loaded ones, are being marketed as quasi-money funds. They are not. They have variable NAVs, which can fluctuate as much as the NAVs of domestic short-term bond funds. Investors discovered this to their sorrow in 1992 when some important currency hedges went awry, and NAV's plummeted. All had total returns less than their yields. Like other short-term bond funds they are also hurt by rising interest rates.

The newest innovation in international fixed-income investing is the emerging markets bond fund. Both Fidelity and Scudder now have them. When first introduced in 1993, they offered high yields and good total returns. It was another story in 1994. These funds were hard hit by currency devaluations and fears of default. Fidelity New Markets Income, which had gained 38.8% from its inception in May, 1993 through December, 1993, lost 16.1% in 1994, and another 20.9% in the first nine weeks of 1995. These funds will probably deliver good returns in the long-run, but with extreme volatility.

Two fund groups—Benham and Scudder—offer no-load mutual funds investing in zero coupon bonds. Typically, the funds hold U.S. Treasury securities that have been stripped of their interest coupons. You buy the corpus at a deep discount from the face value, which is paid when the bond matures. The primary advantage of zeros is that they eliminate the reinvestment risk. You don't have to reinvest interest payments periodically at varying, and possibly lower rates. One major disadvantage: you pay taxes each year on the interest as if you had received it. This is true for both individual bonds and funds. (In fact the Benham fund declares an annual dividend solely for tax purposes, followed by a reverse stock split to maintain the fund's NAV, since the zeros pay no dividend.) This tax disadvantage can be eliminated by purchasing zeros in a tax-sheltered account such as an IRA or Keogh.

The Benham Target Maturities Trust has six portfolios maturing at five-year intervals through 2020. The Scudder Zero Target Fund now has a single portfolio maturing in 2000. When a Benham Target fund reaches maturity, it is liquidated. Shareholders have the option of moving to another fund or taking cash. At Scudder, a target fund is converted into a permanent fund, usually short- to intermediate-term.

Investors interested in holding zero coupon bonds should carefully consider the relative merits of buying a fund versus buying individual securities. The fund's advantages: (1) no-load; (2) low minimum and subsequent investment amounts, typically $1,000 to begin, $100 to add to your investment; (3) greater liquidity: if you want to sell before matu-

Zero coupon bond funds

rity you are not at the mercy of the secondary market; (4) the ability to switch between series; (5) call protection (some municipal zeros can be called, and it's very hard to know if that's happened, since there are no regular interest payments; if there were, you might notice one missing); and (6) easy to invest in an IRA or other tax-qualified plan.

The major negative: fund expenses, which can be as much as .70% per year excluding brokerage fees, taxes, and interest. Benham's management fee is .35% per year. If you are buying a fund with the intention of holding it to maturity, you're paying these expenses unnecessarily. For all practical purposes, you then have an *unmanaged* investment. By buying the bonds individually you avoid the fees—a considerable savings in the long run. Here's a rule of thumb for cost effectiveness: if you plan to hold less than four years, buy no-load funds; more than four years, buy the individual bonds.

If you are a long-term holder, the best way to profit from zeros is to buy the individual U.S. Treasury bonds from a broker when interest rates are high and peaking—then hold them until a particular maturity, which you have selected in order to return your capital at a time when you need it. (We recommend you avoid corporate zeros and municipal zeros unless they are general obligation bonds. You don't want to assume any default or possible premature call risks.) For example, if interest rates are at 8%, a zero coupon bond maturing in nine years could be bought for approximately half its face value, then held until maturity for a guaranteed 100% profit. The only way an investor can lose is if inflation averaged 8% or more over the entire period, an unlikely occurrence. Why take the risk of having to always be correct on your interest rate forecast if such a desirable alternative is readily available?

Zero coupon bonds, whether in a fund or outside, are extremely volatile, rising and falling in response to interest rate fluctuations. At various times zero coupon bond funds have been at both the top and the bottom of the fund rankings. In 1993, the Benham Target Maturities Fund 2020 portfolio was the best performing fixed-income fund, up 35.6%. The 2015 and 2010 portfolios were second and third. Thus, if you speculate in interest rate movements, here is a way to get action. But watch out when interest rates spike up, as they did in February 1994 after the Fed tightened. Your losses can be dramatic. The 2020 Portfolio lost 7.6% that month, and 17.7% by year end! As a rule of thumb, you can figure that the zeros' profit or loss potential is about three times that of ordinary bond funds.

Two fund groups have offered individuals no-load adjustable rate mortgage (ARM) securities guaranteed by the U.S. government or its agencies. The Benham Adjustable Rate Government Securities Fund and the T. Rowe Price Adjustable Rate Government Securities Fund are designed for conservative, income-oriented investors seeking higher yields than money market funds, Treasury bills, or short-term bank CD's. Investors must be willing to accept some fluctuations in the funds' share prices. The prices of adjustable rate mortgages fluctuate less than traditional fixed rate mortgages. As a rule, a $10 share should move up or down only 15-25 cents for each 1% change in interest rates, while garden variety GNMAs investing in fixed interest mortgages would normally move about 45 cents. This lower volatility is balanced by the fact that the ARMs usually have lower yields that vary more frequently and have a greater pre-payment risk. The funds' dividends vary because ARM rates are reset every six to 12 months. Thus these funds may be most appropriate for investors with relatively short time horizons.

The concept has not proven particularly successful. As a result, in March 1995, Rowe Price announced its ARM fund's focus would be broadened to include short-term Government-back securities including Treasury issues and Government agency notes, bonds, and fixed- and adjustable-rate mortgages. To reflect this broader focus, the Fund's name was changed to the T. Rowe Price Short-Term U.S. Government Fund. In making the announcement Price noted that the supply and demand situation in the ARM market had been difficult. We would note that the fund's gain for the last three years ending 1994 was a low 2.0% per year.

ARM funds

These funds—all sold through brokers—invest in bank loans that are used to finance leveraged buyouts and other transactions involving heavily indebted companies. Because they can be tough to sell on short notice, prime rate funds don't buy back their shares on a daily basis, as do all other funds. Investors in these funds can redeem only every three months, when the funds hold quarterly tender offers. The Pilgrim Prime Rate Trust, one of the largest of these funds, is listed on the New York Stock Exchange to provide daily liquidity (although not necessarily at net asset value). These funds are not recommended.

Prime rate funds

Derivatives

Derivatives are such exotic financial instruments that they are virtually unfathomable to the public, and confusing even to some pros. So it's probably not surprising that these mysterious creatures got a number of bond funds in trouble in 1994. The investment climate was very hostile. Rising interest rates turned supposedly prudent risk-taking into unmitigated disasters. Most adversely affected was the Piper Jaffray Institutional Government Income Fund, a supposedly safe short-term fund. It declined in value a shocking 28%.

The universe of derivatives ranges from some that are intended to reduce risks to others that are highly speculative. The most common include options, futures, etc. The fact that some derivatives went awry hasn't persuaded funds to discontinue their use. Derivatives are a weapon that is simply too important in fund managers' arsenals. Some fund groups say they will stick with the conservative instruments and avoid risky, exotic derivatives. Vanguard, one of the more conservative fund groups, noted in a shareholder newsletter that it will continue to use futures, options, planned amortization class CMOs (or PACs), and synthetic short-term notes (or floaters). It will *not* employ interest-only strips (IOs), principal-only strips (POs), inverse floaters, interest-rate swaps, caps, floors, collars, and swaptions.

Can you avoid funds with derivatives? That is difficult to impossible. In late 1994, *Money* magazine sent a questionnaire to 592 retail bond and money market funds. A staggering 292 or 49% refused to answer their questions regarding the funds' derivative holdings. Although derivative holdings should be included in the funds' quarterly reports, they are hard to decipher.

The best advice: beware of a free lunch. If a fund's yield is unusually high compared to its peers, it is not waiving expenses, nor is there any other obvious explanation, the answer may well be that the fund is using derivatives to enhance its performance. There are no giveaways in investing. Higher yields mean higher risks. If that makes you uncomfortable, stay away.

We can offer one note of reassurance. The worst excesses occur among the load funds. They are goaded to use derivatives in order to offset high 12b-1 fees that make their reported performances uncompetitive.

Yield quotations

Until a few years ago, there was great controversy over the yields compiled and quoted in mutual fund advertising, which many investors used as a prime determinant for making their selections. Instead of the more illuminating total return, yields were quoted without reference to gains or losses in principal. As a result, a fund might be tempted to use any means at its disposal to show higher yields. One ploy: ignoring the eventual capital loss of portfolio bonds bought at a premium. For example, if a bond due to mature in 12 years had a 10% coupon, it might be selling for 110. Taking that premium into account, the real yield would be about 9%. And the most accurate comparative measure, called the yield to maturity, would be around 8%. That's because the bond holder gets only 100 at maturity, not the current 110 value. Similarly, some U.S. government securities funds with Government Plus in their names claimed they were enhancing yield by writing covered options on bonds held in their portfolios. Options are no magic potion. The premiums received from the sale of the options are, in effect, a return of capital. They're not interest.

In 1988, the SEC handed down new rules to curtail the ingenuity with which funds misrepresented their performance. Suddenly, they had to compute yields according to a standardized, government-prescribed method that sharply restricted the potential for abuse.

■ Yields must be shown for the last 30 days, except for money funds, which show 7-day yields. Tax-exempt funds can advertise a tax-equivalent yield.

■ Premium income from option writing is excluded.

■ For bonds selling at discounts or premiums, yield-to-average-maturity must be computed, or yield-to-call if there is a likelihood of the bond being called.

■ GNMA funds must reduce their advertised yields by any reductions realized from homeowners repaying their mortgages early.

Two yield figures are available, the SEC yield, discussed above, and the distribution yield, which is based on actual payouts. The funds will generally give you the SEC yield. In fact, information dispensed by automated telephone answering systems comes under the SEC guidelines. But what a fund representative tells you may not. So it doesn't hurt to ask what you're getting. A few funds give both yields.

The SEC figures are not a perfect representation of the yield, but they make comparisons between funds much more reliable. Funds holding discount bonds now report higher yields; other funds holding premium bonds may report lower yields. In practice, these new procedures apply to fixed-income funds, but can apply to equity income funds if yields are quoted for them.

It is important to understand that these reporting procedures in no way affect dividend payouts. Think of the 30-day advertised yields as essentially measuring a fund's earning power. The actual dividend payouts, on the other hand, are different. They do not take into account accruals, and may include short-term capital gains realized by a fund either on the sale of its portfolio securities or by selling options on its portfolio securities (a strategy used by some funds to enhance income). Depending on the length of the month, the dividend distribution could be for 28 to 31 days. The advertised yields are always 30 days. If the distribution yield is well above the SEC rate, say two or three percentage points, you should be very wary.

Outside rating services (including ours) provide a 12-month "distribution" yield by taking the dividends actually received for the latest year and dividing by the NAV. It is not possible for outsiders to compute yields the SEC way because they would need to know every security in the portfolio, information they cannot obtain. Even the funds need expensive software programs to derive their figures.

Are fixed-income funds for you?

Yes . . . if you are a conservative investor who needs stable income with a lower risk of capital loss.

Yes . . . if you lack the capital to properly diversify individual bond purchases.

Yes . . . if you want to diversify against the risks of equity ownership.

Yes . . . if you wish representation in specialized fixed-income areas such as mortgage-backed securities, international bonds, ARMs or zeros.

Yes . . . if you think declining interest rates will generate capital gains.

CHAPTER 10

Municipal bond funds

Before municipal bond funds debuted in 1976, there was no way for individuals to invest small amounts of money in managed portfolios of tax-free bonds. Today, municipal bond funds give that opportunity to anyone with as little as $1,000 to invest. Moreover, even investors, who have the means to spend $5,000 or more for individual bonds can benefit from the muni funds. Here's why:

In addition to offering tax-free income, muni funds provide professional management, liquidity, convenience, and reduced commissions in acquiring portfolio bonds.

Professional management is especially important. Fund managers closely scrutinize their bonds' credit standing. This is a boon to individual investors, who otherwise are at a decided disadvantage because less information is available on municipal bonds than, say, for publicly held corporations. Tax-exempt issues are relieved of many disclosure requirements by the Securities Act of 1933. Surveillance by the rating agencies is spotty and often occurs only when an issue is sold. Furthermore, most of the bond funds permit management to sell their bonds and park the proceeds in money market securities as market conditions warrant, and some funds do so from time to time.

The funds have the ability to buy and sell large amounts, thus avoiding odd-lot fees and commissions that most individual investors would pay. Dividends are almost always paid monthly and can be reinvested without charge. By contrast, owners of individual municipal bonds are at the mercy of a broker when they buy or sell. And individual bond owners receive their interest twice yearly; generally, there's no simple means of reinvesting the proceeds in other tax-free securities.

While stocks trade in an auction market, with quotes freely available in daily newspapers, bonds trade in a negotiated market, mostly by telephone. Thus quotes are not easily available. The prices of individual municipal bonds — and even the unmanaged municipal trusts — do not appear in daily papers. As a result, in the 1970s millions of bond holders were unaware of the extent to which the value of their holdings had declined because of inflation. And investors could be blindsided again. Not so with muni bond funds. Their prices are available daily, and can generally be found in your daily paper's mutual fund tables. Thus muni bond owners know exactly what their investments are worth on any given day.

Should you own taxable or tax-free bonds?

Deciding whether to invest in municipal bonds rather than taxables, issued by corporations or the federal government, is simple. It depends solely on the respective after-tax yields. Check Table 28 to determine whether you can benefit from tax-free income. Find the line with your taxable income (be careful not to confuse taxable with gross income) and read across. If you're in the 28% bracket, tax-free income of 6% is equivalent to an 8.3% taxable yield. In other words, if the going rate for taxable bonds of the same quality is less than 8.3%, then 6% munis will

Table 28

Tax exempt/taxable yield equivalents for 1995				
Single return $0 - $23,350	$23,350 - $56,550	$56,550 - $117,950	$117,950 - $256,500	over $256,500
joint return $0 - $39,000	$39,000 - $94,250	$94,250 - $143,600	$143,600 - $256,500	over $256,500
Tax bracket 15%	28%	31%	36%	39.6%
Tax-exempt yields (%)		**Federal Taxable yield equivalents (%)**		
2.0	2.4	2.8	2.9	3.1	3.3
3.0	3.5	4.2	4.3	4.7	5.0
4.0	4.7	5.6	5.8	6.3	6.6
5.0	5.9	6.9	7.2	7.8	8.3
6.0	7.1	8.3	8.7	9.4	9.9
7.0	8.2	9.7	10.1	10.9	11.6
8.0	9.4	11.1	11.6	12.5	13.2

provide you with greater after-tax income. The higher your bracket, the greater the benefit munis will provide — otherwise, there'd be little incentive to purchase them, since a U.S. government bond, for example, has no risk of default.

When you're doing these computations, make sure you are comparing like bonds; you need to look at short maturities versus short, investment grade versus investment grade.

Relative yields change. Tax brackets change. So it's a good idea to review your choices of taxable versus tax-free funds at regular intervals.

Single-state bond funds

When municipal bond funds started out, they spread their investments over many states. But soon it became apparent that investors could get even greater tax advantages by buying bond funds that invested only in bonds issued within their own states. That's because only muni bonds issued by your own state (or its communities and agencies) are totally tax-free to you. The interest you get from out-of-state munis generally is fully taxable at the state level if your state or municipality has an income, dividends or interest tax. This holds true for both municipal bonds and municipal bond funds. If the fund purchases bonds issued by municipalities outside your state, you will have to pay state and local taxes on the interest you get from them (though not federal income tax, of course). Only that portion of a national fund's assets that is invested in your state's bonds can be exempted from your state tax.

Almost every rule has an exception. Four states—Illinois, Iowa, Oklahoma, and Wisconsin—tax even the income from some or all of their own bonds. On the other hand, the District of Columbia, Indiana and Utah give tax-free status to muni bond interest, no matter where the bonds are issued.

Single-state municipal bond funds did not exist prior to 1983. Now, they are more numerous than national bond funds. The first no-load municipal bond fund investing in the securities of a single-state was the Fundamental New York Muni Fund. Its popularity has now led to the formation of additional single-state no-loads benefiting investors in Arizona, California, Connecticut, Florida, Georgia, Idaho, Kentucky, Maryland, Massachusetts, Michigan, Minnesota, Missouri, Nebraska, New Jersey, New York, North Carolina, Ohio, Oregon, Pennsylvania, Tennessee, Virginia, and Wisconsin.

These single-state bond funds are available from Benham, Dreyfus, Fidelity, GIT, Rowe Price, SAFECO, Scudder, USAA, Vanguard and others.

By sidestepping state and/or local income taxes you can dramatically increase your after-tax returns. A New York City resident who is in the new 39.6% federal income tax bracket can zoom to a combined federal, state and city income tax bracket of 47.1%. That means that a 6% yield from a fund invested in a New York bond fund is worth an after-tax equivalent of 11.3% to a top-bracket New York City resident. Similarly, a California resident in the 39.6% federal tax bracket and a 46.2% combined state and federal bracket would need to get 11.2% from a taxable investment in order to equal a 6% tax-free yield.

To calculate the equivalent taxable yield, divide the tax-free yield by 1 minus your tax bracket denoted as a decimal. For example, here are the calculations for someone in a combined federal and Massachusetts state bracket of 39.28%: 6% tax-free yield ÷ (1.00 - .3928 or .6072) = 9.9% equivalent taxable yield.

Single-state muni bond funds are more likely than national funds to be insured. Which is a good thing, since they aren't as well diversified. The debacle surrounding Orange County, California's default in late 1994, hit the California single-state funds the hardest. However, there's always a downside. Insured bond funds may be a bit more volatile than their uninsured counterparts. That's because with insurance, their coupons are lower, making durations higher.

Table 29

What tax free yields are worth

Tax-free Yield	Tax-equivalent yield Federal taxes only	CA	CT	MA	MI	NJ	NY	OH	PA
				Tax-equivalent yield if free from state taxes					
4%	5.80	6.51	6.07	6.59	6.08	6.23	6.61	6.23	5.96
5%	7.25	8.14	7.59	8.23	7.60	7.79	8.27	7.78	7.45
6%	8.70	9.77	9.11	9.88	9.11	9.35	9.92	9.34	8.95
7%	10.14	11.40	10.62	11.53	10.63	10.91	11.57	10.90	10.44
8%	11.59	13.03	12.14	13.18	12.15	12.47	13.23	12.45	11.93

Tax-equivalent yields are based on a 31% federal tax rate. New York rates include New York City rates.

In deciding whether to purchase a single-state or a national fund, don't automatically assume that a single-state fund for your state is preferable. You have to calculate after-tax equivalent rates of return. A surprisingly wide variation in returns exists, due to the states' differing tax rates and investor demand relative to the supply of municipal bonds in any particular state.

In the five years ending with 1994, about half of single-state muni bond funds underperformed the average general municipal fund. In some cases the differences between individual state funds and a general municipal bond fund are small; in other cases they are significant

Performance of single-state bond funds

Table 30

Long-term single state bond funds

Ranked by 1990-1994 total return

Fund (#)	% gain
Texas (25)	40.9
Florida (71)	39.8
Kentucky (7)	39.5
New Jersey (48)	38.5
Pennsylvania (57)	38.1
Massachusetts (47)	37.8
Alabama (7)	37.7
Louisiana (13)	37.6
Ohio (48)	37.2
Michigan (37)	37.2
New York (83)	36.4
General munis (216)	36.0
Colorado (20)	36.0
Arizona (34)	35.9
Connecticut (22)	35.6
Tennessee (15)	35.5
Missouri (17)	35.0
Georgia (26)	34.7
Oregon (17)	34.6
Virginia (31)	34.4
Minnesota (34)	34.3
South Carolina (13)	34.2
Maryland (29)	34.1
California (94)	33.9
Hawaii (11)	33.5
North Carolina (29)	33.4
All other states (51)	31.2

The number of funds in each average is in parentheses.
Source: Lipper Analytical Services

enough so that there may not be a tax advantage. If you live in California, Hawaii, North Carolina, South Carolina, Minnesota, Virginia, Oregon and Georgia, note that the long-term municipal bond funds in your state underperformed the average national fund. Therefore, investors in those states, and other poorly performing states, should be think twice about buying single-state funds. Our annual *Handbook* lists the combined federal and state marginal tax rates for all states. Using it you can then calculate the after-tax yield of a single-state fund and compare that with the equivalent return for a national fund. The easiest way to do this is to convert both to a taxable yield basis.

Pricing bond funds

Well over a million issues of municipal bonds exist; but only a small fraction of them actually trade on any given day. Thus, no accurate current prices exist for the vast majority. Since the funds need to price their shares each day the bond market is open, they use the services of an outside pricing firm, which estimates the prices of the bonds that have not traded. Such companies price bonds by using a matrix. Essentially that involves applying a mathematical formula that takes into account the bond's coupon rate, maturity, discount or premium and call features. When interest rates are stable, these estimates are reasonably accurate. But in times of flux, it may be another story. None of this matters very much unless a fund suffers massive redemptions that force its managers to sell bonds that may be mispriced (usually overpriced). It's unlikely you will be able to anticipate such situations. But if you think you may need to bail out at an inopportune time, redeem sooner rather than later.

Funds vs. trusts

Unit investment trusts (UITs) are an alternative to no-load municipal bond funds. (There are $87 billion UITs outstanding, 80% of them tax-exempt.) The trusts have fixed portfolios and for that reason can lock in high yields for many years. Their portfolios are not managed; consequently there is no management fee, only a minuscule trustee fee of about .15% annually. On the other hand, the trusts are sold with a 4%-5% sales charge. For the long-term investor, trusts can provide a higher yield than funds. They are liquid and can usually be sold back either to the sponsor or in a secondary market. But the sales charge penalizes short-term investors. Thus, the trusts lack practical liquidity during the early years. If you plan to hold for six years or more—then consider the unit investment trusts. Otherwise, no-load bond funds are more economical. (One exception, bond index funds, which have expenses almost as low as the UITs.)

When the municipal bond funds were first organized, their sponsors claimed that their management ability would enable them to out-perform the unmanaged trusts. The managed funds can go to cash in adverse markets and have the ability to dump bonds whose credit standing has declined.

How has the performance of funds compared with that of trusts? No comprehensive analysis has been done in many years. But early studies showed that in down years (i.e., when interest rates are rising), the funds, with their ability to sell bonds and move to cash, out-per-formed the trusts. In rising markets, when interest rates were drop-ping, the reverse was true. The fully invested trusts outpaced the funds.

Most UITs are acceptable alternatives under certain circumstances. Be sure that you are not buying a problem investment. Check the trust's portfolio before you buy. You're going to be living with it for the duration of the investment. Because these trusts are sold mainly on the basis of yield, there is a great temptation to stretch by buying lower quality bonds. About 25% of the WPPSS (Washington Public Power Supply) bonds that went into default a number of years back were owned by trusts. On occasion, the brokerage firms that under-write bonds put them into retail trusts when they can't drum up insti-tutional interest.

It is hard to follow UITs. No newspaper coverage of their bid and asked prices exists, and no advisory services track them. We suggest that if you own UITs, you leave them in a brokerage account. That way you'll get a monthly or quarterly review of prices, saving you the trouble of having to call the Trust for a quote. Two other tips before you buy. Find out the yield-to-call, as well as the yield-to-maturity, and see how many of the bonds can be called. Unlike mutual funds which reinvest the proceeds from called securities, the trusts return the principal to you. Thus, after a few years, the outstanding value of your investment can be significantly lower. In the early 1990s, most muni UITs made huge return of principal distributions as interest rates dropped. Next, see if the portfolio contains any long-term zero coupon bonds. If their maturities extend beyond that of other bonds, you will not receive face value when the trust is liquidated.

Are municipal bond funds for you?

Yes . . . if you are a high-bracket investor needing tax-free income.

Yes . . . if you want fixed-income investments with immediate liquidity.

Yes . . . if you lack the capital to properly diversify individual bond purchases.

In summary, when purchasing municipal bond funds, keep in mind their quality and maturities. If you live in a state where single-state bond funds are available, consider them first for additional tax savings.

Money market funds

The money market fund was invented in 1972 as a way to allow individuals to benefit from the high interest rates prevailing at the time. Prior to the invention of the money fund, the only place an ordinary person could invest cash was in the bank. And the banks' ability to pay market interest rates was restricted by Regulation Q, a Depression era law that had been passed to prevent banks from overpaying for their deposits and running the risk of going bankrupt. By the 1970s, the situation had reversed. Regulation Q was limiting the interest on bank savings accounts to 4 1/2%, an amount far less than they could afford.

The first money fund was launched by Harry Brown and Bruce Bent of the Reserve Fund; the second a short time later by James Benham. The money fund took advantage of a loophole in Regulation Q, the lack of an interest rate cap on jumbo CDs of $100,000 or more. Using the mutual fund structure, the money funds could buy these jumbo CDs and pass along high market rates of interest—over 8% at the time—to shareholders who had invested as little as $1,000 in the funds. Furthermore, the Reserve Fund had a new innovation that made it unlike any other mutual fund—a fixed share price of $1, thus fostering the impression money funds were like bank accounts. This was accomplished by varying the yield, computed daily, instead of the price.

One further invention was necessary to turn money funds into a preferred way to manage cash, and this happened in 1974 when Ned Johnson of Fidelity brought out Fidelity Daily Income Trust, the first money fund that offered check-writing redemptions. Prior to FDIT, the fund industry had made it hard to redeem shares; now it became easy. Since then, money funds have become the gateway to the mutual fund industry. They have brought in millions of individuals who were afraid to make equity investments. Once in the mutual fund fold, these people were exposed to the benefits of equity and bond fund investing. They turned the industry into a financial supermarket that has become the preferred investment vehicle for all Americans with savings.

Money market funds have three objectives: preservation of capital, liquidity and the highest possible current income consistent with these objectives. While the fixed NAV is not guaranteed, money funds have done an outstanding job of preserving capital. They have virtually instant liquidity, but their yields are extremely variable—far more than for the long-term bond funds. A money fund's yield and total return are identical.

You can use money funds in three basic ways. Probably the most important for the no-load investor is as a convenient "parking lot." Until profitable new stock market opportunities arrive, you leave your assets in a money fund. For this reason, almost every mutual fund group now has such a fund. Money market funds can also be used as a free checking account. There is, typically, a $250 or $500 per check minimum, although a few money funds have no minimum. The great advantage with a money market fund check is that you benefit from the "float," earning interest until your check is cashed and returned to your money fund's custodial bank. Finally, you can obtain money market interest rates that are generally higher than those paid by banks, not only with liquidity but also safety. For all these reasons, some of your cash should stay permanently in a money market fund.

The main types of money funds available for your use:

General money funds

The most common type is the general taxable money fund, which holds a wide array of investments but typically has a preponderance of assets in commercial paper. Most general money funds are "first tier" but a few are "second tier." First tier funds must have all their commercial paper holdings invested in companies of the highest rank; second tier funds can have up to 5% of their commercial paper holdings with lower ranked companies. Money funds' portfolios are not insured, but they have compiled a remarkable record for safety.

There are *risk differences* between general money funds. But in the main they are relatively small, particularly as compared to stock and bond funds. The possibility of a portfolio security defaulting on interest or principal is known, technically, as the credit risk. Since money funds are not insured, this has been a modest concern among investors. It needs to be put in perspective, though. First, money funds diversify like other mutual funds. They don't generally invest more than a limited percentage of their net assets with any individual issuer. The average fund owns securities of more than 30 individual issuers, so the default of a single one should not be catastrophic.

The only time individual investors in a money fund actually lost principal was in the early days of the money funds. In 1978 a small fund, First Multifund For Income, extended its average maturity out over 600 days, betting on a decline in interest rates. When rates rose instead, redemptions shot up. Investors switched to money funds with shorter maturities that had been able to reinvest matured securities more quickly at the higher yields. Further aggravating the situation, the fund did not mark its portfolio to market (that is, price it to current value rather than the value at maturity). The fund finally bit the bullet, selling its securities at a 6% loss. There was no credit problem. First Multifund's principal investment was Citibank paper, which had the highest corporate credit rating. As a result of this loss, the SEC restricted average maturities of 120 days or less. By today's standards, we would not call the First Multifund For Income a money fund.

In the subsequent years several other close calls occurred, due to actual or potential credit losses. This raised the possibility of a loss that would chop NAVs below $1 a share. To avoid that—and the shareholder exodus that would likely follow—advisers reached into their own pockets to make the funds whole.

Because of these close calls, in February 1991 the SEC placed new restrictions on the kinds of securities that money funds can hold. Under current guidelines, no money fund can invest more than 5% of the fund's assets in less-than-top-grade commercial paper. In addition, no single issue can make up more than 5% of the fund's holdings if the issuer is top rate; below that, 1%. The previous limit had been 25%. (Because there's no credit risk, investments in U.S. government securities are not restricted.) Another step taken by the SEC was to reduce the maximum average maturity of the portfolio securities to 90 days.

Unfortunately,these steps didn't prevent a number of money funds from losing money investing in derivatives in 1993 and 1994. In fact, the trade newsletter, *Fund Action,* tallied 16 such close calls in 1993 and the first half of 1994. In every case but one, the fund's managers assumed the loss because they didn't want to be the first fund to "break the buck," as they term it, which means causing a money fund shareholder to lose money.

Then, in September 1994, it finally happened. A small institutional money fund in Colorado, overloaded with derivatives, was liquidated with a 6% loss to its shareholders. The culprit was the Community Bankers U.S. Government Money Market Fund all of whose owners and shareholders were community banks. The shareholders could have been bailed out for a mere $2 million, but there was no point since the owners of the fund were the shareholders. It would simply have been a transfer of money from one pocket to another. No individual investors were involved. The loss, dutifully reported by the press, did not have any effect on mainstream money funds.

We think it's inevitable that a retail money fund, probably a small one, will someday pass on a loss to its shareholders. When that happens, there will be even more adverse publicity, but the chances are the loss will be moderate—less than a couple percent.

Several insured money market funds used to exist, but no longer. Until early 1989, the Vanguard Money Market Trust had both an insured and an uninsured portfolio. The Insured Portfolio, yielded 7.3% for the five years ending 1988, while its uninsured counterpart, the Vanguard Money Market Trust, Prime Portfolio, yielded 7.96% in the same period. The insured fund's yield ranked in the bottom 20% of money funds, the uninsured fund's yield, in the top 20%. That's a steep price to pay for insurance against a minimal risk. In 1989, Vanguard announced that the Insured Money Market Trust was being converted into a U.S. Treasury money fund, a sensible move. Its portfolio securities are, of course, fully insured, and its yield is greater.

Government money funds

The greatest distinction between money market funds is whether or not they hold government or government-guaranteed securities. If you are a very conservative investor, you can choose a fund that buys only government securities. Most major no-load fund groups now have one. Investors in these groups can easily switch from a general money fund to a government-only fund if they feel economic or political storm clouds are gathering. The yield penalty varies. For many years, the government funds underperformed the general money funds by one-half to one-and-one-half percentage points. That has not been the case since 1985. Since then, the government money funds have generally lagged the regular funds by 0.3% or less. In some individual instances, government money funds equalled or bettered the return of general money funds particularly if they were waiving expenses. Treasury-only money funds, tax-free at the state level, easily exceeded it on an after-tax basis.

Government funds invest in Treasury bills, obligations issued by government agencies such as the Federal Home Loan Mortgage Corp (Freddie Mac) or Student Loan Marketing Association (Sallie Mae), and repos. Funds that invest in Treasury bills are the safest. They're backed by the full faith and credit of the U.S. government. They're even safer than insured bank accounts. Agency securities (like the FDIC) have only the moral backing of the government, yet they're considered quite safe. To compensate for the slight addition of risk, agency paper pays around 10 basis points (one-tenth of one percent) more.

Many government funds buy repurchase agreements or "repos." A few funds hold only repos. These are short-term loans collateralized by government or agency securities in which the borrower agrees to buy back the securities at a fixed price including the interest and at a fixed time. A number of years ago repo holders had some scary moments when a few firms dealing in them went bankrupt and the holders didn't have possession of the collateral. That's changed. The SEC now requires money funds to take possession of the collateral, insuring the safety of the investment even if there are problems with the dealer. Repos also pay slightly higher yields.

Like the bond funds that invest only in Treasury securities, U.S. Treasury money funds can pass the state tax exemption along to their shareholders. That can add significantly to your return, in many cases giving them a better after-tax return than the regular money funds— and with greater safety. In addition, short-term securities issued by the Farm Credit Program, Home Loan Bank, Student Loan Program, and the Resolution Trust Corp. can be tax free at the state level. The Benham Government & Agency Fund, which holds such securities, has tax-free pass-through status.

Tax-exempt money funds

These funds invest in short-term municipal securities. Relatively new, they have achieved greater growth since 1983 than the taxables. Historically, their average maturities have been longer than the regular money funds'. When they have longer maturities, the tax-free funds' yields increase more slowly as interest rates rise and decline more slowly as rates fall.

Tax-exempt money funds are appropriate for high-tax-bracket investors who need to keep a portion of their money both liquid and tax-free. When you are considering a money market fund, you need to compare the relative yields of the regular versus tax-exempt funds at your particular tax bracket, just as you would when investing in longer term bond funds.

Single-state tax-exempt money funds

For the same reasons that people in high-tax states are often better served by investing in single-state municipal bond funds, it also makes sense for them to invest in single-state, tax-exempt money market funds. Not surprisingly, fund managers have launched a number of these funds. The first were born in 1984 for New Yorkers. Advisers then followed with single-state money funds for residents of Arizona, California, Connecticut, Florida, Massachusetts, Michigan, New Jersey, North Carolina, Ohio, Pennsylvania, Texas, and Virginia. Single-state funds are available from Benham, Dreyfus, Fidelity, Rowe Price, Schwab, Scudder, the Reserve Fund, USAA, Vanguard, Warburg Pincus and others.

You can't always assume that single-state funds are better for you than national, or even than taxable, funds. You will note that Vanguard has New Jersey and Pennsylvania tax-free money market funds, but no New York T/F money market fund. That's because the fund group found that yields on New York money market instruments were low because too many investors were chasing a limited supply of paper. As a result, Vanguard's national tax-free money fund frequently delivers higher yields—on an after-tax basis—than the average New York T/F money fund. Consequently, the firm doesn't have a New York fund. Investors in single-state money funds should check their current tax-equivalent yields and switch to other funds, taxable or tax-free, when that proves advantageous. However, unless you keep very large six or seven-figure amounts in these cash accounts—and then for significant lengths of time—don't drive yourself crazy by worrying about minuscule differences in after-tax yield.

Some other short-term bond funds, which may appear similar to money market funds, are not classified as money funds. They have variable NAVs, and consequently are listed with bond funds. They typically maintain dollar-weighted portfolios with average maturities not much longer than one year. So their price fluctuations are minimal. But as long as the NAV fluctuates, they can do better or worse than a money fund.

In the taxable category, Neuberger & Berman offers the Ultra Short Bond Fund for investors seeking a higher total return than conventional money market funds provide, minimal risk to principal, and liquidity. It aims to enhance yield by lengthening the average maturity of its diversified portfolio of money market instruments up to 360 days. How much riskier is it? In 1994 the NAV varied from $9.63 to $9.44, a difference of 2.0%. At year-end it had an average maturity of 0.4 years. This fund—and other similar funds such as IAI Reserve, Strong Advantage and Harbor Short Duration—is listed with other stock and bond funds in the papers.

These funds are superior on a total return basis when interest rates are declining, but inferior when rates are rising. When evaluating these funds, call the adviser for latest maturities. One caveat: we recommend you don't write checks on these quasi-money funds. Since their NAVs vary, every check cashed is a sale, with potential capital gain (or loss) tax consequences.

Fluctuating NAV liquidity funds

International money funds invest in money market instruments denominated in foreign currencies. They provide investors with a means to profit from declines in the dollar, or to hedge against such declines. For example, if the dollar was favorably priced against the yen, and you were planning a trip to Japan in six months, you could buy shares of a fund whose money market assets were denominated in yen. That would protect you, to the extent you invested in the fund, by locking in the present exchange rate. Similarly, if your child were attending Oxford, you could purchase sufficient shares of a fund dominated in pounds to lock in a year's expenses. Of course, such a strategy could backfire. If the dollar strengthened, your investment in the local currency would work against you.

No pure no-load international money funds exist. However, Fidelity Investments sponsors the Fidelity Foreign Currency

International money funds

Portfolios, three limited partnerships investing in Yen, Sterling and the Deutsche Mark. Fidelity's funds have no 12b-1 fee, but do have a load which ranges from 0.4% for minimal purchases to 0.2% for investments exceeding $100,000. These money funds don't have fixed NAVs; rather they fluctuate with currency movements. Don't look for consistent performance from these currency funds. In 1990, the Fidelity Pound Performance Fund was number two among all funds, up 36.4%. Seventy-five percent of its gains were due to currency fluctuations. In 1992, with a rising dollar, it lost 12.1%, and in 1994, with the dollar once again declining, it gained 9.9%.

While the funds' maturities are short, in the same range as true money funds, they have a variable NAV because of currency fluctuations. The currencies in which they are denominated have to be converted back to the dollar. The prices of the Fidelity Foreign Currency Portfolios are not carried in the papers, but if they grow large enough, they will carried in the stock and bond listings.

One well-known fund that some think is foreign isn't. The Dreyfus Worldwide Dollar Fund invests around the world, but it differs from the other international funds in that all its investments are dollar-dominated. It has a fixed NAV.

Selecting your money market fund

We believe that yield is only one consideration when you are choosing a money fund, and perhaps a minor one at that. Yield differences among money funds are small.

Some funds have higher than average yields, obtained by temporarily waiving their management fees and absorbing some expenses. When that happens, shareholders get a windfall. That's great, but be wary. These free rides are often temporary. When the Fidelity Spartan Money Fund and the Dreyfus Worldwide Dollar Money Fund first were launched, they achieved double-digit yields by waiving expenses, enabling them to scoop up billions of dollars in a matter of months. Both funds then gradually phased in management fees. If you buy shares in a money fund that is waiving expenses, keep a close eye on the yields; don't expect management to tell you when they stop waiving expenses. Increasingly, mutual fund groups are using this ploy as a marketing strategy to drum up business for new funds. According to the *Donoghue Money Fund Report,* 58% of all retail money funds waived at least a portion of their expenses in 1994.

Since expenses are a major determinant of yields, funds that have historically been top performers are likely to remain so.

Bear in mind that the yields quoted in the papers and by the funds are annualized rates. You get them only if you hold the money fund for a full year—and rates stay at that level throughout the period. But don't bank on either eventuality. Money fund yields fluctuate from week to week. It's far more realistic to think of a 4% annualized yield as a rate that yields 0.33% per month, or even 0.08% per week.

Convenience is important. If your investments are concentrated in a no-load fund group that has a money fund, we strongly recommend you use that group's money fund to facilitate switching between funds.

Here's a checklist of services you should consider in picking a fund:

■ A reasonable minimum amount for check redemption. Most funds require you to write checks for at least $250-$500. However, some have lower minimums. Benham's Capital Preservation Funds, for instance, allow checks for $100. Money funds that are part of central asset accounts usually have no minimums. Some funds will let you write small checks for a service fee.

■ Immediate confirmations. Most funds send confirmations after each purchase and each redemption made directly to you, but fewer send confirmations after each check you've written on your money fund account. Money funds may send regular account statements at monthly or quarterly intervals. If you need this account information more frequently, look for a fund that sends your checks back as you write them.

■ Expedited redemptions. If you redeem today, is the money sent to you the same day or a day or two later? Delay costs you interest. Almost all money funds will redeem via fed wires. This is same-day service. In addition some funds provide other types of bank wires. They take one to two days but usually are free.

■ Speed. How fast your money goes to work for you can differ from fund to fund, and check to check. How soon you can withdraw money invested by check also varies. You can wait up to two weeks after you make a purchase before you have "good" funds. The deadline for same-day investments made by wire or in person can vary from 11 AM to 4 PM.

■ Minimum investments. They usually range from $1,000 to

$2,500, but a few funds have lower or higher minimums. The Fidelity Spartan money funds and Vanguard Admiral funds deliver above-average yields for individuals who can meet high minimums.

In selecting a money fund, *size* has its advantages. Other things being equal, the larger funds should pay higher rates because their expenses are spread over a bigger base. They are also more diversified.

Try to *avoid 12b-1 funds*. While these marketing expenses are usually low compared to the charges levied for stock funds, the distribution benefits are problematical. More important, they clearly cut your yield. The Kemper Money Market Fund and the Cash Equivalent Fund, also managed by Kemper, are very similar funds. They are both large, have similar portfolios and maturities. Yet Kemper Money Market yielded 3.99% in 1994 as compared to 3.60% for Cash Equivalent. The only difference is that Cash Equivalent has a 12b-1 charge of .38%, which is used to pay outside organizations for bringing assets into the fund.

Similarly, *avoid high expense ratio* funds. Since gross yields vary only slightly, a high expense ratio almost always means a lower net yield to you.

Watch out for *additional charges*. Some funds charge for check-writing, exchanges and even withdrawals.

Pay attention to average maturity. The shorter the maturity, the safer a fund is, and the quicker the yield will respond to changes in interest rates. In periods of rising interest rates, funds with the shortest maturities will increase their yields the fastest. On the other hand, if interest rates are declining, funds with longer maturities are in a better position because their high yields are locked in longer.

In the case of government funds, check to *see if state and local taxes are deductible*.

Money funds versus the banks

Many investors find it convenient to keep some liquid funds in bank money market accounts. How much to have there depends on the type of services you need and the extent to which small differences in yield are important to you.

If you're using liquid asset accounts primarily for yield, it pays to compare funds and banks closely. It is important to understand that banks and money funds have totally different ways of determining yield payouts. Money fund shareholders participate in the earnings of a pool of money invested in money market instruments. You get a share of whatever that pool of money earns, minus the fund's expenses.

Not so with the banks. Their payout bears no necessary relationship to what their deposits actually earn (although, of course, they must cover their expenses, which generally are higher than a fund's). They establish their yields based on the supply/demand relationships for the deposits. The yield depends on how high a rate they have to offer to keep the money in the bank.

The banks have discovered that money market account customers are not particularly sensitive to interest rates. (Those who are, generally buy CDs; so the banks now compete strongly with the money funds for this business.) Consequently, in recent years, bank money market accounts have tended to pay significantly less than the money funds.

The banks' major advantage is FDIC insurance. If this is important to you, compare bank yields to the government money funds, particularly those owning Treasuries. They're just as secure.

Note, however, that there is another reason to rest easy when investing in a money fund: shareholders own the assets of the portfolios on which they have claims. Even if every shareholder wanted to redeem his dollars at the same moment, all eventually would get paid. Banks, on the other hand, create money by lending out more than their deposits. They cannot pay every depositor at once; that's why a run on a bank can be devastating.

You can find money fund statistics in *The Wall Street Journal, Barron's* and many other large papers on a once-a-week basis. If your fund isn't listed in the papers, don't hesitate to call. A few funds are embarrassed to list their yields. Most funds have 800 numbers with recorded announcements that provide you with the fund's current yield.

Check newspapers for current yields

CHAPTER 12

A fund to meet your every need

Without half trying, you can find a mutual fund that's as general or as specialized as you might want. As you browse through the landscape, you will encounter investment opportunities that seem alluring, as well as those that are baffling—or downright scary. When you start thinking seriously about funds that you might invest in, be introspective. Don't let a fund's glossy brochures and glowing verbiage entice you into making an investment that is out of line with your goals and risk tolerance.

In this chapter, so that you will be armed with the information you need to make your investment decisions, we will run down the different varieties of specialized mutual funds. For convenience, we'll list them in alphabetical order.

All-weather funds. In the wake of the October 1987 meltdown of the U.S. stock market, this was a hot approach; a number of funds described themselves as all-weather.

We define an all-weather fund as one that long-term investors can safely hold throughout a complete market cycle. Specifically, we see three distinct types of funds that can be used for all-weather investing.

One attempts to time the market or to allocate assets among stocks, bonds and cash depending on market conditions. Ideally such a fund stays fully invested in rising markets, then minimizes losses during bear markets by keeping a high percentage of its assets in cash.

A second approach to all-weather investing is the global asset allocation strategy. These, and the balanced funds (below), are described in length in Chapter 8.

A third way to achieve the goal is to select low volatility funds that don't track the market too closely. Some funds have an admirable record of reasonable profits in rising markets and below average losses during downturns. Analytic Optioned Equity, Gateway Index Plus, Lindner Dividend, the Mutual Series funds and Price Capital Appreciation are among the funds in this category. Another fund whose price moves quite independently of the market is the Merger Fund; it specializes in mergers and acquisitions.

Seldom bull market winners, especially in the short term, the market timing, asset allocation and low volatility funds generally do well over the long run. All-weather investing is a desirable strategy for conservative investors and for long-term investors, particularly in uncertain times.

Balanced funds. They keep a relatively fixed percentages of their assets in a combination of common stocks, preferred stocks and bonds as a matter of policy. Balanced funds have a variety of risk levels.

Bear market funds. Trendy managers brought out several funds in 1994 that promised good performance in down markets. The first, the Robertson-Stephens Contrarian Fund, stocked its portfolio with gold and base metals, and T-bills. It also engaged in short selling, an investing technique used by those who want to profit from market declines. Contrarian Fund was followed by the Lindner Bulwark and Peter Grandich Contrarian funds, which have somewhat similar charters. A still more creative entrant was Rydex Ursa. It uses options and futures to produce returns exactly opposite those of the S&P 500. We believe that bear market funds are for market timers only. Even if they do well in down markets—by no means a forgone conclusion—they will certainly be laggards in subsequent bull markets.

Common stock funds. If a fund invests primarily in common stocks, as more than 2,500 do, it is a common stock fund. This broad classification encompasses many degrees of risk.

Diversified and non-diversified funds. This is a legal distinction that does not relate to whether a fund's investments are concentrated in particular industries, but rather to the magnitude of the investments concentrated in particular stocks. Most mutual funds are diversified. According to the Investment Company Act, they must keep 75 percent of their assets well diversified. That means that they can't put more than 5% of their funds' assets into one stock or hold more than 10% of the outstanding voting shares of a particular company. (However, if a holding grows to more than 5%, they don't have to sell off the excess.) A fund that's classified as non-diversified theoretically could concentrate its entire portfolio in one stock. But to qualify for the specialized tax treatment available to investment companies under Subchapter M of the Internal Revenue Code—a powerful incentive—a fund must keep no more than 25 percent of its assets in the securities of one issuer and at least half the assets (instead of 75 percent) must be well diversified. Non-diversified funds are riskier than diversified funds.

Industry funds. While some think industry funds are the latest fad; in truth, they are not new. Century Shares Trust, which holds insurance stocks, began in 1928. The Energy Fund (now Neuberger-Berman Focus Fund) was founded in 1952. But as the number of funds has continued to grow, so have the industry funds. And no wonder. With their non-diversified portfolios, they can stand out from the crowd. In recent years some industry funds have almost always been at the top of the rankings. This makes it easier for fund managers to achieve one of their primary goals: to sell their shares to investors. In fact some industry funds have been launched basically as marketing gimmicks. There are now five environmental funds (down from 11). None has performed particularly well, but the funds accommodate the public's perception that this is or will be a fruitful area. The one no-load is the Invesco Strategic Environmental Services Fund. We'll discuss industry fund investing in more detail in our section on Sector funds.

International funds. In the 1970s, the U.S. economy was so large that investors could adequately diversify their assets within the domestic market. The U.S. accounted for two-thirds of global GDP and two-thirds of the capitalized value of the world's liquid markets. Over the last two decades, though, these numbers have been whittled down to one-third, as other countries' economies have achieved growth rates two to three times that of the U.S. Today, American investors must look offshore. To disregard international investments means to disregard two-thirds of available investment opportunities. America invented color TV, but now manufactures only a small share of TV sets. If you're seeking world-class steel producers, ship builders, consumer electronics manufacturers and car makers you need to look beyond our shores. If your investment adviser is familiar only with domestic corporations, he would compare the advantages of Ford, GM and Chrysler. An internationally minded investor would also look at Toyota, Daimler-Benz, BMW, Japanese tire manufacturers and even rubber producers in Malaysia.

Diversification in international investments can lower overall portfolio risk. The world's stock markets often have their own rhythms; their cycles don't move in lock-step with our markets. Investing internationally is also a way to protect yourself against weaknesses in the U.S. dollar. When the dollar weakens, foreign funds enjoy the benefit of favorable currency fluctuations in addition to the inherent growth potential of their foreign stocks. (By the same token, a rising dollar hampers the performance of international funds.)

Buying foreign stocks on your own is tough. It's difficult to get meaningful investment information on foreign companies. Accounting, auditing and financial reporting practices vary enormously and are frequently spotty. Many foreign countries lack powerful regulatory bodies such as the SEC, which provides protection for American investors.

Another way to look at it, is that if you invest in the U.S. you usually have only one way to go wrong: picking the wrong stocks. By contrast, you have three ways to go wrong when investing internationally: picking the wrong countries, choosing the wrong stocks or misjudging the currency fluctuations.

Thus, the ideal way for the American investor to exploit today's overseas investing potential is to buy a fund that specializes in foreign investments. Their managers have the expertise to make profitable, rather than perilous, overseas investments.

Global or *international?* These two buzz words cover a significant distinction in investment approaches. An international or foreign portfolio is invested exclusively overseas; a global portfolio is invested both in the U.S. and abroad. The advantage of an international fund is that it gives you the opportunity to allocate your investments precisely between domestic and international funds. You can then easily change the allocations to fit your own preferences. The advantage of a global fund is that the professional money mangers who run these funds are equipped to examine worldwide currency and stock market trends and make domestic/international asset allocation decisions for you.

Sometimes you get international diversification without even asking for it. Our *No-Load Fund Investor* newsletter conducted a survey in 1993 and found that half of all domestic no-loads have, in fact, some foreign exposure. It further found that 17% had 10% or more of their equity portfolios overseas. You should take this into account when allocating between the U.S. and foreign funds.

A wealth of choices exist for the investor who wants to diversify internationally. He can choose among both large and small cap international and global equity funds either in the open-end or closed-end structure. There are choices of objectives. Most international funds are growth oriented, but a few have proclaimed growth-income objectives. Small company international funds should probably be considered as aggressive-growth funds. In addition, international and global fixed-income funds are becoming commonplace.

Some funds can invest in geographic regions such as Europe, Latin America and Southeast Asia. A new category that has become important in the last few years is the emerging market funds. While definitions may vary somewhat, the following countries are generally considered developed or mature markets: in Asia: Japan, Australia, and New Zealand; the U.S. and Canada; and the countries of Western Europe as far east as Germany and Scandinavia. All other countries are considered emerging markets. Emerging market funds invest in developing countries with high economic growth rates, pro-business governments and good long-term potential. Funds with Emerging Markets in their names, Latin American funds, and those investing in the Pacific Basin region (except Japan) all are in this category.

In contrast, many of the general or European funds make most of their investments in the developed countries. They tend to select large-cap stocks in countries that are heavily weighted in the EAFE international index. This is the Morgan Stanley Europe, Australia, Far East Index, which is generally used a benchmark for international performance.

More than 50 funds invest in specific foreign countries. A few are no-loads investing in Japan or Canada, but almost all the others are single-flag funds marketed as closed-ends because of the lack of liquidity in smaller markets. While these single-flag funds provide easy access to specific countries, we think they should generally be avoided unless you have specific fundamental knowledge of the markets and investment potential in these countries.

While the funds are mostly affiliated with major U.S. fund groups, they are run by managers expert at foreign investing. In many cases, American fund managers have teamed up with established foreign investment counselors. T. Rowe Price International, for example, has joined with British-based investment counselors. The Invesco funds are owned by a British investment concern, Invesco Mim PLC, which provides expertise for their international funds.

International funds should be a permanent component of every investor's equity holdings. A 15% to 30% allocation is suitable for most investors. But don't get carried away and invest in a number of these funds. If yours is a small portfolio, figure on selecting a general international fund that can invest in any foreign country. Larger portfolios can benefit from holding several international funds with regional concentrations in Europe, the Pacific (with or without Japan) and in the emerging markets.

Multifunds. These funds invest in shares of other funds. In theory, they offer expertise in fund selection and market timing. In practice, the funds have not been notably successful. Several such funds appeared in the late 60s and early 70s—First Multifund, Pooled Funds, Inc., Fundpack, Hyperion, No-load Selected. They tended to buy into a dozen or more growth funds, spreading their investments. Many of the best performing funds were small, and couldn't stand to take in too much money from one source, especially one that might suddenly redeem its shares. The result was unwanted diversification, which diluted performance. Worse still, the funds' ability to time the market was none too good. Furthermore, their practice of layering investment fees (their own plus the management fee of the funds in the underlying portfolio) significantly increased their real expense ratios. All the original no-load multifunds were liquidated by 1979, although not necessarily because of these shortcomings.

Other multifunds have been launched since then. In 1984 FundTrust, a low-load multifund with four portfolios, was organized. Each portfolio has a different investment goal—Aggressive Growth, Growth, Growth & Income, and Income. Each FundTrust portfolio invests in about ten different funds, both no-load and load. (Because of the size of its purchases, the sales charges are generally 1% or less, and back-end loads are prohibited.)

In 1985, Vanguard offered Star, a multifund whose portfolio consists solely of ten other Vanguard Funds—seven common stock funds, two fixed-income funds, and a money market fund. In 1994,

Vanguard added four other multifunds to the Star series. Star is ideal for an IRA account, since the minimum investment is only $500 and you pay only one annual IRA fee instead of up to ten. Star itself has no management fee. In 1990, T. Rowe Price launched a sort of copy-cat, the Spectrum Fund, with Growth and Income portfolios, to invest in other Price funds. The Income Portfolio invests mostly in fixed-income funds.

Spectrum and Star have been above-average to average performers. The other multifunds in the 90s are performing no better than their predecessors of the 70s. Over the long run, their overdiversification and layering of fees virtually ensure sub-par performance. FundTrust's various portfolios have generally been in the bottom 40% of funds in their categories.

Open-end and **closed-end funds.** Open-end funds, also called mutual funds, create new shares when you invest your money. They will also redeem your shares when you want to get your money out of the fund. Thus the number of shares outstanding in an open-end investment company varies. Closed-end funds have a fixed number of shares and do not sell their shares to investors or buy them back. Shares in these funds are traded on stock exchanges or over-the-counter in the same way that individual securities are traded. We'll take a closer look at closed-end funds in the next chapter. Open-end and closed-end funds both come in many forms, with all degrees of risk.

Option income funds. Fund managers, moving to take advantage of a provision in the Tax Reform Act of 1976, brought out a new type of mutual fund early in 1977. Certainly here is an area where expertise is needed. If you have dealt with stock options, you know how complex the investment decisions can be: which stock to buy or sell options on; what specific option to write; if and when to repurchase the option.

Option income funds are conservative, writing covered-call options on stocks they already own to generate additional income

---

Market timing multifunds

The Rightime Fund, a multifund organized in 1985, is different. Manager David Rights is a market timer who basically uses funds rather than stocks as his equity vehicles. His fund's performance, which depends primarily on the accuracy of his market timing, has been quite erratic, varying from the top to the bottom 20 percent. Overall, his performance has been poor. Others in the market timing multifund category are the Merriman Asset Allocation and Merriman Capital Appreciation Funds, the Flex Muirfield Fund and the Weston New Century Portfolios. As with the Rightime Fund, they have generally done poorly. Yet, any of them can look good temporarily if they correctly time a bear market.

beyond that derived from dividends and capital appreciation. But they aren't magic. When the market is rising, the call options, in which the writer bets that the market will go down, limit upside potential. Managers of conventional equity funds depend solely on dividends and capital appreciation. In contrast to the option-writing funds, however, their potential is unlimited.

During the long-term bull market since 1977, the option income funds were poor performers. Consequently, their numbers have dwindled. At the peak, 21 option income funds existed, most of them load funds. Today only two are left. Analytic Option Equity Fund, the only no-load, typically ranks in the bottom 20% of all funds in its category except in periods of correction, when it shines.

Precious metals funds. No industry group has achieved more popularity than the precious metals funds. Thirty-six gold oriented funds exist, eleven of them no-load. You can buy gold funds that invest entirely in South African gold stocks, funds that totally avoid South Africa by concentrating investments in North America and other parts of the world, funds that offer a mixture, and even funds that keep a portion of their holdings in gold bullion. How their portfolios are structured makes a difference in performance and safety. The North American mining companies are the most popular, but the South African mines have the advantage of longer life and the ability to produce gold profitably at a lower price. The drawback has been the political unrest in South Africa, which along with the currency risk, makes the shares more volatile. United Services Gold Shares, the top-rated fund in four different years, concentrates its portfolio in South African mines. In light of subsequent events, it seems rather quaint today, but the fund actually declined in value by 20% in the three days following South African leader Nelson Mandella's release from jail in February, 1990. The precipitous drop was caused by fears that the country's mines might eventually be nationalized.

Some funds hold bullion, which is typically less volatile than the stocks of the gold mining companies. Although there are exceptions, a rule of thumb is that the shares tend to have a beta of 1.5 to bullion, meaning that their price fluctuations are one and one-half times as volatile as the price of bullion, and bullion is also more liquid. It provides for greater diversification in a portfolio. Most of the gold funds tend to hold the shares of the larger, established gold mining companies. They seldom buy the new ventures, the prospectors. What differentiates the funds is their asset allocation, including cash and bullion, and their distribution by country—i.e., around the world, North America, South Africa, etc.

The performance of the gold funds is erratic, to say the least. In some years they are the best performing, in others the worst. They were the best in 1986, 1987, 1989, and 1993. In spite of their go-go years, gold funds have not shone over the long term. Far from it! In the 10-year period ending in 1994, gold funds were the *worst* performing category in terms of investment objective. The group advanced just 5.3% per year on average. Keep in mind that if you are buying shares of stock, they are subject to the same influences all stocks are subject to—future earnings, which depend not only on the price of gold but the costs of mining it, new gold strikes, existing mines playing out, etc. Because of many structural changes in the world (including the decline of inflation), gold seems on the way to becoming a commodity that will eventually move to an industrially based price.

As with other industry funds, gold funds make sense only if you believe that they have immediate appreciation potential. Although some advisors suggest holding gold funds as a kind of "portfolio insurance," we do not advocate that approach. Here's why: Let's assume that you have $100,000 to put into equities. Say you invest $90,000 in diversified funds and put the other $10,000 into gold funds as "insurance" against financial calamity. Suppose the worst happens; the economy, the markets, the world all get into trouble. Your diversified funds decline 30%, and your gold funds double. That means you lose $27,000 on one side of the aisle, but gain $10,000 on the other side. You're still down $17,000. We don't think the Prudential or GEICO would call that insurance. We'll show you better strategies.

Real estate funds. Real estate has been a traditional investment for people seeking steady, long-term returns. That objective is especially popular in times of inflation. Most real estate investing is direct—owning your own home or personally managing income producing property. Another common investment vehicle is the limited partnership, which invests in a number of different properties. However, participation commonly requires that you have a substantial net worth, and you must tie up your money for a number of years. Yet another way is investing in individual real estate companies, frequently in the form of real estate investment trusts (REITs) or master limited part-

nerships (MLPs). Complementing these vehicles, the real estate
mutual fund has emerged as an investment with good liquidity and
the advantages of active management.

Five no-load mutual funds available to individuals are the Cohen
& Steers Reality Shares, CGM Realty, Fidelity Real Estate
Investment Portfolio, PRA Real Estate, and U.S. Real Estate Fund.
They couple an investment goal of current income with the potential
for capital appreciation. Their portfolios contain many REITs, which
give investors access to investments in shopping malls, medical facilities, office buildings and apartments. They also provide the opportunity for direct investments in companies within the real estate industry. The advantages of the funds: professional management, diversification, low minimum investments and liquidity. Disadvantages: an
investor is several times removed from a pure real estate investment,
having to contend with the movements of the stock markets as well
as the underlying real estate.

The best of the group, Cohen & Steers, averaged 15.5% per year for
the three years ending 1994, ranking it in the top 15% of equity funds.

Regional funds. Some funds specialize in a particular area of the
United States. The IAI Regional Fund in Minneapolis must keep 80%
of its portfolio in the stocks of companies headquartered in
Minnesota, Wisconsin, Iowa, Nebraska, Montana and the Dakotas.
The managers of these funds feel they gain an edge by investing close
to home, but it depends on where home is. The IAI Fund has had
some very good years, but not every regional fund has fared as well.
For many years, San Antonio's USAA Investment Management Corp.
ran the Sunbelt Era Fund, which invested in the common stocks of
smaller, emerging growth companies in the Sunbelt region. The fund
was a loser. In 1989, Sunbelt Era changed its name to the USAA
Aggressive Growth Fund and dropped all geographic restrictions.
Two newer regional funds are the Northwest Growth Fund and the
SAFECO Northwest Fund. Both invest in the Pacific Northwest
region, mainly companies situated in Washington and Oregon. So far
they have been poor to lackluster performers.

Sector funds. In the early and mid-80s, smart marketers discovered
a way to jazz up industry funds. The new wrinkle was to put several different industry portfolios under the umbrella of one fund, add switching
capability between portfolios and a related money fund, and call them
sector funds.

Sector funds can offer you the opportunity to own diversified portfolios in various segments of the stock market. If you think energy stocks, technology stocks, bank or financial service stocks or health stocks are ready for gains, here is a convenient way to buy the sector and obtain a working portfolio of stocks that will benefit if that sector moves. The potential rewards are great because, unlike well-diversified funds that embrace many different industries, you can use sector funds to zero in on those areas of the stock market that are really moving.

This concept was pioneered by the Fidelity Select Fund in 1981. Select began by offering specialized portfolios in six stock market sectors: Energy, Financial Services, Health Care, Precious Metals & Minerals, Technology, and Utilities, and has since expanded their number to a total of 36, including Select's own money fund.

In 1984, two other groups followed Fidelity's innovation. The Invesco funds came out with Invesco Strategic Portfolios and Vanguard offered the Vanguard Specialized Portfolios. Invesco grew to ten portfolios, but now has seven. Two international portfolios and a utility portfolio were pulled out of the Strategic umbrella. Vanguard stayed with its first five portfolios for many years, added a Utilities Income portfolio in 1992, and then in early 1994 folded two sector funds into diversified funds, primarily because of lack of investor interest.

Invesco has one significant advantage over the other two—it's truly no-load. Fidelity Select charges entrance and exit loads, as well as fees for switching between portfolios. Vanguard, the least hospitable to switchers, levies a 1% redemption fee on three of its original funds when money is moved to other funds in less than a year.

Sector funds are frequently hot topics in the press. Newsletters have been organized to cover them exclusively. The reasons are not hard to understand. Since they are non-diversified, they have a better chance of producing superior performance than do diversified funds. Hardly a period goes by without one or more sector (or industry) funds posting first-rate performance, and top-ranked funds generate a lot of publicity and interest.

In 1993 many sector funds did well, as is the case most years. However, as is also normal, the range of performance was wide. Fidelity's sector funds were among the best—and the worst. Performances ranged from +111.5% for Select Precious Metals to -

Chart 31

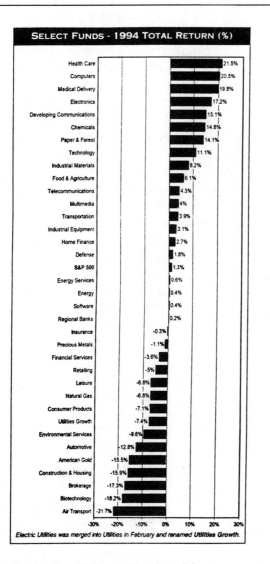

SELECT FUNDS - 1994 TOTAL RETURN (%)

Fund	Return
Health Care	21.5%
Computers	20.5%
Medical Delivery	19.8%
Electronics	17.2%
Developing Communications	15.1%
Chemicals	14.8%
Paper & Forest	14.1%
Technology	11.1%
Industrial Materials	8.2%
Food & Agriculture	6.1%
Telecommunications	4.3%
Multimedia	4%
Transportation	3.9%
Industrial Equipment	3.1%
Home Finance	2.7%
Defense	1.8%
S&P 500	1.3%
Energy Services	0.6%
Energy	0.4%
Software	0.4%
Regional Banks	0.2%
Insurance	-0.3%
Precious Metals	-1.1%
Financial Services	-3.6%
Retailing	-5%
Leisure	-6.8%
Natural Gas	-6.8%
Consumer Products	-7.1%
Utilities Growth	-7.4%
Environmental Services	-9.6%
Automotive	-12.8%
American Gold	-15.5%
Construction & Housing	-15.9%
Brokerage	-17.3%
Biotechnology	-18.2%
Air Transport	-21.7%

Electric Utilities was merged into Utilities in February and renamed Utilities Growth.

Source: Fidelity Insight, Jan. 1995; a publication of the
Mutual Fund Investor's Association.

0.6% for Environmental Services. That encompasses practically the entire spectrum of mutual fund performance that year, from the best to the near worst! In 1994, the range was somewhat narrower. Fidelity again had the best and the worst of the sector funds; its Health fund gained 21.4% while its Air Transportation Fund lost 21.7%.

Sector funds perform much more like individual stocks than do their conventional cousins, diversified mutual funds. This is a negative that concerns us. To explain our concern, consider the fate of the majority of investors who bought Fidelity Select Biotechnology Fund in 1991.

Launched in mid-December 1985, Fidelity Biotech had a lackluster performance until 1989 when the health and biotech stocks took off. Fidelity Biotech, a major beneficiary, gained 43.9% in 1989, 44.3% in 1990, and 99.0% in 1991. The fund was #1 in 1990 and #3 in 1991. Biotech's total assets grew from $40 million at the beginning of 1989, to $1.1 billion in 1991 with $663 million new money pouring in during the final six months. It ended the year with 118,000 shareholders.

However, 1991 proved to be the top. Biotech stocks began a major multi-year correction. The fund lost 26.2% in the next three years. It ranked 3,574th among all funds in 1994. Yet, its shareholder list never fell below 83,000—a decline of 25,000. Its assets are still at almost $400 million, which indicates that large investors were quicker to bail out than small investors. One indication: the average account size is now half what it was at the peak. Those who bought near the top—an unhealthy majority of Biotech's shareholders—have suffered losses. Most investors *bought* too late and either *sold* too late, or more likely, haven't sold at all.

Table 32

Fidelity Select Biotechnology

Year	Annual performance %	Total net assets at year-end $ Mill.
1986	3.5	39.6
1987	-3.3	57.4
1988	4.1	39.9
1989	43.9	69.7
1990	44.3	223.9
1991	99.0	1,146.5
1992	-10.5	799.3
1993	0.7	551.8
1994	-18.2	396.7

Many investors have failed to appreciate how different sector funds are from diversified growth funds. The latter almost always move with the market. Individual stocks, on the other hand, frequently move opposite from the market's direction. In this respect, industry and sector funds are much more like stocks. They may or may not track the market. Consequently, it is dangerous to use the usual criteria—prior track record and management ability—for buying sector funds.

Once a sector fund's stocks fall out of favor, the manager has few weapons to stem the fund's losses. Unlike the diversified funds, he can't buy stocks in other sectors. He could sell his stocks and raise cash, but historically that's been a little used option. When you buy a diversified fund you are really buying the manager, but when you buy a sector fund, you are doing so because you want to buy the stocks in that sector.

Because sector funds perform differently from diversified funds, you should develop your own assessment of an industry's potential for appreciation before you buy a sector fund representing that industry. If you don't have first-hand knowledge of the industry, stay away from sector funds! You are best off if you think of them as proxies for individual stocks. If you like an industry, but are either not sure which will be the best performing stocks, or want to buy several stocks in the industry, then buy a sector fund. In some cases the commissions will be lower than buying stocks individually.

Sector funds are not for buy-and-hold investors or for novices. If sector investing were easy, you would think that Fidelity or Invesco would organize multifunds where their professional money managers would assume the task of switching into the top-performing sectors for you. The fact that they have not done so suggests that these sophisticated professionals appreciate how difficult is the task of divining which sector will be the next winner in the stock market's relentless rotation. Thus, long-term investors are better off sticking to diversified stock funds.

If you are attracted to a given sector, limit your holdings to 5% to 10% of your equity portfolio, and don't hesitate to switch to another sector or a money fund when the sector's move is over. Most of the time you will be better off buying on weakness rather than strength. It can be fatal to buy near the conclusion of a long upward move. Most sector funds should not be held in bear markets. Finally, don't get too caught up with the excitement of sector funds. Despite all the

What sector-fund investors are doing wrong

hoopla in the press, the year-end assets for the Fidelity, Invesco and Vanguard sector funds combined were only $9.4 billion. That's only 1.1% of the total $867 billion invested in all equity mutual funds.

Social conscience funds. Several no-load equity funds aim at purity in their investments. The Pax World Fund's prospectus states that the fund tries through its investment objectives to make a contribution to world peace. It buys shares in companies that produce life-supporting goods and services in such fields as health care, education, food and leisure. The fund avoids liquor, tobacco and gambling stocks as well as companies doing business with the Pentagon. It, and most other socially conscious funds, used to avoid South Africa, but that is no longer the case. Other social conscience funds: the Dreyfus Third Century Fund, which invests in companies that enhance the value of life in America; two Ariel funds, which dropped their loads in 1994; the Domini Social Index Trust, a social conscience index fund. In addition, there are social conscience money funds, such as the Calvert Social Investment Money Market Portfolio and Working Assets Money Fund.

Another fund perhaps falling in this category is the Amana Fund, which is designed to provide investment alternatives that are consistent with Islamic principles. The fund does not invest in such businesses as liquor, wine, casinos, pornography, gambling and banks and associations that are not based on Islamic principals. Muslims do not believe in receiving interest, which rules out domestic banks.

Social conscience equity funds are typically classified as growth or growth-income funds.

Social conscience funds are for people who feel strongly about how their money is invested, to the point that they are willing to accept somewhat lower returns for their principles. Studies have shown that restricting their portfolio managers' options hurts performance. A thorough study of ten no-load and load funds for the five years ending with 1988 was conducted by Samuel A. Mueller, a sociologist at the University of Akron. He found that, risk adjusted, the average social conscience fund produced returns about one percentage point less than the returns that could have been made in comparable funds not subject to the restrictions that the ethical funds have imposed on themselves.

Financial author Timothy Middleton explains the extent of the problem: He interviewed the representatives of eight social conscience funds and found that one or more ignored the ten largest companies in America. All ten are engaged in business activities that some consider antithetical to social goals. General Electric, AT&T, and IBM all have military contracts. Merck, Procter & Gamble, and Johnson & Johnson engage in animal testing. Coca Cola opposes bottle bills. Wal-Mart imports from child labor law violator Bangladesh, and, rounding out the top 10, there's Exxon and Philip Morris!

Another bit of evidence: your intrepid author is one of five investment advisors participating in a fund selection contest sponsored by The New York Times. With the contest 21 months old as of April 1, 1995 (latest figures at press time), I was leading with a 21.1% cumulative gain. In last place was an investment advisor with a portfolio of eight socially responsive funds. His portfolio had gained only 10.5%. One of the reasons: he suffered a huge opportunity loss because there are no no-load international conscience funds.

Investors having trouble finding an attractive social conscience fund might consider putting their money into better performing funds and giving the excess profits to their favorite charity. By doing so you would be following the example of Alfred Nobel. He made millions selling explosives, but then used the profits to create a charitable foundation that has fostered enormous worldwide good.

Special-interest funds. Some funds are differentiated not by what they buy, but to whom they sell. The General Electric S&S Program is a no-load offered only to employees of that company. State Farm Growth Fund is offered only to agents and employees of State Farm Insurance Companies and members of their families. Institutional funds have high minimum investments so only large institutions can afford them.

Utility funds. Some fund groups include utility funds with their sector funds; others hold them out as separate industry funds. Fidelity, with its enormous selection of funds, does both. If you're

Women's social conscience, too

The Women's Equity Mutual Fund is designed to invest in companies that have growth potential and meet the fund's ten criteria on women's issues. These include companies that promote women to senior executive positions or to their board of directors, offer employee benefits that address work/family concerns, choose women-owned vendors, contribute to women's organizations, and present positive images of women. The fund has identified a universe of 300 "pro-women" companies. The fund is, of course, managed by women.

looking for hefty dividend payments, check the individual funds carefully. Some pay large dividends; others do not. In 1994, Stratton
Monthly Dividend Shares paid the most, yielding 8.1%. At the other
extreme, the Lindner Utility fund yielded only 1.4%. Over long periods of time, utility-company stocks have outperformed the market in
general. However, yield-oriented investors got a jarring wakeup call
in 1994 when rising interest rates and a loss of faith in the industry by
the financial community battered utility stocks far worse than other
conservative equity funds.

Value funds. See Chapter 6.

In summary

No-load stock, bond and money-market funds come in an endless and
ever-changing profusion. From funds that buy the entire stock market
to those that invest only in stocks of socially conscious corporations,
from funds that ramble the world looking for bargains to ones that
stay within the Pacific Northwest region, no-loads can provide you
with just about any investment specialty you could want. In the right
time and place, all can help you earn profits. Be cautious, though. Not
every fad and fancy proves profitable.

Closed-end and dual funds

No-loads are bought and sold at net asset value. But how would you like to be able to buy funds at a discount? Such bargain-basement funds exist. These are the closed-end or "publicly traded" funds.

Mutual funds, no-load and load, are called open-end funds. They do not maintain a fixed number of shares. They issue additional shares whenever anyone wants to invest in the fund, and they redeem shares when investors want to sell out. In sharp contrast, closed-end funds issue a fixed number of shares at the time of their initial offering. Thereafter, they rarely change the number of outstanding shares.

Some closed-end funds have been in existence since the 1920s. However, in recent years new closed-ends have been launched at an ever-quickening pace. Some fund advisors prefer to bring out closed-end rather than open-ended funds because they incur a one-time marketing effort. After that, shareholders who wish to buy or sell do so on a stock exchange. Because the fund will not take back shares, closed-ends are a *virtual annuity* for their managers. All fund managers are paid a percentage of the assets under management. Closed-end managers can lose assets only if their portfolio securities decline. In sharp contrast, open-end managers can lose assets if they suffer redemptions—though of course they can also gain by taking in additional money, either from existing or new shareholders.

More than 500 closed-end funds now exist, with total assets over $125 billion (a tiny fraction of the open-ends' $2 trillion in assets).

Closed-end funds come in many varieties. Fixed-income funds are now the most numerous type, accounting for more than two-thirds of the total. Equity funds are divided among four categories; the largest: globals and internationals, accounting for over half of all equity funds. Specialized and diversified funds account for most of the rest. There are also a half-dozen convertible securities funds and six dual-funds. The Adams Express Fund and Tri-Continental Corp. are examples of closed-end general common stock funds. Many of these were started in the 20s. Newer equity funds are more likely to fall in the specialized equity and convertible funds category, which includes gold funds, dual funds and single country and regional international funds.

Unlike mutual funds, some closed-ends have more than one class of shares. Example: Source Capital has both common and preferred stock. The existence of senior securities gives some leverage to the common shares, which increases both risk and volatility.

Closed-end funds offer several advantages:

■ As with open-end funds, they provide professional management.

■ When they sell at a discount, the funds provide investors with real bargains. This is particularly true with closed-end bond funds, which will then generally have higher yields than comparable open-end fixed-income funds, an advantage even if you ultimately sell at the same discount.

■ The closed-end funds do not have to worry about redemptions. (The next chapter discusses how net redemptions can hurt fund performance.) Consequently, they can hold less-liquid securities than the open-end funds. That's why almost all single country funds choose the closed-end structure. The Nautilus Fund, one of the top performers of the 1980s, held 360,000 unregistered shares of Apple computer (32.6% of the fund's assets) before the stock went public. (In 1985, Nautilus became an open-ended fund.)

■ They are easy to margin.

■ The yields of closed-end bond funds are not diluted by new money. In periods of declining interest rates, open-end funds may see the high yields of older bonds diluted by new money pouring in as fund managers take this fresh capital and buy new, lower yielding bonds. This can't happen with closed-ends.

Because closed-ends don't redeem fund shares—they are traded like any stock on a regular exchange or over-the-counter—there is no fixed relationship between their NAV and the current market price. Closed-ends commonly sell at a discount to their net asset value, but at times their price exceeds NAV and the funds sell at a premium. In 1989 single country international funds were very hot and many of these closed-end funds sold at substantial premiums to their NAVs. In 1990, they cooled off considerably; their premiums disappeared, and newer funds went to discounts. When you buy or sell a closed-end, you pay a stockbroker's commission.

You can find the closed-ends' NAVs and discounts from NAVs in *The Wall Street Journal* on Mondays and in some other papers on Saturdays. NAVs and discounts are also available in the weekly *Barron's*.

Closed-ends don't sell at NAV

You should almost always avoid purchasing closed-end funds on the initial underwriting. At that time they are like any load fund, with the price reflecting the NAV plus the salesman's commission. The SEC's Office of Economic Analysis did a study of 64 closed-end funds that came to market between 1985 and 1987. The study revealed that on average, closed-end funds lose significant value during the first 120 trading days following their IPOs (initial public offerings). In this period U.S. closed-end stock funds lost 23.2%, foreign stock funds lost 17.7% and bond funds lost 6.2%. After the first 24 weeks, U.S. stock funds traded at an average discount of 10.0%, foreign stock funds at an average discount of 11.4%, while bond funds traded at approximately NAV. Of course, in all cases, the funds began at a sizeable premium due to the salesmen's commissions, but then trended downward. Finally, the study found these IPOs were far more likely to be sold to individual investors than to institutions.

We believe that closed-ends' prices tend to move from premiums to discounts for several reasons. Since closed-ends are traded like stocks, their market prices are subject to the same laws of supply and demand as are stocks, which may sell for more or less than their book value. In exactly the same manner, closed-end funds sell at discounts or at premiums from their net asset value. Brokers make a great effort to sell closed-ends at the time they are launched because the underwriting commissions are fat. They usually sell enough shares to sat-

Don't buy closed-ends on the initial offering

isfy the demand from all interested investors. Afterwards, the brokers tend to ignore these new funds, thus lowering demand. That's because once the funds are exchange traded, the commissions are the same as for any stock. But since investors are likely to hold them for longer periods than regular stocks, the brokers' second commission is delayed. At that point brokers favor other underwritings, open-end load funds or unit investment trusts, all of which generate higher commissions.

A second reason is that closed-end funds generally lack aggressive advertising or public relations. There's no incentive for the management company to spend its own money for promotion, since that won't bring in new assets. Nor can they levy 12b-1 fees. Thus, most of them languish in obscurity.

Some other reasons that may explain the usual discounts:

■ Poor performance may increase the discount.

■ The market cycle may affect discounts.

■ In some cases there may be a discount because the portfolios contain illiquid stocks.

■ The discount may offset a potential capital gains liability.

A good rule of thumb is to buy a closed-end fund only when its discount is 5% wider than its average annual discount, provided that the discount is not less than the average discount of similar funds. It is difficult to conceive of a reason to buy a closed-end bond fund at a premium. Stock funds selling at premiums should generally avoided, the major exceptions being those funds that own a franchise. For example, for many years there was only one fund that owned Korean stocks. It sold at a healthy premium during those years. It you own a fund selling at an above normal premium, you should consider selling it.

Eliminating the discount

It would be profitable to goose up a closed-end fund's worth by eliminating the discount, and investors have sought ways to do so. The simplest is to open up the fund. As a regular mutual fund, it must sell at its true net asset value. National Aviation and Technology, Stratton Monthly Dividend, the Japan Fund and Alliance New Europe were all closed-ends that were opened up. In many cases the management of a closed-end is enlightened enough to decide that it's in everyone's best interest to go open-end. But, when a reorganization proposal is initiated by outside stockholders the odds are strongly against the fund's becoming open-ended. In such cases management usually resists because its fees are based on the fund's size, which surely will shrink if redemptions are permitted.

In recent years, a number of funds have put provisions into their prospectuses providing for conversion to open-end if certain conditions exist.

In an effort to close the discount, some funds are authorized to purchase shares in the open market or make tender offers. Other funds are guaranteeing a minimum dividend payout. One of the first to try this was the Zweig Fund, which pays a 10% annual distribution. Such payouts are made whether they are earned or not. If the dividend and realized short-term capital gains aren't sufficient, the balance is made up as a return of capital (that is, you get your own money back). Perhaps it could be argued that this is unimportant because over the long run the fund should appreciate by 10% a year or more. On the other hand, it is likely that many shareholders will believe the fund is yielding more than it really is (just as many holders of individual GNMA passthrough securities fail to recognize that part of their dividend is a return of their capital). Such a practice is not desirable. Consider also that the investors in these funds paid a commission to buy the fund. As an investor, you don't get a rebate of part of your commission when you receive some of your own money back. Other funds guaranteeing a minimum payout include: Baker Fentress, The Europe Fund, Gabelli Equity Trust and Liberty All-Star.

Open-end vs. closed-end funds

Which is better? Which should you prefer? Open-end or closed-end funds? While every fund has to be evaluated individually, here are some very general guidelines.

■ Among diversified equity funds, prefer open-end over closed-end. As a generality we believe the open-end funds have more aggressive management since they can be penalized for poor performance. The managers of closed-end funds know that their funds can't be redeemed.

■ Buy specialized closed-ends when no comparable open-ends are available. The single country international funds are prime examples.

■ If the same group manages both open- and closed-end funds, prefer the closed-ends when they are selling at exceptional discounts that are likely to narrow. For example, compare Gabelli Asset to Gabelli Equity Trust or Windsor to Gemini Capital, which both have the same manager.

■ Buy comparable fixed-income closed-ends when the discounts more than make up the transaction costs.

Traditionally, only open-end funds had dividend reinvestment plans. That's changed. The majority of closed-ends now offer the privilege. The closed-end funds obtain the necessary shares either by buying them in the open market or, less commonly, issuing new shares. Reinvestment price is generally the market price if the funds trade at a discount. If the funds trade at a premium, the reinvestment price would be the higher of net asset value or 95% of the market price.

Hybrid funds

In 1993, the SEC adopted a rule allowing some variations on the traditional open and closed-end structures. The new funds, which are called hybrid or interval funds, allow for redemptions at net asset value every three, six or twelve months. That lets management invest in securities that are less liquid than are appropriate for open-ends. Yet, shareholders still have the ability to redeem at net asset value. The fund industry has virtually ignored the SEC's liberalization. At press time, the only group to try the new structure was Piper Jaffray. Its American Adjustable Rate Term Trust Fund, a target fund with four series through 1999, is allowing redemptions at net asset value once a year. The group is proceeding cautiously. Each year it sets a maximum redemption amount ranging from 5% to 25% of assets.

Dual-purpose funds

Dual-purpose funds are a type of closed-end that differs markedly from the funds we've just discussed. A dual-purpose fund achieves two different objectives at the same time by dividing its shares into two classes—capital and income. While each class of shareowner initially puts up half the money, the owners of the capital shares receive all the capital gains and losses from the fund's portfolio but none of the income. The income share owners receive all the income from the portfolio but none of the capital gains. Each class of shareholder gets double the action for his money.

The income shares, which can be considered preferred stocks, have a stated minimum dividend that's cumulative. These shares are callable and will be redeemed at a predetermined price after a stated number of years. For example, the income shares of the Hemisphere Fund were liquidated on June 30, 1985 at $11.44 per share. The assets left over after paying off the income shareholders stayed with the capital shareholders.

Leverage is what makes dual funds interesting. It increases their potential for gain (and loss). Initially, capital shares usually have two-for-one leverage. But this changes with the fund's performance.

Let's assume that the ABC dual-fund began operations with $40 million, $20 million from the capital shareowners and $20 million from the income shareowners. The leverage is 2:1.

$$\frac{\$40 \text{ million (total assets)}}{\$20 \text{ million (capital assets)}} = 2$$

Now let's assume that the market is rising and the fund's portfolio grows to $50 million. These gains accrue entirely to the capital shareowners. The income shareowners are still entitled only to their $20 million. As a result leverage is now 1.67 to 1.

$$\frac{\$50 \text{ million (total assets)}}{\$30 \text{ million (capital assets)}} = 1.67$$

The leverage has decreased. The rule is: as asset value increases, leverage decreases; as asset value decreases, leverage increases. During bear markets when these funds do poorly, leverage is considerably higher than the initial 2 for 1.

Additionally, the capital shares of dual-funds, like all closed-end funds, can sell at a discount from NAV. The effective leverage based on the market value of the capital shares is greater if the shares are selling at a discount, or less if the shares are selling at a premium.

Initially, seven dual-funds existed, all organized in 1967. All have reached their redemption dates. Some of them became no-loads after their income shares were liquidated while others were completely liquidated.

The dual funds have been criticized as being neither here nor there. They had the difficult task of buying stocks for both growth and income in order to satisfy their two classes of shareholders. Most did not succeed. As a result the original dual funds never did generate much investor interest.

Nevertheless, the category is still in existence. One of the original seven dual-funds, Gemini, liquidated its income shares at the end of 1984 However, Vanguard, Gemini's advisor, didn't let the concept die. It now has Gemini II with 10 million capital and 10 million income shares. Its prospectus notes that it is managed for its dual objectives and not to maximize either capital appreciation or income growth. Its income shares have a 12-year life—to 1997. Two other dual funds launched in the 80s are Merrill Lynch's Convertible Holdings Fund and Quest For Value Dual Fund. Dual funds are sold through brokers. Their NAVs and discounts are published along with the closed-end funds. Like regular closed-ends, dual funds are best bought at discounts.

PART III

Mutual Fund Selection and Strategies

How to select the best equity funds

Now that you are familiar with the various types of funds, the next step is to learn how to pick the best funds in each category. In order to do so you need to look at the factors that determine performance. By far the most important is past performance. In this chapter, we'll discuss past performance and other factors that are pertinent in various situations, including the portfolio manager, the fund group, fund expenses, size, cash positions, cash inflow and portfolio composition.

Let us say at the outset that using past performance as the criteria for picking mutual funds is a very imperfect method. It's a matter beyond dispute that past performance is no guarantee of future performance. Nevertheless, past performance is almost universally used as the major determinant of a fund's future performance. The reason is simple: all other ways of forecasting future performance are even less effective; in fact, it could even be argued there is no other way. So, like it or not, you will inevitably wind up making past performance a major criteria in selecting a mutual fund. With that understanding, you'll find that you can maximize your chances of picking a top-performing fund by judiciously choosing which past periods to examine.

Note that the discussion in this chapter primarily concerns diversified funds, where the performance of the manager is paramount. As we pointed out in Chapter 12, you ought to invest in sector and industry funds only after you have done a fundamental analysis of their

Past performance as crystal ball

industries. The methodology is also different for passively managed funds such as index funds. They are discussed in the next chapter.

The long and the short of it

Which time-period or periods to consider is a matter of great controversy. About the only thing the experts seem to agree upon is that you shouldn't buy a fund simply because it made the top rankings over some short period of time. (But even here, we have found exceptions.)

Historically, when load funds predominated, "experts" (usually salesmen) argued that a very long record—at least ten years—was the best predictor of future performance. In recent years analysts have leaned toward shorter periods—usually one-to-five years. Here's our take on the subject.

First of all, there is a very practical reason for selecting shorter time frames. If you limit yourself to funds of great age, you eliminate hundreds of promising candidates. About 67% of all funds are less than five years old; and 85% are less than ten years old. Thus a universe of relatively new funds exists, many of which have already demonstrated top performance.

Furthermore, not only are most funds new, their managers are even newer. A compilation by *Morningstar* found that the average manager tenure is 3.1 years. An old fund run by a new manager is no different than a new fund.

If old funds were better performers than new funds, it might make sense to restrict your selection to this smaller universe. But, that isn't the case. An examination of fund performance over several periods, comparing those funds organized since 1985 to those that are older, shows that a somewhat higher percentage of the youngsters placed in the top 20% of all funds than was the case with their elders, particu-

Table 33

	% of equity funds in first quintile	
	by age over various periods	
	Organized 1985 or later	**Organized before 1985**
1994	21%	19%
Latest 3 years*	24%	15%
Latest 5 years*	24%	18%

* All periods end Dec. 1994

larly over the last three and five years. For example, 24% of all funds organized since 1985 ranked in the upper fifth of all funds for the five years ending 1994, but only 18% of funds organized before 1985 did.

The conclusion: age is not a significant factor when selecting a fund. It is foolish to ignore a fund merely because it doesn't have an extensive performance record. Disregard the advice you so often hear to "concentrate on the ten-year (or some other extended) track record."

What time period is appropriate then? That depends on how you expect the markets to perform in the immediate future. Ideally you want to examine the most recent previous time period during which similar market conditions prevailed. That's the best benchmark for determining how funds will perform in the future.

For example, if you think small capitalization stocks (and hence small company growth funds) will excel in the immediate future, hunt for prior periods when there was a bull market in that type of stock. See which funds did best, then note whether the fund has the same manager as it did in the previous period. Similarly, if you think the direction of the market is South, then look for funds that have done well in adverse conditions.

But you need a prediction to make this information usable. And since predicting is difficult, especially if it involves the future (a bon mot that has been attributed to a wide range of celebrities, ranging from Lord Keynes to Samuel Goldwyn to Casey Stengel), that explains why we aren't all millionaires.

It also explains why opinions on the matter are sharply divided. If all you rely on is a gross five- or ten-year period, the results you get will depend heavily on the on the types of markets that were prevailing during the period. And bear in mind: if you alter your starting and ending dates even slightly, you may get a different crop of winning funds. You need to take a more multi-dimensional view.

Since few people consistently make accurate predictions of the future, here are some practical guidelines you can rely on.

What to do

Begin your quest by examining the current winners, and then seeing which of them have also done well over longer periods of time. You will generally see two types of long-term performance data: presented annually and/or in bull and bear market spans. Either one can be useful, but one warning: If you're investing in aggressive growth funds, you should focus your attention first on bull-market periods. If you investigate down periods, keep in mind that the aggressive funds that fared *worst* in bear markets are the ones most likely to do *best* in a bull market. Volatility can work in your favor.

Keep in mind that you have to compare your potential selection with other similar funds. This way you can quickly see which performed best, given their level of risk. You want to compare aggressive growth funds to other aggressive growth funds; income funds to other income funds. Put another way, an aggressive growth fund that outperforms a growth-income fund in a sharply rising market may not be desirable when you take risk into consideration.

In a long-running bull market, such as the one we've experienced in recent years, the quintile ranks, as presented in our companion publications, have provided reasonable predictive power. In the newsletter, quintile ranks (a quintile of one means it's in the top 20% of funds in its objective category, a quintile of five, the bottom 20%) are shown for seven different time periods ranging from one month to five years.

Short-run performance can measure portfolio momentum. Funds that develop superior momentum have put together a portfolio of stocks that will, in the short-run anyway, most likely continue to outperform other portfolios.

The longer-term record, when available, reassures you that the fund's current performance is due to skill, not luck. If an older fund has been mediocre in the past, and its management has not changed, high-ranked current performance may be due to a few lucky stock picks or market-sector selections. But even here, going back five years is usually sufficient.

Table 34

Stock and bond fund performance comparison

| No-Load Fund | NAV 3/31/95 | Total return percent with quintile ranks by objective | | | | | | | % Cash 3/95 | Total Assets | | Yield % |
		Mar 1995	1995 3 mo	Latest 9 mo	Latest 12 mo	2 yr ann cmpnd	3 yr ann cmpnd	5 yr ann cmpnd		$ Mil 12/31/94	$ Mil 9/30/94	
					AGGRESSIVE GROWTH FUNDS							
AARP Capital Gro⊘..................	32.06	1.8[4]	6.3[3]	8.3[4]	4.1[4]	2.9[5]	5.9[5]	8.3[5]	2.0	631.6	684.1	0.0
American Heritage...	0.76	-6.2[5]	-10.6[5]	-19.0[5]	-29.9[5]	-17.1[5]	-6.3[5]	6.1[5]	10.0	56.9	78.7	—
Babson Enterprise II⊘SC...	16.86	0.9[5]	4.1[4]	2.5[5]	-1.3[5]	5.1[4]	8.0[4]	—	2.6	36.8	38.1	0.1
Babson Enterprise⊘‡SC...	15.68	2.0[4]	3.5[5]	9.2[4]	8.5[3]	7.4[4]	10.5[2]	13.5[3]	7.8	190.5	192.7	0.2
Baron Asset SC..................	24.29	3.2[2]	10.4[1]	22.7[1]	21.0[1]	17.4[1]	16.1[1]	14.0[2]	2.6	87.1	80.3	0.0
Berger 100⊘.............................	15.94	2.3[3]	1.6[5]	11.2[3]	-0.8[5]	7.1[4]	8.7[3]	18.0[1]	18.9	2,113.0	2,225.8	0.0

If a fund achieves quintiles of one or two—meaning that it is in the top 20% to 40%—in most time periods, it generally has enough momentum to continue to be an above-average performer. But don't forget to consider a fund's performance in light of your expectations for the market. If small cap stocks are not in vogue, then the aggressive growth funds investing in them can hardly do well.

The "mountain" is the fund's performance chart shown on an annual basis. The fund is not required to show such a chart. But if the fund has performed well it may elect to use this device to gloat, in its prospectus or in promotional literature. To avoid misrepresentation, the SEC requires that performance data cover the life of the fund, or periods of ten years or longer (over ten years in multiples of five). The longer the period used, the more impressive the "mountain," since money has been growing longer. However, since the periods shown vary from prospectus to prospectus, it is extremely difficult to use these charts to compare different funds directly or even to tell how any one fund has done in recent years.

The "Mountain"

To illustrate just how irrelevant these charts can be, we have shown the mountain for the Mathers Fund in Chart 35. The fund has a fine long-term performance record, but in recent bull market years it has not done well because it has kept too much money in cash through 1993 and, ironically, too little in 1994. The fund had a 5.9% loss in 1994, and only a 7.0% gain per year for the five years ending 1993, ranking it in the last quintile for both periods. Yet when you examine the mountain, it appears that Mathers' performance had gone to the sky until 1994. It would be hard to show a steeper uptrend. The reason the chart looks so great is that the growth (the vertical axis) is drawn with an arithmetic scale instead of the more proper ratio scale.

One point in Mather's favor, though; at least the fund compares itself to the S&P 500. Other funds with inferior long-term performances tend to compare themselves to the Cost of Living index. It's a lot easier for a fund to beat inflation than it is to surpass the performance of the S&P 500.

Thus, you are best advised to make molehills out of a mutual fund's "mountain." And certainly, don't make investment decisions based on them. Your guideline should be numerical performance data for more recent periods.

Chart 35

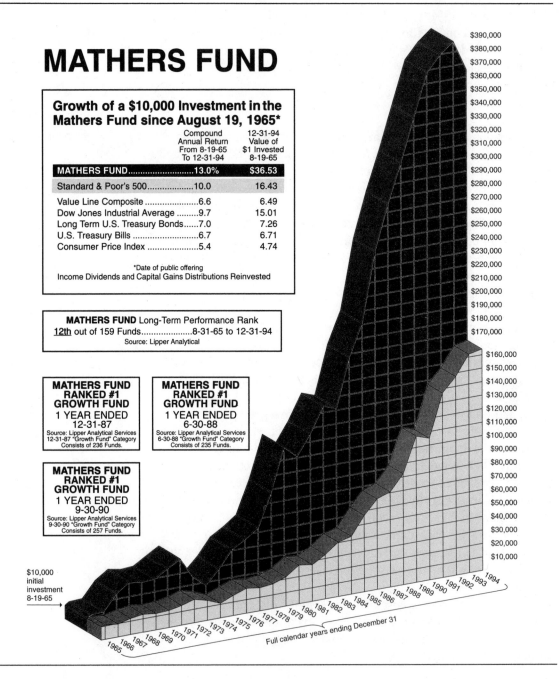

MATHERS FUND

Growth of a $10,000 Investment in the Mathers Fund since August 19, 1965*

	Compound Annual Return From 8-19-65 To 12-31-94	12-31-94 Value of $1 Invested 8-19-65
MATHERS FUND	13.0%	$36.53
Standard & Poor's 500	10.0	16.43
Value Line Composite	6.6	6.49
Dow Jones Industrial Average	9.7	15.01
Long Term U.S. Treasury Bonds	7.0	7.26
U.S. Treasury Bills	6.7	6.71
Consumer Price Index	5.4	4.74

*Date of public offering
Income Dividends and Capital Gains Distributions Reinvested

MATHERS FUND Long-Term Performance Rank
12th out of 159 Funds.....................8-31-65 to 12-31-94
Source: Lipper Analytical

MATHERS FUND RANKED #1 GROWTH FUND
1 YEAR ENDED
12-31-87
Source: Lipper Analytical Services
12-31-87 "Growth Fund" Category
Consists of 236 Funds.

MATHERS FUND RANKED #1 GROWTH FUND
1 YEAR ENDED
6-30-88
Source: Lipper Analytical Services
6-30-88 "Growth Fund" Category
Consists of 235 Funds.

MATHERS FUND RANKED #1 GROWTH FUND
1 YEAR ENDED
9-30-90
Source: Lipper Analytical Services
9-30-90 "Growth Fund" Category
Consists of 257 Funds.

$10,000
initial
investment
8-19-65

Full calendar years ending December 31

1965 1966 1967 1968 1969 1970 1971 1972 1973 1974 1975 1976 1977 1978 1979 1980 1981 1982 1983 1984 1985 1986 1987 1988 1989 1990 1991 1992 1993 1994

$10,000 $20,000 $30,000 $40,000 $50,000 $60,000 $70,000 $80,000 $90,000 $100,000 $110,000 $120,000 $130,000 $140,000 $150,000 $160,000 $170,000 $180,000 $190,000 $200,000 $210,000 $220,000 $230,000 $240,000 $250,000 $260,000 $270,000 $280,000 $290,000 $300,000 $310,000 $320,000 $330,000 $340,000 $350,000 $360,000 $370,000 $380,000 $390,000

Finally, you will find annual performance data in the prospectus or other fund literature. If the numbers differ significantly from published data, check to see the period covered. Funds frequently show these annual figures for their fiscal year, not the calendar year most publications use to put all funds on an equal footing.

The ability of a fund's management is a most significant factor in evaluating a diversified mutual fund. Although the word "professional" carries the connotation of excellence, alas, this is not universally the case. Many professional fund managers do an outstanding job for their shareholders, some are mediocre, and more than a few are so poor that their shareholders would be better off selecting stocks by throwing darts at the financial pages. With the total number of funds surpassing 5,000 and the number of equity funds topping 2,000, the chances of new and mediocre management increases.

How adept is the manager?

Invariably, investors are exhorted to select well-managed funds. But how to evaluate management's ability? Here are some guidelines:

The prospectus may be of some help in evaluating the management of a fund. Since July 1993, the SEC has required that the name or names of the portfolio manager(s) be listed in the prospectus along with the length of service and experience for the last five years. Money funds, index funds, and funds run by committees or teams are excluded from this requirement.

The new regulations mandate that the prospectus be "stickered" for new investors and for current shareholders acquiring additional shares if there is a change in portfolio managers. Other shareholders will receive the news in the fund's next regular mailing.

Many investors select a fund because the manager has received favorable publicity. But write-ups in the financial press don't always indicate true expertise or predict outstanding performance. Nor does a lack of publicity imply poor management. The facts are that financial columns on occasion profile the managers of funds that perform well over short spans and neglect other managers who have been equally outstanding over long periods.

Similarly, television interviews are, at best, an imperfect way to select a fund manager. The most eloquent portfolio managers are not necessarily the best stock pickers! Conversely, some of the best managers are not particularly outgoing, so their firms do not promote them to the media.

The fact that some fund managers are profiled and others aren't is due primarily to their attitude regarding publicity. Some managers love the limelight and eagerly seek it; others shun it. Be skeptical of publicity. Don't select a fund on that basis.

Magazine and newspaper profiles, while they generally make interesting reading, often fail to provide actionable information for prospective fund investors. They should include a measure of the fund's objective and risk, the type of investor who would find the fund suitable, the fund's performance, properly benchmarked, and even the phone number and minimum investment accepted, if it's unusually high. Instead, they all too often emphasize a portfolio manager's winning stock selections. That's not what fund investing is about. If a portfolio has enough stocks, some of them are bound to be winners. In one profile, former New York Times business columnist, Robert Metz, noted in exasperation: "Mr. _____ would rather discuss his successes." The fund manager's strategy is to identify companies with the best growth!!!

New managers

If the fund has a new manager, that may be a reason for caution. At the very least, you'll need to ignore the fund's prior performance record, which was compiled by someone else. However, a 1992 study found that when a poorly performing fund had a change of managers, it is frequently for the better. On the other hand, the replacement managers for top performing funds frequently did not live up to their predecessor's record. We think that's logical.

And then there is the situation where a manager eases out of day-to-day control. In January 1986, John Templeton, one of the most successful fund managers of our time, announced the sale of shares of his privately owned management company to the public. The master cashed in. While the octogenarian Templeton continues as the "public face" of the company, he is no longer president. Mutual fund salesmen still sell the Templeton name, but current shareholders are getting the services of a large, diversified organization which manages more than 70 different funds worldwide (and is now a subsidiary of the Franklin Funds). You may see a Templeton advertisement with Sir John's picture prominently displayed, but in the fine print there will be a disclaimer saying he "is not involved in investment management decisions, which are made by the fund's investment manager."

Here's a situation you may be able to relate to. You own a fund, and you're happy with it. But suddenly you see the fund's manager on TV, and you realize—egad!—he's only 28. Should you worry yourself sick? Probably not. But in any case there may not be a lot you can do about it. Portfolio management tends to be a young man's game. A *Morningstar* study found that 38% of portfolio managers are in their 30s and another 32% are in their 40s.

Old fossil "experts" are frequently quoted as saying the youngsters will get killed in the next bear market, because they aren't old enough to remember the last one. It's hard to say that there's much truth to the assertion. In 1987, almost every growth fund manager was scorched by the October stock market meltdown. When the bull market of the 60s ended, some of the go-go managers who got mangled were quite young. But they were running money more speculatively than is generally the case today. Our best guess: when the next bear market arrives, the type of fund you've invested in will be a greater determinant of your success or failure than the fund manager's age.

The manager is just a kid!

Some managers personally invest large sums of money in the funds they manage. Many others do not. The ones who do will frequently publicize this fact. We agree that when a manager puts his own money into his fund it's a definite plus. However, the converse is not true. We don't see any significance to the absence of personal money in a fund. There could be any number of valid reasons for this. The fund's objective may be different from the manager's personal objective. He may be with a large group, and expect to be shifted around. We're of the opinion that a high salary and frequently a substantial bonus are sufficient to motivate a manager. The personal investments are just icing on the cake.

Does the manager invest his own money in the fund?

There is, of course, expertise in the mutual fund field. But it's difficult to identify. So recognize that the best way to measure a manager's ability is to concentrate on fund results. Continual gains in the value of a fund's shares are the most eloquent testimony to his or her ability.

In summary

The importance of the fund family

With today's exaggerated media hype, it's all to easy to overestimate the importance of the portfolio manager. The fact is that in most cases he is not indispensable. We estimate that in about 90% of the cases, a change in portfolio managers will not materially affect a fund's performance. Here's why:

Most of the time the departing portfolio manager is replaced by another one equally skilled. This is particularly true in larger organizations where the portfolio manager is not as critical as in smaller ones. For this and other reasons enumerated below, when other things are equal you should invest in larger families.

Take gargantuan Fidelity. It has achieved strong performances with young managers who seem to move frequently. Between April 1992 and September 1993 there were 50 management changes at Fidelity funds. As of January 1995, the median equity manager at Fidelity has run his current fund for only 19 months. Thirty percent of the equity managers joined their funds in 1994. Only 17% had run the same fund since 1989. Yet Fidelity has more than its share of top-performing funds. You have to conclude that the group's high turnover of managers has *not* affected performance to any significant degree.

How do they do it? The key to Fidelity's success is the strong organization that backs up its portfolio managers, including an army of skilled research analysts and traders.

Other major fund groups also have solid organizations. As a result, good managers leave all the time—without causing a deterioration of performance. For example, when Roger McNamee ran T. Rowe Price's Science & Technology Fund, some thought he was irreplaceable. Yet the fund has done well since his departure in September 1991.

Because of this tendency, we believe that if you are considering two funds that appear similar, the odds favor buying the fund that is part of the largest group. In May of 1993, we wanted to add an emerging market fund to our newsletter's model portfolios. Both Fidelity and Montgomery had outstanding funds in this category. We went with Fidelity, and subsequent performance proved our decision right.

Still other advantages: Your account will likely receive better service and administration in the larger group. And if the fund should falter, it's a lot simpler to switch to another excellent fund. If you're in a stand-alone fund, there's a time-consuming redemption and reinvestment process.

Don't we share the all-American desire to see the little guy triumph? Sure. And sometimes a Monetta, a FAM Value, a Meridian or a Kaufmann does. But the sardonic cliche is true: The biggest don't always win, but that's the way you bet it.

Sometimes it's hard to tell what you are getting when you buy a fund run by a team or committee. In some cases the committee may be composed of members all having equal voices; or, more commonly, there will be a team leader who makes the major decisions with the rest of the team being essentially assistants or analysts. Only fund management knows the roles played by specific individuals in the everyday business of the fund and the extent to which they contribute to its success or failure. So while you're flying blind to a certain extent, if the fund group has a record of excellence, you aren't taking much of a risk.

Funds run by committees

There has been a marked increase in the number of funds that claim team or committee management since the SEC began requiring funds to name their portfolio managers in the prospectus. Some funds don't want to spotlight their personnel, so they take advantage of an exception to the rules: funds run by committees don't have to name names. A 1994 study by *Morningstar* found that while only 15% of all funds were piloted by more than one person in 1989, the figure is now 35%. Funds who recently made the switch to team management are suspect. It's quite likely that one particular individual among the fund's management is still controls the decision making.

It's just as important to pay attention to expense ratios when you are buying stock funds as when you are buying bond or money funds. It's a mistake to excuse high expenses if the fund is doing well. Now, with the 12b-1 distribution fees, expense ratios are increasing, particularly for the 12b-1 funds with fees of 1% or more.

Watch expense ratios

In the case of stock funds, there's no doubt that superior management can overcome the drag of a high expense ratio in a given month, or even over a one- or two-year period, but it's much more difficult for fund managers to offset this drag over long periods of time. So if you want to be a successful investor over the long haul, it is essential to keep investment expenses as low as possible.

The performance of index funds confirms this axiom. The Vanguard 500 Portfolio is an index fund that buys the stocks that comprise the S&P 500. The fund has no manager or management fee, and it has one of the lowest expense ratios of any fund in the country. In five years ending 1994, the average expense ratio has been .20%, one-sixth that of the average equity fund. Given that its portfolio is an exact duplicate of the S&P index you would think that its performance would also be on a par. But it isn't. In these five years, the Vanguard Index 500 Fund fell 1.2% behind the index, which of course, has no expenses. The S&P 500 index, with distributions reinvested, grew 51.6% in this period vs. the fund's 50.4%. (Over the last ten years, which includes years in which the fund was smaller, it fell 10.3% behind the Index (282.7% vs. 272.4%). If a .20% expense ratio does that to performance, imagine how serious the impact of a high expense ratio can be.

To illustrate, we've compiled a comprehensive list of all funds, load and no-load, that meet two criteria: a 1994 expense ratio of 2% or more, and a five-year performance history. A seventh of all stock funds with five-year records (137 out of a total of 1,029) met the criteria. Overall, these high-expense funds had decidedly inferior performances. Only 26% ranked in the first or second quintile of all funds (the top 40%). Eighty-four, or 61%, ranked in the two bottom quintiles. In other words a high expense ratio fund is more than twice as likely to be below average as above average in terms of performance!

Table 36

Stock funds with expense ratios of 2% or more

**Percent distributions
by five-year quintile performances**

Quintile	# funds	%
1 (Best)	20	15%
2	15	11%
3	18	13%
4	29	21%
5 (Worst)	55	40%
Total	137	100%

Source: returns, 5 yrs ending 1994, expense ratios:
latest through Nov. 1994

To give you benchmarks for evaluating expense ratios, we've calculated medians. As in all our analyses, we try to compare similar funds.
So we first grouped funds by size, since the smaller the fund, the
greater its expense ratio normally will be. We used medians (the middle number in a group) rather than the mean (the average) because a
few funds have extremely high expense ratios, which would seriously distort the picture. We've shown equity and fixed-income funds
separately. The expense ratios for equities include international funds
which typically have higher expense ratios than domestic funds.
Fixed-income funds have lower costs—and keeping them low is more
important, since the funds' expenses are deducted from dividend
income.

    We've also compared the median expense ratio for no-loads to the

What's a good expense ratio?

Table 37

Median expense ratios

Stock funds

Assets in millions	No-loads	Loads	No-load Advantage
$1,000 +	0.92%	1.07%	0.15%
$500-1,000	1.01	1.18	0.17
$250-500	1.16	1.56	0.40
$100-250	1.11	1.51	0.40
$50-100	1.21	1.57	0.36
$25-50	1.25	1.75	0.50
$10-25	1.30	1.75	0.45
$10 and less	1.81	1.83	0.02
Total	1.19	1.56	0.37

Fixed-income funds

$1,000 +	0.49	0.87	0.38
$500-1,000	0.64	1.05	0.41
$250-500	0.65	0.99	0.34
$100-250	0.72	0.99	0.27
$50-100	0.67	0.94	0.27
$25-50	0.85	1.00	0.15
$10-25	0.84	0.92	0.08
$10 and less	0.75	1.02	0.27
Total	0.70	0.98	0.28

Base counts: Equity funds - no-load: 580, load: 1171;
Bond funds - no-load: 445, load: 1415
Data: 1994

expense ratios of load funds. In 1994, the median no-load equity fund had an expense ratio of 1.19%, 24% below the median expense ratio for load equity funds. No-load international funds had a median expense ratio of 1.50%; the ratio for international load funds was 1.92%. Among fixed-income funds, no-loads had a .29% overall advantage.

The essential difference between load and no-load funds, the major reason for the no-load advantage, is the higher 12b-1 fees that many load funds charge. Unlike front- or back-end sales charges, these are continuing expenses and as such are included in the expense ratio. By the way, we excluded institutional funds from the no-load averages; if they'd been included, the no-load advantage would have been still greater. These data clearly refute salesmen's claims that load funds are managed more economically.

All fund expenses affect performance results. But, generally, minor differences in expenses among funds are insignificant compared to the wide variations in performance. Still, you need to screen out the high ratios. Make a point of checking the expense ratio before buying any fund.

Size

Fund size—the total net assets a fund has under management—is another factor affecting performance. Everything else equal, well-managed small funds frequently have an edge over large funds. This advantage is most pronounced in the case of small cap funds.

An examination of fund rankings generally shows small funds doing better than—and also worse than—larger funds. Some small funds land at the bottom of the rankings because of poor management. They can't afford the management expertise provided by larger funds and groups. But if a fund, often a younger fund, has good management it frequently excels. In 1994, 29 of the top 50 best performing load and no-load equity funds had $100 million or less in assets at the start of the year, and 40 funds had assets of less than $250 million. We have tracked these statistics for many years and have found these results are always similar in down-market years. In up-market years, smaller funds are even more strongly favored.

Table 38 shows the 1994 gains of the top 25 diversified no-load stock funds. The largest of the 25 has assets of $1.7 billion; there are only two funds over a billion. They are contrasted with the lesser performance for the 25 largest diversified no-loads, which have assets of $2.8 to $31 billion. We've determined asset category according to a fund's size at the beginning of the year. In 1994, as you can see, there was no duplication between the two lists. There was no duplication in 1993 and only one duplication in 1992. Size militates against aggressive growth. The best performers in 1994 had gains of from 6.5% to 23.8%. Only eight of the largest funds had gains; 17 had losses. Their performances ranged from +4.5% to -8.0%. This is remarkable considering the fact that the markets in 1994 favored the large cap stocks usually held by these big funds.

There are two broad reasons why small funds can outperform large ones. First, as we pointed out in Chapter 5, the small companies these

Table 38

Performance of diversified no-load equity funds

	Best performers	Assets Mill. $ 12/93	1994 % gain	Largest funds	Assets Mill. $ 12/93	1994 % gain
1	PBHG Emg Growth...	36.3	23.8	Price, Rowe Eqty Inc...	2,848.5	4.5
2	Robrtsn Stph Val Gro...	23.1	23.1	Mutual Shares...	3,527.1	4.5
3	Montgmry Growth...	3.8	20.9	Fidelity Eqty Inc II...	5,021.9	3.2
4	Strong Growth...	0.1	17.3	Fidelity Gro & Inc...	7,684.0	2.3
5	Janus Mercury...	126.9	15.9	Fidelity Puritan...	8,988.2	1.9
6	Berger Sm Co Gro...	0.5	13.7	Vangd Idx 500...	8,272.7	1.2
7	Twentieth Cent Giftrust...	164.3	13.5	Fidelity Eqty Inc...	6,641.9	0.3
8	Crabbe Hsn Spec...	29.0	11.5	Fidelity Retrmnt Gro...	2,848.2	0.1
9	Vangd Primecap...	790.9	11.4	Vangd Windsor...	10,610.8	-0.1
10	SAFECO Equity...	194.0	9.9	Vangd Star:Star...	3,628.2	-0.3
11	Fidelity Blue Chip...	1,094.7	9.9	Vangd Wellington...	8,075.8	-0.5
12	Invesco Balanced...	0.6	9.5	Janus Fund...	9,199.6	-1.1
13	Kaufmann...	965.4	9.0	Fidelity Contrafund...	6,193.3	-1.1
14	Longleaf Partners...	397.3	9.0	Vangd Windsor II...	7,616.3	-1.2
15	Janus Enterprise...	258.6	8.9	Twentieth Cent Growth...	4,552.7	-1.5
16	Yacktman...	143.0	8.8	Fidelity Magellan...	31,705.1	-1.8
17	Robrtsn Stph Emg Gro...	169.7	8.0	Nicholas Fund...	3,179.1	-2.9
18	Fidelity Value...	1,716.1	7.6	Twentieth Cent Ultra...	8,362.4	-3.6
19	Warbg Pincus Gro & Inc...	34.5	7.6	Invesco Indust Inc...	3,905.8	-3.9
20	Baron Asset...	64.0	7.4	Dreyfus Fund...	2,870.9	-4.3
21	Fairmont...	18.9	7.3	Vangd Wellesley Inc...	6,011.5	-4.4
22	Merger...	27.2	7.1	Fidelity Balanced...	4,684.5	-5.3
23	Stratton Growth...	24.6	7.1	Fidelity Asset Mgr...	9,094.4	-6.6
24	FAM Value...	220.2	6.8	Janus Twenty...	3,515.9	-6.7
25	Wm Blair Growth...	149.7	6.5	Twentieth Cent Select...	4,938.0	-8.0

funds invest in have greater growth potential than large companies. Secondly, small funds can make meaningful investments in small capitalization companies. Big funds can't take meaningful positions in minuscule companies. Only a small amount of stock is available, and there are legal limits to the amount of voting stock of any one company they can own.

Consider the case of a promising industrial corporation with only $10 million worth of outstanding stock. No single fund can buy more than $1 million. Suppose a fund with $1 billion in assets has $1 million worth of this particular corporation's stock. If the stock doubles, its value is increased to $2 million, but the large fund's total assets are increased to $1,001,000,000, up only one-tenth of 1%.

On the other hand, a $20 million fund has $1 million of the same stock. When the stock doubles, the small fund's total assets increase to $21 million, and its net asset value goes up a very substantial 5%.

If the $1 billion fund specializing in these small growth companies puts no more than $1 million in each, it would need to buy 1,000 different stocks. To properly analyze and manage so many stocks is a difficult undertaking, to say the least. As a result, the larger growth funds prefer substantial holdings in major corporations. Just as important, large funds can't quickly dispose of their huge holdings without depressing a stock's price. Diminutive funds are more nimble. They can sell their holdings almost as readily as individual investors can, without disrupting the market.

Because of the disadvantages of being too large, a number of funds stopped selling shares when they reached a certain size. Acorn, Acorn International, Babson Enterprise, FAM Value, Fidelity Low Priced Stock Fund, Harbor International, Janus Twenty, Janus Venture, Lindner, Lindner Dividend, Monetta, Montgomery Micro-Cap, Montgomery Small Cap, Mutual Shares, Mutual Discovery, Mutual Qualified, Nicholas Limited Edition, Pennsylvania Mutual, Price New Horizons, Price Small Cap Value, Quantitative Numeric, Sequoia, Skyline Special Equities, Strong Common Stock, and Windsor all have stopped sell-

The Windsor Fund's big bets

In 1994, the $11 billion Windsor Fund held $762 million of Citicorp, $426 million of Bankers Trust, $333 million of Aluminum Company of America, $635 million of Chryslers, $490 million of Ford Motor, $396 million of Aetna Life & Casualty, and $412 million of CIGNA. The fund held only 66 common stocks. The average holding was $152 million.

ing shares at one time or another. Most—but not all—are small company funds.

The fact that these funds have closed their doors tells you how important their managers feel modest size is. They are voluntarily depriving themselves of one of the only two ways they have to increase income. (The other way is internal growth through increases in NAV.)

Other funds have taken steps to moderate their growth. In 1980, 44 Wall Street Fund, at that time a hot fund, raised its minimum investment for new accounts to $250,000. The fund wished to keep about 25 different issues in its portfolio and felt a moderation of cash inflows, which often came at inopportune times, would benefit the fund's existing shareholders.

Cloning existing funds is a popular method of relieving pressure on further growth. In 1983, after the Twentieth Century Growth and Ultra funds had grown bulky, the adviser introduced the Twentieth Century Vista Fund. Similarly in 1987, Twentieth Century introduced the Heritage Fund. Although some minor differences exist, all these funds have essentially the same growth objective. Other examples of cloning: the Mutual Series Funds, Windsor II, Babson Enterprise II, and Skyline Special Equities II. Unfortunately, in many cases, when a small cap fund is cloned, the new fund frequently invests in mid-cap stocks. Count yourself fortunate to own shares in funds where management restricts size before the fund becomes too large; it's in your interest. These funds have increased their chances of performing well for an extended period of time.

What's the optimum size? It's hard to pinpoint a number, so let's consider the size of some of the funds that since 1991 have locked out new investors. Janus Venture announced in September, 1991 that its then portfolio manager, Jim Craig, felt that $750 million was about all he could handle. (Unfortunately, Janus permitted the fund to grow by an additional $350 million in the period between the announcement and the final cutoff of sales.) Monetta closed at $500 million in March, 1993. At the lower end of the spectrum, Babson Enterprise closed at $125 million, Skyline Special Equities at $150 million, Nicholas Limited Edition at $170 million, Montgomery Small Cap at about $165 million and Quantitative Numeric at $100 million. Rather than try to provide an iron-clad figure, we believe investors should compare the best performing small cap funds. All else being equal, choose funds with the smallest assets.

Handling fund closings

Some funds close their doors to new sales without warning. There's nothing you can do about that. But others give up to several weeks notice. Should you rush to invest in those funds before they close? It mostly depends on the fund's size. If a fund is already too large at the time it closes, then the damage has been done, and there is no reason to expect good performance to continue. In our opinion, Janus Venture, Janus 20, Monetta, and FAM Value, which closed in the early 90s, were in this category.

On the other hand, the Quantitative Numeric Fund announced in December, 1994 that it would close when it reached $100 million in assets—still a very small size. This fund is likely to be a good performer for years.

But raw size isn't the only criterion. FAM Value closed at $212 million. The Fidelity Low Priced Stock Fund closed and reopened in 1992, and then closed and reopened again in 1993—it began 1993 with $2.3 billion, and went on to do quite well the balance of the year. The difference: FAM Value is a pint-sized shop, while Fidelity has enormous resources to back up a portfolio manager. Similarly, at Janus, Jim Craig finally relinquished control of Janus Venture to spend full time on the Janus Fund. Janus Venture now has two managers who achieved good performances in 1993 and 1994.

When size doesn't matter

As a practical matter, fund size is most significant in the performance of small company funds and then, only when small company funds are outperforming large funds. While small company funds have outperformed larger funds over broad periods of time, their ascendancy tends to run in cycles. For example, in much of the 1980s, large cap stocks were the best performers. When this is the case, large funds—which of necessity own mostly large cap stocks—can do as well as small funds.

In the case of bond and money market funds, size is an advantage. You should prefer larger funds because of their lower expense ratios.

We should reiterate one point. If you choose a small fund in order to maximize performance, realize that it is likely to excel primarily because of its maneuverability and its greater propensity to take risks, not because of inherently superior management. The large growth funds own the stocks of multibillion-dollar companies which are unlikely to go bankrupt in any recession. On the other hand, some emerging growth companies favored by the small performance funds do go under during a recession, and even in booming times bankruptcies in highly competitive fields are scarcely unheard of, especially among high-tech firms.

Many large funds grew to their present size because they performed well in their early years, when they were still small. The Dreyfus Fund is a classic example. Its greatest gains came in the 50s and early 60s, when the fund was quite small and was aggressively managed. Back then, it regularly outpaced the NYSE Index by margins of two or more times. The Dreyfus Fund is no longer a superior performer and is now classified as a growth-income fund.

The Fidelity Magellan Fund, both when it was managed by Peter Lynch, and now under Jeff Vinick, appears to be an exception to the smaller-is-better rule. Defying gravity, the fund has managed to maintain respectable performances despite incredible size ($36 billion at the start of 1995). We think a major reason for Magellan's continual good fortune is the strength of Fidelity's management team. However, if the fund were not so large it might be doing even better.

In 1989, Lynch authored a book on investing, *One Up on Wall Street,* in which he noted: "My biggest disadvantage is size. The bigger the equity fund, the harder it gets to outperform the competition. Expecting a $9 billion fund to compete successfully against an $800 million fund is the same as expecting Larry Bird to star in basketball games with a twenty-five-pound weight strapped to his waist. Big mutual funds have the same built-in handicaps as big anythings—the bigger it is, the more energy it takes to move it."

Is small size a detriment?

Can a fund be too small? The answer is yes. Small funds often lack the wherewithal to afford good managers and purchase top quality investment research. We suggest that you avoid, or at the very least research far more extensively, established funds (say, those five years or older) whose assets are still below $25 million. And if a fund can't attract enough investors in five years to reach at least $10 million, then it clearly should be avoided. (An exception might be made for a rare, limited-sale fund, such as a small fund run in-house for a number of years before being marketed.) Similarly, be wary of a new fund that has attracted reams of publicity, usually because of some unique marketing gimmick, and still remains quite small. One example of this is the Women's Equity Mutual Fund. Two years after its founding, it still has only $1.1 million in assets.

Portfolio diversification

Here's a riddle: Which should an investor prefer, funds with well-diversified portfolios, or those with concentrated investments? A study by *Morningstar* quite clearly tilts toward well-diversified funds for the best combination of risk and reward. Using their star system which measures both return and risk, *Morningstar* found a clear correlation between portfolio concentration and a fund's star ranking. Funds with only one star had 37% of their assets concentrated in their top ten holdings. At the other extreme, the superior, five-star funds had only 22% of their assets in their top ten holdings.

Table 39

Morningstar rating	% Assets in top 10 stocks
*	37%
**	28%
***	25%
****	22%
*****	22%

Source: 5 Star Investor, September 1994

We don't find the results of this study surprising. Fund managers with concentrated portfolios tend to think of themselves as stock pickers, much like a broker. On the other hand, managers of more diversified funds are more knowledgable about modern portfolio theory. They think in terms of structuring portfolios for maximum gain while minimizing risk, not just willy-nilly picking stocks. When in doubt, chose diversified portfolios.

How much cash is in the till?

A fund's cash position is the portion of its assets that are not invested for the long-term. This includes cash and cash equivalents such as short-term government securities, bank CDs and other money market instruments plus receivables, minus current liabilities. The amount of cash it holds should be appropriate for the market conditions.

Here are the rules for an appropriate cash position:

In a bull market, a fund should be fully invested or even leveraged, in order to take maximum advantage of rising prices. Conversely, in a bear market, a high portion of assets should be in cash or cash equivalents in order to minimize losses as stock prices tumble.

In essence this is market timing. As we noted earlier, a majority of equity funds do not time the market to any significant degree. However, a sizeable minority (perhaps a third) of funds do. In a bear market, 20% to even 100% of their assets may be in cash.

In practice you will find three somewhat distinct types of funds that run high cash positions on occasion: market timers, asset allocators, and value funds. Market timing funds vary their cash positions by typically using technical analysis (an explanation of that term appears in the Glossary). Asset allocators move their assets among stocks, bonds, cash and other asset classes by using models to determine which class is expected to have the most potential. The value funds use fundamental analysis to determine whether a stock is over- or underpriced. They sell stocks they feel are overpriced, and remain in cash if they cannot find undervalued replacements. Because stocks tend to be overpriced at market peaks and underpriced at market bottoms, their actions amount to market timing. Technicians sometimes call these people "bottoms up" market timers, while they themselves are "top down" market timers.

> ## Where to find cash position data
>
> Our newsletter, *The No-Load Fund Investor,* is one of the few comprehensive sources of cash positions. It provides current data for virtually all popular no-load equity funds. You can also find cash position data in the funds' quarterly reports, but that information is usually out of date by the time you get it.

Chart 40 shows three funds that have significantly varied their cash positions over the past eleven years. Management of the Strong mutual funds considers itself to be an asset allocator. Janus and Lindner funds probably are best described as value managers. Two fund groups that use technical analysis are Merriman and Flex Funds.

As you can see, fund managers are not infallible when it comes to correctly timing the market. Those who go to cash at the onset of a bear market frequently fail to reinvest in stocks at the bottom. Some fund managers erroneously believed that the rally in the summer and fall of 1982 would be short-lived. This was a classic example in which funds with large cash positions failed to invest fully in order to take maximum advantage of a fast-rising market. Similarly, any number of funds had high cash positions at the beginning of 1991, and consequently missed a good portion of the strong rally began when U.S. troops attacked Iraq during "Desert Storm." Funds like Flex-Muirfield (67% cash), Fontaine Capital Appreciation (49% cash),

Chart 40

Percent of portfolio in cash

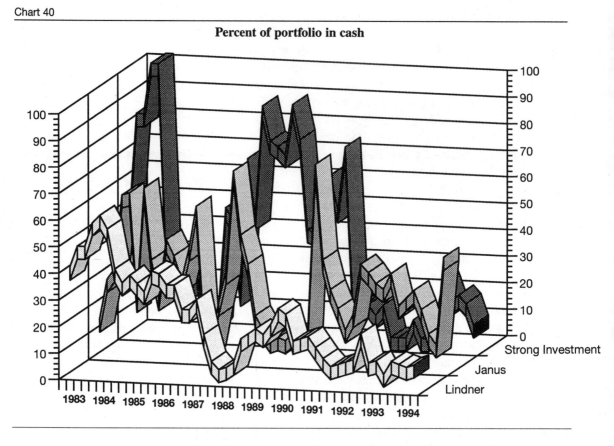

Mathers (92% cash), Strong Opportunity (39% cash) and Valley Forge (80% cash) lagged badly because of their inappropriate cash positions. All ended the month of January 1992 in the fifth quintile.

Mathers and Valley Forge are two examples of funds which maintained inappropriate cash positions during most of the 1991-1993 bull market. Both funds kept more than 70% of their assets in cash. As a result, they both ranked in the bottom 20% of all equity funds in this period.

Value funds seldom carry cash positions over 30%. The funds with higher cash positions are usually congenital bears or market timers. While there may be some exceptions, in general, you should avoid funds with cash positions exceeding 30%.

Funds that do not attempt to time the market feel they lack the ability to forecast the market's direction consistently.

If you do your own market timing, choose a fund that is always fully invested, and then move back and forth yourself between the stock fund and its companion money market fund. If you're a buy-and-hold investor, and want a fund to time the market for you, select one fund that has demonstrated its adroitness.

In sum, a fund's cash position gives you an important indication of how its management views the future. It is also a measure of risk and reward. In a bull market, funds that are fully invested offer the greatest potential for gain. If you are willing to take the risk, by all means buy funds that are completely invested or even leveraged at key market junctures. But, if the outlook is uncertain, look for funds with greater cash reserves.

An investor can obtain leverage in either of two ways. First, invest in a fund that is internally leveraged. Unfortunately, only a few funds use that strategy, and they are seldom the most desirable funds.

Second, you can get more leverage on your favorite funds than they themselves employ by buying their shares through a discount broker which trades in mutual funds. Charles Schwab or Jack White are well-established firms that permit you to borrow to the current 50% margin limit. Using that ability to the fullest would enable you to obtain two-for-one leverage, providing for greater gains in bull markets—as well as much bigger losses during market declines. The procedures are similar to buying stocks on margin. Chapter 22 and the *Handbook* provide more information on discount brokers.

Leverage will maximize profits

Here's an interesting conundrum. If a fund performs well, does that cause it to gain new shareholders? Or, is it the other way around?

For many years it was thought that cash inflow or outflow was a function of performance. But there's another possibility: positive cash flow *produces* superior performance (and negative cash flow, more shareholders taking their money out than putting it in, causes inferior investment results).

This latter theory was put forth by Alan Pope. He is a mutual fund statistician who retired some years ago to Florida.

Pope drew his conclusions after he noticed that no fund, however well managed, ever maintained front-rank performance for more than

Cash inflow

a few years. Absolute size was certainly a factor. But that did not suf-ficiently explain why funds inevitably seemed to stumble. After all, many small funds achieved superior performance for a short time, then declined, even though they had not grown to unmanageable size. So why did they slow down? Pope concluded that cash inflow was a key variable.

■ With new money coming in, he reasoned, a fund's management can buy securities on market dips or simply raise its cash position without selling securities.

■ A positive cash flow means that a fund does not need to sell good or promising equities in order to meet redemptions, or to raise cash for defensive purposes.

■ With fresh money coming in, a fund need not sell existing hold-ings to take advantage of new or special market situations. Thus, decision-making is simpler; a manager has to decide only what to buy, rather than what to buy and what to sell.

■ A positive cash flow minimizes a fund's investment mistakes. Bad investments comprise an increasingly smaller proportion of the fund's asset base. In effect, incoming cash flow dilutes losses.

■ With more money to spend, a fund can attract the advice of the best analysts.

■ With ample cash, fund managers try harder to find promising new investment opportunities.

■ A fund can "bootstrap," directing new money into additional shares of stocks already in its portfolio. If the stock's "float" is not too large such investments can raise its price—and the value of the fund's shares.

To what extent does cash flow aid performance? Pope's research indi-cates that 100 percent cash flow increases performance by 10-14% above the market average. Less than 10 percent cash flow doesn't help much.

Using the method described below, we estimated cash inflow for all aggressive growth funds since 1988 and confirmed Pope's theory. We found a strong correlation between cash flow and performance. In six consecutive years, those funds that, on average, had a cash inflow exceeding 50% did the best. Inflow below 50% reduced performance. Those funds with outflow performed significantly worse.

Table 41

	Aggressive growth funds		
	Annual total return %		
Cash inflow	50% +	0-50%	Outflow
1994	3.6%	-1.8%	-5.4%
1993	19.7	16.1	13.0
1992	12.4	9.4	6.4
1991	60.4	45.4	38.6
1990	-2.0	-7.5	-14.2
1989	28.2	26.1	24.1
1988	27.0	21.3	12.8

Cash inflow also explains why big funds inevitably slow down. They cannot maintain the same rate of cash inflow over long periods of time. If a $2 million fund maintained a 100% rate of new-money inflow, it would have $4 million in assets at the end of the first year (excluding the effects of per share price changes), $8 million at the end of the second year—and over $8 billion by the end of the twelfth year! It is not possible for large funds to grow at the same rate as they did when they were small.

Cash inflow typically starts after investors notice that a small fund is turning in an outstanding performance. Cash flow then enables the fund to maintain superior performance until the additions of new money are no longer meaningful in relation to the size of the fund.

Calculating cash inflow

Usually, the Statement of Changes In Net Assets in a fund's annual or quarterly report has data titled "Capital Share Transactions." Entries in this section show the number and dollar value of shares sold or redeemed. If you don't have the reports, you can estimate a fund's cash flow by noting its per share performance and total net asset figures. Then measure the growth of assets caused by the fund's per share gain for the year. The net inflow of capital is the fund's assets above this gain.

Here is how to calculate cash inflow: Assume a fund started the year with $1 million in net assets. During the year its per share value increased 40%. The fund ended the year with $2 million in total assets. By itself, the 40% per share gain would account for $400,000. Thus $600,000 is the amount of new money that flowed into the fund.

This new-money inflow percentage is 60% of the fund's initial assets.

As Alan Pope points out, the operative word is "flow." Ideally cash should come into the fund at a steady rate. If a fund is inundated with new money it will have trouble investing the largess wisely.

Beware of net redemptions

While excessive cash inflow can present problems, net cash outflow clearly hinders performance. A fund experiencing net redemptions must either keep abnormally large cash positions, thus diluting its performance in up markets, or sell stocks to meet redemptions. The fund tries first to sell the stocks that are the weakest. But eventually it may be forced to sell promising holdings prematurely. A fund in net redemptions is forced to forgo valuable investment opportunities. As its size diminishes, its expense ratio will likely increase. Net redemptions virtually always work to the detriment of the fund's shareholders.

Should you go with the crowd?

Mutual funds, like most investments, go in and out of vogue. Some funds languish for years with little public attention; others are recommended by legions of advisers. In most cases, funds receive multiple recommendations because they currently lead in one or more rankings. In a few cases, public relations plays a part.

That being the case, should you buy what everybody is recommending? We ask this question because investors frequently tell us that they subscribe to several publications, and then feel comfortable investing in funds that have been recommended by several.

To answer that question, we analyzed a summary of recommendations which appears regularly in the Hulbert Financial Digest. This newsletter lists funds that are recommended by three-to-nine newsletters in a given month (out of a base of about 50 fund newsletters). Our methodology was to track those funds recommended the most in January of 1991, 1992, and 1993, and then determine their quintile rank at year end. For example, in January, 1993, four funds had been recommended by nine different newsletters. For all of 1993, these four funds had an average quintile of 3.0. A quintile of 3.0 is exactly average. ("1"s are, of course, the best, "5"s the worst. In the same year, 27 funds had been recommended by three different newsletters. These 27 funds also had an average quintile of 3.0.

In 1991, funds that received the most recommendations did the best, and funds with only 3 or 4 recommendations did the worst. In 1992, the reverse was true. In 1993, the funds with the most and least recommendations did the worst. Averaging the three years we find that funds recommended by 5-7 newsletters did the best, while funds recommended by nine newsletters did the worst. Over the entire three-year period, all funds recommended by three or more newsletters did fractionally better than average (2.9 quintile).

Table 42

Equity funds recommended by three or more newsletters		
# nl's recommending funds	1991-1993	
	# funds recommended	Avg quintile
9	11	3.9
8	7	2.7
7	8	2.3
6	15	2.7
5	27	2.4
4	39	3.0
3	72	2.9
Total	179	2.9

We also took a look at the performance of all funds recommended by three or more newsletters to see if their performance compared to other funds that were recommended by two or fewer newsletters. We found that over the three years, 47% of the recommendations were in the first or second quintiles while only 31% were in the fourth and fifth quintiles.

Table 43

Quintile distribution for all recommendations				
Quintile	1993	1992	1991	3 years
1	33%	15%	34%	27%
2	25%	18%	13%	20%
3	17%	25%	26%	22%
4	7%	17%	17%	13%
5	18%	25%	11%	18%

In conclusion, it seems beneficial to pick a fund that's been recommended by at least a few services, but it doesn't really matter how many. If you're getting your recommendations from newsletters, pick a publication you have confidence in, whose style of investing suits you. Then stick with it.

Track funds on your own

Once you own no-load funds, it's a good idea to follow them periodically. You should review your conservative fund holdings at least quarterly, although monthly is better. And definitely check on more speculative funds at least once a month. If the market has been turbulent, don't hesitate to keep an eye on your holdings weekly. Many newspapers and magazines provide good monthly or quarterly data. But the easiest way to track funds weekly is to follow the total return figures in *The Wall Street Journal, Barron's* and a few major papers such as *The New York Times.*

If your local newspaper doesn't show total return data, see if it has a weekly summary of mutual fund performance in its Sunday edition. You can compute fund performance from this information by simply dividing the gain or loss for the week by the NAV from the preceding week, which you can get by subtracting or from the previous week's paper. Be sure to add to the ending NAV any distributions made during the week. They are noted in the paper with an "x." If you buy aggressive growth funds that are not listed in the papers, call them for their NAVs when the market is in the midst of a major move.

Newspapers list funds alphabetically, either individually or under their group names. (Incidentally, information on some small funds is often not published because the fund has either fewer than 1,000 shareholders or less than $25 million in assets, the threshold levels required by the N.A.S.D. for listing.)

Summary: equity fund selection

Our discussion has analyzed a number of factors that you ought to consider when you are selecting a mutual fund. The most important factor influencing future performance is the fund's performance over various periods in the past. But the other criteria can also be significant. All else being equal—which it never is—we favor the in-depth management at the larger fund groups. In upcoming chapters we will guide you on how to combine the funds you have selected into a portfolio and discuss how long to hold onto your funds. This is the final step to investing success.

CHAPTER 15

Index fund investing

Most investors buy funds that are actively managed. The funds they select have expert portfolio managers who buy and sell securities in an attempt to maximize profits. In previous chapters we described the procedures for selecting such funds.

Yet another investing strategy has much to recommend it. It is passive investing in index funds.

Invented in 1971, index funds are a logical outgrowth of the Random Walk theory. That's the notion that the stock market fairly values stocks. Thus an investor cannot consistently find bargains. Theoretically, that means that you could get just as good results by picking stocks at random. Another way to accomplish the same thing is to purchase all the stocks in a given market or index, or at least a large statistical sampling of them. Then, you wouldn't have to worry whether you did or did not select top-performing stocks. If this sounds like a coward's way out, investing so broadly has much to recommend it. For example, it ensures that you will always match the performance of the market—or whatever share of it you've invested in.

The idea gave rise to the index fund, and over the past two and one-half decades, index funds have found a niche, especially in the investment strategy used by pension funds. When hundreds of millions or even billions of dollars are invested, as is the case with major corporate and government pension funds, it becomes difficult, if not impossible, to beat the market. Some pension funds are so large they virtually *are* the market. Accepting this fact of life, large institutions have adopted the old adage, "if you can't beat 'em, join 'em." They find that they can save substantial sums of money on management fees, research and trading commissions by simply duplicating a broad cross-section of the market, such as the S&P 500, thus automatically achieving the same returns as the overall market.

Wells Fargo Investment Advisors, the leader in index fund management, claims that active management must outperform the market by 2% to make up for the transaction costs and higher management fees. Since the market is in a long-term uptrend, and institutions have far longer time horizons than individuals, they find that indexing can be a profitable strategy. Total assets of equity index funds now exceed $450 billion.

Index funds also have a place in the portfolios of individual investors, and have been available to retail investors since 1976. Here are some reasons why you should consider including index funds in your portfolio:

■ Since the market is in a long-term uptrend, index funds—which by definition are always fully invested—maximize your potential for long-run gains. You won't lose out at the beginning of a strong uptrend, which can happen if an active manager has a high cash position.

■ Index funds have the lowest costs of any investment. That's very important! In the last chapter we showed that high expenses are a major reason for underperformance. They also have low turnovers, thereby minimizing transaction costs and taxes. The Vanguard 500 Index fund, for example, has a turnover rate that has been as low as 4%. Vanguard keeps expenses and turnover low by discouraging market timers. The 500, and Vanguard's other index funds, either have a small sales charge payable to the fund, or they lack telephone switching privileges. One fund even has a redemption fee.

■ You avoid the need to sort out the many contradictory market forecasts. Index funds are as close to a "no-brainer" as you can find in investing.

■ Index funds aren't managed (except, perhaps, by computer). That means you don't have the problem of a star fund manager quitting. You also won't have the problem of the manager's strategy going out of style.

We think index funds will become even better investments in the future because the market is becoming increasingly efficient as a result of better communications, computers, more competition and disclosure regulations.

A variety of investors can benefit from index funds: (1) long-term, buy-hold investors, including dollar-cost-averagers (who are most affected by the drag of high expenses) can profit from the minimal expenses of index funds; (2) buy-and-hold investors who are comfortable with the return and degree of risk provided by the various index funds (betas are 1.00 plus) can benefit; and (3) market timers who are looking for guaranteed (as opposed to potentially superior) performance in their equity vehicles and who want a pure stock fund, rather than one in which a manager may take defensive cash positions in uncertain markets, can get predictability from index funds.

While we believe strongly in this investment category, several factors can make it unsuitable for some investors. If you don't have a five-to-ten year time horizon, or if you can't stand the volatility of a fund that is always fully invested, you are better off selecting a managed fund that may move to cash in a bear market. (In an unexpected downturn, it may not make much difference. The Vanguard Index 500 Fund declined 21.7% in October, 1987, only slightly more than the average diversified fund, which was off 21.0%.) Furthermore, if you aspire to get top performance, you obviously won't find it in an index fund.

Index funds for individual investors have proliferated, so it's now easy to benefit from their relative performance certainty. They tend to fall into distinct categories: (1) pure no-load index funds designed for the long-term investor, which emphasize low costs; (2) somewhat higher-cost index funds or quasi-index funds designed for market timers; and (3) loaded index funds. We recommend funds in the first category, sometimes in the second, but never in the third. Index funds that carry commissions are a contradiction in terms. The point of an index fund for the long-term investor is low cost. You cannot get that with funds that carry commissions.

The second category is appealing to investors who try to make the bulk of their profits by market timing, since they are shut out of most funds in the first category. They can use funds with somewhat higher administrative costs, as long as there aren't any transaction costs. To the best of our knowledge, no basic index funds accommodate timers at this point, but a few funds for timers mimic index funds by using index futures and other strategies to keep their betas around 1.00. The Rydex Nova Fund might be in this category.

In 1991 Neuberger-Berman launched the Professional Investors

Who can benefit from index funds?

Growth Fund, a no-load market timing fund restricted to professional investors. The fund was not a success; it was liquidated in 1994.

S&P 500 Index funds

Index investors began by investing in the S&P 500, a broad group of large stocks, yet a universe that is more manageable than, say, all the stocks traded on a particular exchange (for example, the New York Stock Exchange). Even today, the S&P 500 is the most widely tracked by index funds. At least eleven groups offer S&P 500 Index funds to individual investors. However, there's a surprising variation in the funds' performances. Since all have the same portfolios, the only difference is in their expense ratios. In 1993, their performances varied from 10.0% to 7.7%. In 1994, when the average S&P fund was up 0.9%, the range was smaller.

The leader in the field is Vanguard, whose 500 Index Portfolio, at $9.3 billion, is the largest and best known retail index fund. For the ten years ending with 1994, the Vanguard 500 Portfolio ranked 37th among the 182 diversified no-load equity funds. Some argue that this good performance is due to the fact that as more institutions converted to passive investing, they bought the same 500 stocks, thus driving up the prices of these particular issues.

In fact, a 1987 study by Barr Rosenberg Associates (a firm that advises institutions) analyzed the performance returns of the stocks that comprise the S&P 500 index and found that their inclusion in the 500 *per se* improved performance to the extent that it enabled them to do about 30% better in the 80s than would have been otherwise expected. But other analysts point out that foreigners have a preference for large, well-known companies; the greater liquidity afforded by investing in actively traded stocks with millions of shares outstanding; low costs; and their use as hedges by big stock portfolios, are all reasons why the S&P 500 Index funds have done well in the last decade.

However, Jack Bogle, the chairman of Vanguard and a leading index fund proponent, argues that most active managers also hold their main positions in the S&P 500 stocks, and that the S&P 500 correlates closely enough to the Wilshire 5000 that the "gap is likely explained by statistical noise rather than the growth of indexing." Bogle's research leads him to believe that low expense ratios are the basic reason why index funds, which in theory should do average, actually provide above average performance.

A number of index funds now target other indexes besides the S&P 500. And some even invest passively in set lists of stocks of their own devising. In our opinion this is a welcome addition, because the S&P 500 is dominated by large capitalization stocks. Thus index funds that follow the S&P 500 are all large cap funds. There is a place for funds that track indexes of small and medium cap stocks, international stocks, and bonds. Here we will describe some of the other index funds you may wish to employ. At the end of this chapter we'll show you how to construct an all-indexed portfolio.

The Vanguard Extended Market Portfolio seeks to provide investment results corresponding to the performance of the universe of publicly-traded stocks that are outside the S&P 500. Its strategy is to buy a stratified sample of the small and medium sized companies in the Wilshire 4,500 stock index.

The Vanguard Total Stock Market Portfolio aims to match the Wilshire 5,000, the broadest stock index in the U.S. It combines the Vanguard 500 Fund and the Extended Market Fund in a three-to-one ratio to own the entire Wilshire 5,000 properly weighted, with a lower minimum than would be required to buy them separately.

Vanguard also offers a Small Capitalization Stock Fund, which invests in 500-700 small companies from the Russell 2000 index. Owning the Extended and Small Cap portfolios would be particularly advantageous should the S&P 500 stocks lag. Charles Schwab also has a small cap index fund.

Both Dreyfus and Vanguard now have index funds that are even more targeted. The Vanguard Index Growth and Index Value Funds split the 500 into those respective stocks. Dreyfus splits the Wilshire 5000 four different ways: large company growth, large company value, small company growth, and small company value. We believe these narrowly based index funds are fine for sophisticated investors; however, they do require judgments as to which sector is best. Investors who want a "no-brainer" are better off buying everything: the Total Market Index for equities.

Choose your index—and fund

Quasi-index funds

Not to be confused with index funds are quasi-index funds. They aim for a high degree of predictability relative to the S&P 500 Index. The Vanguard Quantitative Portfolios match the characteristics of the index. But the fund tries to outperform it by weighting its portfolio toward stocks that its computer models identify as the most attractive.

The Vanguard Index funds have very low expense ratios—averaging 0.20%—partly because they do not have portfolio managers. Unlike these funds, Quantitative does have a portfolio manager. As a result, its expense ratio is about 0.48%. Of course, that compares with an expense ratio of well over 1.00% for the average managed equity fund.

You can also invest passively overseas. There are index funds that concentrate in Europe, the Pacific, emerging markets, and even individual countries.

Vanguard also has four fixed-income index funds. They started with a Total Bond Market fund, and then in 1994 added three more with Short, Intermediate, and Long-Term durations. And just to put it all together in one fund, they brought out a Balanced Index Fund, which combines the Total Market and Total Bond Index Funds in a 60/40 ratio.

There is an index fund that holds the 30 Dow Jones stocks. But since Dow Jones & Co. won't give indexers permission to use their magic name, the fund is known as the ASM Fund.

Passively invested specialty funds

A number of funds follow indexes of their own creation or simply invest passively. The Schwab 1000 fund invests in an index of 1,000 stocks. The Benham Gold Equity Index invests in a universe of North American gold stocks. The Benham Global Natural Resources Index Fund holds energy and basic materials securities of companies that are in the Dow Jones World Stock Index. Rushmore's American Gas Index buys stocks of companies that are members of the American Gas Association and the Dreyfus Edison Electric Index Fund buys the 180 members of the Edison Electric Institute, trade associations in their respective fields. The adviser of the Domini Social Index Trust has developed her own index of 400 companies that meet certain social criteria.

Essentially these funds are investing passively. The major difference between them and standard index funds is that they don't have to track a well-known index. This can be an advantage because they reduce their costs by not having to replace stocks simply because Dow Jones or S&P does. Any low-cost, passively managed fund can achieve the same objectives.

While Vanguard dominates the retail sale of index funds, you should be aware of Dimensional Fund Advisors (DFA), a large institutional group in Santa Monica. The group has sixteen domestic and international funds, which are classic examples of funds that achieve good results by investing passively. The DFA Japanese Small Company Fund has twice been the number one fund—in 1987 and 1994. DFA funds are available to individuals through investment advisors participating in Charles Schwab's FAS program. Our *Handbook* has a comprehensive list of index funds.

Index funds are well suited for long-term investors, and for anyone who doesn't want to pay a great deal of attention to their investments. This makes them ideal gifts for a young grandchild. The money isn't typically needed until college. The child's parents, with all the expenses and distractions of a new family, may not follow the financial markets closely. If you can afford only one fund, the best one to buy is the Vanguard Total Market Index Fund — it invests in everything.

Even active investors should consider index funds for their core portfolios. You can invest in an index fund for the long term, through all kinds of markets. Table 44 shows one way to set up a long-term buy-and-hold core portfolio using index funds. Up to half your fund assets can go into this core portfolio; the balance can then be actively managed.

The biggest slice goes into the Vanguard Total Market Index Fund. However, since it's capitalization weighted, it mirrors large cap stocks more than the small cap stocks that are frequently the best performers. Therefore, we've added a small cap index fund. Since a properly diversified portfolio should contain some international exposure, we've added three international index funds. In order to make the figures easy to understand without using fractions, we've totaled the index funds to 100%. If they comprised just half of your portfolio, each percentage figure should be halved.

We think index funds belong in the core portion of almost every portfolio, but they are not a total solution to successful investing. Most investors should have top-performing actively managed funds to balance their risk/reward goals.

Ways to use index funds

Table 44

A sample core portfolio

Vanguard index funds	% Allocation	
Equities	75%	
Total Market Portfolio		40%
Small Cap Fund		20%
Index Pacific		5%
Index Europe		5%
Emerging Market Index		5%
Bonds	25%	
Bond Market Intermediate		25%
Total	100%	

Here's the same core portfolio, but with the bond funds deleted. Bear in mind that this version has significantly more volatility than the balanced version above.

Table 45

Vanguard index funds	% Allocation
Total Market Portfolio	50%
Small Cap Fund	25%
Index Pacific	10%
Index Europe	10%
Emerging Market Index	5%
Total equity index funds	100%

You will note that we made specific fund recommendations for the first time in this chapter. We can do that with index funds. Nothwithstanding the fact that a few authors do it, it just isn't responsible to recommend in a book the more erratically performing, actively-managed funds, We reserve these recommendations for our monthly newsletter.

One final item: if you implement an index fund strategy at Vanguard, as most investors do, you should be aware that their index funds also have a $10 annual account maintenance fee. With the minimum $3,000 investment this amounts to another 0.33% charge, which more than doubles the expense ratio. However, the fee is waived for investments over $10,000.

The first index fund?

Simply matching the indexes is a relatively new concept. So we find it interesting that in 1938, long before anybody dreamed of index funds, a fund was organized that possessed most of the characteristics of today's modern versions. Founders Mutual, the oldest fund in the Founders group, was limited by its original charter to holding 40 stocks that were considered suitable for long-term investments—37 industrials, one insurance company, one railroad and one utility (AT&T). All were selected at the fund's inception. IBM was its largest investment. Other major stock holdings were Eastman Kodak, Sears, du Pont, Union Pacific, and Proctor & Gamble. Whenever new money became available, equal dollar purchases were made in every issue, in effect applying the principle of dollar-cost-averaging. No stock was ever sold but by the end of 1983, 45 years later, the portfolio was down to 36 stocks—four had merged or gone bankrupt. Over the years the fund's performance was, as you might expect, roughly average. In 1983, Founders received permission from its shareholders to shed the original charter and provide the fund with active management. It is now called the Founders Blue Chip Fund.

CHAPTER 16

Guard against newly organized funds

Every year in the early to mid-90s, hundreds of new funds have been launched. On the load fund side, salesmen frequently push brand new funds, thinking their customers will equate them with new issues of stocks. Even with no-loads, heavy publicity sometimes lures investors into buying funds in their infancy. With some significant exceptions, generally you are better off avoiding these babies until they have demonstrated their ability to perform.

In this discussion, we are defining a new fund as an initial offering, the same as a new issue of stock. A fund with even a short performance record is not considered a new fund.

When you buy an established fund, evaluating its performance is comparatively easy because it has a record. And it's relatively simple to get a fix on its investment objective by analyzing its portfolio and volatility. With hundreds—or even thousands—of funds that have a known track record, there is little reason to take the blind risk of buying an unknown entity.

The initial offering of a mutual fund is a totally untested commodity. You have only the prospectus to go by, and it may be vague.

As you might suspect, the performance of new funds varies greatly. We've analyzed the past two decades worth of new funds. Our approach is to track funds during the first calendar year following their organization, then compare their performance with the average of all funds with

The unbearable unevenness of new funds

the same objective. Between 1972 and 1994, 671 new aggressive growth and growth funds have made an appearance. During that 23 years, half of the funds, underperformed the average of their class in their first full year of operation.

We analyzed 473 new growth-income and income funds in the same period, and found that 56% of them were below their group's average in their first full year.

In recent years, we've also tracked international funds, and found half underperformed their peers.

It seems to be harder still for new bond funds to achieve good performance. Of 1,018 new fixed income funds, 57% had below-average performances their first full year.

In compiling new fund performance, we have also been surprised to find instances where new funds, less than two years old, have already been liquidated, merged or had their names changed. Table 46 summarizes new fund performance over the years.

Table 46

First year performance of new funds

Year rated (fund was organized previous year)	Total no. of funds	Above average	Below average	% below
Aggressive growth and growth funds				
1972-1985	167	82	85	51%
1986-90	222	108	114	51%
1991-94	282	148	134	48%
Total	671	338	333	50%
Growth-income and income funds				
1972-1985	71	33	38	54%
1986-90	175	78	97	55%
1991-94	227	99	128	56%
Total	473	210	263	56%
Fixed income funds				
1972-1985	132	60	72	55%
1986-90	363	170	193	53%
1991-94	523	204	319	61%
Total	1,018	434	584	57%

Our methodology gives new funds the benefit of the doubt. Some of them were in operation for more than six months by the start of the first full calendar year that we measured them. Yet the odds of turning in above-average performances were no better than a flip of a coin.

While many new funds are immediate winners, can you reasonably expect to select those heroes beforehand? Without performance records to analyze, it's a most difficult task.

New funds are different from new stocks

New stocks often are profitable because a fixed number of shares is available, and if demand is great, the price increases, sometimes sharply. We've all read about the difficulties of obtaining shares of these new issues in joyful anticipation of windfall profits.

Open-end mutual funds are entirely different, and in fact almost opposite. They can create an unlimited number of new shares as public demand increases. Since all shares are sold at the fund's net asset value, buying early provides no advantage whatsoever.

Some quick arithmetic illustrates this point. Assume a fund has $100,000 of assets and 100,000 shares outstanding. Each share is, therefore, worth $1. Now, suppose a new investor wants to purchase 10,000 shares. In the case of an open-end no-load mutual fund, the new investor would also pay $1 per share—the net asset value. Ten thousand new shares would be created. The total asset value of the fund would increase to $110,000. The number of shares would increase by the same percentage. And the per-share value for both old and new investors would remain the same.

Table 47

Sales don't change NAV

	Total assets	Number of shares	Price per share
Originally	$100,000	100,000	$1
New sale	10,000	10,000	1
After sale	110,000	110,000	1

Unlike stocks, there is no advantage to buying early. You always pay net asset value for mutual fund shares—no more, no less.

Pros and cons of buying new funds

Advocates of new funds make the following points in their favor:

■ *New funds start small.* Because of the excellent agility that it provides, being small is generally an advantage.

■ *A new fund, with all cash in its coffers, has no mistakes to liquidate.* It hasn't done anything wrong yet. This is an advantage, particularly if the fund is started in the middle of a bear market. On the other hand, neither has it done anything right yet. At some point the fund has to invest the money to produce results.

■ *The new fund may offer a tax advantage.* If you buy existing successful funds with substantial appreciation, which is often the case during a long bull market, you are buying somebody else's tax liability (as we discuss in Chapter 22). This can't happen with a new fund.

■ *A new fund may be favored* by a large fund group. Although the fund group will vehemently deny it, we believe that some new funds get first crack at hot new stock issues and other favored stocks.

With the exception of the last point, these advantages do not outweigh the disadvantage of not being able to see a performance record.

When to buy new funds

When it comes to picking mutual funds, there's always an exception. In the case of new funds, occasionally a new concept comes along, or an established concept becomes available without a load for the first time. In these cases—where no established fund is acceptable—consider the new fund. In 1990, *The No-Load Fund Investor* newsletter recommended the newly formed T. Rowe Price New Asia Fund. It was the first no-load to specialize in buying stocks in the fast-growing Pacific Rim countries (excluding Japan). It is managed by Price Fleming International, Inc., which has had outstanding results with four other Price international funds. The recommendation proved a sound one. The fund ranked second among all international and global funds from 1991 to 1993. (The number one fund was a single country fund buying only stocks in Hong Kong.) The *Investor* also occasionally recommends a fund with a short performance record if it appears to be doing better than another recommendation in the same family.

Another type of fund that's perfectly all right to buy new: an index fund. For obvious reasons, age makes no difference.

With the avalanche of new funds in recent years, we are seeing more funds doing quite well in their initial days. Since we suspected that some large fund groups might be favoring new funds in some way, we decided to do some rigorous analysis in our newsletter to see if there is any truth to our suspicion. Our methodology was to take each new fund's first calendar month performance and compare it to the average fund in its objective category. To simplify the study, we restricted it to actively-managed, diversified, domestic equity funds. From 1989 through October 1994, 105 funds met these criteria.

Our first finding was that the new funds did slightly better than average in their initial month. They posted an average 1.1% gain for the month, as compared to a 0.3% gain for the benchmarks. However, this 0.8% differential drops to 0.3% if we compute the median fund, perhaps a fairer measure, since two new funds posted extreme performances their first month. For example, Monetta Mid-Cap Equity posted a 16.7% gain its first full month, 13.1% better than the average growth fund that month.

Table 48

Best first-month's performance

	New fund	Adv. over benchmark
Monetta Mid-Cap Eqty	16.7	13.2
Janus Enterprise	13.9	12.1
Fidelity Emerging Gr	14.8	6.6
Robrtsn Steph Contrarian	6.9	6.4
Janus Balanced	6.4	6.0
PBHG Emerg Gro	10.9	5.8

Our next step was to see if there was any pattern by fund family. Are some of the larger groups favoring new funds? Are they loading them up with IPO's? Are other funds in the group buying the new fund's stocks to drive up the price? And can you profit from this knowledge?

We averaged each fund family's new funds to see if there was any pattern. Families with only one new fund are excluded from the following table.

We want to emphasize that this evidence is all statistical. The results may be due to chance or nothing more than fortuitous timing. (That was certainly the case when the Robertson Stephens Contrarian

Fund was launched in a down month.) Nevertheless, if you like the concept of a new fund or a particular manager's record and want to take a flyer on it, we think you would have a better chance with a new fund from Janus, Fidelity, Strong, Price or Lindner. The odds on Fidelity look particularly good; nine out of eleven of their new funds surpassed their benchmarks.

Table 49

Average difference in total return
New funds versus their benchmarks

Family	# funds	Avg diff
Janus	4	5.5
Robertson Stephens	2	4.4
Lindner	3	2.6
Strong	3	2.0
Fidelity	10	1.9
Price, Rowe	4	1.6
Evergreen	3	1.4
Crabbe Huson	2	1.3
Mean	—	*0.8*
IAI	4	0.6
Royce	3	0.3
Median	—	*0.3*
Benham	3	0.2
Columbia	2	0.1
Dreyfus	5	0.0
Merriman	4	-0.2
Invesco	4	-0.3
USAA	2	-0.4
Montgomery	3	-0.5
Loomis Sayles	3	-0.8
Portico	3	-1.0
Scudder	3	-1.1
Capiello Rushmore	3	-2.1

Flying solo ain't easy

From time to time, well-known, highly successful fund managers leave a large mutual fund company to form his or her own management firm. As a general rule, don't leap blindly into these funds. Usually the manager is leaving a well-oiled machine, with in-depth support, for the dubious advantage of building his own organization from the ground up. It takes courage, but also takes time. Some cases in point.

Gerry Tsai left Fidelity to start the Manhattan Fund in 1967. A huge winner at Fidelity, he did not do nearly as well on his own. Manhattan fund performed poorly until Neuberger-Berman took it over years later.

Richard Fontaine put together an outstanding record at T. Rowe Price. Since 1989, though, he has been the principal in the Fountain funds, a small group of three funds. None of them could remotely be considered a star.

Donald Yacktman compiled a superior record running the Selected Funds. His Yacktman Fund was the fourth worst equity fund in 1993, its first full year. (There was a dramatic turnaround in 1994—which was the time to buy the fund.)

Elizabeth Bramwell, formerly with Gabelli funds, went out on her own in 1994. With about six months' history, her Bramwell Growth Fund is performing somewhat above average at this writing.

In late 1994, Carlene Murphy Ziegler, the co-manager of the Strong Common Stock Fund, and her husband Andrew Ziegler, the president of the Strong funds, left to start their own group. Their new fund, the Artisan Small Cap Fund, had not yet been launched at this writing.

In both of these last two cases, we believe that the funds should be seasoned before investors consider buying them.

Clones

Some new funds are "clones" of older funds. In 1985, for example, Vanguard closed Explorer and Windsor, and then offered in their place Explorer II and Windsor II, in this case with new managements. (Don't look for Explorer II; in 1990 Vanguard folded it back into Explorer.) Other funds have launched clones using the same management—Mutual Beacon and Nicholas II are well-known examples.

In recent years, a number of small cap funds have spun off other funds that appear to be clones, but really aren't. Some examples: Babson Enterprise II, Skyline Special Equities II and Quantitative Numeric II. All of them buy stocks with larger market caps than their originals. In most cases they were cloned because the original small cap fund had closed to new investors, or was about to close.

It's best to evaluate these clones as if they are totally different funds. In some cases they have different policies or managers. In other cases they can perform differently, even with the same policies, because they are initially smaller.

Sales people love to sell new funds

New funds are easy to sell. That's why every fad brings new funds. When options burst onto the investing scene back in the late 1970s, fund groups rushed to bring out option funds. Sales were brisk, notwithstanding the fact that it was an untried concept with no record of success. At their peak there were 21 option funds, 19 of them load funds. None of them has ever done particularly well. They were just a jazzy sounding product—a natural for salespeople. Over the years, salesmen have jumped on a wide variety of new load funds. Frequently the results didn't warrant their purchase. Here's an interesting example from within the same fund family:

Gabelli Asset Fund vs. Equity Trust

In the spring of 1986, Gabelli Funds launched a new no-load, the Gabelli Asset Fund. Because the fund's manager, Mario Gabelli, had a reputation as an outstanding money manager, the fund was an immediate success. Even though the minimum initial investment was $25,000, the fund quickly attracted enough shareholders to be listed in the papers. By the end of September 1986, the fund had $40.6 million in assets, very good for a new fund that didn't belong to an established group.

In August 1986 Gabelli launched a second fund, the Gabelli Equity Trust, a closed-end fund which was sold to investors with a 6.5% underwriting fee (or 7% of the net asset value of the shares). With a good product to market, brokers quickly sold more than $440 million of the closed-end Equity Trust during the underwriting period; that's more than ten times as much as no-load investors were buying on their own. Both funds invest in the same types of companies (although there are some other differences). It would have been preferable to buy the no-load Asset Fund than to pay an underwriting fee to buy the closed end. Furthermore, if you had waited you could have bought Equity Trust at a discount from N.A.V., instead of paying a premium. (One broker, aware of our interest in the Asset Fund, called us to see if we wanted to buy shares in the Equity Fund. We couldn't seem to make him understand why we preferred the no-load.)

Gabelli subsequently launched two more funds: a Convertible Fund, initially no-load, and a Value Fund with a 5.5% up-front load. The Convertible Fund without a load grew to $16 million in its first three months. The Value fund, supported by an army of brokers, raised an astounding $1.1 billion in a matter of weeks—an all-time record for an equity fund. The Gabelli Asset Fund also has a value orientation and, of course, a number of other no-load value funds also are fine investments. No investor needed to pay the load.

One reason why salespeople find new load funds easy to sell is that the funds' sponsors often set a limited period of time for the original underwriting. There is often no commission during this period—only an underwriting fee. After the period ends, the fund is often closed for sales for a short time. In June 1992, Dean Witter Reynolds launched the North American Government Income Trust, a fund that owns U.S., Canadian and Mexican bonds. The initial prospectus noted that the initial offering period was from June 24th to July 24th. A continuous offering period was to commence two weeks later. (In addition, load fund marketers sometimes reduce the minimum investment during the initial offering period, although in the case of the Dean Witter Fund there was no difference.) These sales tactics, albeit successful, are nothing more than psychological gimmicks to make the offering seem more desirable. The underwriting fee is the same as the load. Closing the fund for a short period is done only to force investors to make a decision before the underwriting period ends. You don't save anything, and money can always be invested elsewhere during the closed period.

An artificial marketing period pressures investors

With the huge popularity of mutual funds in recent years, an unbelievable amount of money has poured into the initial offerings of funds. Sales of fixed-income funds were especially popular until 1994, with investors pouring billions into government bond funds, mostly with loads. These new funds aren't superior to existing funds. They don't have greater yields than existing income funds with comparable objectives and policies. It makes no difference whether you buy an existing fund that already owns certain bonds, or a new fund that goes out and buys the same bonds. In either case, you receive the same dividend. The same is true for equity funds investing in dividend-paying stocks. A fund may be new, but it's buying old stocks.

Three no-load short-term global income funds were launched in 1991. They attracted a lot of money, but the new concept's initial results disappointed shareholders. They generally underperformed similar domestic funds in 1992.

New bond funds

In sum, while no absolute rules exist in the selection of mutual funds, and while some new funds will become instant successes, you'll fare better in the long run if you restrict your purchases to funds with at least several months' experience. For growth or aggressive growth funds, which are often more erratic, wait at least a half-year; a year is better. Let somebody else go through the growing pains with new offerings. Don't buy until you see proof of a fund's success.

Watch out for gimmick funds

Be particularly careful before buying new funds that are launched for marketing reasons. The Santa Barbara Fund is an example. It was first offered in May 1986 to participate in the leveraged buyout craze by investing in takeover targets. That concept proved to be a poor one. The fund never got off the ground; it was liquidated in the Fall of 1987.

In 1990, Lord Abbott, a load fund group, launched a new fund called Lord Abbott Equities, which featured an unusual selling point. If, in the year 2000, ten years later, your assets in the fund are worth less than your purchase price, the fund will make up the difference, provided you have reinvested all distributions over the decade. Some deal! The guarantee is backed by insurance which will cost you a stiff 0.5% per year. The guarantee is in nominal dollars—not inflation-adjusted—and in no decade since 1929-38 have stocks declined. It's just a marketing gimmick that salesmen can use to trap the unwary.

Some of the new closed-ends launched in recent years could be considered gimmick funds. Some were single country international funds, launched without great regard for the prospects of equities in the country. Others offered guaranteed yields, which are in part a return of capital.

Don't be gulled by such gimmicks. Insist that a fund specializing in the latest investment fad demonstrate that its concept makes sense before you buy.

Another somewhat unsettling trend: writers of financial newsletters starting their own funds. A number of the best known authors of market timing and stock advisory newsletters have launched funds. One might think that newsletter advisory skills are transferable, but the evidence seems to indicate otherwise. Actually managing money is different from merely recommending action in a publication.

In 1987, Al Frank, publisher of the highly successful *Prudent*

Speculator newsletter, became the sub-advisor to the Prudent Speculator Leveraged Fund. The new fund gained 12.7% in 1988, its first full year of operation. The newsletter's recommendations had a 49.2% gain that same year. Again, wait until these funds are performing before you buy. In 1989, the Prudent Speculator Leveraged Fund was the second worst no-load equity fund; in 1990, it was the third worst. As a result Frank was replaced by another advisor. (Its new management got off to a flying start in 1991 with a 63.8% gain, but the fund then settled back into losing ways.)

Similarly, Stephen Leeb, the editor of the Personal Finance and Big Picture newsletters, is the manager of the Leeb Personal Finance Fund. In its first three years, the fund has been a mediocre performer.

Finally, don't get excited because a firm with proven funds trots out a new one. That's no guarantee of success either. Every fund family now wants a complete product line. The fact that a group has done well with domestic funds, for example, is no guarantee that it will be able to manage a superior international fund.

THE NO-LOAD FUND INVESTOR

Creating a profitable portfolio of mutual funds

It's a New Age dilemma—where to put how much of your assets. The answer, of course, depends on your personal circumstances and your prospects. As either one changes, you want to transfer part of your wealth from one type of investment to another, searching for a portfolio mix that's both right for you and right for the time.

In previous chapters, we explained how various types of funds— aggressive growth, growth, income—were suitable for some investors, but not for others. Here, we put it all together, showing you how to lay out your investments so that your financial portfolio can achieve your objectives. It's wrong to buy a fund, or any security, in a vacuum. You should always consider its place in your overall strategy.

Know what you own

Understanding the securities you own is half the battle. Begin by grouping them according to their objectives. Put the riskiest funds (or stocks) in the aggressive equities section, growth and growth-income funds in the conservative equities section, bond funds (corporate or municipal) in the fixed-income category and any money market funds in a separate section. Group sector funds with diversified funds of like risk levels. Do *not* make gross, undifferentiated categories. Stock mutual funds, for example, is too general a category. Another guideline: don't make distinctions without a difference. Bonds and bond mutual funds should be in the same category.

The categories are not hard and fast. For instance, if you are primarily interested in income, you may want to put growth-income and income funds, which contain high-dividend stocks, in your income category. Growth funds could be lumped in with the aggressive growth category.

Table 50 gives you a model that you can adapt to your own situation. If you own a personal computer, you can set up a sophisticated tracking system. However, you can easily keep your portfolio up-to-date with only an inexpensive pocket calculator.

Here's how to lay out your portfolio: In the first column to the right of each fund's name, write the number of shares you own. Second, put the market price of each. Third, the current market value (price x number of shares = value). In the fourth column, calculate the percentage of your total portfolio that each fund (and each category) makes up. This is essential because it helps you to make certain that your portfolio is in roughly the proportion you have decided on, and allows you to keep it that way.

At least quarterly, update your figures by noting the number of shares and the current price of each fund or security and then determining the worth of your portfolio. That way you can easily keep track of your overall allocations, as well as spotting funds that are performing poorly.

You will also want to take note of the yield you are receiving from your funds. First get your dividend per share for the latest twelve months. If you have owned your fund for more than one year, you will find that data complete in the statements your funds send you. If you don't have the information there, some newspaper tables list per share dividends. Barron's has it. Or you can call the fund directly and ask.

Next calculate your total dividend by multiplying the dividend per share by the total number of shares you own. Finally, figure your yield by dividing your dividend by the market value of your shares.

The yield is an interesting yardstick for comparing various investments. But it is much more important in evaluating bonds than stocks. If you are primarily interested in receiving income from your funds, keep track of current yields (but don't forget total return). Growth stock investors will be much more concerned with the current market value and total return of their holdings.

Table 50

Personal financial assets

Model portfolio

Security	No Shares par value	Market price $	Market value $	% of total	Dividend per share	Dividend total $	Yield %
Aggressive Equities							
Invesco European	1,541.512	12.34	19,022	4.8	0.16	247	1.3
Neuberger-Ber Manhattan	1,575.375	10.59	16,683	4.2	0.01	16	0.1
SteinRoe Growth Stock	642.431	21.19	13,613	3.4	0.15	96	0.7
Twentieth Century Vista	798.671	10.78	8,610	2.2	0.00	0	0.0
Total aggressive equities	—	—	57,928	14.7	—	359	0.6
Conservative equities							
Dodge & Cox Balanced	587.256	47.69	28,006	7.1	1.79	1,051	3.8
Fidelity Convertible Securities	1,526.677	15.68	23,938	6.1	0.80	1,221	5.1
Neuberger-Ber Partners	1,437.444	19.41	27,901	7.1	0.11	158	0.6
Pacific Telesis	200	29.75	5,950	1.5	2.18	436	7.3
Mutual Beacon	1,354.231	32.80	44,419	11.2	0.59	799	1.8
Vanguard Wellington	1,238.562	20.41	25,279	6.4	0.88	1,090	4.3
Windsor II - IRA acc't	1,455.871	17.04	24,808	6.3	0.55	801	3.2
Total conservative equities	—	—	180,301	45.6	—	5,556	3.1
Fixed income							
Janus Flexible Income	851.204	8.89	7,567	1.9	0.72	613	8.1
Fidelity Global Bond	1,174.388	9.67	11,356	2.9	0.69	810	7.1
Fidelity Ltd Term Muni	861.345	9.36	8,062	2.0	0.51	439	5.4
Monthly Payment Series # 276	10	548.00	5,480	1.4	40.05	401	7.3
My company savings plan	800	16.80	13,440	3.4	0.95	760	5.7
Rowe Price Spectrum Income	1,540.431	10.43	16,067	4.1	0.69	1,063	6.6
Cats 0% 8/15/97 - IRA	15,000	0.83	12,450	3.2	0.07	1,050	8.4
USLIFE Income Fund	1,300	9.25	12,025	3.0	0.84	1,092	9.1
Vanguard U.S. Treasury Int.	3,273.057	9.96	32,600	8.3	0.60	1,964	6.0
Total fixed inc.	—	—	119,047	30.1	—	8,192	6.9
Cash							
Dreyfus Basic	31,250	1.00	31,250	7.9	0.03	1,563	5.0
Bank money market account	6,125	1.00	6,125	1.6	0.03	245	4.0
Bank checking account	350	1.00	350	0.1	0.00	0	0.0
Total cash	—	—	37,725	9.6	—	1,808	4.8
Total Financial	—	—	395,002	100.0	—	15,914	4.0
Recap							
Total aggressive equities	—	—	57,928	14.7	—	359	0.6
Total conservative equities	—	—	180,301	45.6	—	5,556	3.1
Total fixed income	—	—	119,047	30.1	—	8,192	6.9
Total cash	—	—	37,725	9.6	—	1,246	4.8
Total Financial	—	—	395,002	100.0	—	15,914	4.0

The simple form you have now created provides you with a wealth of information. It tells you your exact asset allocation. If you are heavily invested in speculative stock funds, you know you will be selling when the market goes down. If inflation surges, you know to what extent you will need to lighten up on bonds. You know how much cash you have on hand. By subtracting the amount you need to keep aside for emergencies or for needs in the near future, you will then know how much is available for investment.

Note that in the model portfolio in Table 50 we included only those assets, primarily financial, that you can control and that have the potential to appreciate. We show an IRA and also a company savings plan, possibly a 401(k), because in many cases, you have the option to move moneys in these plans from equity to fixed-income investments. If you own rental property, that could be listed. All these investments can be adjusted to meet your master plan. We exclude wasting assets like cars, even though they may have considerable liquidation value. That's because if you dispose of a car, you generally need another. It's basically an expense.

If you want to know your total assets, for example for retirement and estate planning, you can easily compose an overall financial statement. Simply add your home, cars, household belongings, equity in insurance policies, pensions and Social Security entitlement. You then deduct mortgages, loans, bills, and other liabilities to get your net worth.

Allocating your assets

Once you know just what you own, you can evaluate your portfolio, and make changes as necessary to ensure that your assets conform to your personal objectives.

In earlier chapters, we characterized the main types of mutual funds and their appropriateness for various sorts of investors. But obviously, just because you are looking for aggressive growth you wouldn't put all your assets into aggressive growth funds. A major part of your wealth should be in more conservative investments for proper diversification. Similarly, even if your objective is current income, don't bet the ranch on fixed-income funds. Some of your money should be in income-producing stock funds to provide you with protection against inflation.

In constructing your own portfolio, apply the principle of the financial pyramid. In this paradigm, safe investments go at the base of the triangle. Every investor should have some foundation investments (money market funds, bank deposits, short-term bond funds, conservative equity income funds). The next level of investment is securities that provide for long-term growth of capital. These should be comparatively conservative, such as dividend-paying growth funds, balanced funds or intermediate-term bond funds.

Depending on your situation, a greater or lesser portion of your portfolio should be in growth investments. Then, a smaller amount of your investments go into more speculative vehicles, which are higher up the pyramid. These are primarily aggressive growth stock funds. And finally, at the top of the pyramid are the highly speculative investments that most investors will omit. At most, a very small amount of your investments will be allocated to such high-risk investments that promise a very substantial return if successful, but may also result in a major loss if unsuccessful. Here, we're talking about initial public offerings, speculative over-the-counter stocks, and the like.

Chart 51

The most important decision you will ever make

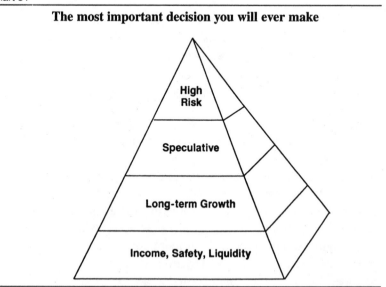

In Table 52, we show three different investment progrmas, each with differing risk levels. We then show sample fund portfolios for each program. This table is taken from the April 1995 issue of our *No-Load Fund Investor* newsletter. An up-to-date version with current fund and cash position recommendations appears every month in the newsletter.

While model portfolios are sometimes categorized solely by risk orientation—for example, a portfolio with nothing but aggressive growth funds, etc.—we don't buy that approach. A portfolio of funds that all have the same risk level is not a complete investment program. Moreover, investors often don't understand which risk category is most appropriate. So we offer various model portfolios oriented by life-style goals. Each portfolio represents a complete investment program—using the concept of the financial pyramid—for all your financial assets. We have not shown the amount of cash you may need for emergencies or for everyday expenses. That depends on your personal circumstances.

The *Wealth Builder Portfolio* is designed for working investors whose goal is capital accumulation. It takes above-average risks to achieve its goals. Current income is not a factor in this portfolio, so bond funds are generally excluded.

The *Pre-Retirement Portfolio* has a more conservative outlook than the Wealth Builder. Designed for investors who are within ten years of retirement, it generally avoids the aggressive growth funds that can suffer the most severe short-term losses. This portfolio normally invests in equity income, growth-income and lower volatility growth funds, as well as fixed-income or money market funds.

The *Retirement Portfolio* emphasizes income and capital preservation and since a major portion of the portfolio is generally invested in equity income and growth-income funds as an inflation hedge, it is usually best suited for couples in their sixties and early seventies who anticipate spending many years in retirement. Bond or money funds provide current income and minimize price fluctuations.

We emphasize that these are models and should be adjusted to your own risk preferences and lifestyle. For example, if you are retired yet are still reinvesting your dividends, the Retirement Portfolio may be too conservative for you. Consider staying with the Pre-Retirement Portfolio. Furthermore, low tax bracket investors should use taxable bond funds; high bracket taxpayers will generally benefit from municipal bond funds. Note that bond fund recommendations are for income; if money funds are recommended, they are for stability and

Table 52

Model investment portfolios

Wealth Builder Portfolio

Fund	Obj	Beta	Cash %	March returns	1995 YTD	Latest 12 months returns	Yield %	Recommended portfolio % Dist.
Janus Mercury	agg gr	*1.26	11	1.4	4.8	14.9	1.1	5%
Montgomery Growth†	growth	*1.25	24	4.1	5.7	20.7	0.4	10%
Lexington World Emer Mkts	int'l	1.13	0	-1.1	-10.4	-12.0	0.0	10%
Price European	int'l	0.78	4	3.7	4.4	7.8	0.9	10%
Price New Asia	int'l	1.19	6	0.5	-2.6	-1.4	0.8	5%
Yacktman	growth	*0.89	12	3.0	9.4	21.7	2.0	10%
Fidelity Equity Income II	gr-inc	0.84	9	3.3	6.9	11.9	2.0	20%
Mutual Beacon	gr-inc	0.67	19	0.5	6.3	11.3	1.7	15%
Price Equity Income	income	0.74	14	1.8	8.1	16.3	3.4	15%
Weighted average	—	0.91	12	—	—	—	1.6	100%

Aggr. Equities 15% — Int'l 25% — Long-Term Equities 60%

Pre-Retirement Portfolio

Fund	Obj	Beta	Cash %	March returns	1995 YTD	Latest 12 months returns	Yield %	Recommended portfolio % Dist.
Baron Asset‡	agg gr	0.97	3	3.2	10.4	21.0	0.0	15%
Strong Growth	growth	*0.96	12	3.5	7.1	15.4	0.8	10%
Montgomery Emerg Mkts	int'l	*0.81	10	-0.7	-10.8	-9.3	0.0	10%
Vanguard Index Europe	int'l	0.79	0	3.9	5.4	9.6	2.0	10%
Price New Asia	int'l	1.19	6	0.5	-2.6	-1.4	0.8	5%
Mutual Beacon	gr-inc	0.67	19	0.5	6.3	11.3	1.7	15%
Price Equity Income	income	0.74	14	1.8	8.1	16.3	3.4	15%
Vanguard GNMA	bond	0.19	5	0.4	5.0	6.4	7.2	10%
Price, Rowe Spectrum-Inc	bond	0.29	5	2.0	6.6	7.3	6.5	10%
Weighted average	—	0.72	9	—	—	—	2.5	100%

Bonds 20% — Int'l 25% — Long-Term Equities 55%

Retirement Portfolio

Fund	Obj	Beta	Cash %	March returns	1995 YTD	Latest 12 months returns	Yield %	Recommended portfolio % Dist.
Vanguard Index Growth	gr-inc	*1.02	0	3.1	9.7	18.1	1.9	10%
Fidelity Equity Income II	gr-inc	0.84	9	3.3	6.9	11.9	2.0	15%
Lexington World Emer Mkts	int'l	1.13	0	-1.1	-10.4	-12.0	0.0	5%
Price New Asia	int'l	1.19	6	0.5	-2.6	-1.4	0.8	5%
Price European	int'l	0.78	4	3.7	4.4	7.8	0.9	10%
Dodge & Cox Balanced	income	0.70	4	2.2	7.8	11.4	3.7	10%
Fidelity Puritan	income	0.69	10	2.3	4.9	7.4	3.3	10%
Vanguard GNMA	bond	0.19	5	0.4	5.0	6.4	7.2	15%
Price, Rowe Spectrum-Inc	bond	0.29	5	2.0	6.6	7.3	6.5	20%
Weighted average	—	0.65	5	—	—	—	3.7	100%

Bonds 35% — Int'l 20% — Long-Term Equities 45%

* Estimated   N = New selection this month   W = Change in portfolio weighting ↑↓   † = Considered aggressive   ‡ = Considered Long-Term

Source: The No-Load Fund Investor, April 1995.

income, particularly, if economic or equity market conditions are unsettled.

To illustrate the differences between the portfolios, we compute their average betas and yields. To give a further indication of risk we include cash positions.

The answer really depends on the amount of risk that you are willing to take, and your time horizon. An all-stock fund portfolio will, over the long-run, achieve higher returns, but at the expense of taking greater risk. Portfolios balanced between stocks and bonds will typically provide lower returns than an all stock portfolio, but will not be subject to as much downside risk. That is why our newsletter's Wealth Builder portfolio, which we've just described, seldom includes bond funds, while the two more conservative portfolios usually do. The Wealth Builder portfolio is for younger investors with longer time horizons. The other two portfolios are for investors who typically have shorter time horizons.

In fact, the level of risk you are prepared to take often correlates with your age. Here's a rough rule of thumb that some planners use: The percentage of your portfolio in stocks should be 100 minus your age. This means a 30-year old should have a minimum of 70% invested in equities; a 65-year old, at least 35%. Many investors don't achieve these minimums. Other planners believe this rule is too conservative. They modify it by suggesting you invest your age in bonds multiplied by 80% and the rest in stocks. For a 60-year old, the formula would be 60 X .80, meaning 48% for bonds and 52% in stocks. The basic rule would have you only 40% in stocks. At age 70, the modified rule would be 44% in stocks compared to 30%.

What percent of your portfolio should be in stocks?

A provocative research study was conducted by Peter L. Bernstein, a noted economist and securities analyst. His research leads him to make a case against the common asset allocation strategy in which the normal portfolio composition is 60% equities and 40% bonds. Many balanced funds use that sort of allocation. It's typical of the approach, for instance among balanced funds managed by Dodge & Cox, Founders, IAI, T. Rowe Price, as well as at Vanguard's Wellington Fund. Bernstein argues that a portfolio allocation consist-

The no-bond study

ing of 75% equities and 25% cash is at least as good, and in many market climates, probably better.

The study was first done in 1988 using the S&P 500 as a proxy for equities, the 30-year Treasury bond, and 90-day Treasury bills. The original research found that from 1954 until the middle of 1988, a portfolio 60/40 stocks/bonds had an annual compound yield of 9.17% with a standard deviation (a measure of risk) of 5.78. Over the same period, a portfolio 75% stocks, 25% cash generated a 10.24% total return—12% more! Yet, the standard deviation rose only 4%, to 5.99%. Thus the stocks/cash portfolio delivered a substantially larger gain with only slightly more risk.

However, most stock market research is maddeningly sensitive to particular time periods. A strategy that works in one period, may not work at all in another. The 1954-1988 period covered many years when bonds were in a bear market, which biased the results toward the stocks/cash strategy.

To take that bias out, the study was redone in 1994 for the two decades from 1974 to mid-1994. That period included the great bull market in bonds, from 1982 when interest rates began to decline, until 1994, when rates climbed dramatically. Not surprisingly, the advantage of the stocks/cash plan almost disappeared. Over the last 20 years, the stock/bond portfolio averaged 11.40% per year, while the stock/cash portfolio averaged 11.18%. The standard deviations were 6.51% versus 6.29%. Thus, the stock/bond portfolio had a 2% advantage in performance at the cost of a 3.5% higher standard deviation.

Bernstein also replicated his study using other asset classes. Instead of using the S&P 500 to represent equities, he substituted a mix of 70% S&P stocks with the remaining 30% in small company stocks. Secondly, he substituted an intermediate-term bond for the long bond. The addition of small company stocks raises both the risk level and returns of the portfolio. Shortening bond fund maturities has the opposite effect. Making these changes improves the risk/reward relationship of both portfolios. The new mixed-stock portfolio plus cash outperformed the new stock/bond portfolio but at a greater risk—though it is not as statistically significant as it appears in the accompanying chart.

Since these latest readings don't show one strategy clearly dominating the other, why should you consider such a radical departure from conventional asset allocation?

Chart 53

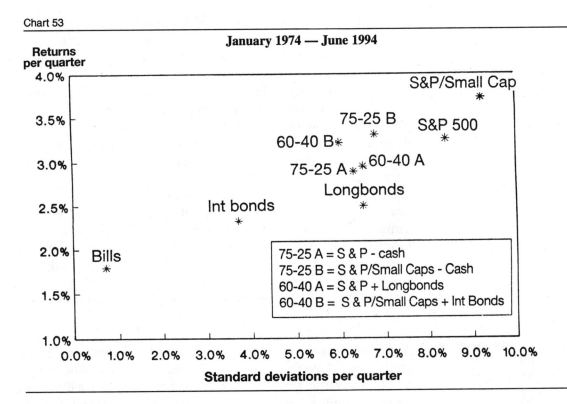

January 1974 — June 1994

Here are three reasons for eliminating bonds and substituting cash in your portfolio:

■ Bonds can suffer negative returns, cash cannot.

■ The original reason for balancing a stock portfolio with bonds is that, historically, the two asset classes did not move in tandem. This has been less true in recent years. Stocks and bonds now decline simultaneously much of the time. From 1974 through 1994, there have been 25 quarters (out of 84) when the S&P 500 declined. Long bonds declined in 19 of these 25 quarters.

■ We believe the great, decade-long bull market in bonds is over. Thus the original study may be more relevant than the update.

When bonds are in a bear market, the stocks/cash plan is clearly superior. When bonds are in a bull market, the two strategies are roughly a wash. This tilts us toward the stocks/cash plan. However, if you feel strongly about the direction of interest rates—and stocks, for that matter—this could change the equation. A substantial decline in interest rates in the remaining years of this century would enhance the appeal of the stocks/bonds strategy. On the other hand, if there is a resurgence of inflation, then bonds will be poison and cash king in your portfolio.

If you believe that the long-term bull market in bonds is essentially over, we suggest one way to gradually switch over to a stock/cash allocation is to stop reinvesting bond fund distributions. Either have the fund send you a check each month, or, if you're at one of the larger fund groups, direct your distributions to a good stock fund or money fund.

Note that following the stocks/cash strategy doesn't necessarily mean you never hold bonds. It means that stocks and cash are your permanent investments. Cash becomes your diversifier and risk-reducer. Bonds are only bought opportunistically, that is if you believe interest rates are about to decline. Then a play in bonds will produce attractive returns. (With a traditional stock/bond allocation, the reverse is true. Cash becomes your opportunistic purchase.)

How many funds should you own?

A common question put to mutual fund experts is, "How many funds should I own?" While it may seem that this is a simple issue, in fact it's not. Of course, this doesn't stop "experts" from responding. But we get the feeling that their answers display no science and little art, typically being made off the top of the head or intuitively. The most common answer we see is, "Not too many funds. Otherwise, you will be diluting your performance." Or: "Enough for proper diversification." Or: "Not so many that you can't easily manage them."

We'd like to provide some solid information in an area where analytical answers seem hard to come by.

As a preface to this discussion, we should remind you that we are talking about no-load funds. So, an investor never has to increase a purchase within any one fund family in order to hit what are called break points—the level in load funds where the commission begins to decline. You don't need to limit the number of funds you own for that reason. On the other hand, the paperwork consideration can be all too real. The more funds, the more paperwork—a bother both in keeping track of your investments and in filing your tax return. If you have a limited tolerance for paperwork, this may be reason enough to prefer a smaller number of funds.

Years ago, we used to take the position that smaller was better when it comes to the number of funds in your portfolio. Over the years, we've modified our thinking. We now believe proper diversification is paramount and a million dollar plus portfolio could easily include twenty funds.

It's the size of your portfolio that should be the major consideration in deciding how many funds to own. If you have only a small amount of money to invest, the minimum investment restrictions that some funds impose can be a problem. People with only small sums to invest need to locate fund groups—such as Montgomery and AARP—that have low minimums. Alternatively, they should consider funds that provide internal diversification, such as balanced funds, asset allocation funds or multi-funds like the Vanguard Star and the T. Rowe Price Spectrum. If your assets are greater, then this problem is eliminated. You can diversify on your own to greater advantage.

We think that owning more funds can provide greater diversification, which is advantageous. When you analyze the model investment portfolios in Table 52, you see that they follow the principle of the financial pyramid. This strategy can entail owning quite a few funds. For example, we allocate most of our money to fairly conservative funds, keeping relatively small portions in the speculative funds categories. However, unless the market is quite high, we think it's preferable to own more than one aggressive growth fund. One diversification we advocate is holding a small cap fund plus an aggressive fund that does not take size into consideration when picking top growth stocks.

In the growth and growth-income categories, it makes sense to diversify between an earnings-driven (growth) fund and a value fund. Completing the financial pyramid, virtually all portfolios should have an equity income fund. And, diversifying into international funds is a must for today's investor. That can be accomplished by investing in one fund; but large portfolios might do better buying two or more regional funds plus an emerging market fund. We don't think specialized funds are necessary, but they can enhance the total return of a portfolio.

Many different types of bond funds exist, providing all sorts of diversification possibilities. Most fixed-income money should be invested in funds with intermediate-term maturities. If you use only one fund, it should probably be one that invests in government securities or investment grade munis. Investors who buy two or more can add a high-grade corporate bond fund, or even global or international bond funds. But don't diversify willy-nilly. Three or more fixed-income funds in the same category, say long-term corporate bond funds, won't provide you with meaningful diversification.

Will holding a great many funds dilute performance? In theory, a portfolio composed of just three or four of the best funds should have greater potential, but it's exceedingly difficult to pick the three or four funds that will turn out to be the best. And even if you do, the portfolio could be dangerously undiversified, since the best—and worst—performing funds at any moment are likely to be similar. On the other hand, more diversified mutual fund portfolios can produce greater rewards for the same amount of risk, or the same rewards with less risk, provided you are diligent in selling off your losers (a practice that's essential no matter how many funds you own).

We did some studies to document this point. For example, we compared the performance and variability of two portfolios of aggressive growth funds over a three-year period. The first portfolio consisted of five aggressive growth funds, the second 20 aggressive growth funds (including the five in the first portfolio). We selected funds to give both portfolios about the same total return (40.5% vs. 40.9%). The larger portfolio had a standard deviation of 5.08, while the smaller portfolio's standard deviation was 5.80. Similarly, we assembled a portfolio of eight funds similar to our Wealth Builder Portfolio. We then compared it to a similar portfolio with 20 funds. Again the results were similar, the larger portfolio had less variability and a slightly higher total return.

Table 54

Portfolio	Total return	Std Dev.
8 funds	53.5%	4.44
20 funds	54.1%	4.21

Can you achieve the same results with low-cost index funds? Yes, but they can't do the whole job. They have relatively high betas, ranging from 1.00 up to 1.12 for the Vanguard Small Cap Index Fund, due to their policy of always staying fully invested. So conservative portfolios need additional funds that would bring down the overall level of risk. Nor do index funds allow you to concentrate on hot sectors of the market in order to maximize your return. We think index funds belong in the core portion of almost every portfolio, but we don't think they are a total solution to minimizing the number of funds you need.

Real estate

Because of its inherent inflation protection, real estate undoubtedly should play a role in most investors' financial plans. However, its exact participation depends heavily not only on your circumstances, but also on your inclination toward the management of property. Generally, individually chosen and managed real estate is your best investment. (If the equity in your home represents 20% or more of your assets, that may well be sufficient.) If sole ownership is impractical, though, you should consider choosing an alternative. A real estate investment trust (REIT) is one possibility. Another is a share in a real estate limited partnership. Within the mutual fund arena, you might consider a no-load real estate fund, although the amount of inflation protection these funds offer is difficult to determine. Bear in mind that a large mortgage can offset the deflation protection afforded by long-term bonds. If that applies, you might consider replacing a regular bond fund with a Benham Target Fund that holds zero coupon bonds. This will give about triple the protection for the money.

While allocating your portfolio is of utmost importance, no set formula can be applied to everyone. You need to tailor your investments to your own situation. Your stage of life has a significant bearing, as does your risk tolerance. The paramount consideration, however, is your specific investment objective. When you are young, the majority of your nest egg will be invested in growth vehicles. Nearing retirement, you begin picking your spots to convert some of your growth stock funds to growth-and-income and fixed-income funds. At retirement, you have to calculate how much income your investments are required to produce in order to supplement pensions and Social Security and provide you with the money you need to finance a style of life that you are comfortable with. Even in retirement, though, you should leave some of your assets in growth stock funds. Otherwise, inflation will gradually erode your purchasing power.

Happily, you can construct portfolios for all seasons by using no-load funds. And you can easily adjust the proportions as your needs change.

Rebalancing

Rebalancing is a strategy designed to maintain a portfolio's desired weightings. For example, you have a portfolio set up with a 5% weighting in gold funds. If, by some chance, gold should double, its weighting in the portfolio will approximate 10%. You would rebalance by selling half your gold holdings, and putting the profits in sectors that did less well.

No question that the theory is sound. The practice, though, is dubious. Some authorities suggest regular rebalancing. Our feeling is that unless the weightings in your portfolio change significantly—over 10%, you probably don't need to bother. You will increase your tax exposure (in a non-qualified account) to gain a marginal advantage. The book *Bogle on Mutual Funds* by Vanguard head John Bogle contains a study comparing two $10,000 investments. Both start with a 50/50 distribution between stocks and bonds. One portfolio is rebalanced annually (enough of the best performing category is sold and reinvested in the other to bring it back to the 50/50 weighting). The other portfolio is not rebalanced. After 25 years, the portfolio that is rebalanced is worth $100,590; the other portfolio is worth $97,910. Annualized the difference is 9.7% versus 9.6% per year. And this is before tax consequences are taken into account!

If your holdings are concentrated within a major fund family, one easy way to rebalance comes cheaply. Just direct the fund group to send the dividends distributed by your overweighted funds to your underweighted funds. This should work well in the long run.

Everyone's got recom- mendations

Maybe it just seems that way because it is our business and we read all the investment literature, but everywhere we turn we encounter investment recommendations. You can't get through an edition of Wall $treet Week without Lou asking his guest for some stock picks. Recommendations are an important feature in all the personal finance publications and investment newsletters (including our own). Brokers live by their recommendations.

All that advice is fine—if properly used. But we worry that many investors don't know how to use it effectively. Here's some recommendations to beware of.

The *fund of the month* or *novelty syndrome.* The obsession of many publications to tout a "hot" fund or stock recommendation in every issue generates a flood of unnecessary recommendations. Not every recommendation will be top-notch. Moreover, the timeliness factor in these sorts of recommendations is usually vastly overstated, since most funds are meant to be held long-term. While our *No-Load Fund Investor* newsletter has continuing model portfolios, a form of recommendation, major write-ups are not a regular feature. It only recommends funds that it thinks are special, or if the recommendation is particularly timely.

The "one best" fallacy. This type of recommendation generally comes about from a reporter's desire for simplicity, although occasionally unsophisticated individuals ask for it. It goes like this. A reporter will say: "I want your one, single best recommendation." In the real world, of course, no such thing exists. Advice has to be conditioned on a fund's appropriateness within a specific portfolio. And while it seems obvious that no single fund could be best for everybody and at all times, this common sense fact tends to get ignored in the quest to be catchy or concise.

It's certainly possible to own just one fund (an asset allocation fund would be suitable). But for a variety of reasons, you are much better off investing in several.

The David Letterman delusion. We're refering to Letterman's well-known top ten lists. In investing, securities that have performed well in the past get memorialized, often in Top Ten lists, or starred (****), honor rolled, given "A's," written up, or singled out in some other manner. Nobody actually says they are recommendations, but most readers assume that they are. Why else is a fund in the limelight? But we all know that good past performance doesn't guarantee future performance. Thus, there is a difference between an acknowledgment of the past and a recommendation for the future. The top fund lists are not forecasts of future performance. The Best Buy recommendations in our *Investor* newsletter are forecasts. They aren't always right, but that is the goal of the recommendation.

Past performance is, of course, the basic starting point for any recommendation. But constructing a sound portfolio involves a lot more than that. If past performance were the only criterion, then many securities would be recommended at their peak. In addition to past performance, you need to look at the future potential in terms of the types of markets you might reasonably anticipate. You also need to take into account such factors such as continuity of management and fund expenses.

In this regard, you should also be wary of "recommendations" that appear in contests sponsored by publications. Such games have little meaning because they typically focus on just a few selections, mandate artificial holding periods, up to a year, and ignore risk. Once the holding period is selected, the ability to make changes is sharply restricted. These rules are devised for the publications' convenience and may bear no relationship to real-world investing. Consequently, the experts in the competition will pick securities differently than when they are selecting for a client. There may be a tendency to pick risky stocks or funds because there is great publicity value in winning, and virtually no penalty for coming in second, or even last. Don't use these contest selections as a basis for your own decisions, unless the objectives and risks correspond to your own.

Unsuitable recommendations. Most recommendations have merit. But that doesn't necessarily mean they are appropriate for you. The most common error is, of course, buying securities—either funds or individual stocks—that are too risky. Many printed recommendations fail to disclose all the risks. In 1994, the United Services funds launched the United Services China Region Opportunity Fund, a fund that clearly had great long-term potential, but also carried great risk. The fund was sub-advised in Boston by Batterymarch, an institutional money manager with $11 billion in assets including $2 billion in emerging market stocks. Your author attended a supper in Boston given by Batterymarch to promote the fund. The president of Batterymarch commented to me that this would be a great fund for dollar-cost averaging, because "you won't believe how many chances you will get to buy low." She was right. The fund proceeded to decline for several months thereafter. We dutifully repeated her admonition in our newsletter writeup. Not many other publications did.

Undeserving candidates. Not all funds or stocks are deserving of a favorable nod. They may be recommended as a result of an effort by a public relations agent, or they may result when a publication looks for something different. Be leary of articles with titles like: "Five undiscovered funds," or "Rookie funds with great prospects." (This last title, in a major magazine, generated a considerable response for a fund that hadn't yet even been launched.)

Sifting through recommendations to find the ones that work for you. The single most important criterion is, "Does this recommended security fit into my portfolio?" If it doesn't, you don't need it, no matter how glowing its prospects may seem. Avoid owning a randomly selected list of securities that don't blend into a coherent whole that will meet your own objectives. This chapter is all about determining the proper fit.

The *bottom line*: to be in control of your portfolio you need to proceed carefully in evaluating recommendations. We have long felt that the best way to deal with your broker's recommendations is to tell him or her, "Don't call me, I'll call you." The same concept holds true with other recommendations. When you perceive a need to make a specific change or addition to your portfolio, then look at the relevant recommendations and pick the best. That way, you'll always be on top of your investments. Don't be a dilettante, picking the trendy fund of the day that some advisor or publication is touting.

You can probably cite the yield on your bond or money fund. You may know your stock fund's exact return. But *your* return may be different from the fund's return. That can happen when you've made additional investments or withdrawn money during the measured period. It's a bit of work, but it's nice to know how well *you* did—as opposed to how well your investments did.

How to compute your investments' exact return

Professional investors can figure the precise rate of return by performing a complex calculation that takes into account the exact timing of cash inflows and outflows. Mutual funds do it every day. But you don't need such precision. Fortunately, it is possible to arrive at a reasonably accurate figure for your return by using a simple formula. Nearly all the information is in the records you need to save anyway. The formula assumes that additions and withdrawals are made in the middle of the measured period. Here are the steps:

1. Compute the beginning value of your initial investment including sales charges, if any. For example, on Jan. 1, your investments are worth $10,000. Then calculate the value of your investments at the end of the period—say, $12,350 on March 31. Calculate net additions or withdrawals—say $2,000—during the course of the quarter.

2. Subsequent purchases are considered to be additions. Dividend, interest or capital gains distributions taken as income are counted as withdrawals. Reinvested dividends are ignored as they are a wash. If you want your computations to be after-tax, count taxes on distributions as

additions. When you pay tax on gains for a security that has appreciated over several years, your calculation will understate the return for the year in which you paid the taxes, and overstate the returns for previous years. You can correct the distortion by allocating a pro-rated share of the tax payment to prior periods and then recalculate your annual returns.

3. Multiply net additions or withdrawals by 0.5 (note that a net withdrawal will be a negative number). Example: 0.5 x $2,000 = $1,000.

4. Subtract the result of step 3 from the ending value. Example: $12,350 - $1,000 = $11,350.

5. Add the result of step 3 to the beginning value. Example: $10,000 + $1,000 = $11,000.

6. Divide the result of step 4 by the result of step 5. Example: $11,350 / $11,000 = 1.032.

7. Convert to a percentage by subtracting one and multiplying the remainder by 100. Example: 1.032 - 1 x 100 = 3.2%. This is your quarterly return.

8. To annualize the figure, multiply the decimal value in step 6 by itself three times and convert the result to a percentage. Example: 1.032 x 1.032 x 1.032 x 1.032 = 1.134 = 13.4%.

9. To get your actual returns for a year, multiply the decimal value (as in step 6) of your quarterly returns together and convert back to a percentage. Example: 1.032 x 1.042 x 0.98 x 1.048 = 1.1044 = 10.4%.

Anyone who wants still greater accuracy should compute their returns monthly.

CHAPTER 18

Choosing a fund family

As mutual funds have expanded the range of their services, fund groups have become increasingly important. More than 135 no-load families now have one or more stock, bond and/or money market funds. Almost 75% of all no-load stock and bond funds belong to these groups, accounting for 90% of no-load stock and bond assets. As a result most investors now ask themselves which *family* of funds is best, rather than which particular fund. This is especially true if you want to use a fund group for your IRA or Keogh, since you can move money around in a tax-qualified plan at will, without worrying about tax consequences every time you switch from one fund to another. (When you are investing outside of a tax-qualified plan, every time you move from one fund to another—unless it's a money market fund—you have either a taxable gain or loss.)

No single fund family is right for everyone, of course. Different groups have different strengths. Your choice depends upon your individual needs. Here are some considerations to help you choose.

The first and most important is the type and quality of the group's stock funds. The greatest differences between families exist here, particularly in performance. Most groups have growth or growth-income funds that perform respectably. But relatively few have outstanding aggressive growth funds. So if that's where you plan to make significant investments, it's an easy basis on which to select a group.

These days, international investments have a place in every portfolio. Since they're very popular among knowledgeable investors, 58 groups now offer them, making it easy for you to allocate a portion of your investments overseas. But be careful. There are wide differences in the quality and types of these various international funds. Invesco, Montgomery, Rowe Price, Scudder, Vanguard and Fidelity have particular no-load expertise in this area.

After you've found one or more groups that satisfy your stock fund requirements, look next at the group's bond funds. The important differences here are in the variety of fixed income funds available, and their operating cost.

First, does your tax bracket incline you toward taxable or tax-free bond funds? Some groups have one kind but not the other.

Next, look for a group whose bond funds have low expense ratios. Vanguard is usually the best among large groups in this regard.

Finally, consider whether the group that you are investigating offers funds with different maturities. Most fund groups have long-term bond funds. Short- and intermediate-term bond funds are less common. Since these are the better performers in adverse markets, their availability makes a group more desirable.

After you are satisfied with a group's stock and bond funds, examine its money market funds. Variety, rather than performance, is the major criterion. A fund group that includes all three types of money funds—general purpose, government-only and tax-free—has the edge.

Another consideration is the existence of specialty funds. Eleven fund groups—Benham, Bull & Bear, Capiello-Rushmore, Fidelity, Invesco, Gabelli, Lexington, Scudder, United Services, USAA, and Vanguard—have precious metals funds.

Is the fund group completely or only partially no-load? Totally no-load is better, of course. If a fund family has a tendency to slap low-load charges on its best-performing funds—Fidelity being the prime example—that practice certainly inhibits your fund selection. We recommend ignoring a group's loads when making your choice.

Tax-sheltered investing

Whether investing for growth or income, mutual funds offer the best investment vehicles for tax-deferred retirement savings plans such as Individual Retirement Accounts, Keoghs and many pension plans.

Good no-load families offer a broad range of investment choices—a vital feature as you get older and need to begin thinking of moving your retirement nest egg from riskier to more conservative investments in order to preserve principal. An IRA account with a mutual fund family provides the opportunity to maximize profits by convenient buying and selling of various equity funds or switching to money funds without having to pay any taxes until you cash in the account, usually years later. And all the paperwork covering years of contributions comes from a single company.

So, for a tax-deferred retirement account, your first choice should be a family of no-load funds. But these days, more and more investors are using an attractive alternative: a discount broker as custodian. (For that matter, you can manage a portfolio of no-load funds in a non-tax qualified account in a discount brokerage account, too. These options will be discussed in detail in Chapter 22.) Finally, it is quite possible to move your IRA from one management group to another as often as you wish, though you may find that the requisite paperwork and time are considerable. All else being equal, it's preferable to stay within one no-load fund group.

Because your income and capital gains are not taxed until you begin withdrawals, the investment strategy for IRAs and Keoghs may be different from the ones you'd use in an account that is not tax-sheltered. However, basic investing fundamentals still apply.

How much risk should I take in an IRA?

This question is trickier than it seems. You are investing money for retirement. So should you choose a super-safe investment because you don't want to take any chances? Or should you seek the greater rewards that often come from taking risks. After all, if you are still young, you want to pile up as big a stake as possible.

Tax shelters offer a super advantage. But just how much you'll accumulate depends on how well you invest your money. If you're putting your money away for many years, the differences are staggering. If you contribute a steady tax-deductible $2,000 a year to your IRA for 40 years, you would have a retirement nest egg of $242,000 at the end of the period—if the money grew at a rate of 5% per year—but $885,000 if you got 10% on your money, and an astounding $3,558,000 if you were able to achieve the difficult feat of gaining 15% year after year. Needless to say, you achieve the higher rates of return by taking greater risks.

Over the long haul, aggressive growth or growth funds should outperform more conservative income funds. Therefore, if you have many years left before retirement, a growth fund is likely to give you the best total return.

On the other hand, if you will need to withdraw your money in a few years, you had better play it safe by investing in a conservative equity or fixed-income fund. You don't want to take a chance that a severe bear market will measurably erode your assets shortly before you are ready to begin withdrawals.

In short, in terms of risk level, *you should take the same amount of risk in a tax-sheltered plan such as an IRA as you take in your regular investment accounts.*

IRA tax consequences

In terms of tax consequences, there are some distinctions. If you're in a bracket where both income and capital gains are taxed at similar rates, your best strategy is to put growth funds in your IRA. Over the long run, you should have more gains to shelter. If you're in a 36% or higher bracket, appreciation has a tax advantage over dividend income because it is not taxed until you sell and is capped at 28%. Therefore, you are better off putting income funds in an IRA. However, bear in mind that most funds realize their profits within a few years, so the build-up of unrealized appreciation is relatively small; certainly, the impact in mutual funds is quite different from an investor's holding onto an individual security for many years.

Which group to select

In addition to applying the techniques we've described for choosing a fund family, some special considerations apply with a tax-free account.

■ Obviously, you don't include a group's tax-free bond or money market funds in your evaluation. Their dividends, which are already tax-free, would be converted into taxable income upon distribution. For this reason, most municipal bond funds don't even offer retirement plans.

■ Make sure that all the group's funds you are considering accept IRA or Keogh accounts. A few groups exclude certain funds from tax-sheltered programs.

You should put your money into a tax-sheltered account early in the year so the income will be tax-sheltered for the entire year. If you haven't decided on a specific fund, start your IRA in the mutual fund group's money market account. Later you can always switch to a stock or bond fund.

A number of years ago, several funds were organized specifically for tax-sheltered accounts. Under pre-1986 laws, it made a lot of sense for investors to put their IRA or Keogh money in them, since the funds disregarded tax consequences in their portfolio strategies. Typically, they bought and sold stocks more frequently than other funds. For many years thereafter most of that advantage was lost, and most of the funds have changed their charters.

One fund still specifically oriented to tax-qualified accounts is the Fidelity Retirement Growth Fund. It restricts its sales to participants in tax-sheltered retirement plans and tax-exempt organizations. In addition, Vanguard Star, a multifund that owns several other Vanguard Funds, is marketed to IRAs. With its assets allocated among several different types of funds, Star provides wide diversification and charges just one IRA fee.

Funds designed for tax-sheltered investments

Whether you are investing for retirement, or putting money into no-load mutual funds for some other purpose, you should select one or more fund families that best suit your needs. In the following sketches, we give you an overview of the major fund groups you are likely to consider. These brief portraits are designed to help you focus your thoughts on the characteristics that you find important in making your choice.

Fund group profiles

Jones & Babson, which manages the Babson funds, was founded in Kansas City in 1960 with one mutual fund, the Babson Growth Fund. The group, the 38th largest no-load family, now has 21 mutual fund portfolios, including seven managed for the United Missouri Bank (UMB), which accounts for about 40% of the assets under management. Babson has always contracted out its portfolio management to the David L. Babson Co. of Cambridge, Mass. for all funds except two from UMB, which are managed by the United Missouri Bank. David L. Babson is an independent investment counseling firm and is a principal owner of Jones & Babson.

In 1994, Babson became the advisor for the Buffalo Group, which is sub-advised by a Kansas City money manager, Kornitzer Capital Mngt. The Buffalo Group will eventually have four funds.

The group's Shadow Stock Fund is derived from the concept in the

Babson

AAII Journal (a publication of the American Association of Individual Investors). The notion is that small company stocks *neglected* by the institutions may produce superior returns. This fund obtains investment research from Analytic Systems and James Cloonan, its principal owner.

The group takes a value-oriented approach to both equity and fixed income investing. In stock funds, Babson tries to emphasize quality stocks, whether large cap, small cap or international. Its portfolios are kept fully invested, consistent with the belief that forecasting short-term market trends is futile.

Benham

A pioneer in money-market mutual funds, Benham introduced the first Treasury-only money fund, Capital Preservation, in 1972. Its chairman and founder, James Benham is still a strong advocate of this ultraconservative style of investing. Since that time, the family has expanded, becoming one of the largest organizers of fixed-income and money-market funds. Benham offers 30 fixed-income portfolios, both taxable and tax-free, short and long-term. Basically, these funds emphasize safety and high income. While the group appeals to investors nationwide, it is particularly strong in California, its home state. About forty percent of its shareholder base resides there. (This may be partly due to the fact that the group's limited advertising budget is concentrated in California.) Benham not only offers seven different funds specifically for Californians, but also has developed an excellent shareholder relations program for its investors in neighboring states. Benham ranks 11th among no-load groups in terms of assets under management.

Not all of the Benham funds are meant for conservative investors. In 1986, the group came out with the first portfolio of zero-coupon bond funds. Given today's constantly changing interest rate environment, these funds can easily be as volatile as aggressive growth funds.

In 1988, Benham broke with its tradition by introducing its first equity offering, an indexed gold fund. It now has five equity funds. And in late 1993, 21 years after launching Capital Preservation, Benham brought out its first general money fund. In 1990 it made another first, becoming the only group to provide limit orders (see Chapter 19 for details).

After a year of discussion, in February 1995, the Benham funds were acquired by the Twentieth Century Group. It appears to be an ideal marriage—Benham is strong in fixed-income, Twentieth in equities. At press time, the combined group planned to managed all fixed-income funds out of Benham's California headquarters; all equities would be managed by Twentieth in Kansas City. It is unlikely that any funds will be consolidated before 1996. The first to be merged will undoubtedly be the two general money funds.

Blanchard

Started in 1986, this New York City group is named after James Blanchard, a New Orleans entrepreneur noted for his investment seminars, newsletters and rare coins. He owns part of the group, but isn't active in its management.

The Blanchard family has grown to eleven funds and now ranks 52th among no-loads in assets. The company uses outside portfolio advisers to manage its funds, most of which take a flexible investment approach. Almost all invest globally. Its two newest funds — Growth & Income and Capital Growth — are advised by Chase Manhattan in a hub-and-spoke relationship.

More marketing-oriented than most fund groups, Blanchard has proven adept at developing innovative niche products. Examples: one of the first actively managed global asset allocation funds, the first no-load short-term global income fund, one of the first funds that could buy bullion (platinum and palladium, as well as gold and silver) and the first open-end equity and debt emerging markets fund.

The Blanchard family is not pure no-load. Many of its funds exact 12b-1 fees. In February 1995, the management company was sold to Signet Banking Corp., a regional bank with branches in Virginia, Delaware and Washington, D.C. With the active Blanchard officers joining Signet, there will probably be little change in the fund's direction, although Signet has stated they will be looking for ways to reduce expenses.

Bull and Bear

Another New York City family, the Bull and Bear group, started in 1977. Initially it had two funds, the Bull Fund and the Bear Fund. The former was always invested 100% long (in other words, it was always fully invested in stocks). The latter always invested 100% short. Shareholders were supposed to switch between the two funds in accordance with their market outlook. Unfortunately, the concept quickly proved unworkable. The Bull Fund was dissolved. The Bear Fund became the group's money fund.

Now, the family has four equity and four fixed-income funds with diverse objectives. With assets of $230 million it is one of the smaller groups. Bull & Bear follows a top-down approach, gauging overall market conditions and making its investments accordingly. An aggressive, performance-driven group, it seeks to outperform the market in both up and down markets, but has been only moderately successful. Its Special Equities Fund has ridden an especially scary rollercoaster.

Bull and Bear has adopted 12b-1 plans for its funds. Like a few other mutual fund groups, it also offers a discount brokerage service.

Columbia

Based in Portland, Oregon, the Columbia group of funds serves as a showpiece for the management company behind it. With 11 funds and $3.5 billion in assets, Columbia is the 27th largest no-load group. But its management company, Columbia Advisors, has more than $13 billion in its investment advisory business.

Columbia uses a team investment approach to portfolio management, though each fund designates one person who is ultimately responsible for the fund's performance. These managers are top-down investors who do sector rotation.

The group's forte is aggressive growth investing; its flagship fund, Columbia Growth, has an above-average long-term record. Over the years, Columbia has added other equity funds including a real estate fund and a full complement of fixed income funds. The group is pure no-load, but does have a fee-based managed account service that provides assistance to large shareholders in investing in Columbia's funds.

Dreyfus

One of the giants—and legends—of the mutual fund industry, Dreyfus manages 151 funds directly and acts as sub-adviser or administrator to another 19. The third-largest no-load family, Dreyfus boasts about 2 million shareholder accounts. Back in the 1950s, Dreyfus was the pre-eminent name in equity fund management. Its lion commercials became synonymous with growth. The venerable Dreyfus Fund, the group's flagship, has now gained 14,514% (including reinvested dividends and capital gains) since its inception in 1951.

But today Dreyfus appeals primarily to income-oriented investors. About 89% of the $80 billion that the firm manages is in fixed-income or money market funds. Dreyfus has made some of its money funds highly visible by waiving fees to enhance yields and engaging in massive advertising. In 1990 its Worldwide Dollar Fund grew to over $9 billion. In contrast, its no-load equity funds have produced mixed results. In 1991, Dreyfus launched an innovative index fund based on the then new S&P MidCap Index. In 1992, four Dreyfus-Wilshire targeted index funds were introduced.

Like rival Fidelity, Dreyfus has opened investor centers that you can visit to discuss your Dreyfus investments face-to-face. Several are in and around the New York area, where the company is located. Others are in Atlanta, Beverly Hills, Boston, Chicago, Denver, San Francisco, Los Angeles, and four Florida cities.

In August 1994, the Dreyfus Corporation merged with the Mellon Bank in a landmark transaction valued at $1.85 billion. That reduced Howard Stein, the old lion who has symbolized and run Dreyfus for decades, to a figurehead. Though Dreyfus will continue to be run independently, it is expected to become more vigorous and creative as a result of the merger. Dreyfus took over Mellon's 35 Laurel funds, and will likely consolidate some of them into its own family.

The General Motors of the mutual fund industry, Fidelity is a sprawling, privately-owned behemoth with more than $400 billion in assets, 215 funds at last count, and a staggering 5.3 million retail customer accounts. It is estimated that Fidelity's trading desk accounts for 6%-8% of the trades on the New York Stock Exchange.

Fidelity Investments

Eighty-nine of Fidelity's retail funds are pure no-load, giving the company more than any other group. If you're looking for a fund—any type of fund—there's a good chance that Fidelity has it; although increasingly you will find a sales charge attached to the purchase, especially if it's an equity fund with a decent track record. In recent years, when Fidelity has felt that a new fund or an existing no-load fund can offer superior performance, the group has made shareholders "pay up." The sales charges on many of Fidelity's popular funds are used to support the firm's massive advertising campaign—the industry's largest. As a result, among all its funds, only 19 are pure no-load retail equity funds. In November 1992, Fidelity reversed course somewhat by waiving loads on 16 of its popular equity funds for IRA and some other tax-sheltered accounts.

Fidelity's fame is due in part to its spectacular Magellan Fund, which has returned 2,059% to investors over the past 15 years—still No. 1 for the broad period. Magellan's assets have grown with its fame. Now by far the largest mutual fund, with more assets than all but 14 entire fund groups, it is no longer No. 1. At least not for recent time periods. Nor is Magellan run any longer by its legendary investment manager Peter Lynch, easily the best portfolio manager of the 80s.

Still, if Magellan fades in the future, Fidelity has plenty of other rising stars it can rely on, ranging from highly specific sector funds to broadly balanced stock, bond and money market funds. Beginning in 1989, Fidelity introduced a line of low cost Spartan funds. Now numbering 34, these funds provide long-term investors with no-load, low-operating-cost investments.

Fidelity is easily the most innovative and aggressive marketer in the mutual fund business. The company distributes pure no-load funds and low loads directly to investors. In addition, through its Fidelity Advisor subsidiary, the firm sells funds with full loads through brokers. Fidelity sells funds to institutions, and also owns a major discount brokerage company (with another 3.5 million customer accounts). Among other things, the brokerage house trades more than two thousand load and no-load funds from over 175 fund families. It is the leader in the 401(k) retirement plan services with 2.8 million participants. Fidelity has a publishing division that has co-published two winning investment books by Peter Lynch, and now publishes a monthly magazine about personal finance called *Worth*. In 1995 it launched an Investment Information Center on the Internet.

Fidelity's customer service is unparalleled in the financial services industry—or, for that matter, in just about any industry. The firm pioneered 24-hour phone service to its retail customers, and its 14,600 employees now operate from operations centers located in its Boston headquarters, Covington, KY, Cincinnati, Dallas and Salt Lake City. In order to serve shareholders directly, Fidelity has set up 79 Investor Centers around the country. The company has telecommunication services for the hearing impaired and offers a CD shopping service. The firm has a directed dividends program which allows shareholders to automatically reinvest dividends or capital gains from one fund into another. It offers consolidated statements covering both its funds and brokerage accounts.

Behind the aggressive marketing is a highly individualized group of fund managers backed by a large array of analysts and traders. By industry standards they are on the young side. Tellingly, their performance often exceeds the market averages in both up and down markets.

Founders

The Founders group of funds, based in Denver, traces its origins to the Founder Mutual Fund, formed in 1938. By tradition, Founders is growth oriented, with eight of its eleven funds seeking various forms of conservative and speculative growth; Founders offers only two fixed-income funds and one money market fund.

The family, which is the 36th largest no-load company, prefers an approach in which it first selects promising stocks, then looks at the overall state of the stock market. Founders does pay attention to the status of a stock's industry group, however, and several industries show up frequently in Founders portfolios. The group has moved away from its team approach to portfolio management; the lead manager is now more important.

Founders has a loyal following in its hometown area, but in recent years its top performing funds have enabled the company to gain more national recognition. At Founders, you can still call to make a purchase and then send in your money later. If Founders customers can't get the answers they need from service representatives, it's possible for them to have their calls bucked to higher-ranking officials—or even to portfolio managers.

Gabelli

Gabelli Funds was formed in 1986 by Mario Gabelli, capitalizing on his superb record as a private-account money manager. The group, which is located in a New York City suburb, now has 15 funds with about $4 billion in assets, ranking it 37th. Gamco, the parent company, manages over $8 billion in all.

Mario Gabelli's basic approach is to buy companies at a discount to private market value—what the operations would fetch based on their assets, cash flow or earnings. The funds emphasize the different aspects of this approach to varying degrees.

Gabelli has long specialized in certain market sectors, notably telecommunications, media and industrial equipment. He sometimes identifies key trends within those areas, then uncovers the companies most likely to benefit. His firm has broadened its research in these niches to a global perspective.

This equities-oriented fund family manages both no-load and load funds. Eight of the funds are pure no loads, four are load funds and two are closed-ends. Gabelli has a habit of switching funds back and fourth between load and no-load. At press time in 1995 two no-loads were scheduled to add loads in July 1995, and Gabelli had just converted its open-end Convertible Fund to a closed-end.

Although Mario Gabelli increasingly has delegated the research to his analysts, the funds still rely heavily on his investment decisions. The firm says it is working to attract new portfolio management talent, but it has had mixed success, although star portfolio manager, Elizabeth Bramwell, who departed in 1994, has been replaced.

Additionally, In late 1994, Gabelli entered into a joint venture with the Westwood funds, a four fund group that uses a top-down investing approach. Gabelli will do the marketing.

Harbor

Twenty-second ranked Harbor Capital Advisors was formed in 1983 to manage equities for the Owens-Illinois pension fund. Harbor's eight no-load funds are managed by outside advisers who also run separate accounts for the pension fund.

The Harbor funds, based in Toledo, are designed to provide different, non-overlapping risk and return characteristics, with something for everybody—conservative to aggressive, equities to bonds, from investments in the U.S. to those abroad.

The money managers are basically left alone. However, the group insists that managers must "add value"—in other words, beat appropriate market benchmarks with reasonable consistency. If they don't, they will be replaced. Among Harbor's tenets of value-added management, the funds hold a relatively limited number of securities and tend to stay fully invested.

Several Harbor funds have excellent records. Among its outside managers are William Gross, the best-known and one of the most successful fixed-income managers in the U.S., who manages the Harbor Bond Fund, and Hakan Castegren, who runs the international stock fund (now closed to new investors).

Minneapolis-based Investment Advisers, Inc., known until 1987 as
North Star, was founded in 1947 and originally served Midwestern
clients. Its flagship fund, IAI Regional, still invests at least 80% of
assets in Midwestern companies.

IAI

Forty-second ranked, IAI has $14 billion under management,
including $1.6 billion in 15 no-load funds (including an institutional
bond fund). Now a subsidiary of Hill Samuel Group in London, IAI
has developed alliances with major investment firms in key international markets, primarily Asia and western Europe.

IAI's equity funds generally are oriented towards earnings growth,
emphasizing a bottom-up stock-selection approach. The bond funds
invest top-down. Based on analysis of the economy, credit cycle and
Federal Reserve policy, managers make judgments on interest-rate
trends, bond sector and duration.

The firm says it prefers a disciplined team management approach
to a "star system.," With the merger with Hill Samuel accomplished,
IAI has several new funds under consideration, the first of which was
launched in early 1995, the IAI Developing Countries Fund

Formerly, the Financial Programs Funds, this Denver-based group
changed its name to Invesco Funds Group in 1991 in order to establish a uniform global identity with its parent company, the British
based INVESCO MIM PLC. Twelfth-ranked, the group now offers 32
no-load funds. Invesco was once pure no-load, but 14 of its funds now
carry 12b-1 fees. Invesco manages approximately $10 billion. For
years, you could purchase an Invesco fund with a $250 minimum
investment. But in 1993, that was raised to $1,000.

Invesco

Invesco follows a rigid set of investment criteria in managing its
funds. An economist first determines the overall economic climate,
then chooses the industries and industry sectors that are most likely
to benefit from that scenario. Accordingly, the family's portfolio
managers then determine the best stocks within the sectors chosen by
the economist.

Invesco's top-down approach reaches to its array of mutual funds
as well as its fund management. The group has the second-largest collection of sector funds in the mutual fund industry, and the only ones
that are pure no-loads. It has the only no-load environmental sector
fund. For investors who aren't hardy enough to withstand the risks of

volatile sector investing, Invesco also offers diversified equity, international, bond and money market funds.

Invesco has two investor walk-in service centers, both in the Denver area.

In 1994 Invesco ignited an industry-wide controversy by very publicly firing its star portfolio manager, John Kaweske, of Invesco Industrial Income and Health, for certain conflicts of interest in choosing some stocks for his fund portfolio. In the wake of Kaweske's dismissal, regulatory authorities took renewed interest in the internal workings of mutual fund management. In the short-run, at least, Kaweske's departure may have hurt the performance of his fund, not to mention throwing a scare into the entire fund industry.

Janus

Still another Denver-based no-load family is powerhouse Janus Capital Corporation, the eighth-largest company. It was founded in 1969 by Thomas Bailey, who remains its head. The firm now serves as investment advisor to 30 mutual funds. Total assets under management: $24 billion.

Bailey oversees Janus's general investment philosophy and strategy—independent fundamental analysis, a bottom's up approach, and an aversion to risk. But the company has added portfolio managers and analysts to accommodate its resounding growth. Janus looks for companies that are undergoing positive changes not yet recognized by Wall Street.

Unlike most other fund groups, Janus' managers don't feel the need to be fully invested at all times. When they buy, they buy aggressively. If they don't see values, though, they are content to hold cash. This frequently results in the anomaly of fairly volatile performance despite high cash positions, since the stocks they hold move. With the company's propensity to maintain significant cash positions in its funds, Janus sometimes lags at the beginning of a new bull market. Over the long run, however, Janus funds have turned in very solid performances.

The family has been trendy with investors the past few years. So popular, in fact, that Janus felt impelled to close two of its best funds, Venture and Twenty, to new shareholders.

In 1993, Janus made a number of changes and additions in its assignment of portfolio managers to better cope with the group's rapid growth. These changes have enabled some of its newer funds, Mercury in particular, to turn in excellent performances.

While Janus is known as an equity specialist, it also manages four fixed-income funds and three money funds. In addition to its own funds, Janus also manages Idex, a load fund group, as well as some insurance annuity funds.

Janus is now 81% owned by Kansas City Southern Industries, which also owns 80% of the Berger Funds. KC Southern is in the transportation and financial services businesses.

Lexington

One of the oldest families in the no-load universe, Lexington was founded in 1938 as Templeton, Dobrow & Vance Management. The renowned Sir John Templeton was the company's initial leader. In the late 60s, after Templeton moved to the Bahamas, some of the funds doing business under the Lexington name split off and formed their own group.

The fund family considers itself value oriented. In fact, Lexington is a highly eclectic group of seven no-load equity funds with an emphasis on global investing and gold. In addition, Lexington has two money market funds and three bond funds. Including both individual and institutional clients, the firm now manages more than $3.8 billion, mostly in private accounts.

The Lexington funds tend to turn in middling performances. Over the last five years their best fund in terms of rank in its category has been the World Emerging Markets, a solid long-term winner, which now has assets of $289 million. Lexington, also has two load funds which came to it by acquisition in 1991 after problems with its previous management. One of these funds, Lexington Strategic Investments, a precious metals fund, was number one among all funds in 1993, up almost 270%!

Lexington has a 24-hour automated telephone service that shareholders with touchtone phones can use to obtain comprehensive account information, duplicate account statements and automated exchanges. Lexington, a wholly-owned subsidiary of Piedmont Management Co., a publicly-traded diversified financial services company, is located in Saddle Brook, New Jersey.

Loomis, Sayles

Loomis, Sayles & Company is one of the oldest investment management firms in the country, having offered investment management services since 1926. Its first mutual fund—Loomis, Sayles Mutual—was introduced in 1929. This fund and its sister, Loomis, Sayles

Capital Development, was spun off into a separate company (CGM) in 1990 because the funds' manager, Ken Heebner, a legend in the industry, wanted to have a greater equity stake in the funds.

In 1992, Loomis, Sayles launched a new group of nine no-load funds without Heebner. The new fund group now manages assets that total about $370 million, of which $76 million belongs to the Loomis, Sayles pension plan for the benefit of its 319 employees. The mutual funds comprise a tiny fraction of the overall $35 billion that the parent company manages, mostly for defined benefit pension plans.

Loomis, Sayles' staff numbers 71 professional investment counselors and 30 researchers. The firm is decentralized, with its headquarters in Boston, but offices in ten other cities: New York, Washington, Chicago, Detroit, San Francisco, Sonoma, CA, Minneapolis, Milwaukee, Pasadena and Palm Beach.

Montgomery

By contrast to mutual fund groups that date back to the 1920s, Montgomery Asset Management is one of the new kids on the block, having been formed in 1990. An independent affiliate of San Francisco-based Montgomery Securities, the firm began by building a group of funds for specific market niches. Its original approach was to develop investment strategies for areas of the markets where investors were underserved, then recruit proven managers who could be expected to significantly outperform market averages. In return, the managers receive considerable freedom and were offered an equity interest in the firm. However, as the group has grown, its newer funds, such as Growth and Equity Income, have been mainstream, garden variety funds.

Ranking 33rd among no-load families, Montgomery has more than $3.8 billion under management. Of that, $2.2 billion is in its funds. According to Lipper Analytical, a statistical firm that serves the mutual fund industry, the Montgomery funds reached $1 billion under management faster than any other fund family in history.

All of Montgomery's 13 funds are no loads: The group has five U.S. and four international equity funds, two bond and two money market funds.

Montgomery's oldest fund, Small Cap, has an excellent record, but it is closed to new investors. The Emerging Markets Fund was the first no-load fund of its type. And Montgomery Growth Fund, managed by Roger Honour, was one of the stars of 1994. In January 1995, it launched the Micro-Cap Fund, for stocks too small to be included in Growth. The fund was started with the announced intention of closing when it reaches $60 million in assets. With Honour at the helm, it reached that target in less than a month and closed, at least temporarily.

Neuberger-Berman

One of the most interesting no-load families, 17th ranked Neuberger-Berman attempts to find out-of-favor companies with low price-to-earnings ratios, good balance sheets, and understated assets—securities that have value now, not ones that may develop value in the future. In 1993, its Guardian fund was named as Consumer Reports' mutual fund of the year.

Believing investors should own equity funds for growth and fixed-income funds for capital preservation, Neuberger-Berman emphasizes growth equity funds, fixed income funds that buy securities with short maturities, and money funds. In 1988 Neuberger-Berman disposed of its only long-term bond fund, believing that bonds are riskier than investors believe—a prescient view considering the bond market debacle of 1994.

Neuberger-Berman is unusual in that the company has added funds by acquisition as well as by launching its own. It took over both its Partners and Manhattan funds from other advisers—and greatly improved them. The group's latest additions: a socially responsive fund and an international fund.

Long located in New York City, Neuberger-Berman now has Chicago, San Francisco and Atlanta offices. It manages approximately $7 billion in 15 mutual funds, and $29 billion overall. Neuberger-Berman is still headed by its founder, nonagenarian art patron Roy Neuberger.

Nicholas

The Milwaukee-based Nicholas Company, which got its start with the Nicholas-Strong Fund in 1968, hit the big time in 1971 when the fund was No. 1 in mutual fund performance. But then the devastating 1973-1974 bear market raged, and Albert Nicholas and Richard Strong parted ways. Strong went on to form his own fund group, described below.

Today, the six Nicholas funds are for the patient, long-term investor. The fund's primary manager is still Ab Nicholas, a former All-American basketball player at the University of Wisconsin. But his son, Dave, has now taken over two of the funds, Nicholas II and Limited Edition, which reopened in 1994 after being closed for several years.

Nicholas is a value-oriented stock-picker who no longer aims for dizzying heights. Today he seeks low-priced, unrecognized companies with solid balance sheets and steady earnings. These criteria usually lead to smaller companies, but larger ones are not ruled out. Turnover in the portfolios is moderate.

This approach seldom launches a fund's NAV into the upper stratosphere. And in the speculative stages of a bull market, Nicholas funds aren't apt to set the world on fire. But over the long term, the funds generally offer outstanding growth and income.

The Nicholas funds do not attempt to forecast short-term swings in the market; instead their goal is to preserve gains and minimize losses through long-term fundamental investing. Sell disciplines are based primarily on fundamental and valuation considerations. The group, the 23rd largest, now has about $4.5 billion under management.

T. Rowe Price

The T. Rowe Price funds, fourth largest of all no-load groups, are the legacy of Thomas Rowe Price, the group's founder, and one of Wall Street's legends. If there were a no-load Hall of Fame, he would be a charter member! Price developed a theory of growth stock investing that hinged on the consistency of a company's earnings, rather than on the phases of the business cycle. His first fund, the T. Rowe Price Growth Stock Fund, was organized in 1950.

Mr. Price retired in 1971. For a number of years after that, the family's funds turned in mediocre performances. However, a turnaround has occurred in recent years. Several of the Price funds have been industry pacesetters.

Price was also an early believer in small company investing. The Price New Horizons Fund is one of the oldest and largest small company funds.

The T. Rowe Price group still accents its growth stock orientation. But with 63 funds, it has become far larger and more diversified than Price probably could have imagined. For example, T. Rowe Price now offers one of the largest selections of fixed-income funds in the mutual fund industry including funds for high-net-worth investors. The company has an innovative international division that manages more than $19 billion in ten mutual funds and private accounts. It launched the first no-load international bond fund and the first no-load international small cap fund. In the past few years, Price has diversified further, offering commission-free real estate limited partnerships and discount brokerage services.

T. Rowe Price is a leader in the growing 401(k) market which has made defined contribution plans so popular. It believes that investing for retirement is the core strategy that ties its products together. In that regard, Price offers a valuable retirement planning guide free, and retirement planning software for a small fee.

With $57 billion in assets under management overall, Price is one of the real forces in the no-load business. The company is headquartered in Baltimore, and also has offices in Los Angeles and Tampa, and an investor center in Washington, D.C.

Rushmore

The Rushmore funds started in 1974 with the formation of the Fund For Government Investors, one of the nation's first government-only money market funds. Rushmore added three other "Funds For" funds before inaugurating the Rushmore label in 1985. The company is located in Bethesda, Maryland, but its leaders chose the name of their firm as a tribute to the presidents on Mount Rushmore (in South Dakota).

In 1992, Rushmore launched a new group of equity funds, the Cappiello-Rushmore Funds. Those funds are managed by Frank Cappiello, the well-known panelist and substitute host on Public Television's *Wall Street Week*. The group now has four funds.

Several of Rushmore's offerings were index funds, originally designed to appeal to market timers. However, frequent buying and selling made tracking the indexes difficult. So Rushmore has merged three of these funds into the Capiello-Rushmore group. One index fund remains; it specializes in natural gas stocks. The Rushmore funds are pure no-loads, with no 12b-1 fees. Switching is free and three money funds provide checkwriting with a $250 minimum which is usually not enforced.

In 1993, the Rushmore Nova Fund, a quasi-index fund appealing to timers, was spun off by a Rushmore executive. It became the Rydex Nova Fund, and no longer has any association with Rushmore.

Unlike some other small operations, Rushmore conducts its shareholder service and transfer agent operations in-house. Rushmore-Capiello has 12 funds with about $1 billion under management.

SAFECO

SAFECO has a conservative reputation, as befits a group of funds whose parent company is a property and casualty insurer. SAFECO has had generations of experience, having managed mutual funds since 1933. A medium-sized group with 15 funds and $16 billion under management, SAFECO ranks 39th among no-load groups.

It pretty well covers the bases. Shareholders can choose from among all the important equity and fixed-income categories. While Seattle-based SAFECO is a national fund family, it caters to its regional constituency by investing in companies located in the Pacific Northwest. About one-third of the firm's shareholders are on the West Coast.

In 1994, SAFECO launched a load fund group, SAFECO Advisors, consisting of eight funds, many of them clones of their no-loads.

SAFECO prides itself on its analysis and its customer service. Its investment research is done entirely in-house, generally using a value oriented, bottoms-up approach. And, unlike many other small and medium-sized groups, SAFECO is its own transfer agent, which means that the fund can often process its customers' account transactions faster—and more accurately—than other funds can. This is one of the benefits of being owned by a large insurance company. The $16 billion of assets under SAFECO's management is split 90%/10% between its parent company and the funds.

Scudder, Stevens & Clark

Another of the mutual fund industry's giants, Scudder offers 94 funds or portfolios and has over 2 million shareholder accounts. Overall, Scudder has more than $90 billion under management; With $30 million in no-load funds, it is the fifth largest no-load fund group, behind Fidelity, Vanguard, Dreyfus, and Price. Scudder's holdings include funds distributed directly to the public, as well as those it manages for other distributors. A notable example: the eight funds it manages for the giant American Association of Retired People (AARP). Scudder also oversees nine closed-ends (eight of them international) and markets a low-cost variable annuity product.

Having been in the investment counseling business since 1919, Scudder has considerably more experience in fund management than most of its competitors. Its Income fund is the oldest no-load (founded in 1928). The group has a strong international presence. A popular misconception among investors has it that Sir John Templeton founded the concept of international investing with the funds that bear his name. Actually, Scudder's International fund is the oldest in that specialty, having been around since 1953.

While Scudder manages such a range of funds that the family defies easy classification, most of its equity funds tend to be conservative. Income is a secondary consideration.

However, it could be argued that bonds are Scudder's real specialty. The group offers a huge array of fixed-income funds, ranging from single state municipals to U.S. government zero-coupon bond funds. Fixed income now accounts for two-thirds of the assets that Scudder has under management.

Headquartered in New York, Scudder has nine walk-in mutual fund centers nationwide. The other facilities are in Boca Raton, Boston, Chicago, Cincinnati, Los Angeles, Portland, San Diego, San Francisco, and Scottsdale.

Stein, Roe & Farnham

Stein, Roe & Farnham, an investment company that was founded during the depths of the Depression in 1932 to manage private client accounts, is now a major no-load fund group, especially on its home turf in the Midwest.

Located in Chicago, nineteenth ranked SteinRoe has 18 funds and manages about $23 billion in assets. At the end of 1994, $4.5 billion of it was in SteinRoe mutual funds. A subsidiary of Liberty Financial, which itself is a subsidiary of Liberty Mutual Insurance Co., SteinRoe offered its first mutual fund in 1949. The group prides itself on its research, the bulk of which is produced in-house.

In 1994, the group launched the SteinRoe Young Investor Fund, which seeks long-term capital appreciation by investing in companies such as Walt Disney, McDonalds, and Toys 'R Us that affect the lives of children and teenagers. SteinRoe views the fund as an educational investment that will enable children to learn basic investment and economic principles. Minor investors get an attractive wall poster, a certificate of enrollment as a young investor, and a welcome kit.

The SteinRoe family is pure no-load: no front-end, back-end or 12b-1 fees. While the company manages a wide range of funds, its strengths seem to lie at opposite ends of the mutual fund spectrum. SteinRoe offers a wide selection of growth funds—and at the other extreme, an array of conservative fixed-income funds, taxable, tax-free and money market, but it has only one conservative equity fund.

Strong

Dick Strong started his own investment management firm to handle private accounts in 1974, after he and Albert Nicholas had parted company. In 1976 he teamed up with Bill Corneliuson, and their new firm offered its first mutual funds in 1981.

Strong has generally followed a flexible investment approach, seeking a combination of income and capital gains for the highest total return. To that end, the funds are structured to give a great deal of leeway to the portfolio managers. They are allowed to move large amounts of a fund's portfolio into cash or bonds as conditions warrant, using asset allocation strategies. In early years, the firm occasionally went fully into cash. But as Strong has matured, market timing has given way to a more temperate investment approach.

Strong portfolio managers are constantly on the road sizing up companies whose stocks they own or are considering buying. This has exacted its toll. In 1992, co-founder William Corneliuson retired from active management of the group. Although only 49, he had had enough of the 80-hour work weeks and constant traveling. His departure has not hurt the firm, since Strong Capital Management now has 39 investment professionals, including a number of talented portfolio managers who were hired from the outside to rejuvenate the company after it had a couple of bad years in the early 90s.

As of year-end 1994, the firm managed about $11 billion of assets, of which $9 billion is in the Strong family of 24 no-load funds (including two that are vehicles for variable annuities). It ranks fifteenth among no-load groups. For a number of years, the group experimented with 1% and 2% loads on its equity funds. In 1992 all sales charges were dropped, and the family regained its status as a pure no-load fund manager.

Management of the fund group communicates well with its shareholders. The company sends out detailed information about its current outlook for the fund, its investments and its philosophy. Rare for a medium-sized firm, Strong's switchboard is open 24 hours a day.

Twentieth Century

The sixth largest no-load fund group, Kansas City-based Twentieth Century began life in 1958 with two funds, Twentieth Century Growth and Twentieth Century Select. Both of them are among the top six performing funds for the 20-year extended bull market period that began in 1975. Twentieth Century was well poised for that long bull market. Though it began life as a load fund group, in 1974

Twentieth Century became an early convert to no-load investing.

Its investment motto: money follows earnings. In other words, stocks with consistently improving earnings tend to continue upwards in price. In essence, the group invests only in companies with at least a three-year history of accelerating earnings. James Stowers, Twentieth Century's chairman, describes stocks as "chicken eggs" or "tennis balls." Chicken eggs, he explains, "don't bounce back after a bear market, tennis balls do." The latter are the stocks of companies with accelerating earnings that he buys.

Unlike other mutual fund groups that rely on individual managers, Twentieth Century runs its portfolios with three-manager teams who make the investment decisions for the equity funds. These individual managers have the authority to make buy and sell decisions as the need arises. A computerized database of over 13,000 companies helps to screen investment choices.

Over the long run, the Twentieth Century growth funds have been top performers. But they are well known for their volatility. Twentieth Century funds remain fully invested at all times, which makes them naturals for market timers. To discourage timers, the company limits switches to four per year. The funds' volatility as well as their minuscule initial and subsequent investment minimums make Twentieth Century funds a natural for dollar-cost averagers—especially young people and/or those who are planning for college bills some years down the road.

Twentieth Century has an innovative college investment program, utilizing the group's Select and Cash Reserve funds. The program initially puts investments intended for college in Select, a growth stock fund. This serves to achieve a build up of the portfolio during the early years. Then, four to six years before a child is going to need the money for college tuition, Twentieth Century gradually moves the investment into Cash Reserves, where it is sheltered from market volatility. If you choose to rebalance from Select to Cash Reserves during a four-year period, Twentieth Century will automatically move 25% to cash each year; if you choose the five or six year rebalancing plans, 20% or 17% is shifted over per year.

For years, the fund family offered only domestic growth funds. Now, with Stowers' son president of the company, it has drastically expanded its product line. Its arsenal now contains a broad array of funds, including several conservative equity funds, two international funds, taxable and tax-free bond funds and a money market fund. At year-end 1994, Twentieth Century offered 24 retail funds, managing assets totaling $26 billion.

In February 1995, Twentieth Century acquired the Benham Group, making it the fifth largest no-load fund group. See the Benham listing for further details.

United Services

The first United Services fund was founded in San Antonio in 1969. It was a standard growth fund run by Clark Aylsworth. During the gold boom of the early 70s, however, the fund changed its orientation forever.

One of the best-performing of all gold funds, United Services Gold Shares, which invests in South African gold mining stocks, has three times been best fund of the year. United Services also has two other funds that hold non-South African gold stocks. One of these funds, Prospector, ran into trouble in 1984 because of some improper portfolio transactions in Canadian stocks. Partly as a result of this problem, Clark Aylsworth retired in 1989, and the firm was sold to the Frank E. Holmes organization. Holmes is a Canadian investment dealer who was instrumental in bringing the Prospector's troubles to light.

United Services had begun a program of diversification several years earlier, and Holmes is continuing it. He wanted a complete range of funds for a wider array of investors. So Holmes added seven new funds, reducing gold-oriented investments from 51% to 18% of total assets by year-end 1992. However, because of the popularity of their gold funds, their assets have climbed; they now account for one-third of United Services assets under management. The group now offers fourteen funds. Eight of them are actively managed equity funds, four bond funds, and two government money market funds that have been yield leaders. Noteworthy: a rarely found no-minimum check writing privilege on the U.S. Treasury Securities money fund.

In 1994, the group entered into a joint venture with Art Bonnel, formerly a portfolio manager at the MIM group. The new United Services Bonnel group now manages one fund, but plans to add more.

The gold fund that had regulatory problems reopened in 1990 with a new name and objective. It is now the U.S. Global Resources Fund, with gold comprising only about 11% of its assets.

United Services has some highly specialized—not to say exotic— funds. For example, the China Region Opportunity Fund invests predominately in China. (Most other China funds concentrate in Hong Kong, and most of the others are closed-end funds.)

United Services used to encourage switching. But lately the company has instituted a modest fee for buying and selling within 14 days.

Also located in San Antonio, the USAA funds are a subsidiary of USAA, one of the largest low-cost, direct marketing insurance companies in the country. The group offers 29 no-load funds with a wide array of objectives including three that invest overseas. With over $14 billion in the funds, it ranks ninth among all no-load fund groups.

USAA

USAA's managers attempt to concentrate on companies that are not receiving heavy attention from the financial community. They do their research in-house, and don't rely on outside recommendations. With a wide variety of both equity and fixed-income funds, USAA is suitable for all phases of the business/economic cycle. USAA also offers a discount brokerage service.

The USAA Balanced Fund is unusual in that it is one of the few balanced funds that utilizes tax-free securities for the fixed-income portion of its portfolio.

If any group of funds is associated with value-oriented investing, it is Value Line. The funds' portfolio managers use the New York company's famous stock-ranking system as one of their primary tools in making their selections. The system is based partly on fundamental analysis, such as a company's balance sheet basics, and partly on more technical trend-following techniques, such as momentum and relative strength. The Value Line system tracks about 1,700 stocks.

Value Line

Value Line's approach has been successful: the Value Line stock selection system is one of the most popular in the country. And the company's mutual fund arm has grown from one equity fund in 1949 to 15 today, spanning the gamut from aggressive growth to bond to money market. That includes two that are available only through variable annuity contracts.

In terms of its size, Value Line's $2.8 billion under management ranks the firm 35th among no-load groups.

While the Value Line equity funds follow the Value Line system to greater or lesser extents, they haven't been world beaters in recent years. Perhaps it's easier to publish recommendations than to implement them. Note also, the Value Line system does not extend to fixed-income funds; those are managed conventionally.

Value Line's patrician founder, Arnold Bernhard, has passed away. But his daughter, Jean Bernhard Buttner, now Chairman and CEO, continues the company's traditional policies.

Vanguard

One of the premiere mutual fund companies, the giant Vanguard group located in Valley Forge, Pennsylvania outside of Philadelphia, is the second largest no-load family. Although it is far smaller than Fidelity—less than half the size, in fact—Vanguard makes a valiant number two.

The firm manages 90 investment portfolios with $138 billion in assets. It has 5 million shareholder accounts. Unique in the mutual fund industry, Vanguard's management company is responsible for administration, marketing and legal support. Consequently, the company is much more aggressive than the average mutual fund group in cutting management costs. Distribution expenses are furnished at cost to the funds, which typically are run by outside managers (though some are managed in-house).

More expense minded than performance oriented, Vanguard's chairman John Bogle decided in 1977 that all sales charges should be dropped. Moreover, Vanguard funds boast exceptionally low expense ratios, making them ideal for long-term investors, particularly those interested in fixed-income investments. Among their lowest cost funds are their four Admiral funds, which have high $50,000 minimum investments.

Vanguard prefers more conservative funds oriented toward long-term growth. The $11 billion Windsor Fund—closed to new investors since 1989 is a prime example. It produces above average long-term results. In addition, the group has several asset allocation funds. Vanguard has 25 general bond funds (plus six other single state bond funds). Because of their low cost structure, they frequently are exceptional values. However, Vanguard tends to offer fewer aggressive funds, and those few have not been winners in recent years.

The family has been in the forefront with low-cost index funds, now offering 14 of them. These funds track both stock and bond indexes. In addition, there's a quasi-index fund, the Quantitative

Fund, which attempts to improve on the S&P 500. So, while you don't get exotic funds from Vanguard, it's most unlikely you'll get any nasty surprises in performance, either: the company aims for predictable long-term performance rather than short-term gains.

Vanguard also offers a discount brokerage service, real estate limited partnerships, and a low-cost variable annuity program with seven portfolios, three of them indexed.

And if you have plenty of money, Vanguard has a program for you. High-net-worth shareholders who have $500,000 or more invested with the Vanguard can qualify for a service called the Flagship Financial Service. It provides shareholders with a personal representative and free literature. In 1994, it introduced an informational service in conjunction with America Online.

Warburg Pincus

Started in 1985, Warburg Pincus Funds is the no-load fund family of a large investment management firm called Warburg, Pincus Counsellors. The firm is a subsidiary of E.M. Warburg, Pincus & Co., which was established in 1965 Lionel Pincus and Eric Warburg, a descendant of the great German-American banking family. Warburg Pincus succeeds E. M. Warburg, a merchant bank founded in the 30s.

Headquartered in New York City, Counsellors manages more than $9 billion, $4.2 billion of it in 15 no-load funds.

Warburg Pincus managers follow a "bottom-up" investment approach, taking a business owner's perspective and evaluation process. The company's portfolio managers favor internal research and on-site company visits, aiming to identify companies with strong management, innovative products and above-average earnings-growth potential.

The group's best fund, Growth & Income, is run by Anthony Orphanos in a highly eclectic fashion. Quite unlike the traditional growth and income fund, this one has, from time to time, had huge weightings in gold and technology stocks. Other strengths of the group include its international and emerging-growth funds.

All of Warburg's money managers have been with their funds since inception and have an equity position in the firm. Some of the funds previously existed in partnership form.

Winning mutual fund strategies

As each year goes by, we read that investors are living in uncertain times. That's certainly true this year—but then, when wasn't it? Just about every year we can remember seemed dicey at the time. In fact, those rare years when the investment climate seemed the most favorable often turned out to be the most perilous. Thus, investment strategies are simply a way to enable you to deal with "uncertain times."

The simplest one—buying and holding—actually works quite well. If you have a sufficiently long time horizon before you need your investment dollars, you can wait out the turbulent times.

A second strategy for coping with the inevitable peaks and valleys is market timing, the art of getting in at the bottom when prices are low, and getting out at the top, when they are high. In theory, it holds far greater potential than the buy/hold approach. That's the theory. The practice is another story. Market timing is exceedingly difficult to implement successfully.

Another approach is a strategy that we call the Flexible Funding Program. It is a way of switching between aggressive and conservative funds throughout the market cycle, staying largely or even fully invested all the while. This approach combines some of the best features of both buy-and-hold and market timing.

A look at stock market history provides a powerful argument in favor of staying largely invested at all times. Since 1975, when the current super bull market began, investors holding funds long-term have undoubtedly done better than market timers who flitted in and out of equities. Table 55 shows how investments in some top growth funds and those in the average fund have done over the past 20 years.

The merits of long-term investing

Table 55

Long-term winners

January 1975 - December 1994

Fund	What $1,000 grew to	Annualized rate %
Fidelity Magellan	$97,151	25.7
Twentieth Century Growth	55,551	22.3
Royce Penn Mutual	48,915	21.5
Sequoia	45,703	21.1
Lindner	45,480	21.0
Twentieth Cent Select	42,519	20.6
CGM Capital Development	39,065	20.1
Value Line Lev Growth	38,565	20.0
Acorn	38,246	20.0
Mutual Shares	37,180	19.8
SteinRoe Special	34,062	19.3
Nicholas	31,912	18.9
Fidelity Equity Income	28,560	18.3
Vanguard Windsor	28,162	18.2
Scudder Development	27,560	18.0
SAFECO Growth	25,765	17.6
Columbia Growth	24,218	17.3
Janus	23,993	17.2
SAFECO Equity	22,522	16.9
WPG Tudor	22,430	16.8
Average diversified	20,407	15.4

A $1,000 investment made in a top performing fund, such as Twentieth Century Growth, at the beginning of 1975 would have grown to $55,551 by December 1994. That's an annual compounded growth rate of 22.2%. The twentieth fund on the list, WPG Tudor, increased over 22 times for an average growth of 16.8% per year. That's remarkable considering that even though it was a strong up period, several severe corrections daunted investors. Remember the 1,000 point decline in the Dow from August to December 1987?

Of course, you would have been hard pressed to know back in 1975 which funds would make the Top 20. You would certainly have had an easier time picking an average fund. Any investor who had done that would have witnessed a breathtaking twenty-fold rise in his investment, which works out to a satisfying 15.4% per year. (And, of course, today an index fund investment can guarantee you an average performance.)

These figures are impressive. But let me personalize them with an anecdote. On Tuesday, October 20, 1987—a panic day for many because the results of the Black Monday meltdown appeared in that day's paper—an elderly man called the Invesco Funds to find out what his investment in the Invesco Industrial Income Fund was worth.

"I've invested $10,000; how much have I lost?" he asked, his voice quavering.

The account service rep at Invesco called up the account on his computer and noted that the $10,000 investment had, in fact, been made in the early 1970s. "Your fund shares are now worth $164,000," he told the investor.

There was silence on the other end of the phone. The representative said he was sorry; he knew that the shares had been worth much more only a few weeks before. Still silence. "Is there anything else I can do for you?" Another pause. "No." As the representative was hanging up, he heard, faintly, "Yippee!"

Time is on your side

Of course, you might well argue that we picked a very favorable starting point to show this terrific long-term performance. And it's true that the period began one of the greatest bull markets of the twentieth century. But you should realize that buying and holding long-term is a reasonable strategy for limiting risk and obtaining the rewards accruing to equity investing.

First of all, realize that it's desirable to take some equity risk. On average, equities gain two-to-three times more than fixed-income investments over the long haul.

Chart 56 shows that the S&P 500 has gained in 39 of the last 50 years, or somewhat more than three-quarters of the time. Thus, a buy/hold policy suggests that you will be okay in three out of four years, but will take your lumps the fourth year. This doesn't mean the losing and gaining years rotate regularly.

Chart 56

Stock market returns, 1945-1994

Summary: Gain years: 39 (78%)   Loss years: 11 (22%)

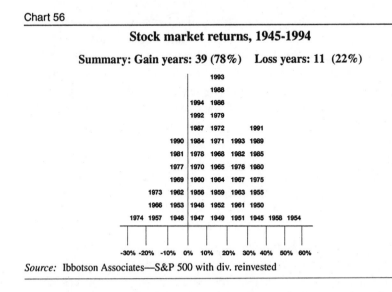

Source: Ibbotson Associates—S&P 500 with div. reinvested

While losses occur in nearly one-quarter of all years, lengthening your holding period will dramatically diminish your chances of losing. If you hold a diversified portfolio of common stocks for five years, you have about a 96% chance of making a profit. If you hold for ten years, you are virtually guaranteed a profit.

Put another way, the last time stocks lost during a ten-year period, was the decade from 1929 to 1938. Never since has a ten-year period

Table 57

How time reduces risk

Total return on stocks, 50 years ending 1994
According to length of holding period

Holding period	# Gain years	# Loss years	% Gain years
1 Year	39	11	78%
Rolling 2 Years	44	5	90%
Rolling 5 Years	44	2	96%
Rolling 10 Years	41	0	100%

Source: Ibbotson, Roger G. and Rex A. Sinquefield.
Based on S&P 500 with distributions reinvested

seen an overall loss. Longer periods are even safer. Since this data series began in 1926, there is no 15-year period in which an investment would have declined.

Your portfolio can go down substantially in any one year. But once you hold for even five years, it's almost impossible to lose much. The largest annualized loss over any five-year period since 1938: -2.3%.

Because time is on your side, long-term investment strategies are the easist way to maximize your wealth. Too often young people in their twenties or even in their thirties see no hurry about starting an investment program. These people are throwing away one of the golden opportunities of their lives. Starting an investment program, particularly a tax-sheltered IRA, even a few years earlier can make a remarkable difference.

We all know the story of the tortoise and the hare. The slow, steady pace of the tortoise enables him to beat the far faster hare. Does it work that way in retirement planning?

How about if we modernize the fable. In our version, we have three racers. We'll call the first one the resting hare. That's because this particular player starts an IRA at age 22, as soon as he begins his working life, putting in $2,000 a year for six years and then stopping. By that time, he has a family and needs all his income for current expenses. Thus, at age 28 he stops contributing and never puts another dime into his IRA.

The second racer does exactly the opposite: he parties away his 20s, and gives not a care to his future. By age 28, he has miraculously matured, and opens an IRA that he faithfully contributes $2,000 a year to until he is 65. Because he started late, he has to sprint to catch up. So, we'll call him the sprinting hare. He's the one in the pictogram with his ears laid back.

And then there's the tortoise. He starts early—at age 22—and he keeps making his $2,000 yearly investment the rest of his working life—to age 65.

Assume that all three IRA portfolios grow at the same 12% annual compounded rate of return.

Does the tortoise win? Of course. We wouldn't alter the famous fable. The $2,000 a year invested from age 22 to 65 grows to a fabulous $2,714,460. But more interesting is the fate of the two hares. *Incredibly, at age 65, both have about the same amount of money!* Even though the resting hare invested only $12,000, his nest egg is now worth $1,348,440, while the sprinting hare, who put in $74,000 after a later start, has $1,363,780. Starting early really pays!

We know that the vast majority of you (we're sorry to say) are too old to get optimal results by using this strategy for yourselves—but show this to your children and grandchildren. Make them start saving *now.* You can make their contribution for them for as great an amount as they earn up to $2,000. Starting young is by far the easiest way to build a very comfortable nest egg for old age.

Even if you didn't get out of the chute early, all is not lost. A late start is better than none at all. If the resting hare invested for the five years beginning at age 35 and the sprinting hare for the 20 years beginning at age 40, the results would again be about the same.

Chart 58

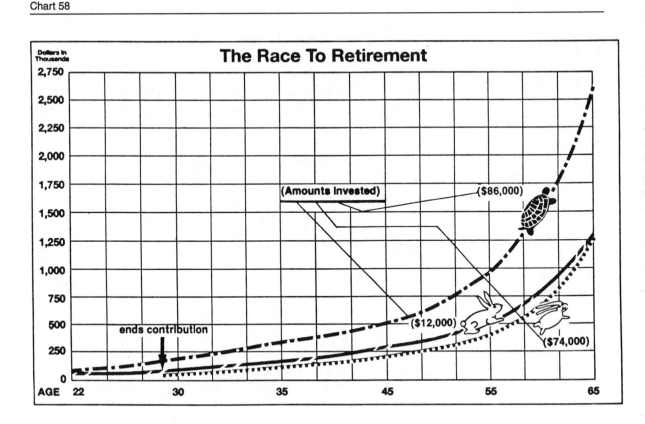

The disadvantages of buy/hold

The principal drawback of a buy/hold strategy is that you need a long time horizon. If you must redeem your money in a few years, then a buy/hold strategy using equities may be too risky for you. Perhaps the safety of a money market fund is preferable.

You also need the psychological stamina to wait out bear markets or even sharp corrections during ongoing bull markets. In the decade of the 80s, on eight occasions mighty Magellan, the best fund in America during the period, dropped anywhere from 10 to 28 percent. After each major decline, some investors got out, and were later sorry that they did.

Thus, the buy/hold strategy is best suited for relatively young investors who have long time horizons and don't need to use their investment dollars to cover ordinary living expenses.

What about market timing?

Consider these facts: Over the past 50 years, a buy-hold strategy would have been profitable 78% of the time. Perhaps market timers can beat this percentage, but they would have to be very, very good. On the other hand, what if a timer makes mistakes? What if the timer is wrong more often than right? Many are. And even timers who have established exceptional records may zig when they should have zagged at any given moment.

Do you want to risk the chance that just at the time when you've entrusted your dollars to the timer, that's the exact moment when his hot hand goes cold? For example, it is doubtful that even 5% of investment advisers moved from fully invested to cash in the days or weeks prior to the October 19, 1987, crash. And bad as that is, being on the sidelines during a strong market advance is even worse. Very few advisors predicted that the stock market would explode on January 17, 1991, the day after the US and its allies went to war against Iraq.

A summary of top market timers invariably produces a wide divergence of opinion. The ten "elves" on PBS's Wall $treet Week voice diametrically different opinions each week. How do you know who is right, and who is wrong? How do you know that the ones who are right aren't just lucky? Worse, when timers do agree, their consensus is usually wrong.

Contrast their generally contradictory market assessments with the pronouncements of experts in other fields. The vast majority of doctors will render a similar diagnosis for a given patient's ailment, for example. We think the divergence of opinions among stock market experts is due to the nature of the markets. Stocks prices always seek a level that balances the bulls and bears.

A few timing mistakes can badly wound your money. For instance, $1,000 invested in stocks over the 40 years ending in 1989 would now be worth $109,000, compared to $7,200 for Treasury bills. However, if you missed the best 34 months of market action during that time, your equity investment would have grown to only $6,900, less than if you'd been in T-bills the entire time! Changes of direction in the market happen so fast that it is harder than ever to be on the right side of moves from the beginning.

And lastly, since market timing means more trips in and out of the market, timing also costs you more in taxes. Unless you are managing money in your IRA or other tax-deferred account, every time you make a sale there is a tax consequence.

Only a handful of funds practice market timing using technical analysis. This year we have identified ten funds. There was an eleventh fund in 1993, the Righttime Growth Fund, but it was merged into Righttime Blue Chip. That there are so few funds is, in itself, is an indictment. If the strategy worked, hundreds of funds would be employing it. Table 59 shows that over the last five years the average market timing fund underperformed the average diversified fund. In 1994, a down year when market timers are supposed to shine, they only equalled the average fund.

Market timing mutual funds

We advocate a moderate approach that's easy to use. We call it the *Flexible Funding Program*. It's an attractive alternative to both the passive strategy of buy/hold and the all-or-nothing approach that most market timers use. It's based on the premise that *you are better off using a theoretically inferior strategy that has a greater chance of success, than a theoretically superior strategy (such as calling market tops and bottoms) that has a far smaller chance of succeeding.*

It is a simple strategy that calls for buying aggressive growth funds when stocks are generally undervalued and the market is rising, then switching to conservative funds when the market reaches overvalua-

Flexible Funding — an effective middle course

Table 59

Total return % of market timing funds
Ranked by 5 year performance

	1994	5 yrs ending 1994 (annualized)
Flex-fund Muirfield	2.7	9.5
Zweig Strategy A	1.1	8.6
Rightime Fund	0.7	8.6
Flex-fund Growth	-0.7	7.5
Rightime Blue Chip	2.3	7.3
Merriman Capital Appreciation	-0.6	6.2
Merriman Growth & Income	-0.2	4.6
Progressive Aggr. Growth	-17.2	0.1
Monitrend Summation	-2.0	-0.2
Zweig Appreciation A	-1.8	
Average market timing fund	-1.5	5.8
Average diversified fund	-1.5	8.6

tion levels. This can be much more profitable than being fully invested at all times in either type of fund. Moreover, when you are largely or fully invested in the market, you have a tremendous advantage because stocks generally rise.

Here's a specific example of fully invested switching using fund performance during 1987, a year with great variation in stock prices. Assume you began the year invested in Fidelity Magellan, an aggressive growth fund. In the middle of the year you became concerned about the high price/earnings and price/dividend ratios and the general market euphoria. So you switched to Puritan, a more defensive fund, at the beginning of July. Bold face in the following table indicates your investment in each half of the year.

Table 60

Switching between speculative and conservative funds

	1987 % Change		
	Jan-June	**July-Dec**	**Jan-Dec**
Fidelity Magellan	**26.1%**	-20.0%	0.9%
Fidelity Puritan	12.0	**-12.4**	-1.9
Switch combination	26.1	-12.4	**10.5**

By switching out of Magellan and into Puritan, you would still have lost 12.4% in the Puritan fund in the second half of the year because of the decline that started in September. However, over the entire year you would have gained 10.5%, giving you better performance than if you had stayed in either fund all year. Even if there had been no decline in the second half of 1987, you would have continued to reap some profits, though not as much as if you had stayed with Magellan. Furthermore, you were also automatically positioned for additional gains in 1988. A market timer who got out in 1987 would still have had to make a correct re-entry decision.

Some investors who correctly exited the market in 1987, never returned in time for the upturn which began in early December 1987. If you had stayed in Fidelity Puritan throughout 1988, you would have gained 18.8%, a far better return than was provided by money funds.

While we describe flexible funding as an alternative to market timing, in another sense it is simply a way of keeping the risk of your fund investments at a level appropriate to current market conditions.

The *Flexible Funding Program,* which can include the use of modest amounts of cash in overvalued markets, is a method that can maximize your profits in the long run while giving you meaningful protection on the down-side.

Advantages of switching while staying fully invested

■ You never leave the stock market, yet you reduce your exposure to risk. This system can sharply tilt the risk/reward ratio in your favor and can work well in the face of considerable uncertainty, since its goals need not be fully attained for it to be profitable.

■ Your temptation to stay with an aggressive growth fund too long is probably less than when the alternative is cash. Few investors sell at the top. However, you can switch to a growth or growth-income fund at any time, knowing you are still in the market and invested wisely.

■ Fully invested switching takes into account the fact that stocks can stay overvalued for years. Stocks were overvalued at the beginning of 1987, but went on to add 800 Dow points before topping out. Many considered stocks overvalued in 1992 and 1993, both up years in the market. You just don't know how overvalued stocks will become or how long stocks will stay overvalued.

■ You eliminate the whipsaw that can occur if you sell and then have to get back into the market at higher prices. Whipsaws bedevil in-and-outers, particularly those making timing decisions based on moving averages.

■ You don't miss the beginning of a new bull market. Traditionally, the biggest money is made in the first few weeks of a strong upturn. For example, when the bear finally returned to his cave in 1975 following the disastrous 1973-4 market rout, 25% of the subsequent bull market gains were made in the first 45 days.

■ In any type of market, some good funds always exist. While 1992 was a lackluster year for equities, the Oakmark Fund gained 48.9%. In 1994, a very trying year, PBHG Emerging Growth Fund was up 23.8%. You need to be in the market to be alert to this kind of opportunity.

■ It's a much more consistent approach.

■ You can use the plan with other strategies, such as dollar-cost-averaging.

In 1991, 1992 and 1993, Flexible Funding worked well for investors who were following the model portfolios in *The No-Load Fund Investor.* The strategy kept investors conservatively invested in equities, notwithstanding the fact that high valuation levels led many other advisors to maintain substantial cash positions, thereby failing to take advantage of three years of profitable opportunities. In 1994, the strategy held losses to under 3%. The *Investor* was one of only two mutual fund newsletters to receive a grade of B or better in both up-and-down markets in the annual *Forbes* newsletter ratings.

Where will the market be in the year 2000?

You still need an opinion on the market in order to implement the Flexible Funding plan. You have to have some sense of when the market is high, when it is low, and where it is going.

Our long-term view is that the rest of the 90s are going to be a period of reasonably good performance for equities. While performance overall in the 90s is not going to be as good as in the 80s, we don't see a repeat of the sawtooth 70s, either, a period when stocks essentially went nowhere. A number of differences between the 70s and the 90s are significant. The declines in the 70s came as a result of the equity overvaluations of the 60s...the rise of OPEC, which extorted billions from the oil-consuming nations...ineffectual presidents—Nixon, because of Watergate; Ford, because he was not elected; then Carter, who initially appointed a particularly weak Federal Reserve chairman, and who failed to correct the twin economic evils of double-digit inflation and high unemployment.

In contrast, the current decade already has in its favor the triumph of capitalism over communism...a peace dividend that will boost economic efficiency...reduced government spending and a vigorous national debate over government waste and excess...lower deficits...our victory in Kuwait, which makes the possibility of OPEC-caused inflation very unlikely...lower international trade barriers as a result of the NAFTA and GATT agreements...Alan Greenspan, who has been an extremely capable Fed chairman...the baby boom of the last 40 years, which will lead to an investment boom as this age group moves from peak spending to peak saving years.

All of this is fertile soil in which the financial markets should flourish.

Here's a 120 year study showing how well stocks can do in periods of low inflation and price stability.

Table 61

Stocks total returns vs. inflation		
	1871-1991	
Economic condition	**Inflation rate of return**	**Annual real rate**
Deflation	-0.2%	5.0%
Price Stability	0.2	19.0
Low Inflation	1.5	11.8
High Inflation	6.6	4.8

In sum, we believe that the Dow can rise to near the 6,000 level by the end of the 90s, ensuring the continued viability of a long-term buy/hold or Flexible Funding strategy.

Dollar-cost averaging

Those familiar words refer to a long-term strategy that can be used in conjunction with the buy/hold or Flexible Funding strategies. It's an especially useful approach if you are making regular contributions to an investment portfolio that you expect to hold for a number of years. Dollar-cost averaging (DCA) can be an effective way to make market fluctuations work for you, rather than against you. You can cope successfully with stock market fluctuations without having to become a market timer.

If you make regular, periodic purchases, investing the same dollar amount each month, you'll be buying more shares of a fund when its price is low, fewer when it's high. You have effectively reduced the risk that you are putting your money into stocks at the top of the market.

No-load mutual funds are the ideal vehicle for employing the dollar-cost averaging strategy. You can easily invest just about any amount monthly—$100, $200 or more—and pay no commissions. In addition, every purchase represents a completely diversified investment. Equally important, mutual funds usually move with the market. However, don't lose sight of the fact that the profitability of dollar-cost averaging is wholly related to the fund's performance. If you are purchasing shares of speculative funds, you'll get different results than if you're buying conservative ones.

DCA probably got its start years ago when most investors bought individual stocks, typically buying the same number of shares with each purchase. But, dollar-cost averaging doesn't work as effectively with individual stocks as with funds. It is harder to invest equal dollar amounts, for one thing, and the commissions on stock transactions will seriously erode small investments. Unlike mutual funds, individual stocks don't always recover after a long decline, as investors who have averaged down sometimes discover to their sorrow.

Here's a specific example of how dollar-cost averaging can work. Assume that both the market and your fund decline, then return to their original levels. You've been investing $100 every month. In the first month, you bought ten shares at $10 each. The next month, the price declined to $9, so your $100 purchased 11.1 shares. In succeeding months, the price dipped still lower and your $100 bought even more shares. Then the market turned up. As the price gradually returned to $10, you were buying fewer and fewer shares. In seven months, you'd spent $700 and owned 81.5 shares. Your average cost: $8.59 a share. With the shares again worth $10, your profit was 16% (Chart 62).

Note that at any time, the value of the accumulated shares is determined by the current share price. In the above example, a loss occurred in some months.

In the previous illustration, the per share price declined $3 and came back. What if, instead, it went up steadily? Say the market is rising. The price starts at $10, then gradually climbs to $13 over the next six months (Chart 63). As the months pass, you are buying fewer and fewer shares because of the increasing price. Thus, your total profit is less than in the previous example—only 12%. Reason: there was less fluctuation in the period. Surprising as it may seem, fluctuations in price produce greater profits than long-term growth can by itself. Consequently, dollar-cost averaging is more profitable with aggressive growth funds than it is with less volatile growth or growth-income funds—although, of course, your exposure to risk is far greater.

In our first example, the fund declined from $10 to $7 and then returned to $10, providing a 16% profit. If the fund had been still more volatile, declining to $5 before coming back to $10, an investor who had conscientiously bought at regular intervals, would have had a substantially greater gain, 34%. The average price would have been $7.45, not $8.59 (Chart 64).

Even with aggressive growth funds that recoup very slowly after bear markets, dollar-cost averaging can make sense. If, for example, you began your investment program when an aggressive growth fund was selling for $10 per share, then kept putting in equal dollar commitments as it sank to $5, and came back to only $7, your profit would still be 5% (Chart 65).

For dollar-cost averaging to work, you have to stick with your program, continuing to buy, especially when the market is at its lowest. If you stop investing during market downturns, you've defeated the purpose of the strategy. Moreover, for the approach to be successful you need time on your side. You cannot stick with the program for a year or two and then abandon it. You need to invest over a number of years, which is why practically speaking dollar-cost averaging works best for people who are automatically contributing each year to a retirement plan or profit-sharing program.

Like most strategies, dollar-cost averaging has its advantages and disadvantages. It's not a panacea. Perhaps its greatest benefit is that it can force you to save regularly—and *make you buy some shares when prices are low.* Too often, investors are perverse. People will buy more of almost any product or service when its price is low than when it is high. Except stocks! Buyer enthusiasm increases as stock prices rise, and decreases when stock prices fall. It's been said that a bull market is when you look in the paper every morning to find out how much your stocks went up the day before. And a bear market is when you don't check the financial pages at all.

Chart 62

Chart 63

Chart 64

Chart 65

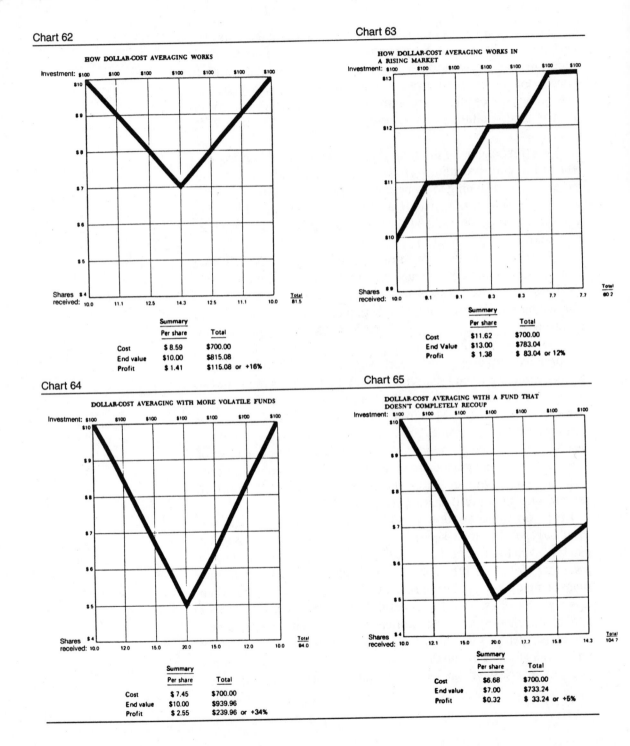

Chart 62 — HOW DOLLAR-COST AVERAGING WORKS

Investment: $100 $100 $100 $100 $100 $100 $100
Shares received: 10.0 11.1 12.5 14.3 12.5 11.1 10.0 — Total 81.5

Summary	Per share	Total
Cost	$8.59	$700.00
End value	$10.00	$815.08
Profit	$1.41	$115.08 or +16%

Chart 63 — HOW DOLLAR-COST AVERAGING WORKS IN A RISING MARKET

Investment: $100 $100 $100 $100 $100 $100 $100
Shares received: 10.0 9.1 9.1 8.3 8.3 7.7 7.7 — Total 60.2

Summary	Per share	Total
Cost	$11.62	$700.00
End Value	$13.00	$783.04
Profit	$1.38	$83.04 or 12%

Chart 64 — DOLLAR-COST AVERAGING WITH MORE VOLATILE FUNDS

Investment: $100 $100 $100 $100 $100 $100 $100
Shares received: 10.0 12.0 15.0 20.0 15.0 12.0 10.0 — Total 94.0

Summary	Per share	Total
Cost	$7.45	$700.00
End value	$10.00	$939.96
Profit	$2.55	$239.96 or +34%

Chart 65 — DOLLAR-COST AVERAGING WITH A FUND THAT DOESN'T COMPLETELY RECOUP

Investment: $100 $100 $100 $100 $100 $100 $100
Shares received: 10.0 12.1 15.0 20.0 17.7 15.8 14.3 — Total 104.7

Summary	Per share	Total
Cost	$6.68	$700.00
End value	$7.00	$733.24
Profit	$0.32	$33.24 or +5%

The value of DCA fades away with time. The strategy doesn't work as well over the long term because of inflation and also because of the overall growth in the stock markets. If the same amount is invested each month, its inflation-adjusted value decreases over the years. Investments of $100 a month, for example, may have made sense 20 years ago, but are truly inadequate today.

One solution is to increase the amount invested each year. We recommend that an investor boost the monthly amount by at least 10% a year, if possible. That's not always feasible. Funding an IRA is an important application of DCA, but obviously you can't increase your annual investments beyond $2,000. Therefore, you need to supplement the IRA with other regular investments.

DCA doesn't offer any guidance on selling. The ultimate value of the investments you accumulate through regular investing depends greatly on the end value. One study of dollar-cost averaging over the ten years ending in 1974 produced a 28.1% loss. The best solution: use averaging in reverse after your accumulation period has ended. A regular withdrawal plan at a fund group would accomplish this objective, which would make the end point less critical.

It might even be prudent to completely abandon averaging once you have accumulated a large sum. As the years go by, each additional investment becomes less significant. If you have built up an account to, say, $20,000, the next $100 is of little consequence. You should be more worried about protecting principal than rejoicing when a major decline provides you with the opportunity to pick up a few more shares at bargain prices.

It's hard to invest significant amounts at bargain prices. While dollar-cost averaging forces you to make at least some investments during bear markets, when prices are low, that's not sufficient in itself. Bull markets traditionally last much longer than bear markets, meaning that the bulk of your periodic purchases will be made when prices are high. The antidote is to double up your purchases during bear markets, when prices are low.

You have less money working for you than if you invested a lump sum. One DCA study found that $12,000 invested over a ten-year period ending in 1988 grew to $21,810. In contrast, if the $12,000 had been invested lump sum at the beginning of the period, it would have grown to $36,747, 68% more. That's because you would have had only half as much money working for you, on average, when invest-

Pitfalls of dollar-cost averaging

ing steadily over the ten years. Of course, if you didn't have the lump sum at the beginning, then investing regularly is your only alternative. But if, say, you receive an inheritance, or a lump-sum distribution from your company's pension or profit-sharing plan, then you need to compare the strategies.

Averaging versus lump sum purchases

Investors are commonly advised to use DCA to spread out a large lump sum over a period of time to avoid the danger of buying at the top of the market. We are frequently asked what time frame to use to dollar-cost average a large sum of money into the market. Those who ask the question should realize that they are really asking a market-timing question. No one answer is correct. If the market is going to rise, then the best strategy is to plunge every penny in immediately. On the other hand, if the market is about to decline, the slower you dollar-cost average, the less money you will lose during the down period. In sum, the number of months it takes to invest the money has a large bearing on the results. Here are some empirical studies that make the point.

We took a sampling of ten funds, ranging from speculative to conservative, and compared their performance to a lump sum purchase over various periods. In all cases, $240,000 was invested.

Table 66 compares the results of dollar-cost averaging $10,000 per month between July 1987 and June 1989 to a lump sum purchase made in July 1987. We picked July 1987 because it was just two months

Table 66

	Total return		
July 1987 - June 1989	**Buy $240,000 lump sum**	**DCA $10,000/mo**	**Lump sum minus DCA**
Gabelli Asset	$351,071	$339,424	$11,647
Mutual Beacon	315,702	311,605	4,097
Price Equity Income	306,911	306,871	41
Vanguard Wellesley	296,984	299,620	(2,636)
Janus	322,203	333,919	(11,716)
Janus Venture	304,640	322,763	(18,123)
Vanguard Wellington	277,807	297,769	(19,962)
Financial Industrial Income	280,977	302,184	(21,206)
Vanguard Index 500	267,267	301,422	(34,155)
Founders Special	283,839	318,513	(34,674)

Table 67

	Total return		
	Buy $240,000 lump sum	DCA $20,000/mo	Lump sum minus DCA
1990			
Vanguard Wellesley	$249,125	$261,186	$(12,060)
Financial Industrial Income	242,201	255,887	(13,687)
Janus Venture	239,045	253,556	(14,511)
Janus	238,218	253,009	(14,791)
Mutual Beacon	220,358	238,181	(17,823)
Vanguard Index 500	231,968	250,823	(18,855)
Vanguard Wellington	233,182	252,804	(19,622)
Price Equity Income	223,819	246,503	(22,684)
Gabelli Asset	228,042	251,534	(23,492)
Founders Special	214,965	249,269	(34,304)
1991			
Founders Special	392,686	312,753	79,933
Janus Venture	354,765	297,268	57,497
Financial Industrial Income	351,067	298,228	52,839
Janus	342,716	293,850	48,866
Vanguard Index 500	312,335	279,266	33,069
Price Equity Income	300,499	268,200	32,299
Vanguard Wellington	296,280	273,175	23,105
Mutual Beacon	282,032	259,142	22,890
Gabelli Asset	283,532	262,777	20,755
Vanguard Wellesley	291,256	276,932	14,324
1992			
Mutual Beacon	294,952	273,070	21,883
Price Equity Income	273,886	259,700	14,186
Gabelli Asset	275,746	264,298	11,448
Vanguard Wellington	258,947	257,426	1,521
Vanguard Wellesley	260,678	259,920	758
Vanguard Index 500	257,896	259,525	(1,629)
Janus	256,476	262,025	(5,549)
Founders Special	259,913	265,943	(6,030)
Janus Venture	257,857	265,367	(7,510)
Financial Industrial Income	242,259	253,760	(11,501)

before the 1987 top and the subsequent crash in October. We expected the averaging strategy to win in every case. But it didn't. A lump sum purchase in three of the ten funds actually produced the best results, even though the money was put in near the top of the market.

This evidence indicates to us that two years is probably too long a period of time to average a lump sum into the market. Two years

Table 68

July-Dec 1992	Total return		
	Buy $240,000 lump sum	DCA $40,000/mo	Lump sum minus DCA
Founders Special	$277,850	$266,834	$11,017
Janus Venture	272,322	264,539	7,783
Vanguard Wellesley	256,353	248,816	7,538
Mutual Beacon	266,541	260,069	6,472
Vanguard Index 500	259,785	253,477	6,308
Price Equity Income	254,600	250,538	4,062
Vanguard Wellington	253,487	249,711	3,776
Janus	262,546	258,924	3,622
Gabelli Asset	261,893	260,037	1,857
Financial Industrial Income	254,268	254,338	(71)

would be preferable only if bear markets lasted that long. But most don't. Note, we did take into account what the money would have earned in a money fund pending each investment in the market.

Next we looked at one-year periods in 1990, 1991 and 1992. Averaging won overwhelmingly in 1990, when the market was flat early in the year and declined precipitously in the third and fourth quarters; it lost overwhelmingly in 1991, when the market exploded in January and went on to have a great year. In 1992, averaging won in six of the ten cases, but investing the lump sum in four conservative funds proved to be the preferable strategy.

Last, we analyzed the two strategies in the last six months of 1992. Lump sum investing was the winner, since the market finished the year with a big surge.

Our conclusion: the strategies are very time-dependent. Which strategy will work better for you depends on how savvy you are about calling turns in the market. If that seems like a dubious activity to you, consider this: up years outnumber down years in the stock market overall. Therefore, more often than not you will do better by not trying to outguess the markets. The superior long-term strategy is to invest a large sum of money all at once, rather than by dribbling it into the market. One compromise, which we favor when the market seems high, is to invest 50% or more of a lump sum right away into conservative equity and growth-income funds, then dollar-cost-average the balance in over 6 to 12 months.

Over the years, analysts have searched for ways to enhance the effectiveness of dollar-cost averaging. One variation that makes sense is to substantially increase the amount you invest when the market declines, and decrease the amount that you invest when the market is high. Various formulas have been developed to implement this.

Value Averaging, a 1991 book by Harvard business professor Michael Edleson (International Publishing Corp.) developed some variations that have potential. The main one, value averaging, calls for the value of your holdings to increase by $100 (or some other set amount) each month. If the market goes down the previous month, you will have to invest more than $100 to meet your goal. If the market increases, a lesser amount would be invested. Under the basic version of the strategy, you would find yourself selling some shares in those months when the market made striking gains in order to limit your portfolio's growth to $100 that month. In an alternative version, you wouldn't sell (which might mean capital gains taxes) but simply wait until your portfolio's actual value was less than the required value before you resumed buying. Edleson's studies found that value averaging was potentially more profitable than straight dollar-cost averaging.

We think the idea is a good one because it enables you to focus more clearly on your goals. With standard dollar-cost averaging, you don't know how much money you will have at retirement time. With value averaging you will know. It's similar to the difference between defined contribution and defined benefit retirement plans. With value averaging you can work back to determine how much money you need to put aside each period to meet your long-range goals. One caution: the correct implementation of value averaging is not as straight-forward as the above description. It pays to buy the book if you are going to try to employ the professor's strategies.

Dollar-cost averaging variations

Let's say your timing is terrible. You had an auto accident the week after you dropped your collision insurance. You bought a beach house just before the hurricane struck. And when it comes to investing, you invariably buy in at the market's highest points. If you sell when the market is substantially lower, that is, of course, a guaranteed way to lose money. But what if you don't sell low? Studies show that even the worst timing need not be fatal for the long-term investor.

T. Rowe Price has calculated the hypothetical performance of annual

How even the worst losers can make money

investments made in the S&P 500 stock index on the *worst day of each year* for the last 22 years. This calculation is similar to a typical dollar-cost averaging program, but with one significant difference. Instead of investing at regular intervals so that at least some shares are purchased at below-average prices, the example deliberately showed purchases chronically being made at the worst time possible, the day the market made its high for the year. In this calculation, an investor deposited a $2,000 lump sum on the day the market peaked each year. Not withstanding this major impediment, the results over the long run are still spectacular.

The two decades includes the horrendous 1973-74 bear market. So, it was very rocky going for a few years. But when the bull markets of the late 70s and 80s began, the investments began to bear fruit. By the 90s, the investments were growing at geometric rates. The gain in 1991 alone was $39,000. By December 1994, the $44,000 invested over the years was now worth $209,951!

Table 69

Buying at the worst time of the year

S & P 500 (with dividends reinvested)

Investment date (S&P high)	Cumulative investment	Value at year end	Cumulative profit/loss
01/11/73	$ 2,000	$ 1,676	$ (324)
01/03/74	4,000	2,675	(1,325)
07/15/75	6,000	5,596	(404)
09/21/76	8,000	8,962	962
01/03/77	10,000	10,182	182
09/12/78	12,000	12,690	690
10/05/79	14,000	17,006	3,006
11/28/80	16,000	24,478	8,478
01/06/81	18,000	25,154	7,154
11/09/82	20,000	32,553	12,553
11/10/83	22,000	41,795	19,795
11/16/84	24,000	46,381	22,381
12/16/85	26,000	63,069	37,069
12/12/86	28,000	76,733	48,733
08/25/87	30,000	82,198	52,198
10/21/88	32,000	97,734	65,734
10/09/89	34,000	130,588	96,588
07/16/90	36,000	128,338	92,338
12/31/91	38,000	169,377	131,377
12/31/92	40,000	184,252	144,252
12/31/93	42,000	204,734	162,734
02/02/94	44,000	209,951	165,951

Similar studies have been done using individual funds. Their results all show that if the market is in a long uptrend, it doesn't matter how egregious your mistakes; the market can still bail you out. Patience and tenacity will be richly rewarded.

Let's turn the study upside down. Surprisingly, even picking the best days to invest doesn't dramatically change the results in the long run. Another study found that if a person had invested $500 at the beginning of each quarter in the S&P 500 stock index, over the 20 years ending 1989 he would have achieved an annualized gain of 11.77%. On the other hand, if he had invested $2,000 once a year at the S&P's exact low, his annual return would be 13.35%. The latter figure is, of course, better, but not as significantly better as you might think it would be, and totally unachievable as a practical matter, in any case. The point is: If you invest regularly in stocks, you will make enough purchases at low prices to do just fine in the long run.

While these results are truly startling, we don't think they mean you can abdicate all judgment. If you are going to invest in stocks you must have an informed opinion about long-term trends. Stocks aren't always in a long-term uptrend. They declined between 1968 and 1974. In the Great Depression, stocks lost 90% of their value—and took 15 years (even with dividends included) to come back. And that period certainly exceeds our preferred time horizons.

Psst. Wanna hear about a technique you could have adopted 19 years ago that would have enabled you to do more than four times was well as investing in the average equity fund.

A speculative way to make big bucks

At the end of each year, buy that year's top-ranked diversified no-load equity fund. Hold it for one more year. Then switch to the new top-ranked fund.

A study by *The No-Load Fund Investor* newsletter found that if you had actually implemented such an approach from 1975 to 1994, an investment of $1,000 would have grown to $52,633. At the same time, an investment in the average diversified domestic stock fund grew to only $11,986. Our methodology was simple. We reviewed the list of top no-load funds until we found the best diversified equity fund available for sale. Since the performances of specialized gold and sector funds are notoriously inconsistent, we excluded them from the study.

We then examined each fund's performance in the year following its

#1 ranking and compared this performance to the average no-load fund.

For example, 44 Wall was the top rated fund in 1975 with a gain of 184.1%. For the purpose of this study, it was bought on Jan. 1, 1976 and held for one year. In 1976 Forty-four Wall gained 46.5%, as compared to a 27.6% gain for the average equity fund. We used the same methodology for the entire 19 years.

The results: If you had simply bought each year's top performing no-load diversified domestic equity fund on January 1 of the following year, held it until December 31, and then switched into the new No. 1 fund, you would have had an average (uncompounded) gain of 23.2% per year since 1976. By way of comparison, the average equity fund gained only 14.0% per year. The top funds outperformed the average fund in 14 of the 19 years. There was one tie. There were only two years with losses, and one year with gains while the average fund declined.

Table 70

How the top diversified domestic no-load equity funds fared

Year	No-load fund	Gain in record year	Gain following year	Average diversified no-load fund
1975	44 Wall Street	184.1	46.5	27.6
1976	Sequoia	70.8	19.9	3.5
1977	Value Line Leveraged Growth	51.1	27.6	11.6
1978	Twentieth Century Gr (3)	47.2	74.2	28.6
1979	Able Associates (3)	79.1	56.7	33.6
1980	Hartwell Leverage	93.9	-13.2	-1.0
1981	Lindner	34.8	27.1	23.7
1982	Tudor (6)	44.5	28.0	21.2
1983	Strong Investment (2)	44.7	9.7	-0.6
1984	Vanguard High Yield Stock	25.2	30.1	27.1
1985	Fidelity OTC (2)	69.0	11.4	13.9
1986	Strong Opportunity (7)	59.9	11.8	0.4
1987	Mathers (11)	26.9	13.7	15.6
1988	Kaufmann	58.6	46.8	22.9
1989	Twentieth Century Vista (5)	52.2	-15.7	-5.8
1990	Founders Discovery (11)	13.1	62.5	33.2
1991	Montgomery Small Cap (3)	98.7	9.6	9.6
1992	Oakmark (2)	48.9	30.5	14.7
1993	PBHG Growth (26)	46.5	4.8	-0.7
1994	PBHG Emerging Growth (2)	23.8	—	1.5
	Average gain	57.1	23.2	14.0
	What $1,000 grew to:		$52,633	$11,986

The numbers in parentheses show the rank among all funds.

If we had included international funds in the study, results would have been somewhat less dramatic. But our top dogs would still have far outperformed the average fund.

Caution: while this strategy produced remarkable results in the measured period, it is a high-risk approach. Don't bet your retirement money on this thesis. In two of the four bear market years, the top-rated fund seriously underperformed the averages.

Another benefit of this strategy is that it reduces the reliance on long-term performance records. For a variety of reasons, not least changes in fund managers, longer track records are less predictive of future fund performance. The immediate past is a far better guide. Documenting this hypothesis, we redid the above study, this time taking the funds with the best five- and ten-year records each year. Again, we recorded their following year results. The outcome was not as good as when we based our selections on the most recent one-year period.

In December 1992, The *Journal's* mutual fund expert, Jonathan Clements, did a similar study using the Lipper data base. His analysis presumed that three investors each bought the top 25% of diversified stock funds (load and no-load). The first investor "bought" the top funds based on the latest one-year performances, the second "bought" on the basis of the previous five-years, the third on the basis of the previous ten-year performances. All three investors then held the funds for an additional five years. To determine which one did best, 19 rolling five-year time periods were evaluated, beginning with 1970-1974. The winner: the investor who bought on the basis of the previous one-year performance.

Wall Street Journal study

Why did the investor who made purchases on the basis of the latest one-year performance fare best? The *Journal* suggests that the answer relates to investment cycles. There are major cycles in equities: small caps versus large, growth versus value. Both rotate in long, multi-year cycles. A great many funds specialize in one of these categories. As a result, if you buy one type of fund after it has been ascendent for, say, five years, you are likely to be buying it at or near the end of the cycle for its kind of stocks. In contrast, buying a fund based on the most recent year's performance gives you a better chance of riding its cycle to completion.

Vanguard's Jack Bogle, in his recent book, *Bogle on Mutual Funds*, undertook a similar study. He took the top 20 funds each year for a decade and calculated their second year results. Averaging all ten years

Table 71

No. years top quartile funds beat average fund		
Out of 19 five-year time periods		
Previous performance base:	**No. years**	**Avg 5 yr gain**
One year	12	95.6%
Five years	6	80.7%
Ten years	8	82.6%
Average fund		84.0%

Source: The Wall Street Journal

together, he found that the top 20 funds returned 17.6% the following year, substantially better than the all-fund average of 13.5%.

Shorting funds

Investors unfamiliar with mutual funds frequently ask if it's possible to short them. That strategy, generally employed with individual stocks, is not universally available with mutual funds. But it can be done.

In February 1987, Fidelity Investments, in a major innovation, began to allow its brokerage customers to sell short shares of eight of its Select Portfolios. But the experiment failed because of lack of customers, and the service was quietly discontinued in November 1989. Fidelity then had second thoughts, reinstituting the service in mid-1992.

You can now short twelve Fidelity Select Funds: American Gold, Automotive, Biotechnology, Energy, Environmental, Food & Agriculture, Health Care, Medical Delivery, Precious Metals, Regional Banks, Telecommunications, and Utilities.

To short a portfolio, you must present cash and/or marketable securities equal to a minimum of 50% of the market value of the shares sold short in addition to the proceeds of the short sale. Subsequently, collateral must equal 30% of the short value of the shares. In order to sell short you will need to open a margin account with Fidelity Brokerage. (You can't margin an IRA or other qualified account.) Commissions are the same as for stock transactions.

Jack White, the discount brokerage firm, also offers a service for short sellers. Subject to availability, White will permit customers to sell short 40 to 50 no-load funds including funds in the Babson, Dreyfus, Evergreen, Founders, Gabelli, Janus, Lexington, Neuberger-Berman, Rushmore, Scudder, Strong, Price, and United Services groups.

Another way to make money on the downside would be to short a closed-end investment company, which is traded on an exchange. A disadvantage of shorting closed-ends is their relative illiquidity. Some of them don't trade many shares daily. A sophisticated investor who was going to execute this strategy would have to plan his short sales well in advance. Undoubtedly, though, such an investor would find equity substitutes, such as index options, more effective vehicles for short sales.

Since 1990, the Benham group has accepted open or limit orders for mutual funds so that investors can specify in advance the prices at which they will buy and sell. Shareholders in a Benham money fund who want to buy one of the group's stock or bond funds simply specify any price lower than the current one and the amount to be invested. If the fund falls to that price, the shares are bought automatically with money from the money fund, just as it would be in a stock brokerage account. Similarly, shareholders in a variable-priced fund can choose to sell automatically whenever the price goes up to a predetermined level. (They cannot place a sell order *below* the market.) The proceeds go into a money fund. Both buy and sell orders expire if the fund does not reach the specified price within 90 days. They can be renewed, cancelled or amended to a new price or changed at any time within the 90 days. The service is free. Benham shareholders are using the service primarily for their Target zero coupon bond funds. The group's equity funds are also getting a play.

You can place limit orders at Benham

Upgrading, the process of replacing average to below-average funds with higher-ranked funds, is a perfectly acceptable investing strategy. We ourselves do it from time to time when a fund's performance falters. Some other advisers use a mechanical approach.

You should beware, though, of advisers who carry the concept to extremes. Some advisers advise selling a fund if it drops out of the top 5, the top 10 or some such, and replacing the fund with a current winner. That's too much. All mutual fund performance is time-period specific. These advisers seldom think through the period of time on which to rank funds, and how far out of their magic ranking a fund needs to drop before it is replaced.

Upgrading mutual funds

As a general rule, as long as the market is rising and the fund is performing reasonably well, stick with it. Fund performance is too erratic for you to do frequent switching to attain a small edge. It just doesn't pay, particularly on an after-tax basis.

The time value of money

Understanding the time value of money is essential to good investing. Which of these two investors obtained the best return? Miss A's fund gained 20% in one year; Mr. B's gained 20% in two years. Obviously, Miss A gets our Shrewd Investor Award. Poor old B's fund grew at an annualized rate of only about 10% a year. Practically speaking, Miss A could have switched into a money market fund after one year, protecting her lead and tacking on additional gains.

This homely example suggests that investors should think clearly about the measurements of investments. Yet, there is an interesting dichotomy in the conventions of calculating investment returns. When discussing stocks and growth stock funds, returns under a year are almost always computed directly, without taking into account the length of time the investment has been held. Even multi-year periods are annualized only part of the time. Fixed income investments such as bank savings accounts, CD's, Treasury bills and money market funds, however, typically are quoted on the basis of annualized returns. When you buy a six-month CD paying a 5% return, the actual return over its life is only 2.5%.

The lesson: always adjust your returns for the length of time you've had the investment. That way you can put the profits from different investments on an equal footing. Similarly, you should reduce multi-year performance data to annualized figures.

This advice is even more urgent for commodity investments. Such things as gold, silver, raw land and art do not pay dividends. A common mistake with land, for example, is to buy too early. If a rise in value is many years in coming, your average annual return may be quite poor, even though your margin of profit is respectable. Similarly, the great auction houses like Sotheby's and Christie's love to publicize the multi-million prices paid for great paintings. But if you adjust them for time, it's another story. For example, in November 1994 Sotheby's sold a Claude Monet painting for $1.8 million. It had been purchased in 1916 for $5,000. The average annual gain over the 78 years: just 7.1%. Stocks did better! (O.K., so hanging your stock certificate on the wall isn't the same.)

Here are some other guidelines: When you are switching between equity and money market funds you should time-weight your returns. If you make a 20% gain in an equity fund over three months, that's an 80% gain annualized. You could spend the next nine months in a money fund and still have a super return for the full year. There is a date attached to every investment you make. The longer your money is invested, the more it has to earn for the return to be competitive.

Because the market can decline very fast, even a small gain on a short sale can, on occasion, be quite profitable.

Some state lotteries award "multi-million dollar" prizes, but actually pay $50,000 a year per million for 20 years. Taxes are withheld each year at the 28% rate. Is this the same? Not by a long shot. If one million dollars were paid at once, it could be invested to throw off $100,000 or more a year, with the principal still in the winner's hands. Four states—Arizona, Colorado, Ohio, and Oregan—actually allow winners a lump sum option. But these states aren't fools. If the winners opt for the lump sum, the states pay them only 40% to 50% of the full jackpot amount. Still, the winners are well advised to take it. By taking a lump sum today of $300,000 ($500,000 less 40% in taxes) and investing it wisely at 10%, they would have $2.4 million at the end of 20 years, and could live off the returns forever.

A 30-year mortgage isn't cheaper than a 15-year mortgage. It only looks that way. (Actually, it's much more expensive in terms of the interest you pay over the long haul.) Similarly, second-to-die life insurance policies (which take longer to pay off) aren't cheaper than individual policies when you take the time value of money into account.

Take advantage of the float. That's another perfect illustration of the time value of money. When you write a check on a money market fund, you hope the recipient will take forever to cash it. Each day of delay puts additional interest in your pocket. Conversely, deposit checks you receive as quickly as possible. And don't retain unused traveler's checks. Why give American Express unnecessary interest income for using your money?

To reduce this discussion to our favorite subject, when you examine a fund's "mountain" (see page 150), be sure to take into account the number of years that have gone into obtaining that performance.

Inflated expectations can damage your fiscal health

At various times during the last two decades, investors' expectations have become, shall we say, greatly inflated. People have thought that earning 15% to 20% per year was normal, even conservative. That's simply not true over the long run. A far more realistic goal with our conservative switching strategy: 12% to 13% per year over a great many years. It's hard not to be influenced by the unrealistic expectations of others. Make sure *your* expectations are realistic.

Seattle money manager Paul Merriman tells the following story: Speaking before an investment seminar in Costa Mesa, CA, he asked the audience, "How many of you are looking for a 12% or greater compounded rate of return?" Almost every one of the 150 or so people in the audience raised a hand. So he asked: "How many of you are willing to lose 50% of your investment in one year in attempting to achieve a 12% return?" No hands went up. "How about a 40% loss?" Again, no hands went up. "Thirty percent?" Three people raised their hands. "Twenty percent?" A couple of dozen hands went up. "Ten percent?" Finally, 40 to 50 hands were raised. Stunningly, more than 30% of this group were unwilling to lose *any* money in pursuit of a 12% plus rate of return. Needless to say, Merriman concluded that the group's expectations were unrealistic.

A summary: rules for successful investing in the 90s

Throughout the book, we have talked about these precepts. Here is a synopsis of our advice:

Invest early and often. This is the real secret to investment success. Make the magic of compounding work for you. Successful entrepreneurs may be able to accumulate vast fortunes in no time. But passive investors in other people's businesses, which is what you are as a stock investor, don't have such ripe opportunities. For you, what counts is the slow steady accumulation of wealth over the long haul.

Make common stocks your core investment. Your potential return is always greater if you own a business or property—or even a small sliver of them—than if you lend money. Thus equities (stocks or real estate) will outperform debt (bonds).

Don't take needless risks. A rational investor is risk averse. You should avoid specific-company risk by diversifying. That's what mutual fund investing is all about. Avoid market risk by diversifying among various markets—stocks, bonds, cash, real estate. Even within the equity category you should diversify. When appropriate, we suggest you consider both large and small growth funds, value funds that buy large and small companies, natural resource funds, and international funds. Generally speaking, you should be cautious about increasing your risk by borrowing.

Understand how much risk you are taking. There is no wealth without risk. When an adviser or newsletter tells you that they can obtain superior rewards without taking risks, you are well advised to run as fast as you can—in the opposite direction. If you are young, you can probably afford to take chances, and you should. When you are older, you will undoubtedly want to guard against losing dollars that you may not be able to replace.

Speculate only with money that you can afford to lose. We would define that as a sum that if lost will not change your life-style or standard of living, one that will not force you to put off a major expenditure that you had planned to make, buying a car or house, for instance, or financing your children's education. Never put more than 25% of your financial assets in the most speculative aggressive growth funds. Don't speculate past your "sleep at night" level. Diversify. Don't forget real estate, particularly home ownership. Don't borrow money to play the market. And that includes not only margin but also such risky endeavors as taking out a home equity loan.

Reduce your equity risk by holding long-term. While equities are risky in the short run, your risk is substantially reduced by lengthening your holding period.

Be optimistic. Bears make the headlines, but it's the bulls that make the money. Never forget that the long-term trend of the market is up!

Avoid zero sum games. Options, futures, gambling are all zero sum games where there is a loser for every winner. They may be fun, but they're not for making money. If you want to make money, invest in stocks; they are a positive sum game, meaning that any number of players can win. And where does that positive sum come from? From the growth of the economy itself, whose fruits must accrue to someone.

Understand that there are no gurus. By that we mean people who can predict the future. There is no perfection in calling the markets—or in any kind of forecasting. Back in 1989, the *Investor* received the following letter in response to a direct mail solicitation. The author wrote in part:

> Thanks for your offer—But I make you an offer—Send me a back issue of *The No-Load Fund Investor.* You seem to be sincere and honest—but I would like to see an August or September 1987 copy— and see if you called the crash. The Mutual Fund Forecaster did not call the crash....*otherwise put this letter in the trash!*

This letter writer strikes us as a loser. He will spend his life jumping from one trendy "guru" to the next and at the end will have little to show for it. He'll be an expert in yesterday's heroes. He should be asking about an adviser's long-term record. An even better alternative is to make core investments in ways that don't depend on predictions. Dollar-cost averaging is one of them. Our Flexible Funding Program is close to being another.

Invest only in what you understand. Restrict your investments to no-load funds, mostly diversified, that you can grasp. Don't invest in complicated limited partnerships that come with 100+ page prospectuses you'll never read. Avoid coins, which have frequently done well, unless you are willing to take the time to become expert in them. Heed the wisdom of Fidelity's Peter Lynch, who says he shuns high-tech stocks because he doesn't understand them, and that of superinvestor, Warren Buffett, who says, "We don't buy things we don't understand." Similarly, the mighty Mario Gabelli believes in "kicking the tires." He doesn't buy international stocks. If John Deere were located in Manheim instead of Moline, or if Pepsico were in Paris instead of Purchase (NY), he wouldn't buy them.

Avoid commission-based financial advisers. Their advice comes with an inherent conflict of interest. Avoid full-service brokers. If you need a broker, use a discount firm that provides executions only. If you absolutely need advice, try this method of working with full-service brokers. Tell them that you'll call them when you need them, and that under no circumstances are they to call you with recommendations, suggestions, tips, research reports, etc. Needless to say, never give a broker discretionary authority or sign an options agreement. Finally, if you need investment advice, get it from an investment adviser. Lawyers and accountants are seldom qualified investment advisers.

Use fee-only financial planners. Similarly, patronize money managers whose fees are based solely on assets under management. Be wary when buying insurance products. Their benefit projections can be misleading.

Primarily the naive are taken advantage of. If you know the ropes, it's relatively unlikely that a broker will try to sell you an unsuitable product because it provides him or her with a high commission. On the other hand, it is, unfortunately, not at all uncommon for them to fatten their incomes at the expense of the ignorant. "Takes time to become knowledgeable," you say. You put in the time and effort when you buy a new car or house or take an expensive vacation. It's your money.

Pay yourself first. Before your paycheck is entirely spent, make sure you have put aside some money for your savings. Many mutual funds have arrangements by which they can instruct your bank to automatically deduct a specific sum each month from your checking account. That way, you never see the money in the first place.

One of the best wealth accumulation devices ever invented is the thrift, profit-sharing or 401(k) plan that many companies offer their employees. Whether on your own or as a participant in a tax-qualified plan, as your account begins to grow, you have the satisfaction of managing an ever-larger portfolio. With a bit of self-discipline, you can eventually control a substantial amount of money. An early start and a systematic plan can lead to a small fortune. In any case, you should be able to accumulate a nest egg sizeable enough to bring you financial peace of mind.

Keep your costs down. That's the essential reason for no-load fund investing.

CHAPTER 20

THE
NO-LOAD
FUND INVESTOR

When to sell your fund

Back in the 50s and 60s most investment advisers counseled clients to buy and hold mutual funds practically forever.

The tumultuous 70s changed all that. The ruinous bear market of 1973-74, plus the disastrous rise in interest rates and inflation throughout the decade caused investors to lose their resolve. Many deserted financial assets for such inflation hedges as real estate and collectibles.

Although the 1980s were one of the best decades in history for financial assets, the belief that mutual funds can be bought at any time and held forever is dead.

Even so, the critical subject of when to sell doesn't receive the attention it deserves. For several reasons: the fund industry has no interest in discussing it; the normal inclination among investors is to buy, not to sell, which is considered a negative activity; and the bulk of the press and independent advisers are similarly oriented to the happier activity of buying. When the notion of selling comes up at all, it is mainly in the context of market timing.

Because buying is more fun for everyone involved, the industry and its salesmen offer simple advice about the best time to buy: Now. Any time is a good time to buy mutual funds, so the rationale goes, because in the long run you are almost certain to make money. Indeed, we ourselves observed several chapters ago that if you hold funds for at least five years, you have a high probability of making money; if you can hold for 15 years, you are almost certain to be ahead. While all this is true, unquestionably you are nevertheless much better off if you evaluate your funds periodically as you would any investment—and sell, when necessary.

The ability to sell at an opportune moment distinguishes the professional money managers from amateurs. The pros understand that paper losses are very real and that it is best to take them while they are small.

By contrast, amateurs are inclined to nurture the often unrealistic hope that their sinking funds will surge sooner or later. Optimism, inertia or both prevent amateurs from taking decisive action. Brokerage commissions and taxes also deter some people from selling. Having difficulty facing up to a mistake is an even more potent psychological roadblock.

Every investor should try to emulate the professionals, especially in terms of dealing with mistakes quickly and effectively. A good example is the way money managers who run emerging market funds reacted in the wake of the sudden Mexican peso crisis in December 1994 and January 1995. Almost uniformly, they were quick to reduce their Mexican stock positions. In contrast, individuals are more likely to sell toward the tail end of declines, often about the time the professionals are getting ready to repurchase.

Mutual funds eliminate most of the reasons that handicap stock buyers. With stocks, for example, most investors buy shares in a particular company once, then hold them indefinitely. Funds are different. Investing in funds is usually an ongoing process. You buy shares at different prices because you are purchasing shares each month, quarter or year by reinvesting dividend and capital gains distributions. Each time you purchase more shares, you are buying at new prices. Not only does that obscure your base price, making you less sensitive to losses with funds than with stocks, it also means that taxes are not such a significant issue in another way. Because the mutual fund manager is required to pass any capital gains exposure along to shareholders, you are likely to pay a small amount of tax each year, rather than having a large exposure when you sell, as you would with an individual stock. So your sell decision is not so likely to be based on your cost basis and tax exposure.

It also helps that selling mutual funds is an impersonal process. You don't need to explain to a broker. You simply talk to a stranger on the phone for a few seconds or, less commonly, send a brief business letter to the fund or its custodial bank.

Unburdened of the load

While the sales commission on load funds can be a real deterrent, when you sell no-loads you have no worry about the sales costs you may have incurred. With no-loads, the most you'll pay is a nominal redemption fee.

Sell for personal reasons

Mutual funds are generally thought of as a nest egg for retirement. And with a great many investors, retirement may be the only reason to sell. But many other circumstances may compel you to cash in your stash: buying a house, facing unexpected medical bills, putting your children through college, even taking an expensive vacation. While funds certainly may be held for the long term, accept the likelihood that you may decide to sell them long before you originally anticipated.

Besides your circumstances, your objectives may change. A person owning an aggressive growth fund may want to switch to a growth or a growth-income fund at retirement. On the other hand, an investor who had been unduly timid might want to exchange some income funds for more aggressive growth-oriented holdings. That could occur because your financial situation improved dramatically, for example, if you received an inheritance, got a better job, or your kids became self-supporting. Under those circumstances, you may want more exposure to speculative funds.

No-load funds, of course, readily accommodate selling decisions for such personal reasons.

Sell when performance lags

Standing pat is no guarantee of a winning hand. Even if your circumstances or objectives have not changed, you are likely to want to switch funds from time to time, so as to stay in top-performing investments.

Here's a case history of a legendary fund that went sour, and how its shareholders reacted. The 44 Wall Street Fund was by far the outstanding success in the stock market cycle that began in 1975 and ended with the 1981-82 decline. From then until 1987 it was one of the worst funds. To see how no-load fund investors reacted, we tracked 44 Wall shareholders through the fund's gyrations from 1974 through 1987.

Forty-four Wall emerged from the 1973-1974 bear market with only 1,500 shareholders. It took investors a while to recognize the fund's outstanding performance in the new bull market. But by 1979, 6,300 astute shareholders had invested an average of $17,095 each in the fund. The following year, 1980, with its achievements widely publicized, its roster of shareholders zoomed to 15,322. In 1980, the fund's minimum investment was raised to $250,000 and some of the 9,000 new 1980 shareholders bought just before the new minimum went into effect. Between 1975 and 1980 the fund gained 1,423%, but no more than 1,500 shareholders fully participated in this huge increase. Most bought along the way; a good percentage bought in near the top.

The next year, 1981, was a down year for the market, and the high flyers, as usual, fared the worst; 44 Wall declined 23.6% and then dropped another 21.5% in the first half of 1982. Relatively few of 44 Wall's shareholders reacted to the fund's poor performance by selling. In 18 months, only 2,200 of 44 Wall's 15,000 shareholders redeemed. (This is the net loss, taking into account new shareholders.) In June 1982 when it was the worst performing of all aggressive growth no-loads, 44 Wall still had 13,000 shareholders. Many more should have sold out, particularly considering 44 Wall's convenient telephone switch privilege.

When the market took off in August 1982, 44 Wall was still a logical choice for the aggressive investor. While the number of new investors added by year-end was small, the fund's assets grew rapidly, far more than could be accounted for by the fund's 36.4% gain in the last six months of the year. Obviously, the big, smart money had come in to reap the bull market profits. Average assets per shareholder, which six months earlier had declined to $7,486, zoomed back to $15,032 at 1982 year-end.

The money stayed in until the end of January 1984. At that time, stocks turned sharply downward and the smart money moved out of 44 Wall. In one month, the fund's assets plunged from $208 million to $93.5 million, far more than the 16% decline in the NAV per share during the same period. But that was the smart money—the large holdings of a relatively few investors. Most investors hung on and absorbed 1984s punishing 59.6% decline. More departed in 1985, 1986, and 1987; yet at year-end 44 Wall still had 5,541 shareholders.

More significant was the greater decline in assets per shareholder as shown in Table 72. At the end of 1987, the value of the average holding of the remaining 44 Wall Street shareholders was only $1,372. The smart investors had taken their profits—or minimized their losses—and gone on to greener fields. What sort of shareholders remained? Most likely investors who either didn't follow their holdings or couldn't bring themselves to sell. Truth is, they had no business buying 44 Wall in the first place. These shareholders were obviously too patient.

Make this your own personal cautionary tale. When long-term performance lags—let alone plummets—as 44 Wall's did, be sure to sell.

Table 72

44 Wall Street Fund

At year end

	Annual performance	Number of shareholders	Total net assets in millions	Avg. assets per share-holder
1974	-52.2	1,500	$ 0.6	$ 400
1975	184.1	2,000	6.7	3,350
1976	46.5	2,000	18.3	9,150
1977	16.5	2,000	16.4	8,200
1978	32.9	3,000	30.6	10,200
1979	73.6	6,300	107.7	17,095
1980	36.2	15,322	193.5	12,629
1981	-22.8	13,516	122.2	9,041
June 1982	*(-21.6)	13,105	98.1	7,486
1982	8.5	13,365	200.9	15,032
1983	6.9	12,915	182.7	14,146
1984	-59.6	11,497	67.8	5,897
1985	-20.1	9,795	42.3	4,319
1986	-16.3	7,066	19.2	2,717
1987	-34.6	5,541	7.6	1,372

*Jan-June 1982

Forty-four Wall Street's woes were detailed in a February 1988, *Barron's* article, which brought this response from a shattered *Barron's* reader:

> To the Editor:
> ...My last check to the fund was invested on Oct. 18, 1982, and for the next five years, I watched in disbelief as, during the great secular bull market, David Baker destroyed my young son's $17,000 college nest egg. When I finally sold on Dec. 10, 1987, only $1,865 was left.
> What do you do when you're too poor to sue?

For some 44 Wall Street investors the only answer is a change of management. That took place on April 27, 1988, when Baker sold to a new company, MBD Asset Management, and its then 26-year-old president, Mark Beckerman, took over. The fund briefly showed some improvement under its new management, but then resumed its losing ways. In 1993, Beckerman finally put the fund out of its misery, merging it into its sister, 44 Wall Street Equity.

If you were a Chicago Bulls fan, and the legendary Michael Jordan decided to retire—as he did at the end of the 1992-1993 season—how concerned would you be about the team's performance? Very, no doubt. And sure enough, in the years following the departure of his Airness, the Bulls were a far cry from the team that won three straight national Basketball Association Championships.

A change in advisers is a reason to sell — sometimes

And a basketball team has five men on its starting team, not to mention a collection of sometimes stellar subs. The mutual fund world is quite different. Often, a fund's success is the expression of one or two exceptionally savvy managers. So, when a manager leaves, the impact can be as dramatic as the departure of a genius like Michael Jordan.

In 1989, Andrew Massie, the portfolio manager for the Scudder Capital Growth Fund and the AARP Capital Growth Fund, moved on to another fund group. The funds haven't been quite as good since. The same situation has prevailed at the Primary Trend Fund. President James R. Arnold, Sr. died suddenly on November 2, 1989. And at the Selected Funds, long-time manager Donald Yacktman, left in April 1992, to start his own fund. Even though the funds' board of directors moved the funds to another well-respected advisor in an attempt to maintain performance, the Selected Funds have suffered since Yacktman's departure.

As in sports, you need to evaluate each significant change in a mutual fund on its own merits. When Joe Montana left the San Francisco 49ers several years ago, the team found another ace in quarterback Steve Young, who was voted Player of the Year in the NFL in 1994 and led his team to the Super Bowl in January 1995. On February 12, 1988, Max Heine, the 77-year-old founder and chairman of the board of the Mutual Series Funds, was killed in an auto accident. Investors who had taken the trouble to acquaint themselves with the group's management knew that a top-notch, well-qualified replacement was already on hand. Michael Price had joined the Heine organization in 1975 and had already earned a reputation as a savvy fund manager and heir apparent. The Mutual Series funds under Price's leadership have done as well as they could have with Heine.

In May 1990, the fund industry witnessed its most significant management change in years. The great Peter Lynch—the Michael Jordan of mutual funds—left Fidelity Magellan. A wizard who had compiled probably the best management record in the history of the business, left the gargantuan fund in the hands of Morris Smith, who previously had done an excellent job of managing the Fidelity OTC Fund. Without question, the greatest part of Magellan's impressive gains had been achieved when the fund was smaller. Still, Lynch had done a very creditable job even after the fund grew huge. In this regard, he was lucky that small company stocks were doing well when the fund was small and large company stocks excelled when the fund was large.

Almost all the Magellan shareholders elected to remain with Morris Smith—and, at the time, we counseled our newsletter subscribers to take a wait-and-see attitude. Then in April 1991, we advised newsletter subscribers to switch to other Fidelity growth funds. In subsequent months the fund did, indeed, underperform other logical alternatives in up markets. Then, in July 1992, Jeff Vinik took over the fund. He improved performance, but the fund still has never regained the lofty levels it achieved under Peter Lynch. In the three years ending 1994, Magellan ranked 44th among Fidelity equity funds—it was outperformed by 21 diversified and 22 Fidelity sector funds. The decision to sell after Lynch left was a correct one, particularly when a simple phone call would switch you into a better Fidelity performer.

Every year some personnel changes are important—and some aren't. Here's a general guideline: The larger the advisory organization, the less likely it is that a departure will cause significant problems. The portfolio manager is not as crucial in a larger organization as in a smaller one, since it is far easier for a larger organization to replace a departing portfolio manager with someone equally skilled.

To document this point we have examined the role of the portfolio manager at Fidelity, the country's largest fund group. Fidelity consistently experiences rapid turnover among its portfolio managers. A study by *Fidelity Insight* newsletter discovered 50 portfolio management changes at Fidelity between April 1992 and September 1993. This means that the people managing the various funds are for the most part fairly new to their funds.

The No-Load Fund Investor did a special study and found that the
median fund manager at Fidelity (as of February 1995) had been running his or her current fund for only 19 months. Of course, a few
managers have been managing their funds for many years. Here's the
breakdown. We've separated sector funds from other equity funds
because Fidelity seems to use them as a training ground before giving a manager responsibility for a diversified fund. We found that
only 21% of all the Fidelity fund managers were in place before 1990,
and in the case of sector funds, only 11%.

Table 73

Tenure of Fidelity portfolio managers*				
Percent distribution **As of February 1995**				
Year began	**Sector**	**Other equity**	**Fixed-income**	**All**
1980s	11%	22%	28%	21%
1990-91	3%	11%	8%	8%
1992-93	25%	50%	36%	38%
1994-95	61%	17%	28%	33%
Total	100%	100%	100%	100%
Median start	Aug. '94	Dec. '92	Sept. '93	July '93

*All stock and bond funds followed by the *Investor*. Load funds and money funds excluded.
Base counts: Sector - 36, Other equity - 46, Fixed-income - 50, all - 132.

Bear in mind that we are measuring tenure on the *current* fund. Many
Fidelity managers managed other Fidelity funds before assuming the
helm of their present post.

This turnover of managers has obviously not affected performance to
any meaningful degree; in fact, to the extent that it indicates a pruning
of weaker managers, turnover enhances performance. Fidelity has more
than its share of top-performing funds.

How do they do it? We think the key to Fidelity's success is its in-
depth organization, which backs up its portfolio managers. Here's the
power behind the scenes at Fidelity Investments. On the equity side: 44
research analysts, 25 assistant analysts, and 24 traders. On the fixed-
income side: another 37 analysts, 18 associate analysts, and 26 traders.
The analysts are typically specialists in various industries or areas (such
as junk bonds, commercial paper or what have you).

Sheldon Jacobs' Guide

We're focusing on Fidelity, here. But other major fund groups have also developed strong organizations, though not as large as Fidelity's. As a result, good managers leave these organizations and there is not a noticeable deterioration in performance. For example, when Roger McNamee ran the T. Rowe Price Science & Technology Fund, we thought he was a god. Apparently, there's more than one in the Price pantheon, because the fund has done very well since he left in 1991, averaging 19.5% per year from 1992 through 1994.

Smaller organizations lack this depth of management. In business, the big usually get bigger and there are good reasons. What should this mean to you as an investor? If two funds have similar performances, one belonging to a small group and the other to a large fund family, the odds favor selecting the latter. You'll probably get more consistently good performance. Your account will probably also get better service and administration. And if the fund at the larger group falters, it's a lot simpler to switch to another excellent investment. When a fund in a small organization veers off the road, you may well have to go through a time-consuming redemption/reinvestment process.

In any case, you are wise to be alert to the possible downside when management changes. Fund management is a people business; the person or group managing a fund is key. If you learn about a management change, investigate the replacement. If you don't feel the new manager is worthy, or if the fund's performance begins to deteriorate, you should sell.

Each year about 7%-10% of funds get new managers. In most cases, performance will not be affected, but there will always be some cases where a manager's departure does make a difference. You need to be aware of those cases.

Watch out for shifts in market leadership

In the early 1970s, a hallowed group of stocks was dubbed the "Nifty Fifty." There was nothing especially sacred about either the nomenclature or the number. It just seemed that roughly that many issues were in that most rarefied of Wall Street categories, the institutional favorites. They were the large-company growth stocks of the era, such household names as IBM, Coca-Cola, Polaroid, Eastman Kodak, Avon, McDonalds, Philip Morris, 3M, Xerox and others. The popularity of the "Nifty Fifty" was so high that their price-to-earnings ratios zoomed to incredible levels. In late 1972, the Putnam Index of 54 growth stocks listed their average P/E as 55 (compared with an average ratio historically of 15).

In the early 70s these were the winning stocks. And the growth funds that specialized in the "Nifty Fifty" were winners too. In its 1973 Survey of Mutual Funds, *Forbes* magazine listed several of these funds on its honor role—David L. Babson Investment (now Growth), Chemical (now Alliance Fund), Istel (now Lepercq-Istel), Massachusetts Investors Growth Stock, National Investors (now Seligman Growth), Pioneer and Putnam Investors.

Then came the savage 1973-74 bear market. Stock prices tumbled and both earnings and price/earnings multiples plunged. By October 1974, the Putnam Index average was only 16 times earnings. In the subsequent bull market, the leadership shifted to smaller, emerging growth companies, energy stocks and firms that thrive in a troubled economy. Funds specializing in the old "Nifty Fifty" never regained market leadership. Only one of the seven funds that *Forbes* honored in 1973 performed as well as the average fund during the next 10 years.

The disparity is illustrated by substantial performance differences between funds even within the same fund group. In the 10 years ending in 1983, the Rowe Price Growth Stock Fund (large-company stocks) gained only 62% while Price's New Horizons (small stocks) did far better, up 171%.

In 1983, market leadership again changed. There was a new "Nifty Fifty," the largest stocks in the S&P 500, the index's driving force. In the next seven years, the S&P 500, loaded with blue-chip stocks, outperformed broader indexes such as the Value Line and the Wilshire as well as the American Exchange and NASDAQ indexes, with their smaller cap stocks.

As a result, the funds holding large capitalization stocks—they're not called the "Nifty Fifty" anymore—were again leaders. Illustrating this reversal is the changed performance of two Price Funds. In the five years ending with 1990, Growth was up 60.8%, while New Horizons lagged with a 20.5% gain.

Similarly, leadership between growth and value funds changes from time to time as we explained in Chapter 6. The moral: When market leadership shifts, shareholders need to move too.

Sell if a fund changes its investing style

A successful small cap fund may grow too large, for example, and be forced to add mid-cap stocks. Or, a fund may find that its usual strategy (say, contrarianism) isn't working, and the fund shifts to a more trendy approach. The ploy may work, but keep in mind that wasn't what initially attracted you to the fund.

Sell when a new concept doesn't pan out

With so many funds angling for the investor's dollar, fund marketeers are always looking for new niches to exploit. Several trendy examples have occurred in recent years. They seemed good when announced and their sponsors gave logical reasons for expecting them to succeed. But success was illusive.

Global asset allocation funds are a good example. What could be a brighter idea than having professional managers deploying your dollars around the world and all over the asset spectrum in order to give you the finest returns? Great idea; hard to implement successfully. Granted, the funds' performance was hurt by the unexpectedly poor showing of gold, and to a lesser extent, international stocks and bonds. But the point is that reality didn't come close to meeting expectations.

Global short-term income funds are another example. They were hurt by unexpected changes in currency rates. Their hedging didn't provide the degree of protection that they had expected. And thus, they frequently underperformed comparable short-term funds investing domestically.

Funds investing in adjustable-rate mortgages are another example of new concepts that were hurt by unforeseen risks.

All these concepts—and many more over the years—held some initial promise. You can't succeed without taking some chances. But if the concept turns sour, don't hesitate to move on to something better.

Conservative fund guidelines

As a rule, sell a growth or growth-income fund when it ranks in the lower half of the funds in its category for one-to-two years. Managers of the growth and growth-income funds are not promising to make money overnight. They are selling on the basis of long-term performance. Investors ought to make a corresponding long-term commitment; so don't sell if a growth or growth-income fund does poorly for a short time. But don't "marry" a fund. You may love your investments, but they won't reciprocate your affection. Remember, you can easily switch to a better-performing fund with the same objective.

As you might expect, you can't expect to apply the same formula to aggressive growth funds that you would to more stable funds. Be much less patient with these gunslingers when they go bad. Keep in mind that aggressive funds take great risks in seeking large profits, and sometimes wind up with substantial losses. So making a long-term commitment may be foolhardy.

Also, think about the greater fool theory. That's the notion that there is always someone even more foolish than you that you can sell your losing investment to. Here's the inverse: the laugh may be on you if other shareholders decide to sell out of a sinking fund and you stay aboard. If redemptions exceed sales by a sizeable margin, the likelihood that the fund will turn around anytime soon is seriously diminished. Hunt for an alternative fund. Even if the first fund's performance lag turns out to be short-lived, the odds still favor selling and buying into a fund that's doing well.

The American Heritage Fund was a high-flyer for three years, but then in February 1994, the fund took a big hit—off 7.9%—as a result of declines in its outsized investment in Spectrum Technologies, a small computer company that had recently hired the former president of Apple, John Sculley, as its new CEO. This was a case where immediate selling was imperative. Redemptions were immediate, Heiko Thieme, the fund's manager was thrown off balance. The fund ended 1994 off 35.4% in a year when the average equity fund declined 1.8%

With both conservative and aggressive funds, it's extremely important that you try to determine the reasons for poor performance. Is it a change in market leadership? If so, is a reversal likely. Is it new management? Has the fund grown too large? Was the fund in the wrong derivatives?

The fund's latest quarterly report can often provide helpful information. The normally superior Strong funds turned in awful performances in 1989. In a February 1990 report to shareholders, the managers explained that the primary problem had been heavy investments in junk bonds. While these speculative securities had been winners for the funds for several years, they were a disaster in 1989. In its report, Strong management announced a change in policy. Henceforth, the Strong funds would limit junk bond holdings to 5% of each fund's assets. The funds have had relatively good years since 1989.

Aggressive growth fund standards are different

Aggressive growth funds take a beating in bear markets

The most volatile funds lack defensive capabilities. The speculative stocks they hold can take terrible drubbings, and most aggressive growth funds view that as simply the cost of doing their kind of business.

During the devastating bear markets of 1969-70 and 1973-74, the average high-performance fund declined by about half! Aggressive funds were also those hit hardest in the October 1987 meltdown, plunging 26% on average, versus a 13% decline for conservative income funds. Hopefully, no bears as grizzly as those lurk in the near future. But obviously we can't be sure. And certainly the markets will experience lesser declines from time to time. From July 16, 1990 to October 31, 1990, for instance, the average diversified equity fund declined 18.3%, while the average aggressive growth fund plunged by 24.4% on average. Bull & Bear Special Equities was at the ursine extreme, off 50.1%. Funds like CGM Capital Development, Columbia Special, Price New Horizons, SteinRoe Capital Opportunities, Twentieth Century Giftrust and Vista and USAA Aggressive Growth—outstanding investments in better markets—declined 30% or more. The S&P 500 was down 14.6% during this period. More recently, even in the relatively mild 1994 downturn, at least 100 load and no-load funds plummeted from 15% to 50%.

If you could accurately predict a bear market, clearly you would't hold aggressive growth funds through it. Alas, most investors make very poor forecasters, and are worse still at acting on their instincts. So we recommend our Flexible Funding Program strategy (explained in the last chapter) as a sound way of minimizing bear market losses.

Sell 12b-1 funds

Many new readers will discover that they own 12b-1 funds (see Chapter 2 for details) with as much as 1% taken off the top annually to pay for "distribution" expenses. It's costly to redeem these funds prematurely since you may well have to pay a contingent deferred sales charge that can cost you 5-6% of your assets in the first year. What's the best way to get out of this bad situation?

If the fund turns out to be a poor performer, there is no good way. You simply have to gulp hard and take your lumps. If the fund is a good performer, it probably pays to wait until the CDSC is reduced (it usually drops to zero within five years). Then switch to a more cost-effective alternative fund.

Here are some other guidelines to help you know when to get rid of a fund:

Sell when the cash position is inappropriate. If you believe the market is about to head south and your fund is fully invested—let alone leveraged—disagree with the fund's management by selling. Conversely, if you are bullish but your fund has a high cash position, switch to another fund that is fully invested in stocks.

Sell when a fund is in net redemptions. If other investors are bailing out in droves, it's almost always symptomatic of serious problems at that fund.

Sell to realize a tax loss. When you need an income tax deduction, selling a losing fund, can be a good way to get it. The money can easily be switched to another fund, and the government will share your loss with you. Under current law, capital losses can be used to offset capital gains. Moreover, you can deduct up to $3,000 against ordinary income. And if you wait as little as 31 days, you can return to the same fund you originally sold without running afoul of IRS wash-sale rules.

Although we have been primarily discussing stock funds, the same principles are even more applicable to bond funds. You should swap or sell them to establish a tax loss. Since the government is primarily responsible for bond losses, it's only proper that Uncle Sam share these losses, particularly since there are no transaction costs to reduce the tax loss benefits. This is one of the funds' great advantages over individual bonds. When selling small lots of individual bonds, the brokerage fees can be killers.

Sell erratic performers. Non-diversified and industry funds often perform erratically. Even diversified funds can show occasional brilliance if they hit it big with a trendy industry group. When the group cools, performance returns to normal.

Sell to rectify a mistake. You may buy a fund because it qualifies under all the guidelines. Yet unaccountably it may fail to live up to your expectations. Investing is an imperfect science. Sell.

Sell proprietary brokerage house funds to move. Funds—such as Merrill Lynch's—in that broker's account, can't be moved should you wish to transfer your account to a different brokerage house. In this case, the only way to close such an account is to sell these proprietary funds. Of course, you'll have to absorb the resulting tax consequences. (See Chapter 3 for details.)

Sell, sell, sell

What if your fund is merged

On rare occasions you may find yourself receiving a proxy statement announcing that management wishes to merge your fund into another one. What should you do? In most cases there isn't too much to worry about because the general rule in the fund business is that losers are merged into winners, rarely the other way around.

The acquiring fund will usually have a better performance record than the fund being acquired. The merged fund's record disappears into oblivion, never again to deter a potential investor. Sometimes there are other reasons. In 1989, the Liberty Fund, a small high-yield bond fund managed by Neuberger-Berman, was merged into the T. Rowe Price High Yield Bond Fund because Neuberger-Berman felt that junk bonds were an inappropriate investment for its shareholders.

Here's a question: because a merger will almost always be approved no matter how you vote, should you retain any shares in the new fund? Or should you sell? Consider these factors. Generally speaking a merger entails no tax consequences. But do read the fine print in the prospectus, and possibly consult a tax advisor to make certain. On the other hand, if you sell, you will have tax consequences.

Next, look at the acquiring fund as if it were a new purchase. Is its objective the same as that of the about-to-be-merged fund? If not, is its

---

Steadman funds — the all-time worst!

The champion *underperformer* undoubtedly is the Washington, DC-based Steadman Funds. Three of the group's four funds rank dead last for the fifteen years ending with 1994. Steadman Technology and Growth declined 71.7%, American Industry declined 64.5%, and Steadman Investment declined 18.4%, all in the midst of a great bull market. Their fourth fund, Associated, gained 46.9% over the fifteen years to rank seventh from last.

Notwithstanding this abominable performance, the Steadman funds still have 21,620 shareholders. Who, in their right mind, would stay with this group? *Barron's,* the weekly financial newspaper, attempted to answer that question, and reported their findings in the Jan. 9, 1995 edition. They failed to locate a single shareholder. Your author was asked to aid in the quest, but I flippantly replied, "They're mostly dead or near the end," which of course became the opening quote in the story. It turned out I was partly right. Under the terms of a legal settlement, shares representing 7%-22% of assets have been turned over to the District of Columbia under the Disposition of Unclaimed Property Act.

With an average account holding less than $600, it's quite likely that the balance of the accounts are for all practical purposes lost. Some might be long-forgotten custodial accounts set up for children, or the accounts of elderly people who are in nursing homes. If by some chance you happen to know a Steadman shareholder, urge him or her to redeem. With expense ratios as high as 13%, there is no hope for making a successful investment in a Steadman fund. And consider this a lesson. Redeem small accounts before you forget about them. All you need to do is move a couple times, and you, too, can be a lost account.

objective compatible with your investment goals? Will the same manager continue to guide the surviving fund? If not, the performance record of the acquiring fund will not mean as much. Is its expense ratio acceptable? If these factors present no problems, you probably should stay with the new fund.

You should also be alert to potential paperwork problems. Make sure that you are being credited with the proper number of shares in the new fund. When you get your first statement, look closely at your number of shares. They will have been adjusted to account for the fact that the surviving fund has a different NAV from the merged fund. Also, double check to make sure that you have all your confirmation slips for your original purchases and reinvestments. Years after the merger, they could be impossible to obtain from the fund.

Here's a situation that doesn't happen very often, but one to be aware of. In February 1995, Gabelli Asset Management proposed that its Gabelli Convertible Securities Fund, at that time a no-load, be converted to a closed-end fund. In our newsletter we strongly recommended that shareholders of the fund vote no, and switch out of the fund when the anticipated approval occurred. The reason, fully explained in the proxy statement (thanks to the SEC), was the strong possibility that as a closed-end, the fund would trade on an exchange for less than its net asset value, giving shareholders an unneeded loss.

Sure enough, a few weeks later 75% of the shares were voted in favor of the proposal, proof again that shareholders will approve almost anything management asks for. With a March 31, 1995 conversion date, we don't have the final chapter. But there was little to lose by selling, and a lot to lose by not. Gabelli did throw a sop to the fund's shareholders. They will be able to sell the fund at market value (not NAV) for another two years without paying brokerage commissions.

When not to sell

Size is not sufficient reason to sell aggressive growth funds. Although we have cautioned against buying such a fund once it gets too large, some large funds continue to turn in good performances, particularly if the market is favoring large capitalization stocks. So wait for a fund's performance to falter before you sell.

Don't sell funds for which you've paid front-end loads so long as they continue to perform. (You've already paid the commission.)

Don't sell a mutual fund for the same reason that you might sell a stock. Many investors believe quite logically that if a stock achieves a certain goal—for instance, doubling or tripling in price—they should sell it. This may be a good rule with stocks. Individual companies seldom go through more than one period of sustained rapid growth. Once they have passed this phase, future growth probably won't exceed that of the economy. The stock then becomes cyclical, moving in harmony with the rhythms of the economy. At this point, most investors who want spectacular growth sell the stock.

Funds are different. A fund is a constantly changing, managed portfolio of stocks and bonds. As long as the manager is performing well and the stock market is gaining, the fund should continue growing. It can never become "fully priced" in the sense that a stock can. Therefore, a fund need never be sold because it has hit some anticipated growth target. Moreover, don't hesitate to buy a fund because its per-share price has risen substantially. In a long-term bull market, it can continue to grow indefinitely.

A word of caution: don't sell after a big plunge. The dramatic stock market meltdown on October 19th, 1887 understandably spooked many investors. Yet, those who hung onto their funds were rewarded; for most funds, less than two years was required to regain the ground lost that October.

Despite what has sometimes been written, there were no massive liquidations of holdings by stock fund managers or shareholders on October 19th. The ICI reports that on that date, only two percent of stock fund assets were redeemed by shareholders, and two-thirds of the redemptions were handled from existing cash postions.

Sometimes after dramatic news, such as the injury or sickness of a major world leader, stocks will sell off. More often than not, this news has no economic consequences. You will be selling at a low if you panic. So, hold on. Eventually the market will rebound.

It's not a good idea to sell a fund with a large unrealized capital loss, if that loss is due to a general market decline. The tax consequences down the road may be less costly than they'd be with an alternative investment, which has no losses to offset against future gains.

In Summary

As a general rule, you will improve your investment results substantially by selling funds that rank in the bottom 50% of those in their investment objective category. Don't be afraid to ditch a dog. Furthermore, never feel that you are locked into a fund—not even a load fund. You paid a sales commission to buy a car, but that doesn't stop you from selling it when it no longer performs. Similarly, you should sell a fund—load or no-load—that gives you the wrong kind of ride.

With funds, most of the reasons for inaction are eliminated. If a fund you own falters and another's performance is superior, you are presented with a simple, actionable decision. You don't have to worry about commission costs. You know that if an aggressive growth fund drops out of the top rankings, it is unlikely to come back in the near future. And even if it did, you'd probably want to bail out simply because of its inconsistent performance.

Mutual funds allow you to invest more professionally. You have narrowed your alternatives and eliminated most of the psychological hang-ups that prevent people from making money in stocks. If you have this attitude, you can invest in "hot" funds with relative safety. Experts have always warned against them because their performance lags after a short time. However, with no-loads the argument favoring the hot funds is strong. Assuming that you can discipline yourself to sell at the opportune moment, the potential for gain is high, and the risk can be kept manageably low.

In updating this chapter for the *Guide*, I was struck by how much it has become the conventional wisdom. This wasn't always the case. The advice in this chapter has survived pretty much intact for more than two decades, since I first gave it in my first book, *Put Money In Your Pocket*, back in 1974. When that book was published, this chapter on selling caused something of a sensation in the investing world. A number of reviewers commented on it. *Money* magazine reprinted the entire chapter. Until this was written, nobody had ever challenged the then conventional mutual fund wisdom: buy and hold forever. Times certainly have changed!—S.J.

An editorial aside

CHAPTER 21

THE NO-LOAD FUND INVESTOR

Understanding the *Investor's* recommendations

Chapters one through 20 are designed not only to enable you to choose mutual funds on your own, but also to understand the specific no-load fund recommendations that we offer monthly in our companion publication, *The No-Load Fund Investor* newsletter.

The newsletter recommends funds, provides up-to-the-minute performance data, investment strategies and fund news. Since we don't have room in the *Investor* for detailed instructions on how to interpret its recommendations, the following guide explains the general rationales for our recommendations. There are, of course, exceptions, which we endeavor to spell out in the newsletter if they aren't covered below.

Unlike the measures of past performance discussed in Chapter 17 (top ten lists, etc.), the *Investor* recommends those funds that its editors believe most likely will achieve superior performance in the future. Recommendations are based on the analysis of fund performance over both the long and the short term. We do not use a mechanical system to recommend funds. We go beyond the quintile rankings and utilize the judgement that our years of experience have accumulated. We look at size, betas, cash positions, and our personal knowledge of management and its history of performance. Some fund groups deliver good performance over the long haul. We try to be patient with these groups if their funds are temporarily out of favor. Conversely, other funds have a long history of mediocrity. Every now and then one of these funds rockets in the standings. We will generally ascribe that performance to luck, and will ignore it until it is proven otherwise. We usually avoid recommending funds with unusually high expenses or 12b-1 fees.

With occasional exceptions (sometimes when a fund is first in a new niche), it is our general policy not to recommend a new fund until we have followed it for several months.

While the *Investor* newsletter follows a number of low-loads, primarily at Fidelity, we do not recommend them as a matter of principle. We make an exception to this rule for funds that charge a .5%-1% load payable to the *fund*, not to management. We highlight these funds with a dagger symbol to make you aware of the charge, but for all practical purposes they are pure no-loads, and we feel free to recommend them. Also a few funds levy a flat up-front fee—$50 to $100. For large purchases the fee becomes nominal. It's a borderline situation. If we like the fund and its concept, we may ignore the fee.

Our policy is to feature two categories of recommended funds. The first can be found in the *Investor's* tabular performance tables where we bold face recommended funds that we believe are the best in their peer group, usually the objective category. In some cases our recommendations refer to sub-categories. This is most often true of fixed-income funds. We bold face what we regard as the best of the short, intermediate, and long-term government and corporate funds, the best of the high yield, investment grade, and single state tax-free bond funds for those states that are covered by three or more funds. Sometimes these funds are not overall winners.

These recommendations are competitive. Sometimes we remove a recommendation simply because many other funds are doing better. However, on occasion we continue to recommend funds with below-average quintiles. The reason is that funds do not perform consistently. If a fund has good management and has performed well in the past, we quite often stick with that fund. The fund's performance may have dropped because the stocks it holds are temporarily out of favor or its cash position is inappropriate. Of course, if the stocks remain out of favor and the fund sticks with them, we will eventually drop our recommendation.

In the equity area we sometimes have standing recommendations on a few funds that tend to maintain high cash positions. These funds do well in down markets, but are usually weak performers in strong upmarkets.

Recommendations in the statistical tables do not imply market forecasts. By this we mean, for example, that while the recommendations for aggressive growth funds essentially apply to rising markets, we don't withdraw them during bear markets. That's because we want to give you time to pre-select the best aggressive growth funds for subsequent bull markets. Or it may not be obvious whether the market is a bull or bear.

The "Best buys" list of recommendations on the back page of the newsletter are our prime recommendations. They do take into account our market forecast (and, thus, may include a cash position). A deletion from Best buys does not necessarily mean you should sell the fund unless it is no longer shown in bold face in the tables. A deletion frequently means that we have found other funds in the same category that have somewhat higher potential, and that we want new subscribers to start with the best available selections. Funds not bold-faced in the tables are OK to sell. If we think a fund should be sold immediately, we will make that very clear in text.

Each newsletter also features three "Best buys" model portfolios, each for a different life style objective. The portfolios should be tailored to meet your individual needs by adjusting for specific risk preferences and time horizons. Similar funds that are bold-faced in the tables can be substituted for model portfolio recommendations. (This is a must if a recommended fund is unavailable in your state.) Investors with sizeable assets should use additional funds for greater diversification providing the total doesn't exceed recommended percent distributions in each category. While the model portfolios may contain either taxable or tax-free funds, if you're in a high tax bracket, substitute munis for any taxable bond funds; if your income tax bracket is low, substitute taxable bond funds for any recommended tax-free funds. The three model portfolios were discussed in detail in Chapter 17, page 198.

PART IV

The Pragmatic Side of Investing in No-Load Funds

CHAPTER 22

THE NO-LOAD FUND INVESTOR

Dealing with your no-load

Knowing the best procedures for buying, selling, keeping records and using the services offered by a no-load mutual can save you time and aggravation—and make you money.

You purchase no-load fund shares directly from the fund, ordinarily bypassing a broker. The exceptions generally involve money market funds, and a very few stock funds. You can buy Merrill Lynch Ready Assets Trust through any Merrill Lynch broker, for instance, or PaineWebber Cashfund through a PaineWebber broker. These transactions and balances are often listed on your regular brokerage statement.

You can always buy shares through the mail, and frequently by phone. The introduction of toll-free calls has revolutionized fund marketing. The vast majority of no-loads have 800 numbers, enabling you to deal directly with the fund, or the fund's transfer agent, at no charge and with a minimum of fuss and bother. That gives no-loads a human voice to handle many of the duties once taken care of by fund salesmen. (Fidelity, Vanguard, T. Rowe Price and others also use their 800 facilities to provide discount brokerage services for stock transactions.)

Funds are supposed to send you a prospectus before they accept your purchase. Those that take telephone orders usually will ask you if you have received the prospectus. If you say you haven't, you may not be able to buy shares on that day. If you say you have, there's a

How to buy fund shares

very good chance that the representative will take your order, particularly if you already have an account in another fund at the group, and are paying via exchange from the group's money fund. Sometimes the group will then send you a prospectus, automatically, a few days later. If not, you can always call again to request it.

If the fund doesn't accept phone orders or you don't want to wait for the prospectus to arrive, send the following letter:

Dear Sirs:

Please purchase as many shares as the enclosed check for $_____ will buy. Register the shares under *(name and address)*. My social security number is _____. Please reinvest all distributions.

Sincerely,

_____

Enclose your check with the letter. A few funds will return your check accompanied by a prospectus, but others will take the order, and then send the prospectus back with the confirmation. In any case, make sure that your order meets the fund's minimum initial investment requirements.

With mutual funds, price is virtually irrelevant. It is never a consideration in either the purchase or sale of a fund. You buy funds in dollar amounts, not a specific number of shares. Funds issue fractional shares to round out your purchases to the exact dollar amount you ordered.

Mutual fund returns are almost always analyzed in terms of percent changes, not in the change in the price of a share—i.e., the fund went from $7 to $10. That's because a discussion of growth in terms of price per share can be misleading if there has been a distribution, which lowers the apparent price. In this case, it would be similar to comparing the price of a stock after a split with the pre-split price. In evaluating a fund, the percent increase *with distributions included* is the only important consideration.

Unlike stocks, the per share price is not an indication of quality. There is no difference between a fund selling at $1.05 per share and one selling at $50 per share. Incidentally banks, which often will lend money against quality stocks but not against very low-priced stocks, occasionally apply the same policy to mutual funds. That's because they just don't understand how mutual fund pricing works. Surprisingly, two discount brokers trading mutual funds—Jack White and Waterhouse Securities—also discriminate. They won't allow investors to margin funds with NAVs under approximately $5.

Like stocks, funds sometimes split their shares—often for the same reasons. Funds split their shares to broaden their market by bringing the price down. This sometimes happens when a fund that has been marketed to institutions at a high per share NAV is now being marketed to individuals. Psychologically, it's comforting to some investors to have more shares at a lower price.

Moreover, a lower NAV means smaller daily cents per share fluctuations, which is also psychologically reassuring. When the Blanchard Short-Term Global Income Fund was launched, the sponsor put a low $1.97 price on it. A few months later the similar Scudder Short-Term Global Income Fund was launched at a $12 price. Since the shareholders of both funds prefer a stable price, the Blanchard Fund's pricing policy has given it a distinct edge. Minor price fluctuations are less likely to produce a one cent price change than in the case of the Scudder fund with its higher NAV.

Forget price per share

Establishing relations with a fund family

If you plan to work extensively with a fund group, we recommend you start by getting prospectuses for all the funds in that group that you think you might use. Be sure to include the group's money fund of your choice. This should be done in advance of the time when you plan to make your purchases.

We suggest that you establish your first account in the money fund by making the minimum investment. Set up wiring instructions, check writing, telephone switch to other funds and all the other features you might conceivably use.

You'd be surprised how long it can take if any problems arise. For example, if the money fund account is in your name and your bank checking account is in a joint name, this might be a cause for delay. Corporations and trusts may have special problems. Once everything is set up and in good working order, deposit the full amount that you intend to invest into the money fund. At that point it can be left there or easily switched to the stock or bond funds of your choice.

It's not a bad idea to test all these services. Switch a small amount. Wire some money back to your bank to see that they have the bank's correct ABA number and to find out exactly how long it takes to process the wire.

By making a trial run immediately, you minimize the chance of a costly disappointment later on. We know of an investor who was an astute market timer but careless in keeping his fund account in perfect order. With all his money in the group's stock fund, he was carefully tracking the market. On October 16, 1987, this investor's indicators gave him a sell signal. He immediately called the group and told them to switch everything to their money market fund. He was told they couldn't do it; the telephone switch privilege had to be set up in advance—and he hadn't done it! By the time this fellow got his account in order, and received the appropriate forms, it was too late. Black Monday intervened. Nowadays, switching privileges are generally automatic, but you still should read the application form carefully. We know of another case where it took one week to wire money from a money market fund to a bank.

Using discount brokers

Active investors should consider buying and selling no-load mutual funds through a discount brokerage firm. The fee is nominal. And if you plan to switch sizable sums between fund groups, or simply want to diversify among a number of fund groups, the convenience of dealing with one broker is well worth the cost. The brokerage firm provides you with regular statements. All your fund holdings are consolidated on one piece of paper, and at the end of the year, you receive just one 1099-DIV for all your funds.

You can execute overnight switching between fund groups using their extended-hours telephone service. This means you no longer have to wait for a redemption check or wire from one fund group before you can invest in another. That always causes a loss of interest on your money, and frequently lost profits, as well. In addition, the major discount brokers have branch offices throughout the U.S., so you can hand carry checks or paperwork to them when time is of the essence. These conveniences are particularly valuable for IRA accounts, where the paperwork involved in switching among several groups is far more onerous.

On the other hand, the infrequent trader or smaller investor can obtain more than adequate service by dealing directly with the fund. That avoids transaction fees.

A number of discount brokers now specialize in mutual fund accounts, but by far the most important are Charles Schwab, Fidelity and Jack White. Schwab and White will let you invest in about one thousand funds; Fidelity, about 2,000. The fees are generally modest and in many cases, free.

Trading funds without paying transaction fees

Many discount brokers now trade certain no-loads without any transaction fees. They are able to do this by having the no-load funds, rather than the investor, pay the commissions. The amounts vary somewhat but range from 0.25% to 0.35%. In the case of 12b-1 funds, the broker's commission is paid out of the 12b-1 fee. For pure no-loads, about 10-15 basis points comes from transfer agent savings, the balance from the manager.

The funds like this approach because they can add investor accounts without having to pay any marketing costs. So the fund realizes offsetting savings. If any charges are being passed onto investors, they are probably minimal, certainly far less than the usual commissions.

At press time, Charles Schwab was offering over 400 no-load funds from 27 families fee-free; Fidelity, 345 from 38 families. (The number of funds changes frequently.)

Some or all of the funds in the following fund groups are available fee-free from one or more of the discount brokers: Alliance, American Heritage, Babson, Baron, Bartlett, Benham, Berger, Blanchard, Bramwell, Bull & Bear, Calvert, Capiello-Rushmore, Cohen & Steers, Crabbe Huson, Dreman, Dreyfus, Eclipse, Federated, Fidelity, Flex, Founders, Gateway, Gintel, Heartland, IAI, Idex, Invesco, Janus, Kaufmann, Leeb, Lexington, Loomis Sayles, Merriman, Montgomery, Neuberger-Berman, Oberweis, PBHG, Pfamco, Pimco, Robertson Stephens, Rushmore, Schwab, Selected, SEI, Skyline, SteinRoe, Strong, Twentieth Century, United Services, Value Line, Warburg Pincus, Wasatch, Weiss Peck & Greer, William Blair, Wright Equifunds, and Yacktman. More are added from time to time.

Four of the five largest groups—Fidelity (except in its own brokerage operation), Vanguard, T. Rowe Price, and Scudder—have declined to participate. Fidelity refuses to cooperate with other brokerage firms for competitive reasons. The other three say they will not participate because of cost considerations. All four do make their funds available for the usual brokerage fees, however.

Nevertheless, with so many fund families participating, the no-transaction-fee services have become desirable for all investors.

This program is not a gold mine for frequent switchers. They still have to pay the usual commissions. If you think you may be in this category, call each brokerage firm for its exact definition. (It's also in our *Handbook.*)

In selecting a discount broker, you are better off dealing with Fidelity Brokerage if you plan to move in and out of Fidelity funds, since that's the only way to get those funds without paying transaction costs. Charles Schwab, the innovator, provides excellent all-around service. Jack White, the third major player is somewhat cheaper.

Not all funds are available everywhere

Mutual funds are organized and operated under federal laws. But, in addition, they must be registered in accordance with the laws of the states where they conduct business. Since it is expensive and time-consuming to obtain registrations in all states, many funds don't register everywhere. Then, too, funds using the most speculative investing methods may not be able to satisfy every state's blue-sky laws and may be prohibited from selling shares in some places.

California and Tennessee prohibit sales of fund shares when

expenses exceed certain levels, although in some cases waivers can be obtained. In the case of California, the limit is 2% of the first $10 million, 1.5% of the next $20 million and 1% over $30 million. Because of these limits, a good many funds waive a portion of their fees to keep their expense ratios down.

If you try to buy shares in a fund not registered in your state, don't be surprised if your money is returned. The reason some funds are cautious is the possibility of rescissions; investors holding fund shares sold improperly can, in some circumstances, demand that the sale be rescinded. In this case, the investor gets back the same amount he paid for the shares, plus interest—regardless of the shares' current value. That's pretty tempting if the value of the fund's shares has dropped. The laws and practices governing rescissions are complex, and vary from state to state. The decisions resulting from a few court cases have not been clear-cut. So fund policies differ.

A few small funds simply ignore these difficulties. Since no-loads don't have sales personnel, they assume that purchases are unsolicited. Investors, after all, learn of the fund through national advertising, publicity, or an advisory service. Those no-loads that make this assumption accept unsolicited orders from states where they are not registered. Their contention: that the purchase is actually consummated at the fund's home office, not at the investor's residence.

If you want a particular fund and it isn't qualified in your state, you may want to try anyway, particularly if you're in no hurry. Our annual *Handbook* lists states qualified. If it's a new fund, they may have added your state recently. The funds should tell you their policy over the phone.

Telephone switching

Modern no-load fund investors can now take advantage of telephone switching offered by practically every fund family. With a simple phone call, mutual fund investors can buy and sell funds as easily as they can stocks. The only requirement is that they move their money around within one fund family or, in a few instances, back and forth to an independent money fund. Groups can offer this flexibility because of their in-house money market funds. Fund managers used to discourage selling because they derived their income solely from management fees, which disappear when you redeem your fund shares. But that is not the case when an investor switches from a stock fund to a money market fund within the same group. The adviser still collects his management fee.

If you're actively managing money in funds, telephone switching offers many advantages:

■ Generally, you incur no commission costs by simply shifting your money from one fund to another.

■ When you sell your shares in a stock fund, the proceeds go into a money market fund, where you immediately begin earning interest.

■ You are switching among working portfolios; hence, you don't have the problem of establishing a position from scratch.

■ Telephone switching is a very good way to sell fund shares. Traditionally, selling mutual fund shares was a problem; the procedure was made intentionally cumbersome by the fund groups. To redeem your shares you first had to read the prospectus to find out the fund's specific procedures. Usually, you'd then need to write a letter. And invariably you'd then have to get your signature guaranteed at your bank or brokerage firm. Then you'd have to settle in for a wait until your letter was received by the fund or its custodian bank. The fund has seven days to mail the proceeds out. Funds usually take somewhat less. But the whole process can easily consume a couple of weeks from the time you decide to sell until you get your money. Now, one telephone call accomplishes your primary purpose—to get out of equities! In the October 1987 meltdown, more than 80% of the money redeemed from stock funds was switched into money market or bond funds.

Caveat: Switching from one fund to another, whether by phone or in writing, is considered by the IRS to be like any other sale. The transaction must be reported as a capital gain or loss on Schedule D.

How telephone switching began

In the early seventies, Fundpack, a Florida multifund, conducted studies which led to the hypothesis that using a stop-loss strategy would produce returns superior to a buy-hold strategy. Fundpack selected a rigid 10% guidepost based on its hypothetical studies. It would sell any funds in its portfolio that declined more than 10% from any point, and would buy back after a 10% rise or an unusually positive news development.

Fundpack's strategy turned out to be a loser. In a mid-1973 special report to shareholders, the firm noted: "But in the neurotic current market decline, Fundpack's prices declined 26% before Fundpack solidified itself. What happened?" The firm went on to explain that, "in whipsaw actions of the market, some of our buybacks declined a second and even a third 10%." Consequently, Fundpack discontinued its strategy in 1975. After adding a money market fund, it became the first fund group to offer telephone switching, thus leaving any stop-loss strategies to the discretion of its shareholders.

When you buy, sell or switch by phone you should keep a record of the transaction. Major groups like Fidelity will give you a confirmation number at the end of the transaction. Keep it until the confirmation arrives. If you don't get a number, get the name of the representative you spoke to and the time and date of the conversation.

Most funds permit unlimited switching. But because it is difficult to manage a fund when large amounts of money are moving in and out, a number of major fund families discourage short-term market timers by placing limitations on the switching privilege. Twentieth Century, Scudder and SteinRoe limit switching to four round trips per year. Funds limit switching to protect their managers against potential disruptions in the portfolio which can result from too frequent in and out activity by market timers. For this reason, a few funds refuse to provide telephone switch privileges. Others won't join the discount broker services that facilitate trading by phone. On the other hand, most of the bigger groups don't care how frequently small investors trade. Instead, they monitor large investors closely.

In 1990, Fidelity and SteinRoe starting curbing the buy and sell activities of investors who relied on certain switch fund newsletters. Fidelity, in particular, notified shareholders whose trading activity coincided with the recommendations of Fabian's Investment Resource newsletter that they would no longer accept buy orders into domestic growth or growth-income funds resulting from Fabian's buy signals. Fidelity told these shareholders that "if you continue to follow your newsletter market timing strategies, you should make arrangements to move your investment to another fund organization." Fidelity adopted this policy because massive amounts of money was being switched at the same time, to the detriment of the funds' long-term shareholders.

Switching has become very popular in recent years. In 1987, a traumatic year, more than one-quarter of fund assets were switched. In recent years, about one-eighth of fund assets move from one fund to another each year.

Almost all mutual funds are priced—the net asset value is computed—at the close of the business day—4 PM Eastern time. As a result, any investor buying or selling a mutual fund gets this end-of-day price, no matter what time the mail or phone call arrives.

This pricing policy has important implications for investors pur-

The only time of day to buy

chasing fund shares by telephone who are looking for that extra tim-ing edge, or who just want all the information humanly possible before making a buy or sell decision. The fact that you can only get the 4 PM Eastern time price can sometimes make or save money for you. But it can also lose you money.

Guideline: When buying or selling by telephone, make your deci-sion shortly before the market's close.

Sometimes the market surges upward at the opening bell because of some important news occurring the previous evening after the mar-ket had closed or just because traders feel the market may have reached a turning point. If you're buying funds, do nothing! The surge may last only a few hours and be inconsequential. You lose nothing by waiting. There was no way you could have gotten an earlier price.

Another situation: It is not uncommon for sharp moves in the last hour or two to continue in the same direction the following morning. If the market is down considerably at 3:30 PM, it may be advanta-geous to wait a day before buying.

The lone exception to the end-of-day pricing practice is at Fidelity, which prices its Select sector funds *hourly*. Select investors can buy in or sell out at any time of the day, and they can day-trade (buying and selling the same day). As is always the case, the funds are for-ward priced. That means you get the next hour's price. The only investors getting the end-of-the-day price are those who buy between 3 PM and 4 PM. If you bought at the 9:30 AM opening, you will get the 10 AM price and you can call them back at about 10:15 AM to find out how much you paid. Hourly pricing can give sophisticated investors an additional edge; but it's not essential—and could be dangerous—for laymen who don't follow their investments closely.

End of the day pricing can sometimes give you a greater edge when buying international funds. Most overseas markets are already closed by 4 PM Eastern Time.

Redeeming your shares

If you've invested in a stock or bond fund that is part of a group with a telephone switch capability, you'll probably find it easier to first switch to the money fund and then write a check for your money.

If you need the money instantly you may want it transferred to your bank by wire. Some funds permit redemptions by telephone; others only by mail. Each fund spells out its redemption procedures in its prospectus. You'll get your money more easily if you follow the directions exactly. If you can't find the prospectus, call the fund on its 800 number and ask for instructions. Here is a sample redemption letter:

Dear Sirs:

  Please redeem all shares (or *number* shares) of XYZ Fund. My account number is _____. Please send proceeds to the address of record as soon as possible.

                                        Sincerely,

_____

It is also helpful to enclose a blank copy of a subsequent investment form. It will have the exact account name and number on it. Send the redemption letter to either the fund or its transfer agent, as described in the prospectus. For large sums, register the letter, requesting a return receipt. It costs more, but you will have a record of the date the fund actually received your request. Your shares should be sold at the closing price on that date.

When redeeming, be sure to find out whether you need a signature guarantee. Mutual funds commonly require that your signature on the redemption letter be guaranteed by a commercial bank or brokerage firm. Having it notarized is not acceptable.

If you want your redemption to be made as fast as possible you should write your redemption letter now, leaving the amount blank if you plan to make only a partial redemption. Take it to the bank and have your signature guaranteed. Then file it with your other records. When the time comes to redeem, send it by overnight mail. This way you will be assured of next-day redemption.

According to SEC regulations, payment for shares redeemed must be made within seven days after the letter of redemption has been received or after issued shares have been deposited with the fund. While checks are usually sent out promptly, it is not unknown for a custodial bank to hold up payment for the full seven days and sometimes longer. Considering weekends and slow mail, it may take as much as two weeks for your check to arrive. So, if you are planning to redeem to meet a specific financial need and have a deadline, allow two weeks between writing your letter of redemption and getting a check back.

Why you need a signature guarantee

You may wonder why that is necessary; why you can't have your signature notarized instead. The answer is that a notary public merely certifies the identity of the person signing the document. The purpose of the signature guarantee is to protect against improper transfer of property interest—in this instance the ownership of mutual fund shares. The guarantor warrants that not only is the signature genuine, but also that the person is an appropriate person to endorse and has the legal capacity to sign. The ultimate effect of the signature guarantee is to transfer liability to the guarantor. This protects the funds from the costs of fraudulent transactions.

Since this is rare, the signature guarantee may not be necessary for small amounts.

Redemptions during panics

In periods of unusual market activity, such as in October 1987, investors worry about getting their money out. Many of these worries are unfounded. If a fund's 800 telephone number is relentlessly busy, you may be able to get through on the fund's regular (non-toll-free) number. Long distance is cheap today. If you anticipate problems, you can check and see if the fund will accept a redemption by fax. The dedicated fax lines are less likely to be tied up. By law (the Investment Company Act of 1940) all mutual funds must redeem shares at a price based on the current NAV per share that the fund next computes after receipt of a redemption order. Funds compute their NAVs every day.

October 19, 1987, when the Dow Jones Industrial average plummeted more than 500 points, was a disaster for most mutual fund investors. If they hadn't sold the previous week, they were, with one exception, locked in for the full 500 point loss. There is very little advice that can be given when such a once-in-a-lifetime event occurs, but it should be pointed out that the investors who were able to get through to their funds and sold out that Monday were actually worse off than those who didn't. As it turned out, there was a 289 point rally over the next two days, which made Wednesday the optimum point to exit the market until the shocks of the aftermath were over. Sometimes, the inability to sell in a panic works to the investor's advantage.

On October 19 and 20, 1987, some fund groups decided to take the full seven days allowed before mailing out checks. Fidelity was one, but by the 21st, had resumed regular daily payment procedures. When the purpose of a redemption is to avoid dropping stock prices, it is not so important if there's a few days' delay in receiving your check.

Under certain unusual conditions the right of redemption can be temporarily suspended. One is when the New York Stock Exchange closes (for other than regular holidays). That's because funds simply can't price their portfolios when the market is closed. The Investment Company Act also permits the SEC to declare an emergency during which mutual funds can suspend redemptions. The SEC has exercised its authority under this section when, for example, major snowstorms have paralyzed the Northeast corridor. In addition, funds may suspend both sales and redemptions during customary local holidays (such as Patriot's Day in Boston), provided adequate disclosure of the holiday closing schedule is given to investors in the fund's prospectus.

Theoretically, funds can also redeem in kind. This means your receiving a proportionate share of the fund's portfolio securities. Redeeming in kind is virtually unheard of in the industry. A few years ago, the ICI conducted a survey of its larger members and found only one redemption in kind. And that was an unusual case in which a shareholder request was being honored. It's not difficult for a fund to redeem in cash. The fund is required to have at least 85% of its portfolio invested in liquid securities, i.e., securities which are readily saleable. In addition, funds keep cash reserves, sometimes have credit lines with banks, and even in the worst of times have some new money flowing in, if only from dividends. In October 1987, the Fidelity Magellan Fund handled approximately $1 billion in redemptions without strain.

When you redeem a fund account completely, most funds do not immediately remove the account from their shareholder records. Therefore, you may be able to reinvest in the same account at a later date, a simpler procedure than having to open a new account. Most funds purge their inactive subscriber records about once a year.

Communicating with your fund group

A few years ago, the funds were publicly criticized for providing account information or accepting buy and sell orders over the phone without properly identifying the caller. While we doubt that this practice caused significant harm, most fund groups now require that callers properly identify themselves. Thus, when you call a fund about your account, it's a good idea to have your Social Security or tax ID number and your account number close at hand before you call. For security reasons many groups have deleted the Social Security number from periodic statements and confirmations, in case they fall into the wrong hands. Don't look for it there.

Mutual fund distributions

One of the most confusing aspects of mutual fund investing is the manner in which distributions are made. Like operating companies, funds declare dividends. But since they are investment companies, they also declare capital gains distributions, resulting from the gains realized when stocks or bonds in the fund's portfolio are sold at a profit.

Federal regulations require that mutual funds distribute at least 98% of their ordinary income and net realized capital gains for the calendar year within that same calendar year. Failure to do so results in a 4% excise tax on the excess not distributed. These distributions must be declared prior to December 31 of each year and paid prior to January 31 of the following year. The distributions are considered as taxable income to investors in the year in which they are declared, even if paid the following January.

Prior to 1986, funds commonly made their distributions in January for the prior year's income. These so-called spillover dividends gave shareholders a full year before they had to pay taxes on the profits. This is no longer possible, having been outlawed by a provision of the 1986 Tax Reform Act. Too bad. It was a great loophole.

Although most municipal bond fund interest is exempt from federal tax, income from "private activity" municipal bonds may be subject to the alternative minimum tax. Your fund will let you know what percentage of its income, if any, is subject to the tax. Additionally, if a muni bond fund sells a bond at a profit, the capital gain is taxable.

Mutual funds commonly offer three distribution options: All income and capital gains distributions are automatically reinvested in additional shares, income distributions are paid in cash while capital gains distributions are reinvested in additional shares, or both income and capital gains distributions can be paid in cash.

Distribution options

For most investors, the first option—reinvestment of all distributions—is best. Your investment compounds and in a rising market will grow faster. Reinvesting dividends is actually a form of dollar-cost averaging.

The logic behind the second option is that you are gaining immediate benefits from the income dividend distributions, but are not eating into your capital. It is important to maintain your capital in real (inflation adjusted) terms. In the case of equity funds, reinvesting capital gains will generally accomplish this purpose. Secondly, while there is no real distinction between dividend income and capital gains, as a practical matter an investor looking for steady income might prefer the second option so he or she does not receive occasional, large distributions that would only have to be reinvested. (Dividends and capital gains are said to be of the same nature because a corporation has the option of reinvesting its profits for further growth, rather than paying dividends. What is the logic of utilities paying out millions in dividends, and then turning around and borrowing or selling more stock or bonds for expansion?) We recommend this option for most retired investors living on their income.

If you take the third option, you receive all distributions in cash. This option can be used to restrict the size of your investment without incurring possible gains by selling. The distributions can then be reallocated to other investments. This option is a good one to consider if you have a sizeable capital gain from a long-term investment in a fund that is no longer performing as it used to.

Don't overlook your bond funds; when interest rates are rising, take their distributions in cash. This option will also simplify your accounting when the time comes to sell. If you purchased lump sum and didn't reinvest distributions you will have only one cost basis;

you'll save a few minutes when it comes time to prepare Schedule D of your tax return.

In addition, be aware that a number of the larger groups offer another option that can be highly desirable. Fidelity, Dreyfus, Vanguard and T. Rowe Price, for example, will direct the distributions from one fund in the group to another fund for reinvestment. You can implement option three by having the cash distributions from a stock or a bond fund reinvested in the group's money fund. This is a convenient way of maximizing your returns until you actually need the money.

Gains—both realized and unrealized—affect you

As with individuals, mutual funds can have realized or unrealized gains on their portfolios, or realized or unrealized losses. These gains and losses have investment implications. As we noted earlier, net realized gains will be distributed to shareholders of record at the time of the distribution. Old shareholders will rightfully pay taxes on these distributions since they received the growth. New shareholders receive no benefit, only the tax liability. If the gain is unrealized there is no immediate tax liability, but certainly a potential one. After several bull market years, many funds will have unrealized appreciation. If they sell appreciated stocks, perhaps anticipating a bear market, the gains will become realized and the tax collector will receive his due. (Of course, that's assuming that an investor holds the fund shares in a non-tax-qualified account. With the increasing importance of IRAs, 401(k) plans and rollovers in individuals' portfolios, tax considerations are diminishing.)

Conversely, realized losses offer opportunities for tax deferral. In a bear market, smart mutual fund managers often realize their losses as they sell losing positions. But, unlike gains, the resulting tax loss benefits are not passed through immediately to the shareholders. The fund doesn't distribute capital gains profits until its losses are fully offset. And because the Internal Revenue Service permits funds to carry these losses forward for five years, shareholders can enjoy a considerable grace period while the fund is accruing new gains. In this situation, there is no tax liability until the shareholder sells the shares at a profit.

While other criteria are more important, don't ignore this valuable plus when you are considering buying a fund. The prospectus or quarterly reports will provide information on gains or losses. During long bull market periods, few funds have capital loss carry forwards. But when the bear comes out of hibernation, it's another story. For example, some bond funds had sizeable accumulated losses in 1994 as a result of the downturn and forced selling to meet redemptions. For example, the $46 million SAFECO GNMA Fund had an accumulated undistributed net realized loss of $2.3 million as of September 30, 1994.

Novice fund investors rejoice when they receive a dividend. More experienced investors aren't always so glad. Here's why.

Reducing the tax burden

Let's assume your fund has accumulated profits and plans to distribute them to its shareholders. The fund now has an NAV of $12 per share and plans to distribute $1 per share in income. The fund goes ex-dividend. (That's when the dividends to be paid are segregated from the rest of the fund's assets. The day that happens the daily papers put an "x" by the fund.) The per share price immediately drops $1 to $11 since funds are always priced at net asset value. A shareholder will soon receive $1 per share in dividends or have the $1 per share reinvested in additional shares of the fund. Either way, the shareholder still has a total equity of $12 per share. If he takes the distribution in cash, he has fund shares worth $11 per share plus a dollar in his pocket. If he reinvests the shares his total equity—number of shares times per share price—is still the same. He has not benefited from the distribution, only incurred a tax liability. That's assuming the investor's account is not in an IRA, Keogh or other tax-qualified plan. This is true even if the distribution is reinvested!

After several bull market years, gains can be sizeable. In December, 1993, the Warburg Pincus Growth & Income Fund declared a $3.77 per share capital gains distribution. On the prior close, the fund's price had been $12.92. The distribution amounted to 31% of the fund's net asset value. If you had bought the day before the ex-dividend date, you would have incurred a whopping tax liability. Similarly, the Manager's Balanced Fund paid $4.67 in distributions. With a prior NAV of $17.58, this amounted to 27% of NAV.

You can minimize your tax liability by carefully timing your purchases. Take the case of a fund that distributes once a year, in December. If you buy just before the distribution, you immediately incur a tax liability. You have acquired a share of the other stockholders' profits. On the other hand, if you wait until after the distribution, the NAV will be lower by the amount of the distribution. You will be able to buy more shares for your money, and have no tax liability until you sell or until the fund declares its next annual distribution.

Incidentally, beware of brokers who "sell dividends." This is the disreputable practice of inducing an investor to buy fund shares in order to receive a dividend distribution in the near future. Buying a stock just before a dividend is declared can be smart. In the case of a mutual fund, you lose.

Many funds will give you the exact dates of their distributions a few days or weeks before they are made if you phone them. When you call, make sure to find out the precise ex-dividend date and the record date (not the date the distribution actually gets paid—often a week or so later). Go by the ex date, usually the day after the record date. In the aftermath of the 1986 Tax Reform Act, most funds now make major distributions in December. So, be especially careful if you are planning to make purchases at year-end.

Money market funds and most bond funds declare dividends daily. In the case of these funds, the advice offered in the preceding paragraphs does not apply since there is no chance for the interest income to build up. Their NAVs are unaffected by the daily distribution of interest income.

If you need to be careful about your purchases, that does not really extend to your sales. In general, it makes no difference whether you sell just before or just after a distribution is made. By selling just prior to a distribution, you will receive a higher price, potentially giving you a larger gain. If you sell afterwards, the price, and your capital gains liability, will be lower; but you'll have to pay tax on the fund's capital distribution. Exception: if the distribution is an income or short-term capital gains distribution, it is fully taxable. On the other hand, if selling prior to the distribution enables you to obtain a long-term capital gain, you will benefit if you are in a high tax bracket.

Know your cost basis

When a fund reinvests your dividend and capital gains distributions, these sums become part of your cost basis. For tax purposes, it's as if the fund had sent you checks for the amounts due and you then returned the money to buy additional shares. And, of course, you paid taxes on each distribution the year it was declared. Here, for example, are the final tax consequences of a ten-year gain through December

1994 on an investment of $10,000 made in the T. Rowe Price International Stock Fund.

Value of shares initially purchased 12/31/84	$17,177
Value of shares acquired by reinvestment of dividends	5,764
Value of shares acquired by reinvestment of capital gains	<u>29,529</u>
Total value of investment after 10 Years	$52,470

While the only money the investor actually paid to the fund during the 10 years was the initial $10,000, if he or she sold the shares on December 31, 1994, the cost basis would be:

Initial investment — Dec. 31, 1984	$10,000
Dividends used to purchase shares	5,382
Capital gains distributions used to purchase shares	<u>27,990</u>
Total Cost Basis	$43,372

Thus, although the original investment of $10,000 is now larger by $42,470, the capital gain reported for tax purposes is only $9,098 (the difference between $52,470 and $43,372). Taxes on the balance of the gains have already been paid. Always save the distribution statements the fund sends you so that you can provide the IRS with the proper cost basis if and when the time comes.

When you sell fund shares, you can use any of several methods for determining your cost basis. The differences can be important if you are making a partial liquidation.

1. You can sell *specific shares*. It is best to do this by letter, specifically identifying by number and purchase date the shares you want

to sell. Keep a copy of the letter; the fund's confirmation statement will be of no help.

2. *First in, first out (FIFO)*. If you don't instruct otherwise, the shares bought first will be deemed to have been sold first. If these were bought at the lowest cost, the tax bill will be higher.

3. *Average cost per share.* You take the total cost of your shares and divide by the total number of shares to get the average. You must make a special election with the IRS to use this method. Some funds are now providing their shareholders with average cost per share data.

4. *Double category method.* You can figure one average cost for long-term holdings and another for short-term holdings. This method is important if you're in a high tax bracket substantially above long-term capital gains rates.

The "wash sale" trap

If you have set up your fund account for dividend reinvestment, don't fall into this tax trap. Mutual funds, like any other securities, can be sold to establish a tax loss. If you sell a security at a loss, you can't buy back your shares until more than 30 days have passed or the IRS will disallow the loss for tax purposes as a wash sale. This potential problem can occur with any fund, but it can really catch you unawares if you make a partial liquidation of a bond fund that pays monthly dividends. That's because any dividend reinvestment is a purchase that offsets your sale. You can avoid this complication, either by making a complete, rather than a partial, liquidation, by switching from a reinvestment to a cash distribution account for at least 31 days, or by specifying which shares you are selling. This tax problem is also a good reason for not establishing a check redemption feature in bond funds with variable NAVs.

Tax-managed funds

One no-load approaches the tax liability problem from the opposite direction. The policy of the Copley Fund is to distribute nothing to its shareholders. The fund reinvests all its income and capital gains. Thus you never have to pay taxes on distributions. (The only time you owe is if you sell your shares at a gain.)

However, since the funds don't qualify for conduit treatment by distributing at least 90% of their income, they are subject to the Federal income tax charged corporations. (And under the new tax law, the funds are also subject to a 4% excise tax.) However, because Copley is taxed as a corporation, it is allowed to deduct 70% of the dividends it receives from other corporations—in this case the shares of the companies in its portfolio.

Some other funds make claims to tax-management, but they aren't exactly the same. The Vanguard Tax-Managed Funds are more properly described as tax-efficient funds. Using various techniques, they seek to minimize distributions, but not necessarily eliminate them.

As a mutual fund shareowner you will receive many types of reports from your fund. You should save some, usually for tax purposes. Read and discard others.

Read and retain: The *prospectus*. This provides basic information you need to know about the fund. Save the current prospectus.

Reports of transactions: Every time you make a purchase or redemption, or the fund declares a distribution, you should receive a confirmation. These confirmations note how many shares you bought and sold and at what price. Funds send individual confirmations, statements that recapitulate previous transactions, usually for the calendar year, or both. In the case of cumulative statements, save only the most recent. These confirmations and statements must be saved for tax purposes until you sell your shares, then for as long as you retain tax records, generally for three years after the date you file your returns. If you are missing a statement, the fund can usually provide you with a duplicate, in some cases at a nominal charge.

If the fund declares income or capital gains dividends, it will send you a form 1099. Put it with your other tax records. Note that the IRS requires that funds treat distributions of short-term capital gains as "ordinary income." The two categories are combined on the 1099, even though they are generally shown separately on the fund's transaction confirmations.

Another form you should retain is the "explanation of tax information" that sometimes accompanies the 1099. It lists the classifications of distributions for your income tax returns. The form explains how the information should be reported. Municipal bond funds usually enclose a form listing dividends by state. You can deduct that percentage of the dividend payment that originates in your own state when paying state taxes.

Record keeping

Sign and return: proxy statements. Do the fund a favor. It needs a quorum of the shares so the annual meeting can be held. Usually it is sufficient to read the front page only. Quite often it says only that the directors and accounting firm will be continued. Sometimes you will be asked to vote for an increase in the management fee or a 12b-1 fee. If you disagree you can vote no. In any case, send it back. If you do disagree with the direction management is taking, your best recourse, as with most public corporations, is to sell.

Read: quarterly and annual reports. If you want to refer to the composition of the fund's portfolio, save these reports until later ones arrive. You can read and discard informational material, such as letters from the president and fund newsletters.

The president's or portfolio manager's letter can be informative, particularly if it is honest. The usually top-performing Windsor Fund did terribly in 1990. In its annual report, Vanguard Chairman Bogle laid it on the line as these excerpts from his letter attest: "The Fund provided a distinctly poor return to its investors during the fiscal year...While the stock ·market environment was unfavorable...the Fund's stunning decline was far larger than that of stocks as a group, and of most competitive funds." Bogle then went on at great length to spell out the details of how they went wrong.

How safe are mutual funds

With the anxiety about the safety of financial institutions, especially banks and S & L's, it's natural that investors frequently raise questions about the safety of money in mutual funds.

Rest easy. While the price of your fund shares rises or falls with moves in the markets, there is little cause for concern in terms of a fund company going bankrupt or defrauding shareholders. Safeguards have been built into the industry by the Investment Company Act of 1940. Here are some of its provisions that protect you. The act prevents:

■ insiders from manipulating the companies to their own benefit and to the detriment of public investors;

■ issuance of securities that have inequitable or discriminatory provisions;

■ management of investment companies by irresponsible persons.

■ the use of unsound or misleading methods of computing earnings and asset value;

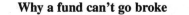

Why a fund can't go broke

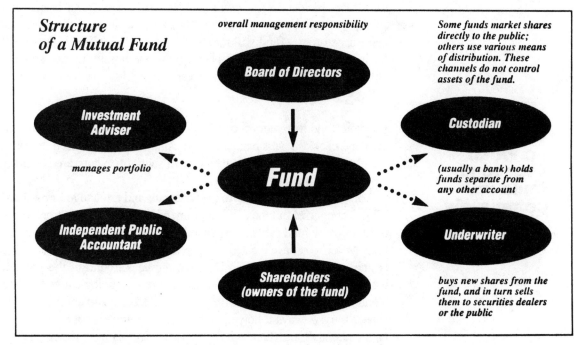

■ changes in the character of investment companies without the consent of investors; and

■ excessive leveraging on the part of investment companies.

The act also ensures the disclosure of full and accurate information about companies and their sponsors.

Mutual funds are organized as wholly separate companies with their assets held by a separate custodian. No creditor has recourse against the assets of your mutual fund to meet the obligations of an investment advisor or underwriter. The funds' assets are held by separate custodians. The advisor's officers and key employees are bonded, and auditing is done by outside firms.

Funds prefer not to issue stock certificates, and will do so only if you request one. T. Rowe Price has eliminated stock certificates entirely. As a general rule it's better to leave your shares uncertificated. It is safer and facilitates selling. If you have certificated shares they must be sent, properly signed, to the fund's transfer agent for redemption. However, there

**Do I want
a stock
certificate?**

is one possible reason for obtaining the certificates: to use as collateral for a loan. Incidentally, if you lose your certificates (fund or corporate stock), you will have to put down 2%-3% of the value of the shares as a deposit before the fund will reissue the shares. The deposit is basically for insurance, to the fund company against the possibility that someone will try to sell the original certificates.

What to do when your fund fouls up completely

Has your fund lost your account? It's happened. Have you failed to get a dividend check? That's happened, too. And have you had trouble getting the matter straightened out? If you're in such a fix, here are some suggestions that may help.

You can always complain to the Securities and Exchange Commission (SEC), of course. But the SEC recommends that you first attempt to contact the senior fund official responsible for shareholder or customer relations. When you have located this person, explain your problem as clearly and concisely as possible. Describe the background of the problem, including the details of any transactions, in chronological order. Then mention the present status of the matter and the adjustment that you feel is necessary. Always follow up with a letter spelling out what you stated on the phone. Some funds won't consider a complaint serious unless you commit it to writing.

If this doesn't get satisfaction, then try contacting the Securities and Exchange Commission Office of Consumer Affairs and Information Services, 450 5th St., N.W., Washington, D.C. (telephone 202-272-7440) or one of its branch offices. The SEC staff will respond to all investor complaints and inquiries, answer questions and where appropriate, contact the fund for its response. When writing to the SEC, include the name and address of the fund advisor, the name of the particular fund, your account number, a brief description of the problem, copies of related documents (for example, confirmations of transactions and monthly account statements) and/or copies of any correspondence regarding the matter. Also include a daytime telephone number where the SEC staff can reach you if they have questions. If you are simultaneously furnishing other individuals and/or securities industry organizations with information copies of your complaint, mention that so there's no duplication of efforts.

Here's a list of the Regional and District SEC offices. The states each covers are listed in parentheses.

Northeast Regional Office, 7 World Trade Center, Suite 1300, New York, NY 10048, 212-748-8000 (CT, DE, DC, ME, MD, MA, NH, NJ, NY, PA, RI, VT, VA, WV)

Boston District Office, 73 Tremont Street, Suite 600, Boston, MA 02108-3912, 617-424-5900

Philadelphia District Office, The Curtis Center, Suite 1005 E., 601 Walnut Street, Philadelphia, PA 19106-3322, 215-597-3100

Southeast Regional Office, 1401 Brickell Avenue, Suite 200, Miami, FL 33131, 305-536-5765 (AL, FL, GA, LA, MS, NC, Puerto Rico, SC, TN, Virgin Islands)

Atlanta District Office, 3475 Lenox Road, N.E., Suite 1000, Atlanta, GA 30326-1232, 404-842-7600

Midwest Regional Office, Citicorp Center, 500 West Madison Street, Suite 1400, Chicago, IL 60661-2511, 312-353-7390 (IL, IN, IA, KY, MI, MN, MO, OH, WI)

Central Regional Office, 1801 California Street, Suite 4800, Denver, CO, 80202-2648, 303-391-6800

Fort Worth District Office, 801 Cherry Street, 19th Floor, Fort Worth, TX 76102, 817-334-3821

Salt Lake District Office, 500 Key Bank Tower, 50 S. Main Street, Suite 500, Box 79, Salt Lake City, UT, 84144-0402, 801-524-5796.

Pacific Regional Office, 5760 Wilshire Boulevard, 11th Floor, Los Angeles, CA 90036-3648, 213-965-3998 (AK, AZ, CA, Guam, HI, ID, MT, NV, OR, WA)

San Francisco District Office, 44 Montgomery Street, Suite 1100, San Francisco, CA 94104, 415-705-2500.

Individual Retirement Accounts (IRA)

Since it's a poor idea to rely on Social Security for your retirement income, sound planning requires you to take some of the responsibility yourself. Mutual funds provide an outstanding vehicle for maximizing your retirement nest egg.

Under the Tax Reform Act of 1986, anybody who has earned income can contribute to an IRA each year, and all dividends and gains building up inside the IRA are tax-deferred until withdrawn. Whether or not you may deduct contributions from your earned income in any given year depends on your level of income and whether you are an active participant in another tax-qualified plan. It's important to realize that over a lifetime, the immediate tax deduction—although undeniably important—is not as valuable as the tax-deferred buildup of assets.

Transferring IRAs

You may have IRA accounts at several different financial institutions. If so, the paperwork is no doubt beginning to mount up and so are the annual IRA fees. A solution: transfer all your IRAs under one roof.

The best places: a brokerage firm that specializes in no-loads or a family of no-load mutual funds. That way you can diversify your investments while making record-keeping simple. Some fund groups now lower or eliminate the IRA fees for large accounts.

Unfortunately, moving your IRA is not always simple. You can transfer your IRAs between institutions in one of two ways. Either do it yourself, once a year, through what is called a "60-day rollover." Or let the institutions handle the process directly, through what's called a custodian-to-custodian transfer. With that approach, you can move money from one fund family to another as often as you want.

Some funds have specialists to advise you on IRAs and other tax-sheltered plans. It's a good idea to review the details with them, particularly when you are dealing with an IRA rollover. Current law makes it almost mandatory to do a custodian-to-custodian transfer of a rollover, at least at the time you receive the distribution from your company.

If you plan to use a tax-sheltered account for frequent switching between management companies, by far the best way to do it is to set up a mutual fund account at a discount broker.

Withdrawal Plans

A mutual fund withdrawal program is a systematic means of obtaining regular monthly payments from dividends and invested principal. It is a logical outgrowth of the fund's capabilities and a highly convenient service. These plans are flexible. You can change the amount of the payout at any time, terminate it at will or withdraw lump sums when you need to. Checks can be sent directly to you, to your bank for deposit or to any third person. While any amount can be withdrawn, it is generally recommended that it not exceed 6% of invested capital annually. If the fund is well managed, its dividends and capital appreciation will be more than enough to cover these monthly payments.

If you want a monthly fixed income, the simplicity of a withdrawal plan gives it a tremendous advantage over stocks. Since most stock dividends are paid quarterly, you would have to own three stocks paying dividends in different months of each quarter in order to approximate the monthly payout principle of a fund withdrawal program. And with stocks, there's no easy way to take out your principal regularly. Moreover, you'd have to pay a commission if you sold stock.

Most fund families offer withdrawal plans; however, they seldom publicize them. If you're interested in setting one up, ask the fund's representative for details. Funds generally require that you have a minimum invested before you can set up a systematic withdrawal program; $10,000 is a common minimum. A few funds will set up a plan if you have as little as $5,000 invested, but then generally permit only quarterly, rather than monthly, withdrawals. This is logical; too small a check makes the plan hardly worthwhile.

The major difficulty with withdrawal plans is that shares of your fund undoubtedly will have to be sold in order to make up the required distribution. These sales, like all others, are taxable events. If your income from Social Security and a pension is sufficient to cover your basic living expenses, you are better off not using a systematic withdrawal plan. It will simplify your life—and your record keeping—if you satisfy your needs simply by taking the fund's income distributions in cash. If that's not sufficient, then take capital gains distributions in cash, then make occasional redemptions to pay large bills. If that's still not enough, then use a withdrawal plan. Obviously, you maximize your assets by refraining from dipping into your principal except when you really need to.

When not to use withdrawal plans

Since a common reason for a withdrawal plan is to supply retirement income, often for an extended period of years, it follows that investors will be better off using a conservative growth or growth-income fund as the vehicle. These funds are less volatile when investing for the long haul. Theoretically, there is no reason why you cannot use an aggressive growth fund. But if it loses 30% in a year, in addition to your withdrawals, you may not sleep very well. Or, more likely, you will feel constrained to abandon the withdrawal program while the fund is dropping, and that would undoubtedly be aggravating.

The major variables guiding your selection should be your other income and your life expectancy. Couples retiring at age 60, have a maximum life expectancy of 30 more years, and they may well be depending upon their funds to provide income throughout their lives. Obviously, taking a long-term view is advisable. So, they should invest a portion in a growth fund, where the opportunity for capital appreciation is greater.

Which funds are appropriate for withdrawal plans?

On the other hand, a couple at 75 has a joint life expectancy of 16 years (meaning that one or the other is likely to live to 91). Since these older folks don't need as much inflation protection, they can concentrate more on investments paying high interest or dividend income.

Table 74

Years in retirement

Expected retirement age	Life expectancy	
	For individual	For couple same age
55	28 years	34 years
60	24	30
65	20	25
70	16	21
75	12	16

Source: Based on IRS life expectancy tables

Some ways withdrawal plans can be used

Although mutual fund withdrawal plans are most commonly associated with payouts to the widowed and the retired, they can serve other objectives equally well. They can be used to:

■ Care for dependents.

■ Pay for school or college expenses. A program can be set up in which the principal is depleted over a specific period, such as four years.

■ Make alimony payments.

■ Pay any regular monthly bill such as rent or mortgage payments.

What if you withdraw money faster than the fund is growing?

If you take your money out at the often recommended rate of 6% a year, and your fund grows at a higher rate, which decent-performing mutual funds certainly should over the long haul, your capital will never be depleted. You can live forever and not run out of money. However, some elderly investors, especially those whose nestegg isn't too large, may find 6% inadequate to meet their current expenses. They need more, even if they have to eat into their capital. If that's you, our best advice is: be careful. To determine the maximum at which you can safely withdraw money, look at the triangular Table (75), which gives the "financial life expectancy" of an investment where the rate of withdrawal from principal is higher than the rate of growth.

Suppose you have $100,000 which is growing at 9% a year, and you withdraw at a 12% annual rate—$12,000 a year or $1,000 a month. Looking at the box where these two percentages intersect shows you that your principal will last for 16 years. On the other hand, if you withdraw at the rate of 11%, it will last 19 years, and at 10%, 26 years. Use the chart in conjunction with standard mortality tables to determine the number of years you'll need a payout. You can also read in the other direction. Assume you need withdrawals of 8% a year for 20 years. Then the right side of the chart shows that you need an investment that pays only 5% a year. Since a wise investor is "risk averse," the money should be conservatively invested. If the fund's rate of return exceeds your withdrawal rate (below the table's base line), then your assets will increase, and you will make your children very happy.

Table 75

Financial life expectancy

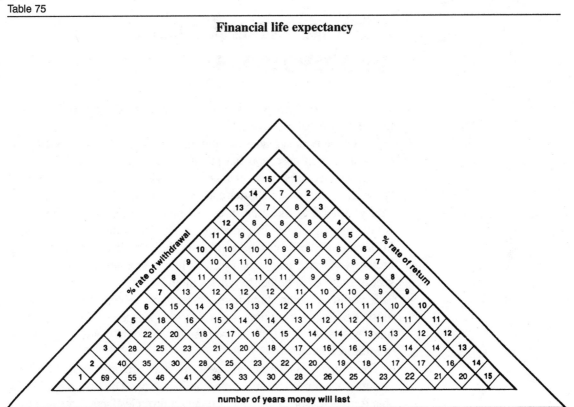

number of years money will last

CHAPTER 23

The mutual fund prospectus

What, me read a prospectus! Why, I'd rather read the fine print in my life insurance policy!

That's the typical reader reaction that prospectuses traditionally have enjoyed. But in case you haven't read one lately, here's some good news: prospectuses have changed. Today's prospectuses—call them "prospectus lite"—are shorter and more readable. They summarize the data you need to make an informed investment decision. Funds now cover the dreariest information in a "Statement of Additional Information." You can request it from the fund if necessary, but most investors will not need to. (In fact, so few are requested that many fund groups don't even bother to typeset them.)

If you're a mutual fund investor, learning about the prospectus is a must. Federal law requires that you get a prospectus when you buy a fund. Always save it. Even if you don't read it right away, you may need to refer to it later.

The primary purpose of a prospectus is to provide "full and fair disclosure" of all relevant investment information. The document is valuable for this reason alone. Occasionally it provides facts that some funds would just as soon leave unsaid. For example: whether a fund is being sued, how experienced—or inexperienced—management is and whether management's fee is abnormally high. These are facts you won't get when you buy stock that was previously issued, or when you select an investment counselor or a broker. Most important, the prospectus generally gives you a clear, detailed explanation of the fund's objectives, not the one- or two-word short-hand descriptions that most advisory services use.

What the prospectus does *not* tell you is how the fund stacks up against others. The SEC prohibits such comparisons.

Even in the era of "prospectus lite," reading through one can be a chore. So we will pinpoint the most important sections first, helping you to zero in the most vital information. Later in the chapter we will cover information of lesser importance.

What you need to read

Investment objectives, policies and types of investments. This is one of the most valuable sections in the prospectus. Mutual fund guides and directories usually provide one word descriptions, or at most short extracts of the objective, and are even less likely to describe a fund's policies. These vital facts should really be read in full in the prospectus. They generally run only a few paragraphs.

A fund's objective—growth, income, etc.—is different from its policy. Its policies are the means it proposes to use to achieve its objective. The fund may have a policy of buying dividend-paying common stocks or of buying bonds to achieve an income objective, for example. A fund's policy spells out what is permitted, for example investment techniques such as borrowing money, selling stocks short, buying warrants or put and call options, writing options, or investing in restricted securities. This doesn't mean that the fund is using the techniques at any given time, only that it can. Lately, funds have had the tendency to list everything they might possibly use—just in case. This gives them far more latitude but makes this section of the prospectus less valuable.

The SEC does ask that emphasis be given to current policies. A fund does not have to disclose policies which it is authorized to follow if it hasn't within the past year and has no intention to. Also, if a policy doesn't put more than 5% of the fund's assets at risk, the policy need only be identified; such as, "the fund may buy options."

If a fund concentrates more than 25% of its assets in any one industry, the prospectus will say so. If a fund provides high income by investing in lower rated bonds, that will be noted.

You should also check the summary or cover page (usually the first page of the prospectus) for warnings or special risk factors. These paragraphs should be read carefully. In 1988, we perused the prospectus of the Renaissance Fund, a new no-load, closed-end, market timing, index fund (it's not worth explaining how that's possible). Under Risk Factors we found the following statement: "There will be no continuous offering of shares of the fund. AS A PRACTICAL MATTER AFTER THE OFFERING MADE BY THIS PROSPECTUS, THERE MAY BE NO MARKET FOR FUND SHARES TO BE TRADED." We investigated and found out that, sure enough, there was no market; there was *no* practical way to sell the shares!

The prospectus for the Strong Growth Funds notes in solid caps that "THE FUNDS MAY ENGAGE IN SUBSTANTIAL SHORT-TERM TRADING, WHICH MAY INCREASE A FUND'S EXPENSES. EACH FUND MAY INVEST UP TO 10% OF ITS ASSETS IN RESTRICTED SECURITIES. THESE INVESTMENT POLICIES INVOLVE SUBSTANTIAL RISK AND MAY BE CONSIDERED SPECULATIVE.

There will also be a notation if the fund's expenses are unusually high.

No-loads generally proclaim their status on the cover page, which will also provide the date of the prospectus. Make sure you are reading a current one, no more than a year old.

All prospectuses must include a **Fee table**, which discloses all the costs associated with buying and owning mutual fund shares. The fee table separately reflects both non-recurring expenses such as front- and back-end sales charges, and recurring expenses such as management and 12b-1 fees. You can generally find that table on page two or three of the prospectus. Fee tables are in a section titled "Fee Table" or "Summary of Fund Expenses" or "Shareholder and Fund Expenses" or "Expense Information" or "Fee information." Checking this table is a must. *If you don't look at anything else in the prospectus, look at the fee table.*

Here's the Fee Table for the Partners Fund. This is the kind of fee table you are looking for. It's ideal.

Neuberger & Berman Partners Fund:
Expense Information

Shareholder Transaction Expenses

Sales Load Imposed on Purchases	None
Sales Load Imposed on Reinvested Dividends	None
Deferred Sales Load	None
Redemption Fees	None
Exchange Fees	None

Restated Annual Fund Operating Expenses Net of Expense Reimbursement
(As a percentage of average net assets)

Management fee	0.66%
12b-1 fees	None
Other Expenses	0.18%
Total operating expenses after expense reimbursement	0.84%

Contrast that with some examples of Fee Tables from load funds, which you would obviously be better off avoiding. The John Hancock Discovery Fund has both A shares (front-end load) and B shares (back end load).

John Hancock Discovery Fund

Shareholder Transaction Costs

	Class A	Class B
Maximum sales charge imposed on purchases (as a percentage of the offering price)	5.00%	None
Maximum sales charge imposed on reinvested dividends	None	None
Maximum deferred sales charge	None	5.00%
Redemption Fee	None	None
Exchange fee	None	None
Annual Fund Operating Expenses (as a percentage of average net assets)		
Management fees	1.00%	1.00%
12b-1 fees	0.30%	1.00%
Other Expenses	0.71%	0.67%
Total operating expenses	2.01%	2.67%

The Fee Table doesn't provide details of the contingent deferred sales charge on the B shares, which is unusual, but those details are spelled out on page 17 of the prospectus as follows:

Year in which Class B shares redeemed following purchase dollar amount subject to	Contingent deferred sales charge as a percentage of CDSC
First year	5%
Second	4%
Third	3%
Fourth	3%
Fifth	2%
Sixth	1%
Seventh and thereafter	None

You'd have to hold this fund for six years to avoid the CDSC sales charge, by which time you'd have paid a total of 6% in 12b-1 fees.

Here's an example of a fund that gives its investors a choice of Class A shares, with the up-front load, or a Class C shares with a level load. The Class C shares have no up-front commission, but the salesman is compensated by a 1% annual 12b-1 fee. Note that the Class A shares feature a 25 basis point (one-quarter percentage point) 12b-1 fee in addition to the load. This is what the industry calls a "trail." It goes to the selling broker in compensation for continuing to work with the investor. As you can see, the presence of a load doesn't necessarily mean that the management fee is reasonable. In the case of the Calvert Strategic Growth Fund, it's a high 1.70%.

Calvert Strategic Growth Fund
Shareholder Transaction Costs

	Class A	Class C
Maximum front-end sales charges on purchases (as a percentage of the offering price)	4.75%	None
Maximum contingent deferred sales charge	None	None
Annual Fund Operating Expenses		
Management fee	1.70%	1.70%
Rule 12b-1 service and distribution fees	0.25%	1.00%
Other expenses	0.65%	0.65%
Total fund operating expenses	2.60%	3.35%

Pay particular attention to the **Per Share Income and Capital Changes** table, which tracks the value of a share throughout the year. This table may also be labeled "Financial Highlights" or "Selected Per Share Data and Ratios." It is placed toward the front of the document because of its importance. The data must be shown for the latest 10 years or for the life of the fund. Using this table, you can review the fund's historical results in per-share amounts, which offer you the most revealing perspective on the fund's investment results. Skip to the bottom of this table where, ironically, the most important information is. That's where you will find two important ratios: expenses to average net assets—the expense ratio—and the portfolio turnover rate. These important data are illustrated in Table 76 for the Montgomery Small Cap Fund.

Ratio of expenses to average net assets, popularly known as the **expense ratio,** is of critical importance. Also found in the fee table (where it may be a projection), this information is presented as a tabulation of all the fund's on-going expenses divided by the fund's total assets. These expenses include the adviser's fee, which generally covers the cost of providing investment advice—office space, bookkeeping, statistical and clerical expenses, executive salaries and promotional expenses incurred in connection with the distribution of fund shares. The 12b-1 distribution fee, and expenses paid directly by the fund— printing and mailing costs for shareholder material and prospectuses, legal and auditing fees, expenses of independent directors (sometimes reimbursed by the adviser) and custodian and transfer agent fees. (One huge bill not included in the expense ratio: the brokerage charge for buying and selling securities. It's considered a capital expenditure. The cost is simply deducted from the value of the holdings, much the way an individual investor would do when buying a stock or bond.)

The total is what's important. Some funds with modest 12b-1 fees have lower overall expense ratios than other funds that don't levy these marketing fees. That's why you shouldn't automatically exclude funds with 12b-1 fees. The goal is to find funds with low expenses. In Chapter 14 we discussed ways you can properly evaluate the expense ratio.

Portfolio turnover rate. Turnover is the annual rate at which the fund buys and sells its holdings. For example, a turnover factor of 100% would be the equivalent of all the fund's securities being sold and replaced during the year. A 200% turnover indicates that stocks were held on average only six months. The rate is calculated by dividing the lesser of purchases or sales of portfolio securities for the year by the monthly average value of the portfolio. Government securities, both short and long-term, and all other securities including options that mature or expire in one year or less, are excluded from the calculation.

Studies of portfolio turnover generally have not found any particular correlation between turnover and performance. Some funds with a very high turnover rate do very well, some badly. And vice-versa: as many funds with low turnover perform badly as do well badly. Interestingly, though, a 1994 study by Value Line evaluated the performance of 531 funds during a five-year period by volatility. That analysis found that among the most volatile funds, high turnover is a predictor of superior performance, and among the least volatile funds, the reverse is true: high turnover is an indicator of poor performance.

One thing is certain. In a bull market, high turnover will increase realized profits, and they will generally be short-term gains rather than long-term. That means that investors must pay taxes on their profits at ordinary-income rates, rather than receiving the more favorable capital gains rate. A way to cope with this taxing problem is to invest funds that have high turnover ratios in tax-sheltered accounts, such as IRAs, profit-sharing plans and 401(k)s. A fund's policy towards portfolio turnover may be covered in the objective or policies section. New funds may estimate what their rate will be.

If you do nothing else, check the above sections in the prospectus. That will help you make informed judgements about your fund.

Of lesser importance

A wealth of additional information is contained in the prospectus. It can be helpful to you, but is not as momentous as the above.

Here's how to understand the rest of the Per Share table. Income from Investment Operations is the net investment income from dividends minus expenses plus the capital gains or losses. In the case of Montgomery Small Cap, dividends were less than the fund's expenses. So this figure is negative. With a large cap fund or a fixed-income fund, the number generally would be positive.

Note also the **Ratio of net income to average net assets** which shows the same data as a percentage. When these two figures are positive, the dividend and interest is covering the fund's expenses. When the figure is negative, the fund will have to dip into capital to meet expenses. In the case of the Montgomery fund shown in table 76, the figure was negative and is titled "Ratio of net investment loss to average net assets."

The next section, Distributions, is the amount paid out to shareholders in dividends and realized capital gains. The sum of these two sections when added to the beginning NAV (top line) equals the ending NAV. Next, the total return for the period is shown separately.

The section called **Management of the fund** describes the fund's adviser (i.e., the management company), and provides a summary of its experience and compensation. This section has become more important because the SEC now requires that the name of the portfolio manager and his or her experience be detailed. Unfortunately, the SEC exempted money funds and those funds run by committee from this requirement. Unhappily, the number of funds run by committee

Table 76

THE MONTGOMERY FUNDS

Montgomery Small Cap Fund

Financial Highlights

For a Fund share outstanding throughout each year.

	Year Ended 06/30/94	Year Ended 06/30/93	Year Ended 06/30/92	Year Ended 06/30/91	Period Ended 06/30/91*
Net asset value—beginning of year	$ 16.83	$ 12.90	$ 13.24	$ 10.05	$10.62
Net investment loss..................	(0.12)	(0.11)	(0.06)	(0.06)	(0.07)
Net realized and unrealized gain/(loss) on investments	(0.47)	4.04	3.25	3.27	2.71
Net increase/(decrease) in net assets resulting from investment operations ..	(0.59)	3.93	3.19	3.21	2.64
Distributions:					
Dividends from net realized capital gains	(1.09)	—	(2.75)	(0.02)	(0.02)
Distributions from paid-in capital ...	—	—	(0.78)	—	—
Total distributions	(1.09)	—	(3.53)	(0.02)	(0.02)
Net asset value—end of year	$ 15.15	$ 16.83	$ 12.90	$ 13.24	$13.24
Total return**	(1.59)%	30.47 %	27.69%	31.97 %	24.89%
RATIOS TO AVERAGE NET ASSETS/SUPPLEMENTAL DATA:					
Net assets, end of year (in 000's)	$209,063	$219,968	$176,588	$27,181	$27,181
Ratio of net investment loss to average net assets	(0.68)%	(0.69)%	(0.44)%	(0.47)%	(0.45)%+
Ratio of operating expenses to average net assets	1.35 %	1.40 %	1.50 %	1.50 %	1.45 %+
Portfolio turnover rate	95.22 %	130.37 %	80.67 %	194.63 %	188.16 %

*   The Fund's shares became available for investment by the public on July 13, 1990.
** Total return represents aggregate total return for the periods indicated.
\+ Annualized.

has increased dramatically since this requirement was adopted—or so the funds would have us believe. (We discussed this issue in Chapter 14.) If there isn't a section called "Management," keep looking. Fidelity, for example, has buried this information at the end of the prospectus under a section titled "Charter."

The prospectus will also note cases where the adviser is controlled by a parent company and whether it employs a sub-adviser. It's not uncommon for a management company to hire another firm to run the portfolio. Dreyfus, for instance, employs Fayez Sarofim to manage the Dreyfus Appreciation Fund. Dreyfus benefits from Sarofim's expertise while retaining the administrative and marketing functions. Similarly, many mutual fund families that lack expertise overseas employ a sub-advisor to manage their international funds.

This section usually includes details of the manager's fee. How big is it? Is it scaled down as the fund increases in size? Are there any incentive features? What portion of the fund's expenses are paid by the adviser out of the management fee? What portion is borne directly by the fund? The management fee used to be 0.5% of total net assets per year, and for many large funds it still is. Small funds can't exist at that level, however, and its very common to see managers' fees in the 0.75% to 1.00% range, particularly for aggressive growth funds. One fund charges 2% of the first $2 million in assets. Many funds with fees based on asset size now list an effective management fee based on the fund's actual size in the prospectus, leaving the details for the Statement of Additional Information.

Approximately 55 funds have incentive, or performance, fees. Here's how they work using the Fidelity OTC Fund as an illustration: First, the fund has two basic management fees: a group rate based on all of Fidelity's assets, and an individual fund fee. In 1994, the group fee was .32% and the individual fund fee was .35%, for a total of .67%. The portfolio is then compared with the record of the NAS-DAQ Composite Index over a rolling 36-month performance period. The difference is translated into a dollar amount that is added to or subtracted from the basic fee. The maximum annualized performance adjustment rate is plus or minus .20%.

In the case above, the incentive fee goes to the adviser, thus directly affecting fund results. However, many fund groups pay their portfolio managers incentives and bonuses for superior performance. Such payments have no direct impact on the fund's management fees.

You will also find the names of the transfer and dividend paying agent in the prospectus. Many funds have you deal directly with the transfer agent when you are buying or selling shares. Some transfer agents represent many funds. Some are inept at administering your account, and you'd like to avoid them. But if the fund you are considering investing in has an excellent track record, you probably won't want to skip it because the fund's administrative side annoys you.

Since the point of the prospectus is to get you to buy, one section will tell you how to **purchase and redeem shares.** Included are minimum purchase amounts, wire or telephone privileges, sales charges, distribution fees and valuation of shares. Minimum initial investments for no-loads, with some exceptions, range from $250 to $3,000.

Sometimes funds raise their minimum investment requirement as a way to cut costs by allowing the fund to deal with fewer and larger accounts. At other times, funds will lower the minimum in order to stimulate sales. You can open an account at the MIM funds if you have as little as $250 in your jeans; AARP Funds require just $500. Minimum subsequent investments are often in range of $50 to $100.

Generally, you invest in a no-load mutual fund by filling out the application form that accompanies the prospectus and attaching your check. The application requests such information as your Social Security or tax I.D. number, the name and address under which you want your shares to be registered, and whether dividends and/or capital gains should be reinvested or sent to you. The application tells where it is to be sent and to whom your check should be made payable.

The prospectus also describes any special purchase or accumulation plans, exchange services and the procedures for redeeming your shares. Always check this section before you redeem. It will save you time and aggravation.

There will be a section that tells you when and how often the fund distributes **dividends and capital gains.**

Once in a while you will find a section called **Pending legal proceedings.** If there are any "material" legal proceedings against the fund, they must be disclosed here. Such disclosures won't usually affect your investment, but you should be aware of them, because occasionally the fund's shareholders have to pay some of the costs of litigation.

Note: A fund can use the same prospectus for a year before it must be updated. Therefore, the fund's latest quarterly or annual report may furnish more up-to-date financial and portfolio data than its prospectus.

Often you may find that several funds are included in one prospectus. This arrangement has become popular because it cuts down on registration and distribution expenses. Instead of printing different prospectuses for each fund and going to the trouble of registering each in all 50 states, the fund company can gain an economics of scale by including a handful of funds in the same prospectus.

It's important to realize, though, that each fund contained in such an umbrella prospectus is separate and distinct. In some cases the

Umbrella funds

portfolios have a common objective. The Vanguard Municipal Bond Fund, for instance, has seven portfolios, each providing tax-free income. The portfolios are distinguished primarily by the varying maturities of the bonds they hold. On the other hand USAA Mutual Fund's five portfolios—Aggressive Growth, Growth, Income, Income Stock, Money Market—have virtually nothing in common but their manager. And the Fidelity Select Fund, with 36 widely disparate portfolios, contains a dazzling array of different investments.

The good news for investors is that these omnibus prospectuses often have drastically lower administrative expenses, and these savings can be passed on to shareholders. But since they are separate entities, switching between portfolios, just like switching between funds, is a taxable event. Capital gains or losses may be realized.

What's in a name?

For your protection, the SEC will not allow a fund to use a name or title that may be deceptive or misleading. If a fund's name implies that its distributions are exempt from federal income taxation—for example, XYZ Muni Bond Fund—then under normal conditions at least 80% of the fund's assets must be invested in securities that will produce tax-exempt income. Similarly if the name indicates a money fund, the fund had better be investing in money market instruments.

Since 1988, the SEC has made bond funds use the word "Municipal" in their titles if a significant percentage of the municipal bonds held by these funds are subject to the alternative minimum tax. Formerly, the word "Tax-Free" could be used virtually interchangably in their titles. Now, if the fund says it's "Tax-Free," it can't present you with an AMT problem.

You will recall in Chapter 8 that we noted how two global asset allocation funds had changed their charters to permit greater flexibility in their allocations. A third global asset allocation fund, the Permanent Portfolio Fund, has not made any changes. It has a problem that the other funds didn't have—its name. The SEC took the position that the word Permanent in the name meant just that. There will be no changes in its objective, even though the fund and its shareholders want them.

Still, it always pays to look beyond the name. One would assume that all the stocks in the Fidelity Dividend Growth Fund paid dividends; but that's not so. Close to half the stocks in the fund's portfolio do not. One supposes that allows them unlimited potential for dividend growth.

As we mentioned, the Statement of Additional Information (SIA) provides more information of less importance. If you're a potential investor in the fund, it must send you this Statement at no charge *if you ask for it*. If you don't ask for it, you won't get it.

The Statement of Additional Information may contain sections that virtually duplicate ones in the prospectus as well as some information considered to be too detailed to put into the prospectus. Sometimes you will find a list of investment restrictions in the SAI but not in the prospectus. These are techniques that the fund has agreed not to use. Most funds agree not to buy commodities and real estate, for example. Just as with the statements of objective and policies, these restrictions cannot be changed without shareholder approval. Similarly, officers and directors, while sometimes listed in the prospectus, must be named in the SAI.

If details of the advisory service contract and the 12b-1 distribution fee are not in the prospectus, they will be listed here. Sometimes this information in the prospectus is so abbreviated that this is one instance where it pays to look further in the SAI.

In addition the SAI has information regarding how the fund allocates the brokerage commissions incurred when buying and selling stocks. If the fund is managed by a brokerage firm or affiliate of such a firm, the prospectus will explain the relationship between the fund and its parent broker, and the percent of the brokerage fees given to the broker-parent company.

Custodian, Transfer and Dividend Disbursing Agent, Counsel and Auditors are organizations who provide administrative and technical assistance. Mutual funds have custodial banks that hold the fund's securities and cash. This is an important safeguard against fraud or embezzlement by the adviser or one of his employees. The transfer agent maintains shareholder records. Sometimes one organization performs both the custodial and transfer functions, but more frequently these duties are performed by separate organizations.

The SAI can be skipped.

Statement of Additional Information

A pat on the back

A philosopher once remarked that a pat on the back is a great incentive to success—if delivered early enough, hard enough and low enough. So, dear dedicated investor, because you have taken the time and effort to complete this intricate journey with us, please consider this book a pat on the back.

You've gotten it early enough (because it's never too late to make money with no-load funds), you've gotten it hard enough (we've pulled no punches in stating the principles of successful no-load investing), and you will have gotten it low enough, if this *Guide* will make you get off your seat and start working on an intelligently conceived and carefully monitored no-load investment program.

Remember, the potential rewards and personal satisfactions are both great. Good luck—and good fortune.

APPENDIX A

How to use stock market indexes

We feel that comparing a fund's performance to the average fund in its peer group is the primary means for you to evaluate funds you hold. We also believe that comparing a fund's performance with stock market indexes, as the popular press generally does and as the SEC requires of the funds, is of limited value. Funds are entirely different from indexes. Their portfolios are often composed of stocks from various exchanges; most also contain cash, at a minimum to provide liquidity for shareholder redemptions; and many also have bonds in their portfolios. Fund performance is reduced by the costs of buying and selling stocks, management fees and the expenses of serving shareholders. For example, an index won't reinvest dividends for you. It won't wire you money. Depending on the amount of trading a fund does and its other expenses, costs can amount to 1%-3% of a fund's assets each year.

By contrast, the stock market indexes have no expenses, no transaction costs, and for the most part include stocks from just one exchange. They are weighted differently than fund portfolios. The fact that funds in general over- or under-perform an index by a few points doesn't mean much, particularly if the comparison is to a universe of stocks such as the Dow Jones 30 Industrials or the S&P 500, which primarily measure large cap stocks. You will find that in years when large cap stocks do well, the funds will typically lag these indexes. In years when small cap stocks do well, funds will generally outperform the well-known indexes. There is no perfect bogey. So, you should use the stock market averages only to give you a general gauge of market direction.

The money fund average provides a different, more relevant comparison. Money funds are an alternative to stock or bond investments. So, they measure the correctness of your asset allocation decisions. In some years you would have done better investing in the money funds than you would have in almost any diversified stock fund. In other years, virtually every stock fund fares better than a money fund. So if you owned a stock fund that did significantly better than a money fund, how important is a fund's performance against some arbitrary index?

Nevertheless, since mutual fund performance is constantly being compared to stock market indexes, you should understand them—the math behind them, how they differ and how and whether to use them.

Benchmarks for every purpose

The granddaddy is, of course, the **Dow Jones Industrial Average**—commonly called the Dow (though there are three other Dow averages). It is composed of 30 blue chip stocks, a roster that is altered periodically. While outmoded by the broader indexes it continues to dominate the news and investors' thoughts because of its historical importance and the fact it is sponsored by Dow Jones, publishers of *The Wall Street Journal*.

Perhaps you have wondered how the average of 30 stocks can be as high as it is, and how it can change more than 500 points in a single day. When the Dow was first constructed by Charles Dow in the last century, it was calculated by simply adding up the prices of the stocks then in the index and dividing by the total number of stocks. But soon there were problems. If a stock worth, say, $60 a share was split, it might be worth only $30 after the split. Some way had to be found to account for the split. Otherwise the index would show a totally artificial decline since splitting a stock doesn't decrease its value, and in fact, frequently results in gains. The solution was to change the divisor to compensate for the split. Over the years there have been numerous splits and each time the denominator has been lowered. In early 1995, the divisor for the 30 Dow stocks was not 30 but .3715! The divisor has become a multiplier. With the denominator so low, if each stock in the index moves just one dollar, the index will gain or lose about 75 points. To get a 500 point disaster—as happened in October 1987—each Dow stock would have to decline $6.19.

Another peculiarity of the index is that the Dow is price-weighted. The high-priced stocks count for more in the average than the low-priced stocks. There's no reason why this should be so; it was just the simplest way to do things in the pre-computer age.

The Dow can be used to compare conservative stock funds which emphasize the large blue chip companies in their portfolios.

The various **NYSE** and **Standard & Poor's** indexes are weighted by capitalization. In computing the index, the price of each stock is multiplied by the number of its shares outstanding. Then all shares are averaged. As a result, these indexes measure market value rather than simply price. This method eliminates the Dow's need to adjust for stock splits. In addition it has the more important result of giving greater weight to larger companies. While the S&P 500 includes many large NYSE companies, the ten with the biggest market value account for 19% of the index's value and movement, the biggest 50 stocks account for about half of the weighting and the bottom 100 only 2.3%. So as is the case with the Dow, a fairly small number of stocks represent the "market."

Similarly, the New York Stock Exchange indexes cover all the common stocks listed on that exchange, but a few large companies have a disproportionate influence on the index.

Because a few large stocks dominate these indexes they sometimes fail to represent the average stock. In 1994, more than 80% of 7,363 actively traded stocks, were down more than 10% from their 52-week highs; more than 58% of them were down more than 20%; and more than 40% were down 30% or more. Putting the broad market indexes on a comparable basis, the Dow Jones Industrial Average and the S&P 500 declined only 3.6% and 4.7% from their 1994 high points. When benchmarking fund performance to capitalization weighted market indexes, we also suggest you use the number of stocks rising or falling as a relevant comparison.

The S&P and NYSE indexes provide a good yardstick for comparing a typical growth or growth-income fund buying large cap stocks. But don't be concerned if your fund lags the Index, particularly when these indexes don't reflect the average stock.

One of the best indexes for mutual fund comparisons is **NASDAQ,** the National Association of Securities Dealers Automated Quotation system. It is a market-value weighted average of what used to be called over-the-counter stocks. Unlike the organized exchanges, NASDAQ has no centralized floor. Instead it is an elaborate network of market makers and broker-dealers connected by a phone and computer system. There are more than 4,900 NASDAQ stocks with a total market value of about $800 billion. The volume of trading on NASDAQ is enormous; in terms of shares, about equal to that of the NYSE. In addition it leads all other U.S. markets in listings of new public companies; about 85% choose NASDAQ. There's a perception that all NASDAQ companies are small, but that's not true. Such giants as Microsoft, Intel, and MCI Communications are traded on NASDAQ. The index is heavily weighted toward technology stocks. Fifteen of the 20 largest NASDAQ stocks are technology or telecommunication companies, and technology in total makes up 29% of the value of the Composite Index. Microsoft alone accounts for 4.4% of the index. The average market cap of the Composite Index is $2.9 billion, not small. NASDAQ's Composite Index is the most important one to watch, but there are a number of sub-indexes for specialized purposes.

An index coming into increasing prominence is the **Wilshire 5000 Equity Index.** This index, which is computed by Wilshire Associates of Santa Monica, CA, measures the performance of all U.S. common equity securities with readily available daily price data. While they continue to call it the 5,000, the index now is composed of more than 6,800 stocks. It is capitalization weighted, with about 83% of its capitalization on the NYSE, 2% Amex and 15% NASDAQ. Wilshire also recomputes the index with equal weighting, but you are unlikely to run across this version. In addition the company computes a sub-index called the Wilshire 4,500, which deletes the S&P 500 stocks. We think this broad measure is a good one for mutual fund comparisons. In fact, we use the 5,000 in the computations of our betas.

The **Value Line Index** provides another useful comparison for mutual fund investors. It consists of 1,618 stocks—1,439 industrials, 167 utilities, and 12 rails. Every stock has the same value since equal changes are treated equally whether the companies are big or small.

Few mutual fund portfolios are weighted toward larger companies, so the Value Line Index is more relevant to growth funds than are the other indexes. An emerging growth fund, for example, may invest about equally in large numbers of small companies. There are actually two Value Line Indexes. The more common one uses a geometric average, the newer one, an arithmetic average. Over time, the geometric average will produce lower results.

The **Amex Market Value Index** is a volatile index that's useful as a benchmark for aggressive funds. The Index has heavy weightings in the securities of consumer goods, service, financial, high technology, and capital goods stocks. Since the volume of trading on the AMEX is slight compared to NYSE and NASDAQ the performance of this index is less important.

There are also some more specialized indexes you should be aware of. The **Russell Indexes** have come to the attention of mutual fund investors because one of them, the Russell 2000, is the basis for Vanguard's Small Capitalization Stock Fund, an index fund. There are three Russell indexes. The Russell 3000 Index consists of the 3000 largest publicly traded stocks in the US, as determined by market capitalization. This index represents about 98% of the investable US equity market. The Russell 2000 Index consists of the 2000 smallest stocks in the 3000 index. It represents approximately 10% of US equities, with an average market cap of $346 million. Finally the Russell 1000 tracks the largest 1000 stocks. Unfortunately, all three are market-value indexes. From the point of view of a fund investor, it would be better if they were unweighted.

The newest index is the **S&P MidCap 400 Index** which Standard & Poor's unveiled in June 1991 as a result of increasing interest in mid-size stocks. The index covers 400 companies with market capitalizations generally ranging from $200 million to $5 billion; the median cap is approximately $820 million. The Index is capitalization weighted, which means the 50 largest companies account for one-third of the Index. Of the companies, 64% are listed on the NYSE, 33% on NAS-DAQ, and 3% on the AMEX. This mid-cap index combined with the S&P 500 Index will together account for 85% of the market value of all traded U.S. stocks.

The most popular benchmark for comparing international funds is the **EAFE Index.** This is the Morgan Stanley Capital International Europe, Australia, Far East Index. It's a market-capitalization-weighted index containing 1,112 companies representing approximately 60% of market capitalization of 20 countries. The Index's total market capitalization is $4.5 trillion, with an average company capitalization of $4 billion. Japanese stocks account for by far the major components of the EAFE Index. Japan accounts for 43% of the Index. Next is the United Kingdom with 16%. The larger the weighting, the more developed are the various foreign markets. Most international funds allocate their investments by referencing this index. When an international fund manager says he is underweighting or overweighting a country, he means compared to the EAFE Index.

APPENDIX B

Glossary of mutual fund terms

Account: Used in such terms as mutual fund account or open account. It denotes an investor's business arrangement or record of his investments, together with reinvestments or distributions and/or withdrawals and charges; an open account is open to further investment.

Acquisition Cost: The load, or sales commission, charged.

Adjustable Rate Mortgage Fund: A fund that invests in adjustable rate mortgage (ARM) securities issued guaranteed by the U.S. government or its agencies. The funds are designed for conservative, income-oriented investors who are willing to accept minimal fluctuations in the funds' share prices. ARMs generally have lower yields which vary frequently since their dividends rates are reset every six to 12 months. (See ARMS.)

Adjustable Rate Preferred: A bond or preferred stock whose dividends are adjusted periodically to maintain a yield within some designated range of a benchmark Treasury security. The dividend is also fixed between floor and ceiling yields, and the stock can be redeemed before maturity.

Adviser: The organization employed by a mutual fund to give professional advice on its investments and management of its assets.

Aggressive Growth Fund: A mutual fund which seeks maximum capital appreciation through the use of investment techniques involving greater than ordinary risk, including such techniques as borrowing money in order to provide leverage, short selling, hedging, options and warrants.

All-Weather Fund: A fund that long-term investors can hold safely throughout a complete market cycle. Market timing, low volatility, and asset allocation funds may be all-weather.

Alpha: A statistical measure representing the difference between the actual and expected performance of a fund given its characteristic volatility. A positive alpha is often considered a measure of management's ability.

Alternative Minimum Tax (AMT): A substitute computation of tax, which ensures that those taxpayers with substantial deductions and credits, pay at least some income tax.

American Stock Exchange (AMEX): The second largest securities exchange in the U.S., located in New York City.

Appreciation: Increase in the value of an asset such as a stock, bond, or real estate.

Arbitrage: The purchase of an asset in one market accompanied by a simultaneous sale of the same (or a similar) asset in a different market to take advantage of the difference in price.

ARMS: Adjustable rate mortgages. The index rate on the loan is periodically reset relative to a base rate. Most follow either a short Treasury index or COFI, which is the 11th District Cost of Funds Index, as determined by the 11th District Federal Home Loan Bank (predominately California). Also see Adjustable-rate mortgage funds.

Asked or Offering Price: The price at which a mutual fund's shares can be purchased. The asked or offering price means the current net asset value per share plus sales charge, if any.

Asset Allocation Fund: A broadly diversified fund that varies its holdings between U.S. stocks, bonds and money market instruments depending on market conditions in order to obtain satisfactory performances in both up and down markets. These funds are sometimes known as Flexibly diversified funds. Asset allocation funds that also invest internationally and in gold are defined as Global Asset Allocation Funds.

Asset Class: A group of securities that share a common systematic risk element. U.S. stocks, foreign stocks, bonds, etc. are all considered asset classes.

Asset-based sales charge: A sales charge deducted from the net assets of a mutual fund under the terms of a 12b-1 plan.

Asset Value: Either total or per share. Total net assets of a fund are made up of market value of holdings plus any other resources such as cash, minus liabilities. Per share is determined by dividing the total by the number of shares outstanding.

Automatic Reinvestment: The option available to mutual fund shareholders whereby fund income dividends and capital gains distributions are automatically put back into the fund to buy new shares and thereby build up holdings.

Back-end Load: A fee paid when withdrawing money from a fund. In the case of a 12b-1 fund, it is designed to recoup sales expenses not collected by the periodic 12b-1 fee, due to premature withdrawal.

Back-testing: The process of testing a trading strategy on historical data.

Balanced Fund: A mutual fund that has an investment policy of always balancing its portfolio, generally by including relatively fixed portions of bonds, preferred stocks and common stocks.

Bankers' Acceptances: Short-term credit arrangements designed to enable businesses to obtain funds to finance commercial transactions. Generally, an acceptance is a time draft drawn on a bank by an exporter or an importer to obtain a stated amount of funds to pay for specific merchandise. The draft is then "accepted" by a bank that, in effect, unconditionally guarantees to pay the face value of the instrument on its maturity date.

Basis Point: A unit used to measure changes in interest rates and bond yields. One basis point equals .01% (or 1/100 of 1%).

Bear Market: A market climate in which stock prices are generally falling.

Beta: A coefficient that measures a fund's volatility relative to the total market, usually as represented by the S&P 500. It is the percentage performance of a fund which has historically accompanied a 1.00% move up or down in the S&P 500. High beta funds have price fluctuations greater than the broad market; low beta funds fluctuate less than the market as a whole. Funds with high betas are consequently riskier than the market, those with low betas are less risky.

Bid or Redemption Price: The price at which a mutual fund's shares are redeemed (bought back) by the fund. The bid or redemption price usually means the current net asset value per share.

Big Board: Another name for the New York Stock Exchange.

Blue Chip: The common stock of well-established companies with a stable record of earnings and dividends.

Blue Sky Laws: Rules and regulations of the various states governing the securities business, including mutual funds, broker/dealers and salesmen.

Bond Fund: A mutual fund whose portfolio consists primarily of fixed-income securities. The emphasis of such funds is normally on income rather than growth.

Bookshares: A share-recording system that gives the fund shareowner a record of his holdings. Used in lieu of share certificates.

Broker: A person who makes securities transactions for others for a commission.

Broker-Dealer (or Dealer): A firm which retails mutual fund shares and other securities to the public.

Bull Market: A market climate in which stock prices are generally rising.

Call Option: The right to buy 100 shares of a particular stock or stock index at a predetermined price before a preset deadline, in exchange for a premium. Options permit a profit from a smaller investment than it would take to buy the underlying stock.

Capital Gain or Loss: Profit or loss resulting from the sale of property or securities. Long-term gains or losses result from the sale of assets held one year or more if assets were acquired after Jan. 1, 1988; short-term - less than one year.

Capital Gains Distributions: Payments to mutual fund shareholders of gains realized on sales within the fund's portfolio securities. These amounts are paid at least once a year if realized.

Capital Growth: The increase in the market value of securities held, which is the prime short or long term objective of many funds. A gain is called unrealized until a security is actually sold.

Cash Equivalent: Receivables, short-term bonds and notes.

Cash Position: Cash plus cash equivalents minus current liabilities.

Certificate: Printed evidence of ownership of securities including mutual fund shares.

Certificates of Deposit: Negotiable certificates of indebtedness issue by a commercial bank to repay funds deposited with it for a definite period of time (usually from 14 days to one year) at a stated or variable interest rate. Money funds generally buy jumbo CDs ($100,000 or more) that are not FDIC insured. They are backed only by the creditworthiness of the bank.

Closed-end Investment Company: Unlike mutual funds (known as open-end funds), closed-end companies issue only a limited number of shares and do not redeem them (buy them back). Instead, closed-end shares are traded in the securities markets, with supply and demand determining the price. Also called *publicly traded* funds.

CMO: A security where a group of mortgage pass-through securities have been put together, and the cash flows are paid out in a specific order or preference to different buyers in order to give structure to the uncertain cash flows of mortgage pass-through securities.

Commercial Paper: Unsecured short-term notes issued in bearer form by large well known corporation and finance companies and certain governmental bodies. Maturities on commercial paper range from a few days to nine months. Commercial paper is also sold on a discount basis.

Commission: A fee paid to a broker or mutual fund salesmen for the buying or selling of securities.

Common Stock: A security representing ownership in a corporation's assets.

Common Stock Fund: A mutual fund whose portfolio consists primarily of common stocks. The emphasis of such funds is usually on growth.

Compounding: The process that occurs through the reinvestment of interest, dividends, or profits. Growth thus occurs at the same rate that the investment itself earns, allowing the reinvested money to multiply, rather than simply adding to the investment.

Conduit: The nature of a fund, which permits it to channel investment dividend income or capital gains to fund shareholders for tax liability, rather than being taxed within the fund.

Contingent Deferred Sales Charge: A sales fee payable when the shareholder redeems shares, rather than when shares are purchased, and which is frequently reduced each year that the shares are held. For example, if shares are redeemed less than one year after purchase, a fee of 5% of N.A.V. might be charged; if redeemed in more than one but less than two years, 4%, etc. Also called a contingent deferred sales load.

Contractual Plan: A program for the accumulation of mutual fund shares in which the investor agrees to invest a fixed amount on a regular basis for a specified number of years. A substantial portion of the sales charge applicable to the total investment is usually deducted from early payments.

Contrarian: An investor who does the opposite of what most investors are doing at a particular time. A contrarian fund generally invests in out-of-favor securities, whose price/earnings ratio is lower than the rest of the market or industry.

Convertible Securities: A preferred stock or bond providing the right for the owner to exchange it for another security, such as common stock, under specified or unspecified conditions of time, price and/or number of shares.

Corporate Obligations: Bonds and notes issued by corporations and other business organizations, including business trusts, in order to finance their long-term credit needs.

CUSIP: The Committee on Uniform Securities Identification Procedures—it assigns identifying numbers and codes to all securities. These CUSIP numbers are used when recording all buy and sell orders. Each fund has a CUSIP number.

Custodian: The organization (usually a bank) that holds in custody and safekeeping the securities and other assets of a mutual fund.

Cycle: A pattern of swings and reversals in a trend that recurs on a regular time schedule.

Daily Dividend Fund: A fund that declares its income dividends daily. The fund usually reinvests or distributes them daily or monthly.

Date of Record: That date on which declared distributions are set aside (held separate, for payment to shareholders at a later date) and deducted from total net assets.

Deflation: A fall in the general price level.

Derivatives: Securities whose returns are linked to, or derived from, some underlying stock, bond, commodity, or other asset. There are two basic types: options and forward type derivatives, which include forwards, futures and swaps. They may be listed on exchanges or negotiated privately between two parties, usually institutions.

Direct Marketed Fund: A no-load or low-load fund whose shares can be bought directly, without going through a dealer, thus avoiding all or most of the sales commission. Investors purchase fund shares through the mail or by telephone in response to advertising or publicity. Also called *direct purchase fund*.

Discount: The percentage below asset value at which an investment company sells in the open market.

Disinflation: A slowdown in the rate of inflation without turning into deflation.

Distributions: The payments of dividends or realized capital gains that a fund determines to pass along to shareholders, who can take them in cash or in additional shares, sometimes in fractions thereof.

Distributor: An organization that purchases mutual fund shares directly from the issuer for resale to other parties.

Diversification: The mutual fund policy of spreading its investments among a number of different securities to reduce the risks inherent in investing.

Diversified Investment Company: A fund complying with statutory requirements under the Federal Investment Company Act of 1940, which specifies that such a fund have at least 75% of its assets represented by cash, government securities, securities of other investment companies, and other securities limited in respect to any one issuer in the amount of not greater than 5% of a fund's assets and not more than 10% of the voting securities of a single issuer.

Dividend: As distinct from a capital gain distribution, represents dividends from investment income.

Dollar-Cost Averaging: Investing equal amounts of money at regular intervals regardless of whether the stock market is moving upward or downward. This reduces average share costs to the investor who acquired more shares in periods of lower securities prices and fewer shares in periods of higher prices.

Dual-Purpose Fund: It differs from other closed-end funds in that leverage is provided by issuing two separate classes of shares. One class, the *income* shares, receives all income from the entire portfolio but none of the capital gain. The other, *capital* shares, receives all the capital gain but none of the income. As a closed-end fund, shares may be purchased or sold only on the open market, subject to a premium or discount from asset value.

EAFE Index: An abbreviation for the Morgan Stanley Capital International Europe, Australia, Far East Index. It's a market-capitalization-weighted index representing approximately 60% of market capitalizations of 20 countries. Japanese stocks have the heaviest weighting in the index, over 40%. Most international funds allocate their investments by referencing this index. When an international fund manager says he is underweighting or overweighting a country, he means compared to the EAFE Index.

Economics: The study of how people use limited resources—personal, commercial, national or international—to achieve maximum well-being.

Efficient Market: Theory that market prices reflect the knowledge and expectations of all investors. Believers of the theory hold that any new development is quickly reflected in a company's stock price, making it impossible for an investor to beat the market over the long run.

Elliott Wave Theory: A pattern recognition technique published by Ralph N. Elliott in 1939, which holds that the stock market follows a rhythm or pattern of five waves up with three waves down in a bull market, and five waves down with three waves up in a bear market to form a complete cycle of eight waves.

Equity: In investments, an ownership interest by shareholders of a corporation. Stock is equity, as opposed to bonds, which are debt.

Equity Fund: A common stock mutual fund.

Eurodollar CDs: Certificates of deposit issued by a foreign branch (usually London) of a domestic bank, and as such, the credit is deemed to be that of the domestic bank.

Exchange Fund: An investment company that allows persons holding individual securities to exchange these securities for fund shares without paying a capital gains tax.

Exchange Privilege: Enables a mutual fund shareholder to transfer his investment from one fund to another within the same fund group if his needs or objectives change. The term is sometimes used by funds, which do not offer telephone switch, to indicate an exchange by mail.

Ex-Dividend: For mutual funds (but not for securities listed on a stock exchange), that date on which declared distributions are deducted from total net assets. On the day a fund goes ex-dividend, its closing net asset value per share is computed minus the distribution.

Expense Ratio: Annual expenses (not including interest and income taxes paid) divided by average net assets.

Family of funds: A group of mutual funds under the same management. Fund families frequently provide convenient telephone switching between funds.

FANNIE MAE: Nickname for the Federal National Mortgage Association.

Fed: Nickname for the Federal Reserve System.

Fedwire: High speed computerized communications network connecting the Federal Reserve banks, their branches and other governmental agencies. It enables banks to transfer funds for immediate available credit.

Fiduciary: A person vested with legal power to be used for benefit of another person.

Fixed Income Fund: A mutual fund investing all or a major portion of its assets (normally 75% or more) in fixed income securities.

Fixed Income Security: A debt security such as a bond and a preferred stock with a stated return in percentage or dollars.

Flexibly Diversified: In contrast to a balanced fund whose portfolio at all times must be diversified among a generally stated minimum or maximum percentage of bonds/preferred/common stocks—flexible diversification means that management, at its discretion, may allot the percentage for each type of security.

Float: The period between the writing of a check and the debiting of an account for that amount. Money fund shareholders can earn interest on the float when they write checks on their accounts.

Forwards: A derivative that commits both buyer and seller to trade a fixed amount of an asset at a specific price on a future date. A common type is a foreign exchange forward. No money changes hands until the forward expires, at which point the contract is often settled in cash rather than by an exchange of the actual asset.

FREDDIE MAC: Nickname for the Federal Home Loan Mortgage Corporation, and also the mortgage-backed securities it issues.

Front-end Load: Sales charge applied to an investment at the time of initial purchase.

Fully-Managed Fund: A term generally used when a fund's prospectus permits assets to be converted to debt securities or all cash at management's discretion, for timing purchases and sales.

Fundamental Analysis: Analysis of corporate balance sheets, income statements, management, sales, products and markets in order to forecast future stock price movements.

Futures Contracts: Standard forward agreements traded on exchanges. They are obligations to buy or deliver a quantity of the underlying commodity or financial instrument at the agreed-upon price by a certain date. Most contracts are simply nullified by an opposite trade before they come due.

General Obligation Securities: The obligations of an issuer with taxing power that are payable from the issuer's general, unrestricted revenues. These securities are backed by the full faith, credit and taxing power of the issuer for the payment of principal and interest; they are not limited to repayment from any particular fund or revenue source.

Global Asset Allocation Fund: A broadly diversified fund that typically invests across a number of markets to provide a hedge against declines in the U.S. stock market. Their holdings may include U.S. stocks; international stocks; U.S. bonds, often governments; international bonds; gold or gold mining shares; cash equivalents, and sometimes real estate securities. They seek satisfactory performances in almost all foreseeable economic climates - inflation, deflation, stability. Also see Asset Allocation Fund.

Global Fund: A fund that invests in the securities of the U.S. as well as those of foreign countries.

GNMA Fund: A fund investing in GNMA securities issued by the Government National Mortgage Association, a corporation that helps finance mortgages.

Growth Fund: A mutual fund whose primary investment objective is long-term growth of capital. It invests principally in common stocks with growth potential.

Growth-Income Fund: A mutual fund whose aim is to provide for a degree of both income and long-term growth.

Hedge: To offset. To safeguard oneself from loss on a risk by making compensatory arrangements on the other side. For example, to hedge one's long positions with short sales, so that if the market declines the loss on long positions will be offset by profit on the short positions.

Hedge Fund: A flexible investment fund for rich people and institutions. The minimum investment is typically $1 million, and since they are restricted to less than 100 investors, they do not come under the same regulations as mutual funds. Hedge funds can use aggressive strategies that are unavailable to mutual funds. Historically, they were simply funds that had a policy of hedging long positions with short positions. In the 1960s the term was used to describe any aggressive fund.

Illiquid: According to SEC regulations, open-end investment companies (mutual funds) can invest no more than 15 percent of their capital in illiquid investments. This rule is aimed at assuring that the funds will be able to redeem their shares on demand. Real estate restricted issues, letter stock-securities requiring registration before they can be sold, are considered illiquid. (See Liquidity.)

Incentive Compensation: The fee paid to a fund manager based upon performance in relation to a market index such as the Dow Jones Industrial Average.

Income Dividends: Payments to mutual fund shareholders of dividends, interest and short-term capital gains earned on the fund's portfolio securities after deduction of operating expenses.

Income Fund: A mutual fund whose primary investment objective is current income rather than growth of capital. It usually invests in stocks and bonds that normally pay higher dividends and interest.

Incubator Fund: A fund that is run on a small scale in-house for a period of time, and then is publicly offered to investors if its private record has been good.

Index Fund: A mutual fund whose investment objective is to match the composite investment performance of a large group of publicly-traded common stocks represented in a stock market index.

Individual Retirement Account (IRA): A retirement program for working individuals. An individual may contribute and deduct from his or her income tax an amount up to $2,000 per year. An Individual Retirement Account may be funded with mutual fund shares.

Institutional Investor: A bank, insurance company, mutual or pension fund that invests other people's money on their behalf. It typically trades securities in larger volume than individuals.

Interval fund: A hybrid between an open-end and closed-end fund that only accepts redemptions on a specific time schedule, say once a month or quarter.

Industry Group Index: The grouping of stocks comprising a specific industry group such as the Oil and Gas and Computer Technology Indexes listed on the AMEX.

Investment Advisor: See Advisor.

Investment Company: A corporation, trust or partnership in which investors pool their money to obtain professional management and diversification of their investments. Mutual funds are the most popular type of investment company.

Investment Company Act of 1940: The federal law governing the registration and regulation of funds.

Investment Objective: The goal—e.g., long-term capital growth, current income, etc.—which an investor or a mutual fund pursues.

Junk Bonds: Low-quality, high-risk bonds that typically offer above average yields.

Keogh Plan: A retirement program for self-employed individuals and their employees based on tax-saving provisions. A Keogh plan may be funded with mutual fund shares. Named after former New York Congressman, Eugene J. Keogh. (Also known as H.R. 10 Plans.)

Legal List: A list published by a state government authority, enumerating or setting standards for securities proper for money held in trust.

Letter Stock: A form of restricted security so-called because it is generally accompanied by a letter stating that the stock has been purchased only for investment and will not be offered to the public until registered. See Restricted Security.

Leverage: The use of borrowed money, primarily to increase volatility.

Liquidity: The ease of converting an asset to cash and/or the minimal effect on price that such liquidation incurs. (See Illiquid.)

Liquid Asset Fund: A money market fund.

Load: The sales charge or commission for buying into a mutual fund.

Load Fund: A fund whose shares are sold by a broker or salesmen with a sales charge. The *Handbook* generally describes funds with a sales charge greater than 3% as load funds (see Low-load mutual funds).

Long Position: That part of a fund's portfolio which represents securities purchased for price appreciation in a rising market.

Long-term Funds: An industry designation for all funds other than short-term funds (money market and short-term municipal bond). The two broad categories of long-term funds are equity and bond and income funds.

Low-load Mutual Fund: A fund with a front-end load of approximately 3% or less.

Management Company: The entity which manages a fund, as distinct from the fund itself. Officials of both, and even of a company distributing shares or acting as a broker may be the same persons.

Management Fee: The amount paid by a mutual fund to the investment adviser for its services. Industry-wide, fees generally range from 0.5%-1.0% a year of a fund's assets.

Market Timer: An investor who attempts to time the market so that shares are sold before they decrease in value and bought when they are about to increase in value. Sometimes the strategy calls for frequent buy and sell decisions.

Money managers: Professionals employed by mutual fund companies to invest the pool of money in accordance with the fund's investment objectives. Also called portfolio managers.

Money Market Fund: Also called a liquid asset or cash fund, it is a mutual fund whose primary objective is to make higher interest securities available to the average investor who wants safety of principle, liquidity, and current income. This is accomplished through the purchase of short-term money market instruments such as U.S. Government securities, bank securities, bank certificates of deposit and commercial paper.

Money Market Instruments: Include the following types of short term investments: U.S. Government securities, certificates of deposit, time deposits, bankers acceptances, commercial paper and other corporate obligations; also included within such term are short-term repurchase agreements backed by any of the foregoing instruments.

Mortgage-backed Securities: *Passthrough* securities created from pools of mortgages that are packaged together and sold as bonds. The monthly payments of interest and principal on the underlying mortgage debt are passed through to investors.

Moving Average: A mathematical transform which is the sum of the current value plus (n-1) previous values divided by n. The result smooths fluctuations in the raw data.

Municipal Bond Fund: A mutual fund which invests in a broad range of tax-exempt bonds issued by states, cities and other local governments. The interest obtained from these bonds is passed through to shareowners free of federal tax. The fund's primary objective is current tax-free income.

Municipal Securities: Include a wide variety of debt obligations issued for public purposes by or on behalf of the States, territories and possessions of the United States, their political subdivisions, the District of Columbia, and the duly constituted authorities, agencies, public corporations and other instrumentalities of these jurisdictions. Municipal Securities may be used for numerous public purposes, including construction of public facilities, such as airports, bridges, highways, housing, hospitals, mass transportation, schools, streets, water and sewer works, and gas and electric utilities. Municipal Securities may also be used to obtain funds to lend to other public institutions and to certain private borrowers. Municipal Securities are generally classified as either the general obligation, revenue, or industrial development type.

Mutual Fund: An investment company that pools investors' money and is managed by a professional advisor. It ordinarily stands ready to buy back (redeem) its shares at their current net asset value; the value of the shares depends on the market value of the fund's portfolio securities at the time. Most mutual funds continuously offer new shares to investors.

NASDAQ: An automated information network which provides brokers and dealers with price quotations on securities traded over-the-counter. NASDAQ is an acronym for National Association of Securities Dealers Automated Quotations.

National Association of Securities Dealers, Inc. (NASD): The trade association charged by federal law with policing the SEC regulations applying to mutual funds and over-the-counter securities, but not those traded on stock exchanges.

Nest Egg: Assets put aside to provide for a secure standard of living after one's retirement.

Net Assets: A fund's total assets less current liabilities such as taxes and other operating expenses.

Net Asset Value Per Share: A fund's total assets—securities, cash and any accrued earnings—after deduction of liabilities, divided by the number of shares outstanding. It is synonymous with the bid price, and in the case of no-loads also the offering or market price.

Net Investment Income per Share: Dividends and interest earned during an accounting period (such as a year) on a fund's portfolio, less operating expenses, divided by number of shares outstanding.

Net Realized Capital Gains per Share: The amount of capital gain realized on sale of a fund's portfolio holdings during an accounting period (such as a year), less losses realized on such transactions, divided by number of shares outstanding.

No-Load Fund: A mutual fund selling its shares at net asset value, without the addition of front-end or back-end sales charges. The fund may have a redemption fee or a 12b-1 fee of no more than .25%.

No-Load Fund, "pure": A mutual fund selling its shares at net asset value without the addition of low sales charges, long-lived redemption or 12b-1 fees.

Non-Diversified Investment Company: A fund whose portfolio does not meet the requirements of the Investment Company Act of 1940 to qualify as a diversified investment company. For example, a fund which (as to 50% of its assets) may invest up to 25% in the securities of one company.

Off-the-page Advertising: A way to permit no-loads to sell shares directly from a print advertisement without first sending a prospectus.

Offering Price: Same as asked price, which is net asset value per share plus any applicable sales commission.

Open-end Investment Company: The more formal name for a mutual fund, indicating that it stands ready to redeem its shares (buy them back) on demand.

Options: Give purchasers the right, but not the obligation, to buy or sell a fixed amount of a given asset at a specific price within a certain time period. Buyers pay a premium to acquire them. While the buyer can never lose more than the premium paid, the seller's potential losses are unlimited.

Option Income Fund: The investment objective of these funds is to seek a high current return by investing primarily in dividend-paying common stocks on which call options are traded on national securities exchanges. Current return generally consists of dividends, premiums from expired call options, net short-term gains from sales of portfolio securities on exercises of options or otherwise, and any profits from closing purchase transactions.

Over-the-Counter Market: A trading network composed of dealers nation-wide who trade issues off the regular stock exchanges.

Passively Managed Fund: Similar to an index fund, it invests long-term in a universe of stocks that do not necessarily correspond to a recognized index.

Payment Date: The day on which a distribution is mailed to shareholders. Usually is later than the declaration date, which is the day the distribution is announced by the board of directors; and also usually follows the date of record, which is the date the distribution goes ex-dividend. Only shareholders as of the date of record are entitled to the payment.

Performance: The percentage change in a fund's per share value over a specified period of time. As used in the mutual fund industry, it generally includes the value of the income and capital gains dividends distributed during the specified period.

Performance Fund: An aggressive growth fund seeking maximum capital appreciation through relatively speculative techniques.

Portfolio: The group name for securities owned by a fund.

Portfolio Managers: See *Money Managers.*

Portfolio Turnover: Generally given in percentage of total assets in a year; 80% of the dollar value of a portfolio's holdings, for example, were changed in a year. See Turnover Ratio.

Preferred Stock: An equity security generally carrying a fixed return in percentage or dollars, which must be paid before common stock can share in earnings or assets.

Premium: The percentage above asset value at which an investment company sells in the open market. Applies generally only to closed-end funds whose shares must be purchased or sold only through a broker and not through the fund.

Prepayment risk: A danger to investors in mortgage-backed mutual funds, such as GNMA funds. When interest rates fall, many homeowners will refinance their mortgages. When the older mortgages are paid off early, the fund will have to reinvest the money in lower yielding securities.

Prospectus: The official booklet which describes the mutual fund and offers its shares for sale. It contains information as required by the Securities and Exchange Commission on such subjects as the fund's investment objectives and policies, services, investment restrictions, officers and directors, how shares can be bought and redeemed, its charges and its financial statements. A more detailed document known as "Part B" of the prospectus or the *Statement of Additional Information* is available upon request.

Proxy: Enables shareholders not attending a fund meeting to transfer their voting power to another person, usually fund management, to vote on fund business at the meeting.

Prudent Man Rule: The rule which enables a trustee to use his own judgement in making investments as long as he acts conservatively. The rule comes from an 1830 court decision.

Publicly Traded Investment Company: A closed-end fund.

Qualified Dividend Funds: are offered to corporations that want to take advantage of a provision in the tax code that allows U.S. corporations to exclude 70% of the dividends they receive from federal taxation. Funds invest in high-yielding common and preferred stock.

Qualified For Sale: Qualified by reason of registration with the SEC or in accordance with state's regulations.

Real Estate Investment Trust: (REIT). An investment company that specializes in real estate holdings. Cannot be a mutual fund because investments are considered illiquid (see *Illiquid*).

Redemption Fee: The charge levied by a few funds when shares are redeemed.

Redemption Price: The amount per share the mutual fund shareholder receives when he cashes in his shares. The value of the shares depends on the market value of the fund's portfolio securities at the time and any redemption fees.

Red Herring: A preliminary prospectus.

Registrar: The organization, usually a bank, that maintains a registry of the share owners of a mutual fund, and the number of shares which they hold.

Regulated investment company: A fund that meets the income and diversification criteria required under law to avoid corporation income taxation.

Reinvestment Privilege: A service provided by most mutual funds for the automatic reinvestment of a shareholder's income dividends and capital gains distributions in additional shares.

Repos: A short term for repurchase agreements.

Repurchase Agreements: A sale of securities with the concurrent agreement of the seller to repurchase the securities at the same price plus an amount equal to interest at an agreed-upon rate, within a specified time, usually less than one week, but, on occasion, at a later time.

Restricted Security: One which requires registration with the SEC before it may be sold to the public. Because of this restriction, the security may not be considered a liquid asset and therefore may be priced at a substantial discount from market value.

Revenue Securities: Securities repayable only from revenues derived from a particular facility, local agency, special tax, facility user or other specific revenue source; certain revenue issues may also be backed by a reserve fund or specific collateral.

Revenue Anticipation Notes: Issued by governmental entities in anticipation of specific future non-tax revenue, such as Federal revenues available under the Federal Revenue Sharing Programs. Some such notes are general obligations of the issuer and others are payable only from specific future revenues.

Reverse Repurchase Agreements: Ordinary repurchase agreements in which a Fund is the seller of, rather than the investor in, securities, and agrees to repurchase them at an agreed-upon time and price. Use of reverse repurchase agreements may be preferable to a regular sale and later repurchase of the securities.

Risk-free rate: The rate on a short-term, default-free security, usually a Treasury bill.

Sales Charge: An amount charged to purchase shares in a mutual fund. The charge can range from 1.0% to 8.5% of the initial investment. The charge is added to the net asset value per share in the determination of the offering price. Also, now known as a *front-end sales charge*. See *Contingent Deferred Sales Charge and 12b-1 Plan*.

Sales Force Marketing: A method of distribution whereby funds sell their shares to the public through brokers, financial planners, and insurance agents. Some fund organizations sell shares through a captive sales force-salesmen employed by the fund organization to market only the shares of its associated funds.

Sector: Particular group of stocks, usually found in one industry.

Sector Funds: A number of separate industry portfolios grouped under the umbrella of one fund. Adviser usually provides easy switching by phone between portfolios and a related money fund.

Securities and Exchange Commission (S.E.C.): The agency of the U.S. government which administers Federal securities laws.

Senior Securities: Notes, bonds, debentures or preferred stocks, which have a prior (senior) claim ahead of common stock to assets and earnings.

Service fee: A payment by a fund to brokers, financial planners, and money managers for personal service to shareholders and/or the maintenance of shareholders accounts. Transfer agent, custodian and similar fees are not considered service fees. Also see *Trailing Commission*.

Short Sale: The sale of a security which is not owned, in the hope that the price will go down so that it can be repurchased at a profit. The person making a short sale borrows stock in order to make delivery to the buyer and must eventually purchase the stock for return to the lender.

Short-term Funds: An industry designation for money market and short-term municipal bond funds.

Single-state Funds: These funds invest in the tax-exempt securities issued by governmental organizations of a single state. Investors receive earnings free from both federal and state taxes. Single-state funds can be both short- and long-term.

Social Conscience Fund: A fund that invests in the securities of companies that do not conflict with certain social priorities. Some social conscience funds do not invest in tobacco stocks, defense stocks or South African stocks.

Specialized Mutual Fund: A mutual fund specializing in the securities of certain industries, special types of securities or in regional investments. Gold funds and sector funds are examples.

Split Funding: A program which combines the purchase of mutual fund shares with the purchase of life insurance contracts or other products.

Stability: Relative volatility in a declining market. For example, a fund rated above-average for stability, is one that declines relatively the least.

Standard Deviation: The variations in performance from a long-term average. Standard deviation differs from beta in that it measures variability within a fund, while beta measures it in relation to an outside index.

Stock-index Options: Options give holders the right, but not the obligation, to buy (a call) or sell (a put) a specified amount of an underlying investment by a certain date at a preset price, known as the strike price. For stock indexes, the underlying investment may be a stock-index futures contract or the cash value of a stock index. For example, there are options on the S&P 500 futures contract and on the S&P 100 index.

Target Fund: A fixed income fund whose portfolio matures within a given year. Generally structured as a series fund with each series maturing in a different year.

Tax Anticipation Notes: Issued by governmental entities in anticipation of specific future tax revenue, such as property, income, sales, use, and business taxes. Some such notes are general obligations of the issuer, and others are payable only from specific future taxes.

Technical Analysis: Research into the supply and demand for securities based on trading volume and price studies. Technical analysis uses charts or computer programs to identify price trends in order to foretell future price movements. Unlike fundamental analysts, technical analysts do not concern themselves with the financial position of a company, such as earnings, etc.

Telephone Switching: Process of selling one mutual fund and buying another at the same time by telephone. Switching is often between stock, bond, or money market funds within the same fund family.

Total Return: A comprehensive measure of a mutual fund's performance, including price changes, realized capital gains and dividend distributions. See Performance.

Total Return Fund: A fund whose objective is to obtain the highest possible total return, i.e. a combination of ordinary income and capital gains. Funds usually invest in a combination of dividend paying stocks and bonds. Similar to a balanced fund.

Trailing Commission: Also called a trail, it is a small commission periodically paid to a broker or a financial planner to service an existing shareholder as long as money remains in the fund. A typical trail might be .25% per year. It is often paid out of the 12b-1 fee. Also see *Service Fee.*

Transfer Agent: The organization which is employed by a mutual fund to prepare and maintain records relating to the accounts of its shareholders.

Treasury Bills: Marketable U. S. Government securities with an original maturity of up to one year.

Treasury Bonds: Marketable U. S. Government securities with an original maturity of ten years or more.

Treasury Notes: Marketable U. S. Government securities with an original maturity of from two to ten years.

Turnover Ratio: The extent to which an investment company's portfolio is turned over during the course of a year. Calculated by dividing the lesser of purchases or sales of portfolio securities for the fiscal year by the monthly average of the value the portfolio securities owned by the mutual fund during the fiscal year. Excluded from the numerator and denominator all U.S. Government securities and all other securities whose maturities at the time of acquisition were one year or less.

12b-1 Plan: Allows the fund to pay a percentage of its assets to cover the distributor's sales and marketing costs. Also, see *asset-based sales charges.*

Underwriter or Principal Underwriter: The organization which acts as the distributor of a mutual fund's shares to broker-dealers and the public.

Unit Trust: An investment company with an unmanaged portfolio that is liquidated after a specified, limited life span. In the U.K. the term refers to an investment company very much like American mutual funds.

Unrealized Appreciation or Depreciation: The amount by which the market value of a security or a portfolio of securities, at a given time, is above (appreciation) or below (depreciation) the cost price.

U.S. Government Obligations: Debt securities (including bills, notes, and bonds) issued by the U.S. Treasury or issued by an agency or instrumentality of the U.S. government which is established under the authority of an act of Congress. Such agencies or instrumentalities include, but are not limited to, the Federal National Mortgage Association, the Federal Farm Credit Bank, and the Federal Home Loan Bank. Although all obligations of agencies and instrumentalities are not direct obligations of the U.S. Treasury, payment of the interest and principal on these obligations is generally backed directly or indirectly by the U.S. government. This support can range from the backing of the full faith and credit of the United States, to U.S. government guarantees, or to the backing solely of the issuing instrumentality itself. In the latter case of securities not backed by the full faith and credit of the United States, the investor must look principally to the agency issuing or guaranteeing the obligation for ultimate repayment, and may not be able to assert claim against the United States itself in the event the agency or instrumentality does not meet its commitments.

Volatility: The relative rate at which a fund share tends to move up or down in price as compared to the change in price of a stock market index or a mutual fund average. For example, a highly volatile fund is one that usually rises or declines far more than the average fund.

Voluntary Plan: A flexible accumulation plan in which there is no definite time period or total amount to be invested.

Whipsaw: Losing money on both sides of a price swing.

Withdrawal Plans: Many mutual funds offer withdrawal programs whereby shareholders receive payments from their investments at regular intervals. These payments typically are drawn from the fund's dividends and capital gains distributions, if any, and from principal, to the extent necessary.

Yield: Income received from investments, usually expressed as a percentage of market price; also referred to as current yield. Usually computed on the basis of one year's income.

Yield to Maturity: The yield earned on a bond over its full life. Includes capital gains if the bond was bought at a discount from its face value.

Zero-coupon bond: A bond that is bought at a price below par with no coupons. Your return is the difference between the purchase and sale price, or par if held to maturity. Zeros accumulate and compound interest at the same rate that prevailed when the bond was bought.

INDEX

How You Can Save $65 While Earning More Mutual Fund Profits!

Please see the SPECIAL NO-RISK OFFER on the opposite side of this tear-off Order Form for:

- 12-month subscription to *The No-Load Fund Investor* newsletter

- *The Handbook for No-Load Fund Investors*

SPECIAL OFFER: $99 FOR BOTH!
($65 savings over regular price of each separately.)

▼ Detach along perforation and mail

FROM

_____

_____

_____

THE **NO-LOAD** FUND INVESTOR, INC.
PO Box 318
Irvington-on-Hudson, NY 10533-0318